Cipriano Baca,
Frontier Lawman
of New Mexico

ALSO BY CHUCK HORNUNG

*Fullerton's Rangers: A History of the
New Mexico Territorial Mounted Police*
(McFarland, 2005; paperback 2011)

Cipriano Baca, Frontier Lawman of New Mexico

CHUCK HORNUNG

McFarland & Company, Inc., Publishers
Jefferson, North Carolina, and London

LIBRARY OF CONGRESS CATALOGUING-IN-PUBLICATION DATA

Hornung, Chuck, 1943–
Cipriano Baca, frontier lawman of New Mexico /
Chuck Hornung.
    p.   cm.
Includes bibliographical references and index.

ISBN 978-0-7864-7332-8
softcover : acid free paper ∞

1. Baca, Cipriano, 1859–1936. 2. Frontier and pioneer life — New Mexico. 3. Peace officers — New Mexico — Biography. 4. New Mexico — Biography. I. Title.
F801.B14H67 2013   363.2092 — dc23   [B]   2013013699

BRITISH LIBRARY CATALOGUING DATA ARE AVAILABLE

© 2013 Chuck Hornung. All rights reserved

No part of this book may be reproduced or transmitted in any form or by any means, electronic or mechanical, including photocopying or recording, or by any information storage and retrieval system, without permission in writing from the publisher.

On the cover: Cipriano Baca at Mogollon, New Mexico, 1913; sheriff star (Hemera/Thinkstock); background texture and paper image (iStockphoto/Thinkstock)

Manufactured in the United States of America

*McFarland & Company, Inc., Publishers
Box 611, Jefferson, North Carolina 28640
www.mcfarlandpub.com*

To the memory of
Cipriano Baca's lovely daughter
CIPRIANA BACA RANDOLPH
and also to my best friend and beautiful wife
V. J. HORNUNG

Table of Contents

Acknowledgments ix
Introduction 1

1. The Early Years 3
2. A New Life in Arizona Territory 12
3. Diaper Days in Deming, New Mexico Territory 19
4. Grant County Peace Officer 33
5. The World Turned Upside Down 45
6. A New Life in Mogollon 54
7. Socorro, New Mexico Territory 63
8. Miss Mary Ann Berry 75
9. The Baca Boys of Socorro County 81
10. Baca Family Life 87
11. Life in Santa Fe 94
12. Return to Silver City 100
13. Luna County Sheriff 104
14. Deputy U.S. Marshal Cipriano Baca 132
15. The New Mexico Territorial Mounted Police 139
16. Lieutenant Cipriano Baca 142
17. Private Detective and Company Police Officer 180
18. The Mogollon Years 195
19. State of New Mexico vs. Cipriano Baca: Murder 206
20. A Broken Family 219
21. The Wartime Rangers 223
22. The Sunset Years 235
23. The Question of Eva Paiz 244

24. Crossing the Great Divide 251
25. Epilogue 256

Chapter Notes 259
Bibliography 273
Index 281

Acknowledgments

"Think of the past, of the time long ago; ask your father to tell you what happened, ask the old men to tell of the past." — Deuteronomy 32:7

I owe my life and all that I am to the Creator of the Universe, who has blessed me, sustained me, strengthened me, loved me, and given me the courage to write this book. I am sure I have not always pleased Him and followed His path for me, but He has never let me down. *Maranatha!*

When I was a young man, I had the honor to have Fred Lambert as a friend. At the time, Lambert was the last living ranger who had served with the New Mexico Territorial Mounted Police, and from him I heard many stories about these legendary frontier peace officers. During our many long discussions, while sitting around the kitchen table of his small home in Cimarron, New Mexico, Lambert encouraged my desire to research the public and private records of these territorial police and to record their stories for future generations.

One of the subsequent articles I wrote for a series published in the now defunct *Real West* magazine was a brief biography of the Mounted Police's first lieutenant. This article contained most of the information known about Cipriano Baca in 1980. The *Real West* piece had been seen and read by a grandniece of Baca's namesake daughter who gave her Aunt Ann a copy of the publication. Later, via the publisher, Mrs. Cipriana Baca Randolph sent me a letter. She said simply, "Thank you for writing such a lovely article on my father." Cipriana's letter began our friendship, and that began over a quarter of a century of research that has produced this book about her father. My sole regret is that I was so slow with the research and writing that Cipriana did not live to see the project completed for publication.

No person who undertakes to write a historical biography does so alone. I am grateful to many individuals from numerous libraries, historical societies, and government archives whose staffs have guided me through the necessary research. Baca's story developed *poco a poco initio ad-infinen*—little by little from beginning to end.

Many people have helped me along the trail as I tried to discover the nature of the man who was Cipriano Baca. Chief among these persons was Cipriana Baca Randolph. This gracious lady willingly shared with me her family memories, archives, and photographs. Louise Nazarine-Baca, wife of Cipriano Baca's son Florentino, freely shared her perspective of the Baca family. Eloise Sanchez, Cipriano Baca's "unknown" granddaughter, provided information about her mother Eva Paiz and her grandmother Manuelita Montoya-Paiz. I thank you ladies for your generosity.

This biography owes a very special thank-you to John Amos, Cipriano Baca's grandson, and Jim Stauder, the great-grandson of Effie Berry Stauder, for sharing Baca-Berry family stories, traditions and photographs. Charles Jensen, of Albuquerque, did diligent Baca genealogy work. Alexander King, of Los Angeles, plowed unbroken ground and did yeomen genealogy work on the Baca and Paiz families. I thank these guys for their valuable assistance and generosity.

Arturo Roman, archivist at the Deming-Luna County Mimbres Museum and Custom House at Deming, NM, generously shared his file of Cipriano Baca data, and Holly Zuni, judicial specialist for the Seventh Judicial District Court, helped the author search the dusty basement storage vaults of the courthouse at Socorro, New Mexico looking for the records of Baca's murder trial. Barbara Zamora, ad valorem assessment advisor, helped search for Baca's old tax records, and Lori Frank, administrative assistant to the probate judge, found Baca estate records at the Bernalillo County Courthouse. Santiago Romero, Jr., engineer and surveyor, provided the author with land locations and data concerning the Mogollon ghost town. Nancy Brown-Martinez, reference coordinator for the Center for Southwest Research at the University of New Mexico; Jeffrey Bridges, adult services librarian at the Socorro Public Library; and the staff at the Miller Library at Western New Mexico University at Silver City also provided assistance on our voyage of discovery.

The families of Captain John F. Fullerton and Captain Fred Fornoff generously shared their family memories and gave encouragement in our quest to uncover the saga of the New Mexico Mounted Police. My friends among the "family" of descendents of Mounted Police offered advice and encouragement with this biography. Sharon Spears graciously read the Baca manuscript and gave good advice concerning grammar and sentence clarity.

My wife and our sons gave loving support during my lonely years searching archives records, newspaper files, and conducting endless hours of interviews seeking the truth about the men of the New Mexico Mounted Police. Ron and Pat Fuss always made our research trips to Albuquerque fun. Toffee and Yael, the family cats, kept me company while I wrote the numerous manuscript drafts and gave final approval to each page.

I can never forget Charles Fredrick Lambert, the last living member of the territorial rangers, because his guiding spirit is always present when I work on a New Mexico Mounted Police project.

> "Two roads diverged in a wood, and I —
> I took the one less traveled by,
> And that has made all the difference."
> *The Road Not Taken*, Robert Frost, 1916

Introduction

> "[Lieutenant Cipriano] Baca is said to be a fearless and capable officer, speaks both languages fluently and has a natural instinct to hunt criminals."
> — *Tucumcari News*, 23 June 1906

Imprimis is Latin for "in the first place," and that is how any biography of Cipriano Baca should begin. In the first place, he was not an average man of his era. Because of his Hispanic heritage, some people discriminated against him and others rewarded him. Cipriano was the scion of a prestigious Spanish lineage tracing their heritage to the arrival of the Conquistadores in the New World; the Bacas were among the first settlers in *Nuevo México*. Baca's father was a man of property, and at various periods during his life, Cipriano was financially secure and part of the landed gentry. He, however, shared his father's fate and died a poor man.

Baca married three times and fathered 12 children. Six of his children died before their second birthday, and he lost one wife to divorce, one to a tragic accident and the third to complications of childbirth. Cipriano had a paramour and a daughter he could not acknowledge. Most children who knew him loved this peace officer legend, but he was unable to cope with the stressful demands of being a working single parent raising four small children in a frontier mining town. Baca was tenderhearted, but he could also be as cold as steel and lethal when he was determined to do his duty. Cipriano Baca was a man of honor and principles living in an age of personal and corporate greed and selfishness.

Cipriano wore many peace officer badges during his half century of public service. He was first an undercover range detective who helped Deputy U.S. Marshal Wyatt Earp with his clandestine return to Arizona Territory in the summer of 1882 to finish his vendetta against the Cochise County Cow-boys. Later, Baca was a Grant County deputy sheriff, a constable at the Mogollon mining camp and Socorro County deputy sheriff; he was elected Socorro County tax assessor; and he served as a deputy U.S. marshal at Socorro, yardmaster of the New Mexico Territorial Penitentiary, and chief deputy sheriff of Grant County. In 1901, the territorial governor appointed Baca the first sheriff of Luna County. He became constable of Deming, again served as a deputy U.S. marshal, and in 1905, the territorial governor selected him as the first man to serve as lieutenant of New Mexico's territorial rangers under captains John F. Fullerton and Fred Fornoff.

After leaving the rangers, Baca was a railroad detective, and during this time, he discovered the killer of Pat Garrett and the real motive behind the murder. Later, Baca was marshal at the Dawson coal-mining camp, constable at Mogollon a second time, and a mine guard and deputy sheriff at different camps in northern New Mexico. Baca returned to the rangers in 1918 before becoming the deputy sheriff at Tyrone. Before his death, Cipriano was the cattle brand inspector at Albuquerque and deputy sheriff.

Cipriano Baca, just four days short of his 78th birthday when he died, is buried between two strangers in Albuquerque's Sunset Memorial Park. He had served as a New Mexico peace officer for 52 of his earthly years. The old lawman's grave lay unmarked for 68 years until his grandson John Amos once told the author, "I am glad that I was able to honor my grandfather with a worthy headstone to mark his eternal rest and tell the world he was proud to have been a territorial ranger."

John and Belva Amos honored the author by reading the final draft of this manuscript, and John made a few comments and reflections concerning this biographical effort.

> I know that Aunt Ann [Cipriana Baca Randolph] was a strong supporter of you writing her father's biography and was excited with each new discovery. I know that Aunt Ann and Aunt Louise Baca helped with their personal remembrances of my grandfather's story. Aunt Ann would have really enjoyed the finished work as much as Belva and I did. Grandfather Baca seems to have lived in a transitional era of our country's history — the sunset of the Old West and the sunrise of our modern world through the birth pains of the Great Depression.
>
> My Aunt Ann was always the solid bedrock of the Baca children. She was very close to her father and never wavered in her loyalty to him, unlike my mother or the other Baca children. My mother (Maisie Hill Baca Amos) spoke little about our grandfather because of the estrangement discussed in this book. I probably learned more about my grandfather Baca from that article you wrote for *Real West* magazine and now this full biography than collective family memories have ever told me. You made some interesting revelations and filled the gaps in our family history. We are both pleased and delighted with the book; you made the adventure come alive. Perhaps your work is a reinforcement of what I instinctively already knew about my grandfather. Aunt Ann was right to have believed that you would tell an honest story about her father.

In this biography, the author has attempted to resurrect the life, the era, and the legend of Cipriano Baca while separating fact and fiction, and now you the reader, and history, are the final judge of our deed.

> "Let another praise you, and not your own mouth; a stranger, and not your own lips."— Proverbs 27:02

1

The Early Years

"Father never seemed to talk about his early life to any of us children. Aunt Jovita told us the most."—Cipriana Baca Randolph to the author 13 Dec 1982

Many early Spanish records spell the family name Baka, Vacka, or Vaca. Genealogists specializing in Spanish heritage searches have traced New Mexico's Vaca/Baca family lineage to the early 1600s and a man named Don Cristobal Cabeza de Vaca/Baca who was part of Don Juan de Onate y Salazar's San Gabriel colony, the first permanent Spanish settlement in the Nuevo Méjico province. Onate was the provincial governor from 1598 to 1608. The Vaca/Baca patrons returned to Nuevo Méjico in 1692 when Don Diego de Vargas resettled the Spanish land grants after the conclusion of hostilities with the Pueblo Indians.[1]

The Baca family coat of arms dates to the early 1200s and a man named Martin Alhaja, and the archives of the Spanish Empire in Madrid preserve the heraldic record. The old-style Spanish reads, *Un Escudo Jaquelado de Oro y Gules, Con Una Bordura de Azur, Con Seis Cabezas de Vaca, de Plata.* The center of the crest is composed of a *jaquelado*, a checkerboard battlefield, with eight gold and seven red squares. To honor the valor and heroism of his most valiant *caballeros*, the king awarded *el ajedrez*, a chess symbol, to place on their personal coat of arms. King Alfonso VIII of Castile commanded, as an extra special honor, that a border of blue standing for justice, praise, perseverance, vigilance, and loyalty surround the checkerboard of the new coat of arms. A cow's head recalled Alhaja's service at the Battle of *Las Navas de Tolosa* where joint Spanish armies defeated the Muslim Moorish invaders on July 16, 1212. Alhaja had marked a mountain escape route from the Moor's trap with cows' skulls. By royal command, the cows' heads were to be silver color in recognition of the humility, innocence, and truthfulness of the brave sheepherder who defended women and orphans and made a conquest without bloodshed. A head placed upon the border recalled each of these elements. Cabeza de Vaca, the head of the cow, became the emblem of the new family surname.[2] Cipriano Baca's descendants claim a relation to the Spanish New World explorer Cabeza de Vaca, who descended from the original titleholder Don Martin Alhaja.

* * * * *

Cipriana Baca Randolph, one of Cipriano Baca's eight daughters, told the author that her Grandfather Baca's homestead was located near present-day Martinez. The sleepy village on Suisun Bay, northeast of San Francisco, California, has been the Baca ancestral home since the early 1800s, but the family's heritage had began decades earlier in Nuevo Méjico.

Jose Teofilo Vaca, Cipriano's father, was born at the family home in *Partido de la Cienega y Ranchos*, on Sunday morning, January 9, 1826. The parents christened the baby four days later in the Saint Francis de Assisi Parish church. The Cienega-Ranchos were located on the south side of the Rio Santa Fe, north of its junction with the Rio Galisteo before that creek empties into the Rio Grande a few miles north of Santo Domingo Pueblo. This area was southwest of *La Villa Real de la Santa Fe de San Francisco de Assisi* in what then was the Mexican Province of Nuevo Méjico.

Teofilo, as the boy would be called, was one of the many children born to Don Juan Manuel Vaca and his wife Maria Dolores Bernal Vaca; among Teofilo's brothers and sisters were Juan Nepomuceno Tomas (Nepono), Marcos Anastacio, Maria del Roario, Magdalena, Maria Bacillia, Jesus Maria Simon (Chipeto), Maria Francisca, Jose Dolores Alejandro, and Maria Antonia Polonia. Don Juan Manual Vaca kept a small red-leather-covered notebook that he used to inscribe important personal events. This diary, written in Spanish, contains the birth dates of all his nine children.[3]

Juan Manual Vaca had been born to Jose Miguel and Maria Dolores Vaca, at the Vaca Rancho, in the early 1790s. On Thursday, June 15, 1815, Juan married Maria Bernal; they settled on the Vaca Rancho with the rest of the clan. It was here that Juan and Maria started their family. The Vaca children received a basic education in the local church school and learned to read and write Spanish. At some point during his life, Teofilo learned to speak English. Teofilo's mother Maria Dolores Bernal Vaca died on January 31, 1841, and rests in the church grounds at Santo Domingo. That spring the 14-year-old seasoned ranch hand joined his widowed father on a small caravan of wagons for the trip westward across the plains and mountains of present-day New Mexico, Arizona, and Nevada on into California, the Pacific Coast *El Dorado* of the Spanish southwest.

Juan Manuel Vaca and his friend Juan Felipe Pena had heard about the ranching and farming opportunities around a big bay on the north coast of the western Mexican province. Juan Manuel's father, Jose Miguel Vaca, had traveled to the Santa Fe area in the early 1800s when he was still a citizen of the Spanish Crown. The 1821 Spanish census records Vaca's name among the first settler families to locate along the *Rio Grande del Norte*.[4]

Two decades later, the Vaca family felt the press of Anglos for their land, so the two men called Juan made the difficult trip west to explore the settlement offer of land in California. That distant province needed Hispanic settlers to hold the Mexican claim to this land so coveted by the Russian and British empires. Even the new government of the American republic had turned an eye toward these distant western lands under the expansion policy of Manifest Destiny.

The first recorded attempts by European settlers of the Rio Grande valley to open trade with their fellow Spaniards on the west coast were two expeditions led by Franciscan friars in 1776. The expeditions reached their objective, but they were unable to establish the commerce route. Decades later this dream of a Spanish Trail became a fait acompli, and two-way traffic became a reality. The Spanish Trail was a 1,120-mile horse and mule path, never a wagon road, that left the Santa Fe Plaza and ran northward into present-day Colorado and on up to the Green River in Utah before heading south to cross southern Nevada before entering California. This route avoided the massive canyon of the Colorado River, the desert of Arizona, and the hostile Indians.

It was necessary to transport all goods via the backs of mules in mile-long pack trains. New Mexico merchants sent raw wool from their large flocks of sheep and locally spun textiles to California, while the New Mexico traders brought back vast horse and cattle herds. A trip over the Spanish Trail, between Santa Fe and Los Angeles, took at least two and a half months. A trip westward began in the fall before the winter snows fell, and the return trip east left California in the early spring to avoid the high waters on the Green and Colorado rivers.[5] The Vaca-Pena party traveled this route in the autumn of 1841. After reaching the Pueblo of Los Angeles, these immigrants moved up the coastal *El Comino Real* toward San Francisco and their new home. Vaca and Pena found the northern California countryside to be fertile. They received a promise of a generous land grant, issued under the terms of Mexico's settlement law of 1835, from *Commandante* M.G. Vallejo. The two men applied for the land that became the Vaca-Pena Grant or the 45,000-acre *Los Puntas Rancho*. On Thursday, January 26, 1843, after the two families had been on the land for two years, the Mexican government issued a land grant title. The highest point on the grant was the 2,817-foot Mt. Vaca located about 20 miles northeast of present-day Vacaville.[6] In 1850, during the first American census of California, Juan Manuel Vaca's land holdings were valued at $30,000.[7] This was a massive sum of money for that era and when converted into today's dollar value this would equate to almost $700,000.[8]

By the end of 1841, the Vaca and Pena pioneers had settled in California. At some point, Juan Miguel met a widow named Dona Estefana Martinez and the two married in 1845. Vaca became a stepfather to two daughters. Together the couple had a son that Juan named Miguel in honor of his father. A few years later, the marriage broke apart, and by 1850, the Juan Manuel Vaca household was presided over by a 31-year-old "servant" named Juana who used the last name Vaca. There is no record of a third marriage for Juan Manuel Vaca; he died on May 15, 1856, at Vacaville.[9]

The 1850 decadic federal census paints an interesting picture of the Vaca homestead in Solano County, California. Juan Manuel and his housekeeper lived in a house on the family rancho. Also settled throughout the grant were three other house compounds. The eldest son Nepono headed one, and the next oldest son Marcos and another son Chipeto shared a third house. The third-oldest son, 25-year-old Teofilo, headed a fourth dwelling housing himself, two women and four children: Raymunda and Guillermo, both seven years old, Mariano who was five, and two-year-old Manuel. One woman was Teofilo's 37-year-old sister Magdalena; the other woman was most likely a widowed sister-in-law named Jesusita, age 23. The four Vaca brothers jointly operated the family ranching and farming business, and their father ruled the grant as a patron.[10]

In 1846, the United States and the Republic of Mexico entered into armed conflict over the fate of Mexico's northern provinces. Soon after the start of the struggle, an American army marched across the continent to California and after brief fighting claimed the lands of the ill-fated California Republic as a prize of war. Late in 1848, men discovered gold along the banks of the Sacramento River near John Sutter's Fort. This event unleashed a stampede for wealth known today as the legend of the California 49ers.

The federal union received California as the thirty-first state on Monday, September 9, 1850. This congressional measure, along with establishing New Mexico (which included present-day Arizona) as a territory, was only part of the massive legislative compromise that allowed citizens of certain sections of the nation to own slaves legally and certain areas where human bondage would remain illegal. The Compromise of 1850 did successfully avert a massive armed civil conflict, but the agreement was unable to cure the ulcer nagging at the soul of the nation. A decade later, the festering ulcer exploded in a fiery fury causing the near death of the ailing federal union in a war between the northern and southern states. During these years of uncertainty, the gold rush that started in 1849 brought thousands of newcomers to the Vacas' peaceful pastoral lands on the inland waterways north of San Francisco Bay.

Many of the massive influx of Anglos who flooded into California from the eastern states found no gold in the rush for riches. Some of these luckless prospectors developed roving eyes towards the Vaca brothers' land grant because to their way of thinking they were "Americans" and had a right to "requisition" any "Mexican" lands they wished. The Vaca brothers had a different point of view, but the new California state legislature soon enacted a controversial law that supported the "americanos'" idea of land ownership.

Into this bubbling caldron rode William Carey Jones. He arrived from Washington carrying a commission from the secretaries of the State Department and the Department of the Interior to make an investigation of California's land grant problems. Jones's 60-page status report, coupled with copies of the pertinent Spanish and Mexican laws governing the issuance of land grants, published in 1850, was used for the next 16 years as the courts tried to determine the true ownership of all of the Spanish and Mexican land grant claims in California. The Vaca brothers held a valid land grant under the terms of the 1848 Treaty of Guadalupe Hidalgo and were able to prove their claim and retain title to their vast holdings.[11]

Another part of this monumental 1850 agreement would have long-range effects upon the Vaca family because the compromise removed military control and authorized the formation of a civil government for the former Mexican province of Nuevo Méjico. At the time, no one suspected that one of Teofilo and Encarnacion Vaca's children would become one of the foremost enforcers of the American laws that now governed the family's original New World homestead. Later generations Anglicized the Vaca family name to Baca.

Overwhelmed by the newcomers' encroachment of his estate, Juan Manuel Vaca gave each of his children a land inheritance with the hope that they might be able to manage it, but local deed records contain multi-listings of Vaca grant lands being sold or traded by Juan Manuel's children. There is also a deed, dated Saturday, December 13, 1851, for a nine square mile parcel of land in Contra Costa County, made out to William McDaniel from Juan Manuel Vaca. McDaniel wanted to plot a town-site and open the area for agriculture and a settlement. Vaca finally agreed to the sale under condition that Vacaville became the new town's name. The area developed as a fruit- and nut-growing center, and in 1892, the town incorporated and a town government was established. Today, the almost 100,000-population Vacaville community is home to two California state correctional facilities and is a neighbor to the strategic Travis Air Force Base.[12]

* * * * *

The Vaca-Briones family records are unclear about Encarnacion Briones's birthplace. One family tradition has her birth either in Spain or on board the ship that brought her family from the old country to the shores of El Dorado. However, church records seem to establish her birth as taking place on March 25, 1831, in San Rafael across San Pablo Bay from Martinez. Two days later, Don Felipe Santiago Briones and Maria Manuela Valencia had their daughter christened Maria de la Encarnacion. Her mother taught her homemaking and the proper conduct of a young Spanish-bred lady. Her father died when she was nine years old. It is unknown how Teofilo Vaca first met the pretty *Senorita* Encarnacion or how they conducted their courtship, but they married on Tuesday evening, November 6, 1849, at the Church of Saint Francis of Solano in Sonoma. The couple's first child, Prudenciana, was born in September 1850 and christened in the church at San Leandro at Alameda. She died young. The first statewide census conducted by the new state of California in 1852 contains the "Teofilo Vacka" family's information.

The young couple bought some farm property on the Boca Land Grant owned by her family. Ramon Briones signed and dated the deed document, written in flowery Spanish script, on Wednesday, December 17, 1851. The homestead was located near the farms of Marcelino, Casimiro, and Ramon Briones in the Martinez/San Pablo township of Contra Costa County.[13]

The enumerator of the 1860 federal census taken in the Martinez Township of Contra Costa County, California, noted that Teofilo Baca's real estate and livestock holdings were valued at $8,000 (about $145,000 in today's dollar value). A decade later, Teofilo's lower property value reflected the slow recovery from continued unstable livestock prices following the high demand and inflated prices paid during the years of the War between the States.

The Baca-Briones union produced eleven children between 1850 and 1870. Teofilo recorded his children's names and baptismal data in his father's small red-leather memorandum book. There were seven Baca daughters. The oldest was Prudenciana (September 14, 1850, to April 20, 1851). The second daughter was Maria Jovita (February 14, 1856, to February 10, 1955), followed by Luisa, called Louise within the family, who was born in 1861, married Jose Juan Cenon "John" Pena, and lived to around 1918. Dolores Juana, called Lola, was born in December 1863, and died in October 1888. Maria Fidelena Manuela, nicknamed Illena, was born in April 1866 and died in May 1888, just five months after her wedding to Jose Aneceto "Seto" Pena. Prudenciana II was born in 1869 and lived into the second decade of the 1900s, and Maria de Jesus, the last child, was born in August 1870 and died four months later. Cipriano had two older brothers. Florentino was born in October 1852 and died in March 1914, while Placido de Jesus was born in October 1857 and also died before the Great War. Cipriano's third brother, Maximiano, had been born in August 22, 1854, but the baby boy only lived until November 21 of that year.

The old family baptismal record lists Baca's name as Sipriano, but at one point in his life, he spelled his name as Cypriano. To avoid confusion we will use a standard spelling of Cipriano in this biography. He was born on Monday, September 26, 1859, the youngest son and the sixth child of Teofilo and Encarnacion Baca. Over his lifetime, Cipriano kept a close relationship with his older sister Maria Jovita Baca Walker, and "Aunt Jovita" became the most popular Baca relative among Cipriano's children. She was just four days shy of her 99th birthday when she died in Los Angeles.[14]

Cipriana Baca Randolph loved her Aunt Jovita and held a deep spiritual connection for her Hispanic heritage. She proudly told the author about her family treasures,

I have one of the Briones family heirlooms. The grandmother's mother brought three small red trunks with her from Spain. In one of these trunks were five Spanish shawls. These were to be part of her daughter's trousseau. I have the one that Aunt Jovita managed to hang on to and some day my daughter can pass it on to her daughter.

We still have one of those little red trunks in the Baca family. It is wood, painted red with flower designs, edged in brass and studded with brass headed nails. Aunt Jovita would use that trunk when she came to see us. On one of her visits, she was complaining to mother that her trunk was too small and she liked a very large trunk like my mother had. Mama liked the red trunk so she offered to trade her and they did.

After Mama died Grandma [Berry] took the trunk home and kept it until we children were older. She divided Mama's things [among us] and gave the trunk to [my sister] Maisie. Some years later Maisie's landlady was holding the trunk for unpaid rent. My brother Florentino found it out and paid the rent and took the trunk. His oldest daughter [Sally Gilberson Baca] now has it.[15]

Cipriana Randolph could recall very little about her father's boyhood. The Contra Costa County, California, public records for the 1860s and 1870s contain few references to Hispanic families, but it would seem likely that Cipriano attended some public school or St. Catherine's Catholic Church's parochial school established under the direction of the Dominican Fathers in Martinez. Baca's contemporaries considered him an educated man, and surviving records show that Baca wrote a clear legible hand and could read, write, and speak both English and Spanish fluently. Cipriano often wrote his name as "C. Baca," but on official reports, he used his full name.[16] In a writing tablet a youthful Baca mocked a ditty done by a youthful Abraham Lincoln in 1824; "Cipriano Baca is my name. And with my pen I wrote the same. I wrote in both haste and speed and left it here for fools to read."[17] Baca became an avid reader and some of his books survive.

* * * * *

Samuel Langhorne Clemens was a young man in the fall of 1865 and was living in San Francisco. A few years later, using his famous pen name, Mark Twain, he wrote about his adventures on the western frontier in a book called *Roughing It*. "It was just after noon, on a bright October day," wrote the humorist. Clemens/Twain went on to describe his firsthand account of an earthquake. He wrote, "The ground seemed to roll under me in waves, interrupted by a violent joggling up and down, and there was a heavy grinding noise as of brick houses rubbing together."[18]

The three shocks to the San Andreas Fault hit the Bay Area at 1:15 P.M. Sunday, October 8, and were recorded as a 6.3 magnitude shift running east to west. The bay tide rose to an unusual height. The San Francisco *Daily Alta California* reported that the walls of many buildings were cracked and that ceiling plaster had fallen in most of the houses in the city. A story in *Harper's Weekly* magazine said, "The rush from the Catholic Church on Vallejo Street was so great that the doors to the main entrance were carried away, and several persons were injured by being trampled upon." No one reported any deaths, maybe because it was Sunday and the town's business section was not open.[19] Cipriano had turned six years old just 13 days before, but his experience with earthquakes was enhanced three years later.

The San Francisco *Daily Morning Call*, of October 22, 1868, told the world, "The earthquake was quite severely felt at Vallejo, many chimneys toppling down, but no serious injury occurring." Vallejo was only a few miles southeast across the inlet from the Teofilo Baca rancho near Martinez. The newspaper went on to say that Naval Captain Mitchell, stationed at the Mare Island Navy Yard near Vallejo, told a reporter that "the ground shook so violently as almost to throw him off his feet, the shock being accompanied by a frightful rumbling sound." The newspaper also noted, "Several people took to the water, considering the stream much more safe than *terra firma*—which was *terra firma* no longer."[20]

This quake ruptured the southern segment of the Hayward Fault from Berkeley to Fremont. The Seismological Laboratory at Berkeley estimated that the quake caused a right-lateral strike-slip motion for this event that resulted in a 1.9-meter fault shift and a tremor of 7.0 magnitude. Five deaths and over 30 injuries received treatment because of the early-morning vibration. It was 7:53 on a bright Wednesday morning when the earth moved, for about a minute, across northern California and Nevada. The *Daily Morning Call* said, "Many acted as if they thought the Day of Judgment had come. For a time the excitement was intense, and the panic was general."[21]

Within a day of the quake, the San Francisco Chamber of Commerce felt compelled to issue a damage estimate for their city, because there was so much concern about the city's survival in light of the 1865 quake. Now three years later there was a new quake. A day after the dust settled, the Chamber's inspectors predicted, "the total loss on property will not exceed $300,000."[22] When this estimate converts into present dollar value, it reaches well over $4 million.

"I will set it down as a maxim that the operations of the human intellect are much accelerated by an earthquake," wrote Mark Twain in an essay published in one of his early works. "There is no incentive to rapid reasoning like an earthquake."[23]

The human mind is a complex organ and it is uncertain how knowledge of a person's youth is retained and what causes one to later recall forgotten events. We may never know what effect these two childhood earthquakes had upon the personality of Cipriano Baca, but his daughter Cipriana recalled that while the family was living in Socorro, New Mexico Territory, during 1906, the town suffered two small earthquakes that sent a wave of panic throughout the community. Our biographical journey will reach that point later in this narrative.

* * * * *

In the fading ink of Teofilo Baca's personal journal can still be seen his thinking concerning human experiences. He reasoned that a man's experiences are not things that happen to him, but how he is able to use the knowledge learned from these events. Someone once said that the frightening thing about family heredity and a child's developmental environment is that parents provide both. This was true for young Baca in a positive manner because as he grew older, Cipriano absorbed what today we refer to as the Hispanic culture and became cognizant of his own classical Spanish lineage. The Baca heritage had passed through the generations of the Vaca/Baca family with a tradition of public or military service that pervaded the generations to reach Teofilo and Encarnacion Baca's children. The Bible contains a proclamation that there is a season for all things. On the California frontier of the 1860s, however, there was little or no time for a prolonged boyhood. A boy was a child one day and a man the next. It was so with Cipriano Baca.

"Father may have been a farm hand when he was young, but I never saw him do any

[home] gardening until he was older," Cipriana Randolph recalled. "After I had married he lived in that little house in Albuquerque. He had a small vegetable garden behind his house there. It was the Depression and many people grew their own food in those days. I don't know how good [a gardener] he was, but he had one."[24] Baca's destiny was not to work the family lands.

Cipriano Baca's teenage years present a few problems for a present-day researcher because many early records are in faded Spanish and many wished-for documents were not preserved. Historians may never know how involved Teofilo Baca and his extended family were in the 1870s California agriculture export business. Wine and grain seem to be the most likely products that the Vaca/Baca ranchos may have developed for markets outside of northern California. It is also possible, based upon Cipriano's proficiency as a meat cutter, a fallback trade throughout his life, that the Baca brothers may have been meat contractors.

Cipriana Randolph recalled that her father had first left California in 1875 as a strong healthy 16-year-old, and spent a couple of years traveling along the Pacific Ocean trade circle in the Orient. There is no clear documentation concerning these months, and Cipriano Baca does not seem to have ever discussed this adventure with his friends. This ocean voyage may have been some type of seaman apprenticeship or a way for a young man to grow up by learning strong discipline. It is possible that Cipriano was sent abroad to learn about the family's overseas business investments.

It is also possible that none of the above ideas is correct. Cipriana Randolph had no written documentation to support her recollection. The paper trail on this teenage Baca adventure is so thin that no clear picture develops, but one fact is for sure: this completely uncertain two-year drama took a toll on the youthful Cipriano Baca's health. He seems to have developed something like tuberculosis and returned to his California home in poor physical condition.[25]

It is possible that the allying Cipriano stayed with his older sister Maria Jovita at Martinez upon his return to the Bay Area because among Baca's personal papers is a Western Union telegram dated July 5, 1877. The aged paper addressed to Jovita, from their uncle Jesus Baca at Davisville, said, "Your Father is dead."[26] Don Teofilo Baca had died at the Putah Creek ranch, and the *Chronicle*, published in nearby Vallejo, carried his obituary a couple of days later.[27]

The author of Proverbs, in verse 20 of chapter 6, admonishes his readers concerning obedience to their parents saying, "My child, keep your father's commandments, and do not forsake your mother's teachings." Cipriano had done both of these directives, but now he was on his own. There is another ageless maxim that says a boy becomes a man when his father dies. Cipriano Baca was now a man. He would never forget his Spanish heritage even when others despised him because of his cultural lineage. Young Cipriano wanted to regain his health and make his own future, establish his own reputation and become someone whom others would respect because of his deeds and not disdain because of his cultural lineage. He had an inner determination to follow that dream.

Following his father's funeral, Cipriano Baca left El Dorado, taking with him his memories, dreams, and lessons learned from his parents, his extended family, his friends, his siblings, and memories of the covetous greed of the California 49ers and their descendents. Once planted, the seeds of justice would grow slowly before they broke the surface and sprang forth to give birth to a law enforcement legend. The youthful Baca set his face east toward the rising sun and never looked back. He never again resided within the state of California.

"While I cannot document this, Aunt Jovita told us that Father went to Arizona for his health," recalled Cipriana Randolph. "It seems he was supposed to have TB and [he] went to Arizona for [the mineral water] treatment. He lived on cattle ranches. He fully recovered his health and I never knew of him being sick until his last year."[28]

2

A New Life in Arizona Territory

"Remember the days of old, consider the years long past, ask your father, and he will inform you; your elders, and they will tell you."—Deuteronomy 32:07

The word "Arizona" has a pleasant ring to the ear. There are two schools of thought concerning the origin and meaning of the name for the 48th state. One interpretation is that Arizona is the Spanish corruption of the Aztec Indian word *Arizuma*, translated as "silver-bearing," as in mineral rocks. The second explanation claims origin in the Pima Indian word *Arizonac*, translated to mean the "little spring place." Since both definitions have a ring of truth, the reader is free to decide.

* * * * *

"I really don't know much of what Father did [on those Arizona ranches]. I do know that he did live in Arizona for a while before he went to New Mexico," Cipriana Randolph remembered. Baca was making above-scale pay for a range rider when he left the Arizona Territory, but he had started out working as a day laborer earning a small fee and board before advancing to a range hand. By 1880, following some roaming, Baca seems to have taken root at the Sanford Ranch in Pima County. "I do remember him [her father] talking about a Chinese cook and how he never did learn to like that kind of food. I don't remember ever having Chinese food until after I married [Walter Randolph] and moved to California."[1]

The 1880 census taken for the Cienega Valley in Pima County, Arizona Territory, shed some more light on Baca's location and occupation. Twenty-year-old Cipriano was working as a "farm helper" for Don Alonzo Sanford. The wealthy farmer from Honeoye Falls, Monroe County, New York, had married a young woman from Virginia and escaped the civil conflict in the east by moving to the westernmost section of New Mexico Territory. A year later, these lands became Arizona Territory, and Sanford's ranch was growing so that by 1880 he employed his Virginia-born brother-in-law, Baca, and two English-born laborers, plus a Chinese cook to help operate the home place. Sanford had a young wife and three young daughters. Sanford had established a large ranch on Cienega Creek located in Stock Valley about 19 miles north of Camp Crittenden and four miles south of the Total

Wreck Mine. Sanford's place had become one of the six largest farm and livestock operations in Pima County, and the ranch headquarters became the center of social life for the neighboring ranches. It was a common scene for area dances, elections, and other local celebrations.[2]

Sanford posted a newspaper notice concerning use of his personal DS letter brand in January 1875 and claimed he did not sell any cattle marked with that brand. This was a warning to butchers not to buy any of his missing cattle. In late 1880, two of Sanford's neighbors retaliated by accusing him of rustling a few of their cattle, and the confrontation almost reached bloodshed before it was finally settled in court.[3]

Cipriano Baca was highly educated and possessed keen business skill for a young man of the late 1870s, especially for a Hispanic. Sanford was quick to understand these qualities and accorded Baca a measure of respect and trust beyond his years and social statues as a "Mexican" range hand. How long Cipriano worked on the Sanford place is unknown, but circumstances would indicate that he lived at the Sanford farm-ranch for an extended period. Baca earned additional compensation acting as a beef contractor and butcher for his employer before he ventured out as a freelance operator conducting business with the builders of the railroad across Arizona toward New Mexico.

Cipriana Randolph recalled an interesting detail about her father's Arizona days:

> One thing I do remember about the Arizona time was that Father said he knew Wyatt Earp. Father said Earp was tall and blond and had a commanding manner. He said that Earp had a younger brother [named Morgan] that attended a dance at the [Sanford] ranch were he worked and that he was surprised at how much they [the Earps] looked alike.

In Stuart N. Lake's research notes for his 1931 classic biography of Wyatt Earp, there is a reference to Morgan Earp having some disagreement with William "Curly Bill" Brocius and Charles "Pony Diehl" Ray, first rank riders with the Cochise County rustlers known as the Cow-boys, while he was attending a social at Sanford's place. This incident is possible because Morgan operated a gambling concession in Tucson, enjoyed social functions, and was disliked by the Cow-boys. Some considered Morgan Earp a dangerous man with a quick temper and, like his older brothers Virgil and Wyatt, had a history of riding as a stagecoach express messenger and serving as a peace officer in Kansas, Montana Territory, and Arizona Territory. Deputy U.S. Marshal Wyatt Earp would kill Bill Brocius during his Vendetta Ride in March 1882.

> I remember that Earp story because I was visiting Father for Christmas about a year or so after he left the rangers [Herb McGrath's 1918 New Mexico Mounted Police force] after the Great War. I saw him in Albuquerque at the other place [Baca's rented house] and he showed me a copy of a *Saturday Evening Post* story he was reading about old Tombstone.[4] Then he said he had helped the man in the story. I asked who and he said Wyatt Earp. I was a teenage girl and the name Wyatt Earp didn't mean anything to me, so I asked who he was. Father said Earp had been a well-known gambler and lawman in the Tombstone area. Father said he and the man he worked for had gone to Tucson for some supplies and someone pointed Earp out to them.
>
> Father seemed to think very highly of Earp. I thought it was funny when he said he would like to see a book or movie about Earp's life. Years later every time I saw that TV show [*The Life and Legend of Wyatt Earp*] I would think about that visit with my father and wish that I had asked him more about his life [in Arizona].[5]

Destiny always seems to have its own plan, and destiny had a road map for both Wyatt Earp and Cipriano Baca. The paths of these two officers would cross again months later in the mountains between New Mexico and Arizona.

* * *

At some point in the early 1880s, his 28-year-old cousin Teodoro Baca, a butcher by trade, and another west coast friend named Fleishman, who was a storekeeper, had joined Cipriano in Arizona Territory. In the 1880 census for Pima County "in the country" section in the Whetstone Mountains, at a supply center for the Southern Pacific Railroad, Cipriano's older cousin Teodoro Baca is listed as operating a traveling meat-selling business and driving wagons and stagecoaches for John D. Kinnear.[6] The 40-year-old merchant operated a six-horse hitch stage and express operation between Tucson and Tombstone officially called the Arizona Mail and Stage Line, but most people simply referred to the business as the Kinnear Express Line. The stage line charged $7 for a one-way ticket and advertised that they served "good meals on route at reasonable rates."

Teodoro and Cipriano Baca may have supplied some of the meat for these stage line roadhouses. They had a herd of cattle that was free grassing near the railroad construction crews building across southern Arizona headed toward a junction with the railroad crew heading west across southern New Mexico. The Baca team would stop at a crew camp and would butcher enough beef to fill the day's demand, while Fleishman sold the men much-needed personal items.

Baca's outdoor life, with its dangerous edge, may have seemed like the good life to a young man looking to have a successful future in the livestock business. It is not surprising that Cipriano soon caught the eye of a local young lady. As his financial situation continued to prosper with the expanded interest in developing the natural resources of the twin territories of Arizona and New Mexico, Baca also had visions of settling down with a wife and family.

The Baca family records are incomplete for the period covering Cipriano's stay in Arizona Territory and human memory could recall little. "I don't know just how we kids knew that Father had been married before he married Mama," recalled Cipriana Randolph. "The boys [her brothers Gilberson and Florentino] and I have talked about it a little, but I don't think either of them knew

Cipriana Baca attended public school in Chama and high school in Albuquerque. She graduated from Albuquerque Business College and attended Highlands Normal School, now Highland University, at Las Vegas. Here she met and married Walter Randolph of California (Cipriana Randolph).

any more than I did. I assume that Father probably was married near where he was born the first time."

Cipriano Baca could have returned to California to find a wife and returned with her to Arizona Territory. It is very possible that Cipriana guessed wrong about the location of her father's first marriage. It seems more likely that her father first married not in California, but in the land of Arizona. One record has been located that seems to indirectly support an Arizona marriage for Baca. One of the questions asked of adults on the fifteenth federal census, taken in 1930, concerned their age at the time of their first marriage. Baca told a census enumerator that he had been married when he was 21 years old. This age fits within the short time span when Baca lived in the Arizona Territory.[7]

When the author questioned Cipriana Randolph further concerning her father's first marriage she expressed the belief that her father's first wife "and a young girl named Eva" had died. "I cannot recall how we kids came to know this, but I do know that we all seemed to know it for a long time." It is most likely that Cipriano's sister Aunt Jovita Walker told the Baca children about their father's first wife and the infant daughter.[8]

Cipriana Randolph's lack of personal knowledge concerning her father's early marriages is very understandable, because she was a 10-year-old girl when her own mother died, and in the nineteenth century it was not customary to discuss the deceased except upon a rare occasion. In the Hispanic culture there is celebrated an annual *Dia del Muerto*, Day of the Dead, to honor deceased loved ones, but it is unclear if the Baca family honored this cultural festival.

Conjecture would lead one to assume that this first marriage ended in death or a divorce. A death or divorce in the 1880s was a seldom-discussed family tragedy; thus, it is understandable that Baca family stories may not recall such an event. Arizona law did not require maintenance of natural death records, and no legal evidence yet located supports an assumption that a divorce ended Cipriano's first marriage. The search continues on this matter.

* * *

On Saturday, July 2, 1881, Ohio native James Garfield became the second president to fall at the hands of an assassin. Over the next 80 days, the nation stood captivated by the daily medical reports concerning the president's recovery. The first shot grazed the 49-year-old Garfield's right arm, but a second .44 caliber bullet struck him in the back and pierced the first lumbar vertebra. This is a nonlethal wound by current medical standards, but with 1880s-style medical care, the wound became infected and the slow poisoning finally stopped his heart. President Garfield was in office only 199 days. It is very likely that Cipriano Baca followed the president's fluctuating medical condition along with most of the nation's middle working class who, like him, had concerns about their personal economic future.

Cipriano, like most men, would have worn a black armband during the country's days of national morning. Baca must have been relieved and his doubts allayed when the nation's economy continued to grow under the new president, and his own financial situation continued to prosper with the expanded interest in developing New Mexico Territory's natural resources.

Cipriano Baca's service as an undercover agent for the Southwest Cattle Raisers' Association is the most difficult area of his law enforcement career to document. By the very nature of undercover work, there is an element of anonymity from the public record and newspapers. Add to this the fact that early 1880s field records for many cattlemen's associations no longer survive. It is easy to see that this lack of a paper trail severely hinders any detailed analysis of Cipriano's contribution to establishing a safer ranching environment in the Arizona–New Mexico border region.

On the southwestern frontier, a *cowpoke* was a person who worked the stockyards herding the cattle from pen to market, and a person that worked a ranch was a *cow-herder* who was paid about $50 a month plus board for dawn-to-dusk work. Unlike the romantic way latter-day novels and Hollywood would depict them, the term *cow-boy*, on the frontier, was reserved for the "roughs, thieves and bandits" who roamed Texas, Arizona and New Mexico with impunity. The Salt Lake City *Tribune* said, "The cowboy is a cross between vaquero and a highwayman, which intensifies the worst qualities of each type." Tucson's *Arizona Daily Star* pointedly said, "They are law-breakers of the most flagrant character." Meanwhile Tucson's other newspaper, the *Arizona Daily Citizen,* continued the incrimination saying that anyone "who attempts to defend Arizona cowboys by restricting the term to its literal meaning of herder simply makes an ass of himself."

C.M. Chase, in a letter dated late November 1881, described the Cow-boy situation in southwestern New Mexico Territory to his friends back home in Vermont. "The cow-boys, or roughs and thieves, are so numerous that no man ventures any distance from the village [of Deming] without his Winchester rifle, ready to repeat 12 or 16 times without reloading. With this element constantly on the watch for plunder, a man's life goes for naught." In Arizona Territory one outspoken newspaper editor wrote, "The stock industry is to-day paralyzed all through the section they [the Cow-boys] roam. The Cow-boys are outlaws, their hand is against the law-abiding people of the Territory, let them be dealt with accordingly. Let the public consider them outlaws, depredating upon the rights and property of the people, and wherever found let them be shot down like the Apache."[9]

Everett B. Pomroy, United States attorney for Arizona Territory, in a situation report to Attorney General Wayne MacVeigh, dealt with the misdeeds of the "Cow-boy" clan. He described these men as "the lawless element that exists along the border, who subsist by rapine plunder and highway robbery; and whose amusements are drunken orgies, and murder. The evil is one that feeding upon itself does not exhaust it, but causes it to thrive. It is now assuming alarming proportions. This element in certain isolated sections has long defied the local authorities, it now threatens to brave the constituted authority of the government itself." An article in *Harper's Monthly Magazine* added to the concern by calling the Cow-boys "terrorists" who where "scourges of whole districts in Colorado, New Mexico, and Arizona."[10]

During this period of turmoil, Cipriano Baca's personal papers allude to his doing undercover work for the Southwest Cattle Growers' Association gathering information concerning Cow-boy activities. It had become crystal clear to government leaders and powerful business executives that blunt action was needed. An extralegal unwritten extermination order was issued to a select group of manhunters; clean out the Cow-boys in southeastern Arizona Territory and southwestern New Mexico Territory.

After relocating to New Mexico Territory, Cipriano Baca continued to use his meat contractor position to keep watch for illegal livestock activities in the massive longroper haven in the Animas Valley of southwestern Grant County. Back in Arizona, the *Arizona*

Daily Star of Tucson was demanding that the Cow-boys "be hunted down like reptiles, and made to answer the penalty of their crimes, without the law's delay."

A letter published in the Chicago *Tribune* gave a clear explanation of what the writer called the "Gospel According to St. Gosper." It described Gosper's message as,

> the most suitable and eloquent sermon ever addressed to that class of human vermin [the Cow-boys]. The substance of it, as posted up in good print at the Post Office, is that the Hon. Mr. [John] Gosper, Acting Governor of Arizona, offers a reward of $500 to any person who kills a highway robber. To this, Wells & Fargo [Express Company] add an offer of $300 for the arrest and conviction of robbers of their express matter, but the Governor's proclamation is the one to win.[11]

Deputy U. S. Marshal Wyatt Earp answered the clarion call with a bloody sweep of the Cochise County water holes during the spring of 1882. He and his small posse quickly sent some of the area's rustlers to Valhalla and caused others to seek new locals for practicing the ancient art of the running iron. Now Tucson's *Arizona Daily Star*, the Democrat newspaper who had led the charge to rid Arizona of the Cow-boys, decried the deadly actions of Wyatt Earp, a Republican, and his federal posse as renegade lawmen "who used their commission as warrants for rapine and murder" against the Cow-boy, who it turns out where really peace-loving Democrat ranchers. A reporter for the *Kansas City Journal* stated the matter simply saying that Wyatt Earp "broke up the terrible rustlers" and "has killed within our personal knowledge six men, and he is popularly accredited with relegating to the dust no less than ten of his fellow men."[12]

In mid–April 1882, Deputy U.S. Marshal Wyatt Earp and his posse left Arizona Territory. They stopped overnight in Silver City, en route across New Mexico Territory to seclusion in Colorado in the wake of his bloody raid against the Cow-boys, and left a couple of horses in the care of a Wells Fargo undercover operative. They sold the other horses of the posse members. In old age, Wyatt Earp said he clandestinely returned to Arizona Territory later that summer and killed John Peters Ringo, a man he suspected in the assassination of his brother Morgan and a leader of Cow-boys. Some historians have postulated that the Wells Fargo Express Company, the Santa Fe Railway, and the Southern Pacific Railroad provided Wyatt Earp with the logistical assistance and financial support he needed to complete this undercover operation. This theory says that Earp reached the Arizona–New Mexico border via the railroad from his Colorado sanctuary and someone provided him with a horse to reach his secretly assembled posse in the mountains of southeastern Arizona Territory.

A freighter discovered the body of John Peters Ringo on Friday, July 14, 1882. The corpse contained a bullet hole in the head. In a strange twist on truth, during the late 1950s, this outlaw was lionized as an "Arizona frontier marshal" in a 39-episode CBS television series carrying his name.

Cipriano Baca's daughter may have unknowingly supplied support to the claim that Wyatt Earp had returned to Arizona and killed Johnny Ringo.

> Later [in the early 1880s] when father was a meat contractor [and butcher] selling Arizona beef to [railroad construction] buyers at Deming [New Mexico] he made friends with the Wells Fargo man [stationed in that railroad junction community]. Father was some kind of special officer for the [Grant County] sheriff [Harvey Whitehill] at Silver City [and special deputy under George H. Stevens, sheriff of Graham County, Arizona, as well as an undercover agent for

the Southwest Cattle Growers' Association] and the Wells Fargo man knew that about father. So one day he asked him to deliver two horses to a U.S. marshal up in the gap west of that mining town [Steins] on the railroad before you reach Arizona. Father spent two days camped out [at the old Butterfield stage station site] watching for the man. Then one day he saw a man step off the train up in the pass. That man was Wyatt Earp. Father gave him the horses and gear and Earp gave my father a twenty-dollar gold piece and Earp rode off for Arizona.

Cipriana Randolph was unable to provide a date or other data concerning when her father said he delivered a horse to Wyatt Earp, but a July 1882 meeting would fit the time frame of Cipriano's known whereabouts. If this chronology is correct, then this account could lend vital support for Earp's claim he clandestinely returned to Arizona Territory and killed Johnny Ringo; Earp was acquainted enough with the outlaw to call him Jack. If the horse delivery account related by Mrs. Randolph is true, then Cipriano Baca likely played a minor supporting role in one of Arizona Territory's enduring outlaw-lawman folk tales.

In 2001, historians gained another piece to the Vendetta Ride puzzle with the discovery of a carbon copy of a previously unknown letter purportedly written by Miguel A. Otero. This unsigned 1940 letter details the former territorial governor's youthful role as legman for Don Miguel, his namesake father, who as a vice president of the Santa Fe Railway, made every effort to shield Wyatt Earp's federal posse during their April 1882 stay in Albuquerque. The letter claims that Don Miguel's monumental task, undertaken on behalf of a political and economic cabal that reached all the way to President Chester A. Arthur's desk in the Executive Mansion, was successful. Representatives from the Santa Fe Railway, the Southern Pacific Railroad, the Wells Fargo Express Company, and a vast network of national business interests and conservative political concerns composed the cabal.[13]

If the events described in the so-called Otero Letter are true, then it is premiere evidence to substantiate the claim that Deputy U.S. Marshal Wyatt Earp had substantial and influential backing in his crusade to eradicate the Cow-boy outlaws in Arizona Territory.

3

Diaper Days in Deming, New Mexico Territory

"When my husband sent for me in the spring [1883] he wrote and said for God's sake bring some tablecloths, for all they know out here is oil cloth and I had rather run my hand over a snake then feel of them. I brought only a few pieces of silver and a few dishes and these tablecloths."
— Mrs. Ed Pennington, August 1938

Cipriano Baca was in his early 20s when he lost his first wife, but he was not detoured by this personal setback. Once again, Baca sought a new future in a new area. This time Cipriano and his cousins and friends chose the terrain and confines of a new railroad settlement in the high desert country of southwestern New Mexico Territory.

The first non–Indians to see the area around present-day Deming where Spanish adventurers led by Juan Bautista de Anza, Spanish governor of Nuevo México, mapping a trade route from Santa Fe to the mining developments at Airzpe deep in the Crown Province of Sonora. Anza's expedition occurred in November 1780, but it left no permanent settlements along its survey route.[1]

"Deming is fairly well sheltered from winds, and has a most excellent water supply," said the Santa Fe Railroad's 1902 travel promotional booklet *New Mexico's Health Resorts*. "This region has a summer climate a little cooler than the State of New York, and a winter climate a few degrees warmer than that of Charleston, S.C." The writer forgot to say Deming had very little humidity.

The town today called Deming was first located about ten miles east of the present site and dubbed Little Chicago. However, on Tuesday, March 8, 1881, representatives of the Atchison, Topeka and Santa Fe Railway and the Southern Pacific Railroad gathered near a water source known as Mimbres Springs to drive a ceremonial silver spike connecting these two rival transportation companies. The site of this remote ritual proved to be the prologue to a new town site.

With the connection of these two railroad giants, America had its second transcontinental rail line, and this system held a huge commercial advantage. This new southern route made it possible to travel or ship commerce from the Atlantic to the Pacific coast in relative comfort unaffected by the harsh winter weather of the northern route. A 50-mile spur line soon connected Silver City to draw business from the area mines. A second spur went south from Deming to intersect with the line connecting to Arizona's mining interests in southeast Cochise County. These two short lines provided the border country mines with direct access to the big ore smelter in El Paso. The east-west railroad also provided the area's large ranching operations ready access to shipping pens to distant meatpackers. Kansas City was 1,149 rail miles east of Deming.

The earlier settlers in Deming were a diverse population. Chinese laborers built the railroads to this junction point, and some of them stayed in the area to maintain the system. Mexican nationals who came north to work in the mines where they earned about $24 for a 60-hour workweek also made Grant County their home. Other nationalities arrived and added their skills and culture to the small American melting pot of humanity. Day laborers earned $2.25 a day, carpenters earned $3.50 and stonemasons could command $5.00. Potatoes cost $3.25 a bushel, butter was 45 cents a pound, and flour sold for $4.50 a hundred pounds. No one doubted that the economic power structure in the infant community rested with the Anglo population.

The Santa Fe and Southern Pacific companies quickly became economic and political forces in the life of "their town" developing in southeastern Grant County. One of the projects the two rail lines undertook was the construction of a joint occupancy depot, and each railroad built their roundhouses and repair shops near this new depot. Railroad employees set up housekeeping in a tent community near their work sites, and Little Chicago faded into history. Charles Crocker, a Southern Pacific official, named the new railroad junction community to honor his wife Mary Anne Deming's mother and father. A year after its founding, Deming boosted of a school, several hotels and saloons, business houses, a newspaper and a federal international customs house.[2]

The Ed Pennington family was among the first wave of settlers in the new town of Deming. Pennington had been born in New York City in 1843 and moved to California with his father when he was eight years old. He learned the printer's trade before joining the Union army in 1863, and following his discharge in 1866, he settled in Little Rock, Arkansas, and married. The couple decided the future lay in the westward expansion, so they relocated to New Las Vegas, but since they were both "lungers" and suffered from tuberculosis, they needed a drier climate.

In 1938, the 84-year-old Mrs. Pennington recalled the early days in Deming,

> My husband decided to come to Deming and as he was a newspaperman he bought the *Headlight,* and later the Deming *Tribune* and the *Democrat* and combined them all three into one paper.
> When my husband came to Deming he said that he [had] thought Las Vegas was the end of civilization, but God help this country. People were living in all kinds of make shift houses when we came in here. One family up on the hill was living under a piece of oil cloth stretched over two poles with a hole cut in the oil cloth to put the stove's pipe through. This family lived in this place for over a year. When we arrived here [in Deming with the children] Ed had rented us a room for $30 a month and we had to carry water three blocks.

When Ed Pennington left home, he would remind his wife to keep the doors locked and to stay inside their cabin. "It wasn't only the Indians that he was afraid of, but as there were always fights on the street. He was always afraid that we could be hurt." Pennington served Deming as a peace justice. When the area became Luna County, he became the first county assessor and later county clerk. Ed Pennington is remembered as Deming's longtime postmaster following his appointment in December 1904.[3]

The legend of Dan Tucker says he was born in Canada and spent his youth in Indiana. During his early youth he learned to be a machinist before he started his killing ways while living in Colorado. Tucker was slender of build with blue eyes and light hair with "a shy and retiring disposition." His normal dress was reported to be a blue flannel shirt tucked into overalls, with light calfskin boots and a large dark sombrero. Tucker was reputed to have been extremely efficient with a pistol, but his weapon of choice was a double-barreled shotgun for use "in the line of duty" upholding his brand of law and order.

Shortly after his arrival in southwestern New Mexico, Tucker became one of Grant County Sheriff Harvey Howard Whitehill's deputies, and in April 1878 he became Silver City's first town marshal. He held the dual job until January 1880, when he left Silver City to work at the mining camp of Shakespeare. In this wide-open village, Dan Tucker renewed his friendship with Curly Bill Brocius and the Cow-boy rustlers of Arizona Territory's San Simon Valley and the infamous John Kinney band of thieves. Tucker had worked with some of these men during the "El Paso Salt War of 1877" and the ill-fated "Mine Owner's War" in Old Mexico.

In the fall of 1881, Whitehill reemployed Tucker and sent him to the new railroad junction of Deming to keep a lid on the influx of unsavory characters. Within days of reaching Deming, Tucker used his deadly shotgun, sent three men into the afterlife, and wounded two others. In February 1882, the *Southwest Sentinel* of Silver City reported, "Everything is quiet in Deming." Years later, the *Silver City Enterprise* printed a matter-of-fact statement: "Dan Tucker informs us that in the course of his duty as deputy sheriff he has been obliged to kill eight men in this county, besides several in Lincoln and Dona Ana counties."[4]

Killing can become a way of life, and Tucker was no exception. His willingness to take human life almost cost him his own life at the hands of a lynch mob bent on revenge for Tucker's killing a very popular fellow deputy sheriff. Tucker finally stood trial for this murder and narrowly escaped with his life. In 1884, he gave up being a peace officer and tried his hand at being a businessman.

It is uncertain if Cipriano Baca and Dan Tucker were ever friends or even knew each other, but the odds are in favor of that prospect because of Baca's undercover work with the cattlemen's association. Deming was a small town, and Tucker operated the Eclipse Restaurant and Saloon and Baca conducted a meat market. Within a few years, Tucker left Deming and settled in California where he died as a lonely and forgotten man.[5]

Tucker's successor also earned his page in Deming history. He was a skirt-chasing drunk. Once he abused alcohol so badly that he stumbled into another man's house and crawled into bed with his startled wife. The woman got up and went to locate the deputy's wife so she could lead her wayward husband home. The *Silver City Enterprise* summed up the laughable incident by sarcastically mocking the officer: "Model deputy sheriff, this fellow."[6]

* * *

With the organization of a civilian militia to guard against Indian raids, a vigilante group backing a killing deputy sheriff to control the rowdy elements, and an influx of eastern settlers with families, a frontier civilization slowly took root in Deming. C.M. Chase wrote about primary business development in New Mexico Territory, saying,

> Here changes are rapid, society is forming, values are unfixed, business channels are being cut, emigration is pouring in and during this process of formation opportunities for profitable

investment are numerous, springing up every day and every hour, and those who can best judge of results in this formation process, best comprehend the sources and causes of growth, and guess nearest at future supply and demand, are the ones who can invest with the chances of profit.[7]

Cipriano Baca's short-lived Arizona romance had ended, so he and his Baca cousins, Manuel, Patricio and Teodoro, and their friends looked for new adventure. The men were astute enough to recognize the business opportunity found in south central New Mexico now that the railroad had opened up the world's trade markets to that vast, sparsely populated area. Cipriano, still recovering from his tuberculosis, may also have appreciated the area's healthful dry desert climate.

By the time of the 1885 New Mexico territorial census, the Baca cousins had established a ranch on the Mexican border near the village of Palomas, bought town lots in Deming, invested in area mining operations, and conducted other commercial business enterprises in Grant County and the newly formed Sierra County. Teodoro and his bride Mariana Lopez Baca settled in Silver City, while Manuel, his wife Maria Lugarda Susana Alvarado Baca, their six children and his brother Patricio lived on the Baca ranch. Fleishman and his two brothers and a sister and their families became Cipriano's next-door neighbors. They all engaged in the business, religious, and social life of the bustling and youthful Deming, a settlement of 1,000 souls.

How did the Baca cousins become so successful so quickly? The answer is simpler than it might appear at first. Land and water are the keys to the cattle business, and southern Grant County had quality land. "The grazing territory is unlimited and the grass very rich, but there is no water, and unless windmills will furnish the supply, there is little to be expected from that source," wrote C.M. Chase about his visit to Deming in late November 1881. "The water is good, but runs from 40 to 60 feet under ground."

"The climate is delightful, the best out of doors. The sharp, clear sunshine is a trifle too much for comfort. The rainy season comes usually in July and August... sufficient to keep the prairie covered with bunches of grammar grass." Sandstorms was the only complaint that Chase had about the country. "When you hear about a 'sandstorm' in Southern New Mexico, don't imagine that the term is used as a figure of speech. During these storms it is next to impossible to travel or do outdoor work." The Baca cousins homesteaded rangeland and dug water wells. They already had the nucleus of a small cattle herd; therefore, they just needed to settle into a program of breeding and range management.

A financial exercise based upon 1881 cattle prices will present a simple explanation of how the Bacas could have developed their ranching enterprise. If they had purchased a straight 2,000-head herd consisting of 1,000 cows and two-year old heifers, 650 yearling steers and heifers, and 350 two-year old steers at an average cost of $15 per head, the cousins would have invested $30,000. At market time, a 2,000-head rancher would normally sell about 350 three-year-olds and the best of the two-year-old steers at about $25 per head for a sell price of $8,750. Now factor in that 1,000 breading cows will normally provide about 75 to 80 percent calves or say 750 additions to the heard, for 2,750 cattle. Subtract the 350 cattle sold at market and the Bacas had 2,400 cattle left on their range with a value of $15 each, or $36,000. The real ranch profit, minus ranch expenses, would be the $8,750 for cattle sold, plus the $6,000 value of new stock for a total profit of $14,750, or 34 percent first-year return on the investment.[8] Within a few years, the Baca cousins could have developed a highly successful cattle operation and a small chicken and sheep production business for Cipriano's Deming butcher shop. Life was good.

The beginning of the end for the Baca brotherhood started when Patricio died on Friday, December 23, 1887. The beloved and jovial middle brother was buried in Deming's new cemetery after the Christmas Sunday holiday. By the end of the 1880s, the two remaining Baca brothers had left Grant County, and for the first time since Cipriano left California, none of his relatives surrounded him. The effect that situation may have had upon Cipriano's mental health is unknown, but from this point forward he seems to have been driven by some internal force to succeed in the capitalistic world of the 1890s.

No records have been located to suggest that Cipriano and his two former partner cousins ever again saw each other or maintained any meaningful contact. Manuel took his family south into Old Mexico and settled in the mining country near Cananea. Meanwhile, Teodoro returned to California with his family in tow and established a home in the high desert country at the trading center of San Bernardino, near the homestead of the Earp brothers' parents.

The term "fleshewer" as used in early official records denotes a person now called a butcher, but it is doubtful that Cipriano had ever heard the arcane title. Over fifteen years after Baca first settled in Deming, P.J. Bennett, the *Deming Herald*'s editor and publisher, remembered that Cipriano had "resided here in the early days, when the only building that marked the present city of Deming was the one now occupied by Henry Myers as a meat market." The article continued by saying that Cipriano Baca had "herded his beef cattle on the site where the seat [courthouse] of Luna County rests now."[9]

Cipriano had first gone into partnership with a man named Raithel in the Pioneer Meat Market. In 1884, the two men advertised their business with a large box ad placed in the center of page one for the Christmas Day issue of Charles Greene's joint newspaper, the *Deming Tribune* and *Lake Valley Herald*. The focal point of the advertisement featured a steer head looking left across the page just under the paper's masthead. The Raithel & Baca business was the "Leading Meat Market" in the young settlement, selling only the choicest beef, mutton and pork cuts as well as headcheese and bologna. The meat market was also the source for pork and liver sausage and claimed "Honest Prices and Full Weight Guaranteed." The meat purveyors also made another business promise to their customers in a catchy sales gimmick: "I can't sell ya nothing, but the best I can sell ya."[10]

Congress authorized a limited meat inspection program, managed by the Department of Agriculture's new Bureau of Animal Industry, in May 1884. In the spring of 1891, the federal government began to issue meat inspection stamps so the buying public had a visual symbol of the grade and quality of the meat they purchased. This style of inspection ceased in 1953.[11] Provisions of the 1884 law affected Baca, not just because he was a rancher and a meat contractor, but because he was also an undercover agent for the Southwest Cattle Growers Association.

Cipriano Baca bought out his meat market partner in the spring of 1885. He rechristened the retail business the Deming Meat Market and started supplying the new business with beef from his own Mimbres River Cattle Company. The business continued to grow, and when he could no longer supply all the meat he needed, Baca used his contacts with area ranchers and his past reputation as a top dollar negotiator, to become a successful region-wide meat supplier.[12]

The Mimbres River Cattle Company was formed on January 3, 1884, with $500,000 in land and livestock and incorporated on Tuesday, July 7, 1885, and the papers where recorded in the county clerk's office at Silver City. Five years later, the territorial tax assessment roll noted that the Mimbres River Cattle Company owned a home range in Grant County and additional acreage in neighboring Sierra County's Lake Valley precinct. The Lake Valley area was excellent rangeland and part of the Black Range mining district. The mining bug soon bit Cipriano Baca.[13]

The Mimbres people were an ancient Indian tribe. They lived in the valley of the river with the same name that heads in the Black Range and flows south toward Deming on the way to Old Mexico. *Mimbres* is Spanish for the osiers that line the riverbanks and are used to weave baskets or wickerwork. The Indians lived in the area from 200 to 1400 C.E. and produced a very distinctive black-on-while painted pottery and chalcedony arrowheads. At first, the Mimbres lived in pit houses, but finally established pueblos. Mimbres buried their dead in earth mounds with the head of the corpse placed in a pottery. These burial pots are highly prized today by artifact collectors; thus, most area burial mounds have suffered illegal raids and desecration by pottery hunters.

Lake Valley, now a Sierra County ghost town located in what today is ranching country, was home to renegade Apaches and foolhardy prospectors in the late 1870s. These tranquil rolling foothills on the eastern edge of the Mimbres Mountains were the scene of a huge silver strike in 1878 that in a few years produced over $3 million of shining metal. By the early 1880s, the boomtown was a hub for a lawless element that finally required intervention by the territorial militia and death dealing peace officers like Isaac "Jim" McIntyre and Timothy Isaiah "Long-Haired Jim" Courtright to restore order to the region. Cipriano Baca was one of the capitalists who invested in mining property located within the Lake Valley district.[14]

The 27th Territorial Legislative Assembly convened in Santa Fe in December 1886. These lawmakers were very favorable toward the New Mexico livestock industry by enacting some protectionist legislation. They also passed laws dealing with irrigation rights, established bank regulations and for the first time defined what constituted murder within the territory. The summer range drought was broken before the legislators left for home. A massive blizzard, containing double-digit-below-zero temperature and strong winds, settled over the Rocky Mountains west until February 1887. This weather front devastated America's livestock industry from Montana to the Rio Grande. Millions of dollars worth of livestock were lost to the cold and snow. The Mimbres River Cattle Company took heavy losses, but Baca was able to maintain a small heard to rebuild the operation.

In the late 1880s, Baca was still proudly advertising his quality beef in Ed Pennington's *Deming Headlight*, with advertisements saying he gave the "Highest Cash Price Paid for Hides [$5.00 for top quality]" and that "Orders by Mail or Telegraph Receive Prompt Attention." Baca was a visionary when it came to salesmanship; an electronic mail-order business in the late 1880s? One can only wonder how successful an Internet business Baca could have developed.

Twenty-five dollars was the advertising rate for a seven-inch space run over a three-month period, twelve issues. Baca used his investment wisely for public relations and business promotions by always using this notice, "$100 Reward for Anyone Caught Stealing from Our Slaughter House." There is no record that Baca ever paid a reward for theft from one of his businesses.[15]

On a Saturday in late September 1888, Cipriano took lethal action on the streets of Deming. With one quick pistol shot, he dropped a vicious dog in front of his meat market. The animal had attacked and savagely bitten the eight-year-old son of Col. J.A. Lockhart. The father and son had been attending to business at a nearby store when the animal set upon the youth. "Deming is overrun with good for nothing, worthless, and in many cases, dangerous dogs," editorialized the *Deming Headlight*, "and if our precinct officers are unable under the law to get rid of them for the protection of the people, then the people should certainly protect themselves." At first, Dr. Stovall had concerns about young George Lockhart, but the boy recovered quickly. Concerned citizens who feared this incident might have involved a case of rabies swiftly dealt with the dog problem.[16]

Cipriano Baca suffered two personal losses in 1888. He received news in May that Mara Fidelena Manuela Baca-Pena, his

Taken at Deming, New Mexico, in about 1885, Baca gave this small fading *carte de visite* to his sister Jovita who gave it to sister-in-law Mary Berry (Mary Baca photograph album/ Cipriana Randolph).

younger sister he called Illena, had died just five months after Cipriano had seen her happily married. In October, Baca received a telegram concerning yet another younger sister. This message notified him of the death of 23-year-old Lola, Dolores Juana Baca.

In early March 1889, Baca sold the Deming Meat Market to Albert Lindauer. Months later Lindauer passed the market on to Henderson and Company just as the meat and hide market was on the rebound. The sheep industry was also on the upswing because of the enhanced price of wool in eastern markets, and the "baa-baa-baa" of woolies echoed in valleys all across New Mexico. The economic rebound also gave birth to a new wave of livestock thieves.[17]

Baca took his meat market money and invested in Deming's growing livery stable business. Baca treated his horses with care; it was just good business. However, Cipriano could not be called sentimental when it came to horses; to him they where a capital investment. Baca viewed horses as a means of transportation, and once he rode a horse to death during a long and difficult posse chase.

Cipriano operated the Elephant Corral and Livery Stable where he bought and sold horses, rented buggies, hacks, matched teams, and saddle horses. Six months after he took over as the preparatory of the Elephant Corral, the *Deming Headlight* noted Cipriano's latest effort: "C. Baca is now operating the Silver avenue stable in place of Henderson; a change for the better." The old decorative brick livery and blacksmith shop still stands and is on the New Mexico State Register of Historical Buildings as part of Deming's Silver Avenue Historic District.[18]

* * *

Proverbs 12:04 says, "A good wife is the crown of her husband." The 25-year-old Cipriano Baca married Mary Linda Keefe, often called Marie, in Deming on Saturday, March 19, 1887. The Reverend Margeson performed the ceremony witnessed by R.F. Stovall and Clara J. Trisel. There are no family records that indicate when, where, or how Miss Keefe made the acquaintance of the dashing Mr. Baca. A mystery of equal proportion surrounds their courtship.[19]

Marie Keefe was the 19-year-old daughter of Dr. Thomas and Kate Keefe. Mrs. Keefe once described her eldest daughter, saying, "She is just such a woman as people on the street will turn their heads to look at a second time." Marie, about five feet six to eight inches tall, womanly shaped, weighed about 160 pounds. Cipriano stood six feet tall and weighed around 200 pounds.[20]

Marie had a 14-year-old sister named Sherry, a seven-year-old sister named for her mother and a brother named Edward who was five. Keefe was Irish born and educated, while his wife was a native of New York State. The couple had migrated to California in the late 1860s and lived in the San Francisco Bay area where Keefe worked attending the troops stationed at the Presidio. In the 1870s, Keefe moved his family to Winters in Yolo County, about 15 miles north of Vacaville, where he operated as a druggist.[21] Keefe also traveled the northwest and Trains-Sierra country seeking new business fields, including the infamous mining town of Bodie.

Always seeking wealth and adventure, Tom Keefe began to follow the Southern Pacific Railroad construction crews working eastward from California across Nevada to Arizona. The railroad allowed men like Keefe to travel with their crews because physicians, pharmacists, and medical facilities were very limited on the frontier. These mobile medical personnel were sometimes the only first-aid person in the section camps. This type of transient practice could be adventurous, but not always lucrative, so these "doctors" often had a second profession.

The work crew that Keefe accompanied left southern California and moved east toward the mountains and the Colorado River. In Arizona, the multi-culture company of workers made it through unfriendly Apache Country and finally built over the mountain pass into southern New Mexico. The Southern Pacific Railroad building gangs now raced east across the plains toward their rendezvous with the Atchison, Topeka and Santa Fe Railway Company crew racing toward them from their base along the Rio Grande. The two outfits met at the future site of Deming on Tuesday, March 8, 1881.

In the spring of 1882, Thomas Keefe opened an office on Pine Street in the new frontier settlement of Deming. He advertised a business card that said he was a "Physician and Surgeon" and that his office had "A supply of drugs and chemicals on hand." It is uncertain what type of chemicals Keefe stocked or for what purpose he used these chemicals. Maybe he made his own brand of "snake oil" treatment or "horse" liniment. A newspaper card for P.J. McGrath, a building constructor, advertised, "All Kind of Work Promptly Attended

To." The card also noted that McGrath shared office space with Dr. Keefe; it is unclear how long this relationship lasted.

By late June of 1882, Thomas Keefe had made a small fortune and decided to leave Deming. "Dr. Keefe, who has so faithfully attended to the wants of the sick and afflicted, leaves for California. The Dr. has made money in Deming and now goes to a country where he can enjoy the fruits of his labor. He took the roll of greenbacks he made in Deming with him," reported the *Deming Headlight*. "The Headlight is under no obligation to the Dr. for his kind and neighborly attentions, and we wish him abundant success wherever he goes."[22]

It is unclear what Keefe's California destination may have been, but he ultimately persuaded his wife to return with him to New Mexico Territory. The Keefe family was prominent in Deming society by late 1884. Doctor Keefe established his new office on Gold Avenue next to the William Drug Store. He was the area's "Examining Surgeon for the Travelers Insurance Company, Hartford, Conn." Keefe became an active member of the Deming Lodge No. 12 of the Ancient Free and Accepted Masons and served as chairman of the lodge's board of relief. Cipriano Baca's friend A.B. Laird was the grand senior warden in 1884. This gives cause to wonder, did the membership committee ever consider Baca, a burgeoning business leader, for membership in this secret society of mutual aid and friendship? Did social status and/or racism play a silent role in this unanswered question?

Cipriano Baca, like many young men of his era, joined a social club. Many of Baca's future associates, including Miguel A. Otero, chose to become members of the uniformed division of the fraternal Knights of Pythias. Baca made many political contacts at gatherings of the Knights.[23]

It would seem that Baca's father-in-law never lost his wanderlust. From time to time, he would seek business deals and employment that offered a high rate of return for his efforts. A short time after Marie's wedding, the Keefe family left Deming and returned to California. They moved to Washington Territory in 1889 where Tom and Kate separated amidst charges of spousal abuse; she called him churlish. We will discuss this phase in the life of the Keefe family in a later chapter.

Since he lived only 15 miles from Vacaville, had Tom Keefe known the Baca family? Had he cared for the health needs of the family? Did Cipriano Baca and Tom Keefe become acquainted somewhere along the railroad building in Arizona? These are intriguing questions, but at this date, no evidence has been located to verify the theory of a prior Baca-Keefe acquaintanceship.

* * *

It is worth noting that in late October 1881, a man using the name Thomas Keefe had been a witness to key events surrounding the deadly fight on Fremont Street near the back entrance to the O.K. Corral in Tombstone, Arizona. The Earp brothers—Chief of Police Virgil and his deputy brothers Wyatt and Morgan—assisted by special policeman Dr. John H. Holliday had attempted to arrest members of the Cow-boy gang. The encounter ended in the death of three of the suspected troublemakers, Tom and Frank McLaury and Billy Clanton, and the wounding of all the peace officers except Wyatt. This deadly, failed arrest attempt spawned a series of killings that still cause heated debate among historians and Wild West enthusiasts studying southeastern Arizona's rustler troubles and border depredations during the early 1880s.

Tombstone's Thomas Keefe was summoned, on Thursday, November 10, to testify at the preliminary hearing to determine if the city lawmen should be held for trial on a murder charge resulting from the exchange of bullets. The court record lists Keefe's occupation as a "carpenter" and relates that he had lived in the Trans-Sierra mining camps of White Pine, Pioche, and Virginia City, Nevada between 1869 and 1872. Keefe said that he had then lived in San Francisco for about a year and in Oakland for about eight months before he moved to Bodie in the late 1870s.[24]

Bodie, California is located in a shallow depression at an elevation of 8,375 feet, east of the snow-tipped Sierra Nevada range. The town of 5,000 souls, named for area prospector Waterman S. Bodey, is surrounded by mostly barren mountains, with Bodie Mountain at 10,195 feet to the west and Bodie Creek running north and south parallel with Main Street. A preacher of the Gospel visiting Bodie called the settlement "a sea of sin, lashed by the tempests of lust and passion." The gold claims along Taylor Gulch played out in the early 1880s, fire consumed 90 percent of the town's buildings in 1932, and the townsite, now a dwelling place for ghosts, has been a state historic park since 1962.

Keefe served a few days in the Bodie jail because of a domestic dispute. The *Bodie Morning News* said that Tom Keefe, who had a "generally good reputation," got up one morning in early March 1879 and left town. Eight months later he returned to find that his wife had taken up with a man named Don McShannon. Mrs. Keefe claimed that she believed her husband had deserted her. Keefe claimed he had gone to the Yankee Fork country of Idaho to do some carpenter work. During their argument, the wayward "carpenter" allegedly hit his unfaithful wife and threatened to kill her. Keefe claimed that someone shot at him during the confrontation. The Bodie constable arrested Keefe for intent to commit murder with a knife, but in his justice court trial, the peace justice reduced the charge to simple assault and a jury found him not guilty.[25]

This was not the end of Keefe's troubles in Bodie. In the year since his domestic troubles, according to the Bodie *Daily Free Press*, Keefe had "acquired some notoriety by having a very remarkable head put on him on two or three occasions" during some of his drunken brawls. On a Sunday evening in late October 1880, Keefe engaged in conversation with a fellow "sophisticate" named Thomas Hamilton near the Kingsley Livery Stable. The two men disagreed on some point, and Keefe drew his pistol and shot at Hamilton. Keefe's bullet ripped through Hamilton's coat on the left side, passed through his vest and shirt, put a gash on his stomach and settled in the lining of his coat on the right side. This was the second time in a year that Hamilton had escaped death during a disagreement with someone.[26] Thomas Keefe soon left the Trans-Sierra Country in search of new adventure.

In the aftermath of Tombstone's Fremont Street fiasco, Thomas Keefe assisted Dr. Nelson S. Gilberson with his initial examination of Billy Clanton and then later gave a detailed description of the Cow-boy's wounds at the justice of the peace hearing. He next helped Dr. William Miller as he injected Clanton with two shots of morphine to ease the dying man's pain. Keefe later seconded the county coroner, Dr. Henry Matthews, with his attempt to make the fatally wounded Tom McLaury comfortable during his final moments. The Tombstone "carpenter" had, in some manner, assisted all three doctors who attended to the Cow-boy wounded on that bloody Wednesday afternoon in late October 1881.

The 1881 and 1882 Tombstone business directories listed a "Keefe & Co, liquor saloon, 412 Allen" while an 1883 directory did not list the Keefe saloon, but did include this entry:

"Keefe, Thos., carpenter, res. Dragoon Saloon, Allen st., bet. 3d and 4th." The Tombstone Keefe, "a carpenter and builder by occupation," was a witness to Mrs. Mary Woodman shooting William Kinsman, an Englishman, in front of the Oriental Saloon. He testified about the attack before the coroner's inquest held by Pat Holland in February 1883.[27]

Was the early 1880s Tombstone saloonkeeper and/or carpenter lodging in a saloon the same man who was a respected physician in early Deming? Did this man then become Baca's father-in-law? Is he the same man who worked the Washington mining camps in the 1890s? The known facts provide a tight timeline into which the actions of the Tombstone Keefe and the Deming Keefe could be judged as being the same individual. The jury of historical fact is still considering these questions. If the answers are yes, then other questions concerning possible discussions between Keefe and Baca present themselves. Among the questions seeking answers would be what the men knew about the Cow-boy troubles and the deeds of Deputy U.S. Marshal Wyatt Earp and his brothers.

* * *

Deming is located in "that part of New Mexico infested by Indians and roughs, who denominate themselves Cow-boys," wrote C.M. Chase to his eastern readers in late November 1881. He continued, saying,

> During the past three years, within a radius of 50 miles around this depot [Deming] over 500 persons have been slaughtered by the Indians. Cook's canon, in sight from this village, goes by the name of Death's Canon, on account of the various fights and slaughters which have taken place there. During the troubles last summer, the Indians came down this canon, passing within sight of this village, in their flight for Old Mexico. The women in the village were in a corral at the time; and the men were for several days standing guard.[28]

The Indian troubles in Grant County became so bothersome that at one point the editor of the *Silver City Southwest Sentinel* expressed his regret that his newspaper felt "the necessity of constantly warning the settlers to be on their guard against the hostile Indians, and their depredations and outrages." Arizona governor F.A. Tritle and New Mexico governor Edmond Ross considered the Indian problem of such concern that they held a face-to-face meeting in Lordsburg to discuss how to utilize their territorial militias to assist the military to end the Indian raids.

"The Indians under Geronimo had been causing the settlers a lot of trouble stealing horses and killing people that were not around town," Mrs. Pennington told a WPA field historian over fifty years later. "In the day time we would watch them [the Apaches] on the mountains with field glasses and at night we could see their fires." When the newspaperman left home, he would remind his wife to keep the doors locked and stay inside. "It wasn't only the Indians that he was afraid of, but as there were always fights on the street. He was always afraid that we could be hurt." With the organization of a civilian militia to guard against Indian raids, a vigilante group backing a killing deputy sheriff like Dan Tucker to control the rowdy elements, and an influx of Eastern settlers with families, civilization slowly took root in Deming. "By 1885 it was safe for a woman to go anywhere."[29]

* * *

Following their honeymoon in the spring of 1887, Marie and Cipriano Baca set up housekeeping in Deming. Mrs. Baca quickly joined her mother as part of the community's social structure, while her husband worked hard to develop his Mimbres River Cattle Company, the Elephant Corral and Livery Stable in Deming, and his growing portfolio of mining stock.

Within weeks, at 3:13 P.M. on Tuesday, May 3, 1887, earthquake shocks hit Deming. The shock waves traveled as far north as Santa Fe from their center in Sonora, Mexico. Over 200 people died during this adjusting of the Earth's crust, none in New Mexico. This was not Baca's first earthquake, nor would it be the last one that Cipriano would know.

In the early fall of 1888, Marie took the train to San Diego to visit with her grandparents, while Cipriano remained in Deming. During Marie's absence Baca tended to the family businesses, but he and the citizens of Grant County did take a day off to have some fun. When the appointed day arrived, large crowds gathered in both Silver City and Deming to witness an unusual sporting event: a match race between an equestrian and a bicyclist. This strange occurrence had taken root in the whiskey-inspired brains of two El Paso–based gamblers named Clayton and Bolton. The men had been celebrating after a Fourth of July horse race when they began arguing over whether a man riding one of the currently popular velocipedes could win a distance race with a man on a horse. Jeff W. Clayton confronted his friend with a wager. Clayton said he would pay his companion $2,500 if a cyclist of Bolton's choice could beat his horseman in a race from Silver City to Deming. Clayton added two additional side wagers to the original: an extra $100 if his horse did not finish the race in less than five hours and another $100 if the horse did not beat the bike rider by at least half an hour.

It would be a good assumption to believe that Bolton did not study the proposal too long before agreeing to the contest. He knew the road from Silver City to Deming ran over very rough terrain and that the last 15 miles wound its way through gravelly sand. The two-wheel velocipede was a bicycle that was once described as having a "front wheel as high as a man's head and a hind wheel about half as high as a medium sized sheep dog." Bolton also understood the belief that a horse could not sustain a full gallop over a prolonged distance in rough country. He weighed his facts and accepted Clayton's challenge.

Both men set about selecting their standard bearer and preparing for the contest. Bolton bought a new bike and contracted with H.J. Kennedy, a member of the Ramblers Bicycle Club of Denver, to peddle the course. Clayton paid $350 to Tom Lyons for his racehorse Rattler and employed a local range rider named Jim Keith to pilot the animal. On the day of the race, the side bets had reached over $5,400 and were heavily in favor of the young horseman because the locals felt it would take an extra strong athlete to propel his cumbersome bicycle over the rough countryside.

Thursday, September 13, was a wonderful fall day. The contestants assembled in front of the Timmer House to await a shot signaling the start of the race from the pistol held by "Uncle Harvey" Whitehill, a former Grant County sheriff and the Democratic candidate for reelection to his old office in November.[30] Silver City was "festooned with gaily-colored bunting," and the rousing serenade of the town band added to the festive mood. A large crowd had gathered in Silver City to witness the start of the race and to crowd into the picture taken by a local amateur photographer, O.C. Hinman. He was also the Silver City undertaker and a furniture salesman. Cyclist Kennedy appeared decked out in a "cricket cap" and a candy-striped turtleneck sweater.

It was at this point that Cipriano Baca became a participant in the proceedings. Baca said he had been punching cows over on the Mimbres and had ridden over to witness the event. Mounted astride a pinto pony, Baca volunteered to accompany the contestants along the trail to bear witness to the honesty of the race. No one objected to this arrangement as long as the race was between the two official jousters. Whitehill fired his pistol and the racers were off. A telegraphic message notified the Deming community that the contestants were en route.

Crowds gathered at select points along the route to cheer their favorite racer and as they neared Deming, the on-looker became more numerous. A large crowd awaited the competitors in front of the Depot Hotel. Race enthusiasts and other curious individuals had arrived in Deming that morning via train from El Paso. There was a carnival atmosphere around the railroad tracks, and the Ladies' Aid Society's homemade ice cream was a big seller. As the day grew warmer, the sale of bottled beer increased.

Cipriano Baca rode his pinto along with the two men during the three-hour and forty-six and one half minute race.[31] One tale told is how Baca, while loping along on his pinto, was seen glancing over his shoulder at the horse and rider and the bicyclist following him while simultaneously pulling the string tight on a Bull Durham bag with his teeth. This is the sort of tale that produces legends.

Baca raced full out the last few miles and reached the finish line a full minute ahead of Jim Keith and Rattler. The future territorial ranger slid his pinto to a halt and executed a 180 so that he sat facing Keith as he reached the hotel a short distance ahead of Kennedy. No one knows how much money was won or lost on this sporting event or even if Baca made a bet concerning the abilities of his pinto pony. One fact is clear. This race introduced Baca to the wonders of bicycle riding and started him on the road to becoming a two-wheel enthusiast himself.

This event in Baca's colorful life is just another example of the somewhat difficult exercise it is to separate fact and myth when recounting his saga. In 1942, C.L. Sonnichson, an honored history professor at what is today the University of Texas at El Paso, published a book containing a whole chapter dealing with the horse-velocipede race. This account is given from the point of view of the man who claimed he rode the winning horse. In the Sonnichson version a young Silver City attorney and newspaperman named S.M. Ashenfelter is the man who jokingly raced a Cow-boy on a two-wheeler the 48 miles from the county seat to Deming. Twenty-five years later, the *Silver City Independent* recalled the race and said it ran over a 53-mile course and concluded in three hours and 45 minutes allowing adequate time for spectators to consume large quantities of "refreshments" in honor of the occasion.

The El Paso professor did get Baca's part in the event correct. He wrote,

> One man- some say he was a Mexican named Cipriano Baca; others that he was a Mormon- actually groomed a pinto pony and got him into the contest. There were no large bets on this horse. His owner just wanted to see what he could do.[32]

"It is said," noted the *Silver City Independent* marking the silver anniversary of the race, "that the bicycle had the best of the race until it struck the sandy roads between Faywood [about 30 miles southeast of Silver City] and Deming, when the horse passed it and won easily. There were lots of deadgame sports in those days, and thousands of dollars changed hands on the results.

It would seem that all parties missed the boat by not wagering on Baca and the Pinto pony. According to the *Herald* of St. Johns, Arizona, not having bet on the Pinto pony was a costly mistake. The paper reported,

"Another horse, Wilson's pinto, traveled with Clayton's horse [Rattler] and beat it a few minutes. Neither horse seemed the worse for the trip." Baca's Pinto was the real winner, but the nation's major sports magazines, Chicago's *Sportsman and Breeder*, the *Clipper* and the *National Police Gazette*, disregarded this fact and gave the victory to the cowboy and his racehorse.[33]

On Friday, September 21, 1888, the *Deming Headlight* reported, "Mrs. C. Baca has returned from a visit with the old folks at San Diego."[34] Marie Baca had missed the great bicycle-horse race, but she most likely heard a firsthand account of the event from one of the participants.

4

Grant County Peace Officer

"Grant County has never had a more efficient officer."
— Silver City Enterprise 30 Oct 1896

In the last verses of the 16th chapter and the first verses of the 17th chapter of Deuteronomy are contained the six principles of administrating justice as set forth by lawgiver Moses. It is written that a person in authority should render a righteous judgment and not pervert justice. All persons must be treated the same by the law, a person in authority should not accept a bribe to sway his judgment, a thorough investigation should be made to determine the facts, and only reliable witnesses should be used to substantiate the truth. In a life-or-death situation, two witnesses must agree on the facts to pronounce the truth. Vigilantes still ruled southwestern New Mexico by lynch law when the Baca cousins settled there in the early 1880s, and Cipriano was still developing his own personal code of justice. It is unclear when he set his principles to stone, but we do have a clue.

Written in pencil on the back page of a book once owned by Cipriano Baca is a quotation by Ben Franklin: "Justice will not be served until those who are unaffected are as outraged as those who are." It is interesting to speculate as to what prompted Cipriano to have copied that message into a commemorative volume on the life and death of President William McKinley. Is it possible that Baca had adopted Franklin's commentary as part of his own creed of justice?[1]

* * *

Thirteen words composed the sentence contained in the "Curbstone Gossip" column of the *Deming Headlight* for February 15, 1889: "Mrs. Cipriano Baca has gone to La Ascension, Mexico, for a short visit." There is no other information provided in this issue of the *Deming Headlight* or any of the remaining future issues of this newspaper.[2]

Six months earlier Marie had traveled to San Diego to visit her parents. It is only supposition, but circumstances would suggest that Mrs. Baca went to see her mother and doctor father to seek their advice on her pregnancy. It is possible that she had experienced trouble with a previous gestation.

El Pueblo de la Ascencion de Jesus is located about 50 miles south of Columbus, New Mexico, on a fork of the Rio Casas Grandes, seven miles west of Laguna de la Ascencion, in the Mexican State of Chihuahua. This community honors the miracle of Christ's Resurrection, a tenet of faith among members of the Roman Catholic Church. Believers felt the little church in the village was a prayer conduit for people seeking renewed faith. Cipriano's cousin Manuel had taken his wife and six children to live in the region around La Ascencion following his brother Patricio's death in December 1887. Jose Manuel Baca finished his days in the Mexican State of Sonora accompanied by his wife Maria Lugarda Susana-Alvarado Baca. Maria Baca died in California in 1947.

The Baca women had become friends when Maria lived on the Baca cousins' ranch outside of Deming. Marie and Cipriano Baca had been married almost two years when she made the journey to La Acencion. Marie may have visited with Maria after losing her fetus. This idea is only speculative because no contemporary documents support the hypothesis, but this supposition does seem to fit the circumstances and the time frame.

* * *

James A. Lockhart, a onetime member of the vigilantes at Las Vegas, won election as Grant County sheriff in the fall of 1890 and named A.B. Laird as his chief deputy. The *Silver City Enterprise* endorsed this appointment saying, "You can bet that both are lead horses that will stay by their friends through all kinds of weather." Within days of taking office, Lockhart was flooded with applications for a deputy's appointment or by constables seeking a special deputy's commission. Sheriff Lockhart sent all the applicants a letter saying he would grant no special commissions to any constable "simply to enable them to charge the county sheriff's fees for services which they are required to perform for a less fee as constable."

Lockhart was one of Baca's many Deming friends and, unlike other men who wanted a special deputy commission, he asked Cipriano to be part of the new team and continue as a nonsalaried/fee-based special officer. Baca knew both the local Hispanic and Anglo population as well as the land along the border country. Baca accepted his friend's offer, but he continued to earn his main support with his Deming businesses, mining interests, and cattle ranch.

The Hispanic population of Grant County held a different concept of law enforcement than their Anglo neighbors. Sheriff Lockhart understood that the Hispanic culture was a people-centered society where laws were flexible and that they should be less important than the people who lived by them. The dominant Anglo society, however, centered on a rule of law and the concept that all people must obey the law at all times.

In the 1890s, there were Mexican federal statues restricting gambling, the selling of liquor, and the use of child labor, and granting women certain social rights. Mexico's law books contained these federal mandates, but few of these Mexican national laws saw enforcement in the northern states along the U.S.-Mexico border.

* * *

In late January 1891, the *Silver City Enterprise* printed a short item about a woman named Minnie Lee being arrested in Deming by an unnamed officer and brought to Silver City to be housed in "hotel de Lockhart for some time." Some suspected Lee of stealing two $20 gold pieces but "had so adroitly concealed the money on her person that it was sometime before the officer found it."[3] It is fun to speculate about Baca being the unnamed officer trying to search a woman in the Victorian era of morality and physical conduct toward the "gentler sex" even if suspected of criminal activity.

Even if Baca had not been the unnamed officer that arrested and searched Ms. Lee, Sheriff Lockhart did need Baca's services early in March. A Silver City judge had given William "Bronco Bill" Walters the excitement of "sojourning in the county Bastille and enjoying the hospitality of Sheriff Lockhart. He had the invitation to remain until the next session of the grand jury." Bill had different plans. The soft-spoken, dark-eyed, dark-complexioned cowhand "was not inclined to sponge on the sheriff," so he escaped from the basement jail in the Grant County courthouse and went to Old Mexico. The 135-pound, square-jawed, but reluctant county guest was soon located across the international border in Palomas.

Lockhart employed Baca "to go down and get the prodigal." The arrest scenario enacted like a classic B-grade western motion picture script. Walters, allowed considerable freedom in the jail corridors because of his good behavior, had been smuggled a .38 caliber revolver by "one of his friends who is not being cared for by the sheriff" the day before his escape. The *Silver City Enterprise* said, "There are strong suspicions that members of a very respectable Silver City family are implicated in the rescue of the criminals."[4] Decades after the events transpired an area cowboy named "Salty John" Cox claimed that rancher Henry Holgate had provided the pistol.[5]

Bill asked the jail guard to look at his new pistol and then requested that the jailer release him and a fellow inmate. The guard "complied with [Bill's] wishes with considerable alacrity." The second prisoner walked the guard a few miles out of Silver City while Bill mounted a waiting horse with "a desire to reach the land of Montezuma at as early an hour as possible."

Bill rode south while the guard walked back to the county seat and a meeting with Sheriff James Lockhart. The next night, Bill "purloined a fresh horse from Henry Holgate at Deming and continued his journey." When Bill reached Mexico, he sent the horse back to Holgate with a thank-you note for the horse's use.

Bronco Bill was now "congratulating himself on the moral courage he had displayed in denying himself the pleasure of a prolonged visit at the county boarding house." Sheriff Lockhart knew that Walters would know his regular deputies and "ascertain that the sheriff was anxious to have him return and remain a few weeks longer as his guest he would be very careful about getting outside the limits of the Mexican republic."[6] A few days later, Cipriano Baca was in Palomas, Sonora, Republic of Mexico.

Walters had worked on the Diamond A Ranch of the Victoro Land and Cattle Company and was well liked by the management. "He was a tough one, a dead-hard hombre [who] had been an outlaw all his life," recalled Walt Birchfield, a cattleman and member of the early 1900s range detectives known as Scarborough's Rangers. The range riders' leader George Scarborough had once captured Walters. "A good hard worker, a real ranch hand [who would] wrangle horses, cook, cleanout mud holes, punch cows, anything." Birchfield also recalled, "You could trust any of those cowpuncher outlaws if they was [sic] working for you. They'd do anything for you. They'd even risk their lives for you."[7]

Baca was able to locate Walters, but he was suspicious of everybody and wanted to know what Baca was doing in Palomas. Cipriano told him honestly that he was in Old Mexico "collecting overdue bills," so Bronco Bill relaxed his guard when Baca suggested that they jointly sponsor a dance that night. Baca said he would cover the cost of the "Mexican spirits" if Bill would supply the music. Bill liked the idea of "señoritas [young ladies] gaily tripping to the inspiring music of the violin." A suggestion was made that a violin player could be found just a few hundred yards north across the line in a Columbus dance hall.

A few more drinks and Bill was ready to go to New Mexico and get the musician. Baca found him a horse and "volunteered to go along for company." Cipriano also "took a bottle along to keep up their spirits." Safely back in New Mexico Territory, Special Deputy Sheriff Cipriano Baca quickly relieved Walters of his two pistols and "a pair of bracelets were slipped on his wrists." Bill Walters now understood Baca's comment about being in Mexico on a "bill" collecting job, because the toughest "Bill" in that section had just been collected.[8]

Three years after Baca's death and almost four decades after the event, Cow-boy storyteller "Salty John" Cox gave a less dramatic account of Walters' arrest that differed substantially from the contemporary newspaper accounts. Cox claimed that Columbus, New Mexico, dance hall owner John Good had been the man that crossed the Mexican border to Palomas and convinced Walters to attend a *baile* (dance) at his place. Cox claimed that Baca was present at the dance hall and simply arrested Walters and took him to jail at Silver City. Cox was not present at the *baile* and provided no source for his version of the capture of Bronco Bill.

Sheriff Lockhart was happy to see his prodigal guest, but "he neglected to kill the fatted calf." Baca earned a prisoner escort fee plus boarding and mileage fees for this south-of-the-border adventure, while Bill received leg irons in a jail cell. Walters was in the county lockup because of a mishap with a practical joke that ended with Bronco attempting to rob a miner and discharging his firearm in the mining camp of Separ. "Salty John" Cox recalled that Walters was "always in a good humor, but bad to drink … [and] would do anything for devilment." A jury convicted Walters of his October 1890 misdeeds of shooting up a boarding house at Separ and sentenced the 22-year-old Texan to a year at hard labor in the territorial penitentiary.[9]

It would seem that Cipriano Baca had an aura of *confianza*. Even outlaws felt a need to trust him. Unlike many Hispanics who used humor as a coping mechanism, Baca seemed to be happy by nature. However, in the flick of an eye he could turn serious.

Baca's relationship with Bronco Bill did not end in 1891. Eight years later in Phoenix the *Arizona Republic* noted that Deputy Sheriff Cipriano Baca was the officer that transported Walters from the custody of the Santa Fe prison to Socorro.[10] The habitual outlaw was on trial again.

* * *

During the 1891 session of the New Mexico Territorial Legislative Assembly, the lawmakers enacted a bill that authorized a county sheriff to appoint five full-time deputies if his county had at least 15 voting precincts. A county with more than 15 precincts could add an additional deputy per each four additional precincts. This law replaced one that had been in effect since 1864 that had put a four-deputy cap on a sheriff regardless of the size or population of the county. These deputies would assist the sheriff with tax collection duties, tax foreclosure sales, business license fee collection, *baile* or dance permit sales, policing polling places on Election Day, courtroom bailiff duty, regular and grand jury panel selection notification, serving court orders and summons, crime investigation, prisoner transport, and guard duty at the county jail.

This new deputy sheriff law did not address the issuance of special deputy appointments. These nonsalaried officers had the same authority as a full-time deputy but were paid by private funds from mining companies, stock associations, railroads, and express companies. Often a small community or a very remote trading center might pledge to support fully a "subscription deputy" to police their area under authority of a special commission. A sheriff would sometimes choose to add a small stipend, from his own income, to the deputy's subscription levy to ensure the continued political support of his nonsalaried employee.

In the 1890s, a New Mexico sheriff did not receive an established salary from the territory or his county. He earned his income from a statutory service fee structure for serving warrants and court summons. The county officer received payment according to the method set forth by territorial law. A sheriff or deputy was authorized 12 and a half cents per mile actually and necessarily traveled to apprehend a criminal. This was the same rate paid to transport a prisoner to trial, to return a prisoner to the proper jurisdiction for trial, or to deliver a convict to the territorial prison. A sheriff could also collect $1.00 per day for food and lodging for himself, his prisoner and one guard. Territorial law allowed county officers to collect rewards for wanted men. The sheriff still had to play a successful political hand because the county commissioners had to approve all claims he made against the county treasury. Party affiliation and support was vital to a sheriff's financial success and, thus, the monetary success of his deputies.

There was, however, a financial disincentive for a peace officer to trail a suspect out of the territory or out of his jurisdiction. New Mexico territorial law made it almost impossible

The Grant County courthouse is the large brick building, with the tower, located at the head of Broadway in downtown Silver City. The sheriff's office and county jail were located in the basement. The current courthouse replaced this structure in 1930 (Jim Stauder Photograph Collection).

for an officer to collect reimbursement for his trip expense if he was unable to capture his suspect and return his prisoner for trial. This law hampered aggressive pursuit of criminals and quite often resulted in a financial burden for diligent officers like Baca.[11]

The Walters arrest unmasked Cipriano's eight-year undercover status. Sheriff Lockhart was impressed with his friend's easy manner and firm control with men, so Lockhart offered Cipriano a job as a full-time salaried deputy sheriff. Baca had already sold his Deming livery stable business and would soon liquidate his Mimbres River Cattle Company operation. If Cipriano discussed the peace officer proposition with Marie, she must have accepted the idea because they relocated to the mountainous county seat. Baca joined the other Grant County deputies and soon began to police the 7,000-square-mile county and helped safeguard its 5,000 citizens.

One of the men that Baca became friends with was William Harvey Kilburn, the Silver City marshal and son-in-law of former Grant County sheriff Harvey Whitehill. Kilburn served as city marshal on three different occasions: 1888–1891, 1895–1897, and 1903–1904. He was killed while attempting an arrest. Deputy Sheriff John Collier, who would succeed Baca as lieutenant of the New Mexico Territorial Mounted Police, apprehended the killer.

Deputy Sheriff Cipriano Baca soon discovered that not all law enforcement assignments were as exciting as the Walters' capture. He spent most days serving court summons, conducting repossession sales, transporting prisoners, and performing court duty. Once, every so often, Baca tracked down a wanted man — or woman.

In August 1891, a hotel operator notified the sheriff's office about two men he had registered at his establishment, accompanied by two young women he suspected were underage and not related. Baca and another deputy sheriff went to the hotel and confronted the men who confessed, and Baca arrested them for immoral conduct with under-age females. The cow-boy confidence men had seduced the two motherless teenagers into running away from their father's ranch. These "men of the world" promised the teenagers a life of adventure in the city.

The girls' father had come to Silver City in search of his daughters and arrived at the hotel just as the lawmen were taking their charges to jail. The enraged father threatened to kill the men if the sheriffs would step aside. "The cowardly ruffians jumped behind the officers and begged in terrified tones for protection," but the officers told the distraught father "they could not stand to have prisoners in their charge shot down," reported the *Silver City Enterprise*. The father backed off the attack, and the men received lodging in the Grant County jail to await action of the next grand jury.

The father took his daughters back to their ranch. That evening when the girls went off to milk the cows, their father put a pistol to his head and shot himself. "The shame and disgrace had been too much for the brave, proud, sensitive man, rather than witness the shame of his daughters exposed to the public gaze in a court of law, he chose death ... he could not brave dishonor."[12] The newspaper said nothing about the shame, disgrace, or future welfare of the two teenage girls who must now survive without a mother and with the guilt of their father's suicide.

In the fall of 1891, Baca was central to another case involving a woman when he arrested a wife who was running from a loveless and troubled marriage. Cipriano trailed the woman from the Silver City area to Lordsburg where he arrested her and the elderly neighbor rancher who was trying to help her escape. The fugitives were taken into custody upon a charge sworn to by the woman's husband under provisions of a federal law, known as the Edmund Act, against providing assistance in breaking up a marriage. The 22-year-old woman and her two young daughters were all forced to return to their unhappy family life. The 60 year-old-rancher faced the bar of justice.[13]

While Baca was occupied with court duties, Sheriff Lockhart sent Deputy Victor Culberson to the Black Range country to settle a cattle-rustling outbreak. Culberson ended his tour by arresting a prison escapee who was doing most of the thieving and earned a $125 reward for his effort.[14] A few years later, Culberson resigned from the sheriff's staff and accepted an appointment as the general manager of the GOS Cattle Company in Grant County.[15] Nearly two decades after Culberson and Baca served as Grant County deputies, Vic was able to do Cipriano a huge political favor.

It may have been the easiest arrest Cipriano ever made during his long stint as a peace officer. In the middle of July 1892, the *Silver City Enterprise* reported what it called a "shooting scrape" that had taken place in the western part of Grant County along Mule Creek. Two men engaged in a heated debate over a ranch that ended when both men began shooting and one man received two bullets in the stomach. The man who was left standing rode into Silver City and surrendered to Baca. William Morris had a preliminary hearing before Judge Givens, and based upon the testimony of witnesses to the feud he was discharged on a self-defense plea.[16]

The third week in October 1892 was a bloody few days in the history of Grant County. The *Silver City Enterprise* carried headlines that told the story: "Foul Play Suggested," "Shooting at Pine Cienega," and "Mysterious Murder." In the first investigation a rancher's horse was found wandering loose near Cooney, northeast of Silver City. When the horse was found, it had blood on its neck and mane and more blood on the saddle. The newspaper noted, "There is a great deal of interesting conjecture as to how the horse and accoutrements became covered with blood."

Concerning the second incident, the *Silver City Enterprise* told their readers that they didn't have all the facts, but they wished "to relieve the present depression and stagnation in the local items of interest" so they where reporting what they knew. The paper said three men "kindly volunteered to annihilate each other" at Pine Cienega resulting in one wounded and the others being lodged in the "dormitory in the Grant County bastile [sic]."

In the third incident reported on by the *Silver City Enterprise*, a teenage boy and a Mexican helper at his father's ranch where waylaid and killed at their camp near Gila Hot Springs. The newspaper said the "strangest part of the mystery is that nothing was taken from the camp," including five burros and guns and ammunition. An evening rain, fortuitously for the killer, washed away all tracks and no one was arrested for these murders.

A couple of years earlier the federal government declared that the frontier era was over and the nation had been settled, but someone forgot to tell the marauding bands of Indians and outlaws. For a week in mid–October 1892, Grant County, New Mexico Territory, was ground zero for the Wild West mythology. Baca had been the supervisor for the field investigations for these three crimes. None of these cases had a fairy tale ending.[17]

* * *

James Lockhart turned over the Grant County sheriff's office to Andrew Laird in January 1893. This was Laird's second time to be sworn in as sheriff. He had first won election in the fall of 1886 but had been defeated for reelection two years later by Harvey Whitehill. Laird asked Baca to remain in the sheriff's office and appointed Cipriano as his undersheriff or chief deputy. The new sheriff vested Baca with authority to conduct the routine police business of the county, while he would handle the tax collection duties and the official paperwork. Due to the increased land values in Grant County, Laird was required to post a $100,000 performance bond. Sheriff office records for Grant County attest to the success of the Laird-Baca partnership. Taxpayers received efficient fiscal management, quality countywide police protection, a clean jail, timely court process service, and a safe courtroom operation.

Mixed in between his official duties as chief deputy sheriff, Cipriano and Marie enjoyed a social life among Grant County's leading citizens. In early January 1893, "Colonel" and Mrs. Baca attended the Knights of Pythias Ball at Deming. The *Silver City Enterprise* commented on the dance, saying that "those who were fortunate enough to be present enjoyed an evening of merriment and revelry never to be forgotten. The ball-room of the [railroad] depot was beautifully decorated, and the faultlessly arrayed ladies and uniformed knights as they lightly tripped to the music of a splendid orchestra, made an impressive scene." Six months later, Baca served on the reception committee for the Territorial Silver Convention. The gathering was a social who's who of power brokers. The Christmas season offered another round of parties and receptions for Cipriano and Marie.[18]

One of the outside office duties that Chief Deputy Baca performed a couple of times each year was to visit Lordsburg and his old Deming stomping grounds to notify potential jurors that their services might be needed at the next term of the district court to be held in Silver City. On one such occasion, Baca felt an urge to forego his favorite dish of ice cream in favor of a tall glass of cool Deming water, because one of the city leaders told him that a recent chemical analysis had proved the town's water supply to be the purest in New Mexico. Deming's *Headlight* reported the scientific findings and had their report by saying, "Comment is unnecessary."[19] Baca's opinion of the water's quality is unknown. On other occasions, Marie and Cipriano would return to Deming to attend Sunday-afternoon baseball games or Saturday-night dances with longtime friends.

The nation's leading financers became concerned about the health of the American economy early in 1893. The collapse of the Philadelphia and Reading Railroad signaled the beginning decline of other investment markets. The value of grain, cotton, steel, and timber futures led the market downturn and more railroads began to fail as European-held American stocks and bonds where sold at a loss. By early summer, more banking houses failed and an economic crisis swept across the nation. Congress repealed the Sherman Silver Purchase Act in October in a belated effort to curb the drain of gold from the federal treasury, but the measure was too late to stop the devastating loss in all sections of the economy. Baca's dream of becoming wealthy by investing in silver mining stock lost luster almost daily as the nation's growing prosperity in January had turned into the Panic of 1893 by May and slid into a deepening depression by the year's end.

In late August 1893, Chief Deputy Baca took deputies Frank McGillinchy and M.P. Moore with him to Lordsburg to take seven illegal Chinese field hands into custody and transport them to the county seat to await the arrival of deputy U.S. Marshals who had the legal duty to transport these federal prisoners before a federal magistrate court. Baca and McGillinchy had known each other since the early days of Deming when McGillinchy had stood for election as constable in 1888. The two friends had spent Sunday afternoons each fall watching football games played on South Gold Street near the site of the present courthouse.

In September, while in the Lordsburg area serving court papers, Baca's suspicious nature combined with his sharp memory of wanted notices led him to a Texas fugitive who was working as a stock tender on a ranch near Separ. Cipriano arrested Benito Morales without incident, escorted the fugitive to Silver City, and placed him in the Grant County jail until an El Paso County deputy sheriff could arrive with extradition papers for the man's transfer to Texas jurisdiction. The rangers in the Lone Star State wanted Morales for murder, escaping custody, and horse theft. A Texas deputy sheriff, carrying official documents and a one-way train ticket so Morales could visit the Pass City at taxpayers' expense, soon arrived in Silver City.[20]

The next week, Chief Deputy Baca was riding the mountain country searching for a gang of suspected stock thieves. Just after dusk on Saturday evening, September 9, Baca rode up to a roadside bar near the hamlet of Hanover called Ernest's Place. A detachment of 10th Cavalry troopers, on patrol from Fort Bayard, were bivouacked nearby for the night. The water at Ernest's Place was free for all men and horses. Ernest also offered equality for all men to pay the current market price for his "cheap whiskey." Many off-duty black cavalrymen had gathered in the barroom getting a head start on the evening's celebration by the time Baca rode into the settlement.

When Cipriano entered the little barroom, "the fun waxed fast and furious," and Ernest asked the lawman's assistance in restoring order. Baca "arrested two men who seemed to be making the most disturbance, put the nippers on them, and deputized two Mexicans present to guard them while he paid his attention to quieting the remaining and less combative revelers." A couple of hours later, the two men Baca had arrested where sober enough to release into Sergeant John Logan's custody. Logan took up a collection from among the merrymakers and paid each of the Mexicans five dollars for acting as prisoner guards. "Deputy Baca rode on to Central, and from her rocky citadel above the Kneeling Nun could once more bless the peaceful scene."[21] The simple events of this barroom adventure would play a major role in Baca's future in Grant County.

In late September 1893, Baca and another deputy joined resident deputy M.P. Moore in maintaining order at the Territorial Irrigation Convention held in Deming. The local bicycle club and tennis club each held a tournament, and the two clubs jointly hosted a dance for the delegates. Happily for the three county officers most of the convention's events were conducted peacefully, and Deming proved to be a congenial host city.[22]

Sheriff Laird and Chief Deputy Baca left Silver City escorting four prisoners to the territorial prison at Santa Fe on Tuesday, December 5, 1893. These men were an odd quartet; one was a convicted murderer sentenced to 40 years of hard labor, one was a Mexican given time for robbing two Silver City stores, the third man was a petty sneak thief, while the fourth member of the group was a black soldier dishonorably discharged and given two years on the chain gang for assaulting the constable at Fort Bayard.[23] They completed the trip without difficulty, and Baca and Laird took a few hours to do some early Christmas shopping on the plaza of the Ancient City.

Shortly after the New Year's celebration had become history, the Grant County jail had a special visitor. "The county jail was inspected by an ENTERPRISE reporter this week and found to be in first class condition. The prisoners are satisfied apparently with their treatment."²⁴ This was high praise for Baca's leadership because one of his duties as chief deputy was to supervise the jail operation and the jailer. The jailers were Will Rose and Dick Knight. Later that year Knight would challenge Baca for the Republican Party nomination for sheriff of Grant County.

In the early spring of 1894, bands of unemployed men styling themselves "Commonweal" or "Industrial" armies begin marching on Washington to demand federal government public works programs for those out of work because of the financial Panic of 1893. An Ohio man named Jacob Coxey led the largest of the bands; thus the media named the whole movement Coxey's Army. These tattered pilgrims caused a wave of both sympathy and fear as the nation's law enforcement agencies were concerned about how this uprising might affect the day laborers in their area. Democrat Party members controlled both Congress and the White House for the first time since 1859, but the best these leaders in Washington could do was lower the tariff rate on imports, create a national income tax, and repeal the law requiring the federal government to purchase a set monthly quota of silver that was mined in the western states and territories. At least one of these new measures managed to hurt every person living in Grant County, but fortunately, none of these "aid-to-the-working-man" measures lasted very long. The Supreme Court ruled that the income tax measure was unconstitutional in 1895. When the Republicans regained the White House and control of both houses of Congress in the 1896 election, they reestablished a substantial protective tariff and formally adopted gold as the monetary standard to back the nation's paper currency.

In April 1894, the fear of a labor riot gripped mine owners in Grant County. The *Silver City Enterprise* headlined the story "Desperadoes Defy Deputies" and told how Sheriff Laird, Chief Deputy Baca, and Deputy Coultey had traveled to Pinos Altos, seven miles northeast of the county seat, to contain a race/labor war between Mexican and European-born miners. Neither management nor workers wanted a repeat of the mine labor disputes that had erupted at Tracy City, Inman, Oliver Springs and Coal Creek, Tennessee, two years earlier and had ended only after many deaths on both sides and a civic black eye for the Volunteer State.

There had been almost daily acts of intimidation and threats by both sides in the Pinos Altos troubles. It is still unclear what sparked the violence that erupted in a lively exchange of gunfire between the two labor groups and only ended with the death of a Mexican laborer. Upon their arrival at the mining camp, the three Grant County officers made a number of arrests and restored some order, but racial tensions continued for many more months.²⁵ Meanwhile, across the nation, labor unions were gaining ground, and 1894 would witness the devastating dispute between railroad workers and management that resulted in the use of federal troops to restore order.

Theodore Roosevelt, a young aristocrat working for the Civil Service Commission, was concerned about the changing attitude of America's working class. He expressed his concern when he wrote, "The time of the great social revolutions has arrived." He continued to expand on that belief. "We are all peering into the future to try to forecast the action of the great dumb forces set in operation by the stupendous industrial revolution which has taken place during the present century. We do not know what to make of the vast displacements of population, the expansion of the towns, the unrest and discontent of the masses."²⁶ The future president was not alone in his uncertainty.

During the years Baca held office in Grant County, the *Silver City Enterprise* kept the local populace informed about his professional actions and political prospects.

> [Chief] Deputy Sheriff Baca returned Monday [June 25, 1894] from a long trip into Arizona after a horse thief. As usual, Mr. Baca got the man he was after. Mr. Baca is as efficient an officer as ever served in Grant County, and would make a first-class sheriff. It is altogether probable he will be a candidate on the republican ticket. If so he will be a sure winner.[27]

The Democratic-leaning *Silver City Eagle* and the *Silver City Sentinel* were each less than positive about Baca's prospects of becoming the county's next sheriff.

A short time later, A.J. Loomis and H.L. Oakes, the editors and publishers of the recently established *Silver City Eagle*, handed Sheriff Laird, his jail staff, and indirectly the entire deputy corps a black eye of criticism in an exposé entitled "County Jail Delivery." The newspaper reported that at about three o'clock on Friday afternoon August 17 two inmates of Grant County's basement hotel for undesirables left the county's care without prior notice. The prisoners gained freedom to walk the corridor in front of the cells and just opened a hall window and made their escape. There is no record of Baca's reaction to the bungled guard duty operation, and one can only suppose that the two fugitives enjoyed their vacation from the street gang labor.[28]

The Grant County Sheriff's Office was back in the news the next week. About nine o'clock on Monday morning, August 27, 1894, 14-year-old Flora Fluri was walking on the dirt road that ran between Silver City and Central near her family's milk ranch about four miles east of Silver City. She was about a half mile from her house searching for some missing burros when attacked in what the *Silver City Eagle* called "An Attempt at Rape." During the incident, a man "...drew his revolver and attempted to intimidate her into submitting to him," but she screamed for help and "during the struggle Miss Fluri's clothing was torn into shreds but the villain was foiled in accomplishing his purpose." The reporter added, "This is the first attempt at rape in this part of New Mexico in years." The family notified the sheriff's office of the assault, and Chief Deputy Sheriff Cipriano Baca responded to Mr. Fluri's request for help.

Tuesday afternoon, acting upon the girl's description that her attacker was a young Mexican who rode a black horse, carried a black-handled pistol, and was "accompanied by a spotted dog," Cipriano rode out to Miguel Gomez's place prepared to arrest him upon suspicion. The young married man was able to convince Baca that he had been home constructing a chicken coop during the time of the attack. Chief Deputy Baca had almost been correct in his assessment of who the assailant had been; Gomez had a younger brother who resembled him. Nestor Gomez still lived at his father's house about three miles north of Silver City. The younger Gomez brother rode a black horse, and the family dog was a black and white spotted mutt.

Chief Deputy Sheriff Cipriano Baca arrested Nestor Gomez upon suspicion of attempted rape and attempted assault with a weapon. Miss Fluri selected the 19-year-old suspect in a "Mexican lineup" on Wednesday morning. The young man had seen the young girl at the Sunday-night *baile*, in the village of Central. A preliminary hearing justice bound Nestor Gomez over to the Grant County grand jury on a $2,000 bond. In November 1895, a district court jury cleared Gomez of the rape charge, but convicted him on the assault with a weapon charge. The judge sentenced Gomez to six months at the Territorial Penitentiary as prisoner number 879.[29]

At some point in late summer 1894, Laird and Baca had a talk about the upcoming county election. The sheriff told his chief deputy that he was not planning to seek reelection but intended to run for county tax collector. After this talk, one can assume that Cipriano and Marie had a similar discussion. Unfortunately, for the sake of history, no one now knows what Mrs. Baca may have thought about her husband's desire to become the high sheriff of Grant County. With or without Marie's agreement, Baca made an official announcement concerning his intentions in mid–August by placing business card ads in the area newspapers saying that he was "a candidate for the office of sheriff of Grant County, subject to the action of the Republican [Party County] Convention" to be held in Silver City in September.[30] Baca now became the physical embodiment of the Benjamin Franklin admonition, "Be civil to all, social with many, known to few."

The *Deming Headlight*, the Democratic voice in the southeastern part of Grant County, commented upon Baca's announcement to seek the Republican nomination for sheriff: "Mr. Baca is well known throughout this county, has made a most efficient [chief] deputy, and although on the wrong side, is in every way qualified." A few days later, Deputy Baca engaged in one of the least popular functions of a sheriff and took center stage at a "sheriff's sale" to dispose of a debtor's assets to satisfy past-due tax obligations. This was a subtle public demonstration that Chief Deputy Sheriff Cipriano Baca could handle the distasteful and unpopular duties of the sheriff's office.[31]

5

The World Turned Upside Down

"Life is the first gift, love is the second, and understanding is the third."—Anonymous

The cool weather of autumn often comes quickly in the high country. Sometimes the first snow can arrive without any advanced warning that winter has arrived. This can be an omen of a difficult winter. If Cipriano Baca felt some foreboding concerning the closing months of 1894, as Indian summer had turned quickly to fall and fall was now rushing headlong toward winter, he left no record for future historians.

Cipriano Baca most likely felt that his future looked rosy. Marie had discovered two new breakfast products, and she tried to get her husband to eat these as occasional replacement to his classic eggs, potatoes, tamales, and hot coffee. The hot dish, Cream of Wheat, and shredded wheat cold cereal were new to the grocery shelf. Marie lost the battle to change her husband's breakfast habit, but Cipriano did become a huge fan of the new Juicy Fruit chewing gum.

The die was cast. Cipriano was organizing his followers to make his first run for elective public office. He was determined to win the Republican Party nomination to become the ninth person to serve as Grant County's chief law enforcement officer since the county's formation in the spring of 1868. What Cipriano needed most now was campaign money and delegate support at the county's Republican Party Convention, so Baca went hunting for both.

The Grant County Republican Central Committee, chaired by businessman J.A. Ancheta of Silver City, met and set the dates for the events leading up to the general election to be held on the first Tuesday in November. Each of the county's precincts was instructed to hold a caucus of registered party members on Saturday, September 8, and by using a formula based upon the number of party votes cast in that precinct at the last general election, they would select their precinct's voting delegates to the county convention to be held ten days later at Silver City.

The Grant County Republican Party held their convention on Tuesday, September 18. At the appointed hour the Republicans gathered, and the first order of business was the election of convention officers. Next, the convention proceeded to select delegates to the territorial convention two days later in Socorro. These county delegates where bound to vote to nominate candidates for territorial office that had been approved by the county convention. The county convention finally took up the selection of candidates to run for county office.

The convention secretary noted, "Nominations for sheriff being in order, W.H. Newcomb [of Silver City] placed in nomination Cipriano Baca. P.H. McDermott [of Carlisle] nominated Richard S. Knight, and W.H. Taylor [of the Lower Mimbres] nominated George O. Perrault. The nominations were closed." Three men where then appointed as tellers to count the ballots. "The result of the first ballot was as follows, Baca 44, Knight 27, Perrault 22, scattering 1. The second ballot resulted, Baca 52, Knight 25, Perrault 16. Mr. Baca's nomination was declared unanimous." W.B. Walton, editor of the Democratic-leaning *Deming Headlight*, had a different opinion of Baca's nomination success. In an editorial comment, he said, "Cipriano Baca was not the choice of the republican party for sheriff but was selected by the members of the 'ring.' Baca will find out that ring politics don't 'go' in Grant county any more by November."[1]

The *Silver City Enterprise*, a Republican voice in Grant County, evenhandedly reported the results of the Democrats' county convention. "The choice for sheriff—Baylor Shannon [of the Bear Creek or Mangas Precinct]—is exceptionally strong, as Bay has an army of friends in the county. His opponent will by no means have a walk over." The *Deming Headlight* openly endorsed Shannon; "Bay has energy, courage, and good judgment. He is a sterling democrat. As county commissioner, he has done his work conscientiously, and the same may be expected of him, if he should be elected sheriff."[2]

A small group of discontents from both the Democrat and Republican parties formed a Populist Party movement and held their own nominating convention. Following some hard pressure by his friends and family, Captain James E. ("I'm not sure I'm a Populist") Foster, from the Mimbres Precinct, accepted nomination to seek the sheriff's post against Baca and Shannon. To Foster's credit he did campaign hard for the job and earned 166 votes on Election Day.

* * *

Samuel Langhorne Clemens was a caustic writer who used the nom de plume Mark Twain. Caustic or not, Clemens' comment, "Let us endeavor so to live that when we come to die even the undertaker will be sorry," used in 1894 *Pudd'nhead Wilson's Calendar*, seems to have captured the real essence of who was the person known as Mrs. Mary Linda Keefe Baca and called Marie by her friends and family.

This close up is from a group picture of Grant County officials taken in front of the courthouse in Silver City. Baca was the under-sheriff of the chief deputy sheriff of the county. He had charge of the jail and field operations. The county jail was in the basement of the county office building as seen behind Baca in the picture (Mary Baca Photograph Album/Cipriana Randolph).

There remains scant information about the personal life Marie and Cipriano Baca shared together during their seven years as husband and wife. Very little is known of Marie's personality or of her pleasures and dislikes. It is known that she was very compassionate and held a deep love for her family and friends. No pictures of her or any of her personal correspondences seem to have survived her passing. Since New Mexico did not require registration of births until early in the 1900s, it is uncertain if the couple had any children. Cipriana Randolph recalled having heard something about a child named Eva and that Marie was pregnant at the time of her death, but nothing has been located to support that belief. A contemporary newspaper record of Marie's life journey and her untimely death is almost nonexistent. The record of private moments during the Keefe-Baca union is a historic void. In the final analysis, Marie Baca was like most Victorian-era wives; they were just a shadow along the path of their husband's life and left little or no trail of their own earthly sojourn.

There is no public record to suggest that Marie Baca ever accompanied Cipriano to a political rally or did any campaigning on his behalf. It is also possible that the 25-year-old Marie was not attracted to the combative nature of frontier politics and sought to escape the rancorous Grant County sheriff's election campaign. Maybe Cipriano felt that he was going to be away from home so much that this might be a good time for his wife to visit some of her family and perhaps celebrate the impending birth. A few days after the celebration of her husband's victory at the Republican Party's county convention, Marie left Silver City for an extended trip to the west coast. Most likely Marie planned to return in time for the holidays and to witness her husband's swearing-in ceremony.

Marie took the spear line from Silver City to Deming and at that point connected with the transcontinental route to the Pacific. She had not seen her family in two years. Evidence that surfaced after her death suggests that Marie first visited with a sister in San Francisco and met an old girlfriend who was having marital problems. Marie convinced her friend to take a vacation and accompany her on a visit to her invalid mother who lived in Seattle. The two women spent a pleasant visit with Mrs. Kate Keefe at her one-story cottage on Main Street. Marie also visited with her other sister and her family. Thomas and Kate Keefe had left New Mexico Territory in February 1889.

Marie Baca also took the opportunity to visit her father who was living in Everrett, about 20 miles up Puget Sound; her parents had been divorced for a few years. The visit of father and daughter was not pleasant and Marie left with some ill feelings after only a short stay. Upon her return to Seattle, Marie and Captain Edward D. Griffin, a family friend from San Francisco Bay, renewed their acquaintance. The sea captain would always stop to check on Mrs. Keefe when he had a layover in Seattle and often delivered letters and packages to Mrs. Keefe from her daughter in San Francisco.

When Captain Griffin's ship was ready to sail, he got permission from the company manager in Seattle to transport the two ladies back to San Francisco. A pleasant sea voyage in late fall was much preferable to the arduous, dusty, and cold stagecoach and train trip back south. Before she left to begin her journey back to New Mexico, Marie gave her mother a turquoise ring and her young niece a small diamond ring. Mrs. Keefe told a *Seattle Telegraph* reporter that her daughter was traveling with a lot of "beautiful jewelry and diamonds amounting to $300 or more."[3]

The reader should not miss the financial implications of Marie's journey. A West Coast trip of the magnitude Marie Baca was enjoying would have been expensive even by 1894 standards. She was also giving quality gifts and traveling with a collection of expensive jewelry; $300 in 1894 dollar value equates to over $8,000 in current dollar value. Cipriano Baca was not an average fee-earning deputy sheriff working on the closing frontier of New Mexico Territory. Baca's business investments had made him one of the nation's pioneering upper-middle-class citizens in an era of struggling day laborers. Baca's wealth may have been a factor in his sheriff's race. Some not so fortunate Anglo day workers may have resented a well-to-do "Mexican" becoming their sheriff.

A major economic depression, marked by numerous labor strikes over reduced wages for workers, had jolted the United States just a year earlier. A person might work 12 hours a day just to earn $2.50; the average worker earned between $400 and $500 a year. Between a third and half of the nation's population barely had enough to eat daily, while capitalist owners earned millions of dollars annually and paid no income tax. By the end of 1894, 642 of the nation's banks had failed, one-quarter of all heavy industry lay idle, and over 22,500 miles of the nation's railroad tracks were in receivership. On Independence Day 1894, President Grover Cleveland had sent federal troops to break up a labor strike in Chicago; 30 people died, 60 persons were injured, and 700 persons were arrested in this crusade for higher wages.[4]

The sailing ship *Ivanhoe*, named after the lead character in Sir Walter Scott's 1820 novel of the same name, was a 1,610-ton ship measuring 202 feet long and 39 feet wide, with a seven-and-a-half-foot deep hold. The vessel, built at the shipyard in Belfast in 1865, was constructed of timbers lumbered in the forest of Maine. The *Ivanhoe* sailed the Atlantic for 20 years before she made the hazardous journey around "the Horn" to provide an additional decade of service along the Pacific Coast.

In 1894, the collier *Ivanhoe* was a jointly owned cargo ship of Arthur Cornwall and George Bull of San Francisco, and piloted by Captain Griffin, a native of Bangor, Maine, and his 18-man crew; two mates, a carpenter, 13 seamen, and two Chinese cooks. The 42-year-old captain and his crew where based in the San Francisco Bay area. Griffin, a lifelong bachelor, kept a room with the Folger family. The captain first went to sea when he was 10 years old, yet he was well educated for his time and occupation.[5]

On Friday evening, September 14, 1894, the *Ivanhoe*, with lowered sails, was towed into Seattle harbor by a tugboat and was anchored to a buoy. The *Seattle Press-Times* reported that the ship "will load coal for the Black Diamond yards at San Francisco." Thirteen days later, the *Press-Times* noted, under its "Water Front" news column, "The ship Ivanhoe was towed out [of the harbor] today with 2250 tons of Black Diamond coal for the company's San Francisco yards."[6] Along with the coal, the ship's manifest maintained by N.H. Martin, general manager for the Black Diamond Coal Company in Seattle, listed four passengers. Mrs. Marie Baca and Mrs. Dr. Irene Mullin, her traveling companion, had joined family friend, Captain Griffin, for a peaceful and relaxing non-port-of-call cruise to San Francisco. Allan P. Folger, a 22-year-old naval student, fledgling navigator and member of the family where Captain Griffin lodged, was one of the two male passengers. The other was Frederic J. Grant, the dynamic young leader of the Republican Party in northwestern Washington State. Later, one newspaper account claimed that a man named Edward Allardyce had been a stowaway on the *Ivanhoe*. Captain Griffin, his crew, and his passengers all sailed toward the setting sun and thus journeyed into the mist of naval history.[7]

5. The World Turned Upside Down

The *Ivanhoe* moved through the Straits of Juan de Fuca that separated Washington State from British Columbia. In the closing days of the War between the States, the CSS *Shenandoah* made a series of raids upon Union shipping in these straits during June of 1865. This stretch of waterway off Port Renfrew has earned the nickname "The Graveyard of the Pacific" with just foundation; at this writing, 137 major tragedies are charted in these straits.

The last settlement *Ivanhoe*'s passengers and crew saw along the Washington coast was the village of Neah Bay and the Makah Indian Reservation. After sailing around the tip of the Olympic Peninsula in northwest Clallam County, Captain Griffin would have seen the coastal lighthouse on Tatoosh Island, about a half mile off the Cape Flattery point. The lighthouse, first constructed in 1855, had been enlarged and updated over the years and was now the pride of the Washington coast.

On October 11, the *Seattle Press-Times* reported that weather out at the Cape Flattery banks had been "very rough weather" with some hail. Four days later the newspaper headlined a front-page story "Ship Ivanhoe Overdue" and reported that the "ship is at least seven days overdue and the owners are expressing much anxiety." Two days later another ship arrived from San Francisco with reports of "unusually heavy sea off the cape," and the next day another ship reported "heavy weather" during the voyage northward.[8]

The *Seattle Press-Times* continued its coverage of the missing *Ivanhoe* on Wednesday, October 17, with another front-page feature. The column featured an interview with channel tugboat captain Libby explaining that once the *Ivanhoe* rounded Cape Flattery, Captain Griffin spotted an incoming storm and probably made a run for the open sea just ahead of it. "In order to get back into his right course he [Captain Griffin] might have to tack and tack for days. It would be very annoying of course, but certainly a very common experience with sailing vessels." In nautical terms, "tack" is a method of sailing against the prevailing wind. Two days later, the 22nd day in the wait for news of the *Ivanhoe*, the newspaper still said, "there is nothing to cause alarm."[9]

The *Seattle Telegraph*, the state's only Democratic newspaper, broke the news concerning the identity of the passengers aboard the *Ivanhoe*. N.H. Martin defended the seaworthiness of the *Ivanhoe* and added his ideas about the ship. "My opinion is that she encountered a head wind and beat [it] out to sea to get a clear sail down the coast. She may have lost some spears or sails and is now working her way slowly toward San Francisco. Capt. Griffin is a good sailor and I think the vessel will turn up all right." Two days later, the *Seattle Press-Times* reported that someone had sighted wreckage off Cape Flattery, but the newspaper continued to express hope that the passengers and crew were still alive.[10]

There was a report that the *Ivanhoe* was last seen by its companion steamship, the *Robert Sudden*, the evening they had sailed around the tip of Cape Flattery. No distress signal was given. Later reports, in the archives of the Maritime Museum of British Columbia, say the *Ivanhoe* was listing badly off the western edge of the Umatilla Reef and may have capsized due to carrying an overload of coal in the cargo hold. It is unknown if any lifeboats where launched before the vessel sank. Three months after the supposed date of the ship's sinking, pieces of the *Ivanhoe* washed ashore about 150 miles to the north of Cape Flattery along the Canadian coast in British Columbia. There were no survivors and no one ever found bodies from the *Ivanhoe*. The Sea has no mercy.

The *Seattle Press Times*, of December 7, concluded that all hope had faded and that the *Ivanhoe* and her human cargo were lost. In mid–December, the *Silver City Enterprise* reported that the U.S. Coast Guard Revenue Cutter Service had discontinued the search for any *Ivanhoe* survivors and officially considered that all persons aboard the doomed ship had drowned.[11] The Coast Guard had spent over a month searching the coast from San Francisco north to the Canadian border. The local tugboat services had checked the inland waterways to Seattle with no results. Two dozen families lost loved ones to a winter storm and an aging sailing craft; simple words cannot do justice to the tragic personal horror of that storm-tossed nightmare.

Marie Baca's loss at sea does not seem to have been a campaign issue, and it is unknown how or when Baca first learned of his wife's fate. The message may have come from one of her sisters because it is doubtful that her invalid mother or estranged father would have made the contact. It is doubtful that the Diamond Coal Company had any idea how to reach Marie's husband.

It was over a month before one of the Seattle newspapers identified the passengers aboard the *Ivanhoe*, and then they centered upon the importance of Frank Grant. Later, a reporter located Marie's mother and interviewed her, but his published account spelled Marie's married name as "Bara" and then added to the confusion by calling her mother "Mrs. Kiefe." Baca's first alert may not have happened until Marie's San Francisco sister alerted Baca to the possible accident or some newspaper reporter finally connected the "Marie Bara" listed in local newspapers as missing aboard the ill-fated steamship *Ivanhoe* and Marie Baca, the daughter of Dr. and Mrs. Thomas Keefe. It is very likely that Marie was dead for many weeks before Cipriano learned of her tragic passing.

The distance of a century makes it difficult to comprehend how the news of his young wife's fate would have influenced Baca's ability to campaign. Custom would have dictated that Baca conduct a subdued effort, if not voluntary outright suspension of his active involvement in the political process. None of these things took place, so it is fairly certain that Baca was unaware of the tragedy that befell him until long after the fact. This assumption is further supported by the fact that the *Silver City Enterprise*, a strong Baca booster, made no mention of the *Ivanhoe* disaster and that it was two Democratic newspapers that first told Grant County citizens about Baca's grief. The *Deming Headlight* first published a news item originating from the West Coast saying that Marie Baca had most likely died aboard the *Ivanhoe* mishap in late September. The *Silver City Eagle* reprinted the *Deming Headlight* account on November 7, four days after the general election.

One can assume that Baca and members of the Keefe family corresponded concerning the *Ivanhoe* mishap and maybe even consoled each other with their joint grief. It is possible that such letters will yet be located in a forgotten family history file in some historical society archives. There is no tombstone to mark Mary Linda Keefe Baca's passing, so these pages are her epitaph.

* * *

By the first of October 1894, political campaigns were in full swing across the nation. This was the era when women with social breeding did not publicly discuss politics, and no woman living in New Mexico Territory could vote except in some local school board elections, but women and children did attended the dances, barbeque or fried chicken dinners, and the rancorous campaign rallies. These events were hosted by the candidates for the party faithful. There was always a speech or two or three to pep up the partisan effort to get out the vote.[12]

Baca often attended these political shindigs in company with Anglo members of the Republican ticket like Judge Porterfield, J.N. Childers, or Andy Laird. However, in Deming and Lordsburg or some of the other largely Hispanic-populated areas, Baca was the star attraction. Grant County's Democrat and Republican candidates often crossed paths along the campaign circuit and sometimes even appeared in the same town or village in back-to-back town hall meetings.

A lot of food, beer, and hot-air speeches were consumed in the name of freedom and democracy or just plan entertainment. Ben Franklin is often quoted as having said, "Beer is living proof that God loves us and wants us to be happy." He is also credited with believing that three men could keep a secret, but only if two of them were dead. The Democrats soon learned that truth.

Thousands of years before the Shannon-Baca contest took place, the author of the book of Proverbs caught the essence of their contest when he wrote, "Truthful lips endure forever, but a lying tongue lasts only a moment," and later he concluded that "scoundrels concoct evil and their speech is like a scorching fire." These words of wisdom proved to be true in Grant County, New Mexico Territory, during the fall of 1894.

Baylor Shannon held one of his first campaign rallies at the Carlisle mining camp located about four miles east of the Arizona border. The present day ghost town's only claim to fame is that Herbert Hoover, the future president, held his first mine engineering job in that camp when he was hired as the assistant superintendent of the Steeple Rock Mine. During his remarks to the friendly crowd, Shannon used a debate technique known as subreption to accuse Cipriano of having once accepted a bribe to release a prisoner. The Democratic candidate, who had a slight limp as the result of a fall from his horse, concluded his speech by saying that he even had a signed affidavit to prove the charge. It took a few days before news of Shannon's blistering charge of Baca's misconduct in office reached the Republican candidate who was doing his own glad-handing.[13]

Shannon based his bribery charge against Baca upon an affidavit signed by Lafayette Fox, a private assigned to Troop G of the 10th U.S. Cavalry, to effect that Baca accepted a bribe to release him during the barroom incident at Ernest's Place in September 1893. Baca publicly denied the charge, and Republican operatives quickly went to work ferreting out the truth behind the Fox affidavit. The Democrat rumor mill went into high gear while the *Deming Headlight* and Silver City's *Sentinel* and *Eagle* repeated all the accusations as truth. The hatchet job grew so wild that one of the architects, Ed Young, and the Democratic candidate for probate judge were "ashamed of it and came out and denounced the trick."[14]

The plan was simple. A Democrat partisan named Dell M. Potter was drinking in George Parker's Saloon in Central one evening when he overheard Private Fox telling some other soldiers about the incident at Ernest's Place. Potter knew that Baca was going to seek the Republican nomination for sheriff, so he got Fox really drunk, took him before J. Crockett Givens, the local justice of the peace and a notary, and had him sign a trumped-up statement claiming he gave Baca $15 for his freedom. The Baylor campaign held the false document until after Baca started his general election campaign. Potter gave the affidavit to Shannon. In mid–October, Potter went back to the saloons in Central to elitist more affidavits, only this time Baca's friends discovered his trickery. Baca, accompanied by J.R. Johnson and J.W. Weety, confronted Potter at White's Corral, but the man denied the plot until he was later confronted by men who witnessed his attempt to buy more false affidavits from soldiers. The *Silver City Enterprise* now had enough evidence of misconduct and broke the story of the fake affidavits. The newspaper used two inflammatory subheadings, "Candidates in Collusion with Criminals" and "Suborning Perjury," to make their point.

Potter left Grant County the morning after he had a meeting with Shannon, Young, and two other Democrat Party leaders. Fox and some of the other soldiers, four sergeants and two privates, who where present at Ernest's Place signed affidavits concerning what had really happened that night. Sergeant John Logan, the squad leader, testified he had offered to compensate Baca for his services in restoring order in the barroom but that Baca had refused any money.[15]

Two weeks before the general election S.M. Ashenfelter, now the editor of the *Deming Headlight* and remembered from the 1888 bicycle-horse race, published a yellow-journalism exposé entitled "The Baca-Fox Matter." Ashenfelter denied that any Democratic candidate for Grant County public office had anything to do with the supposed false affidavits incident directed against Baca; he alleged that the misguided fraud was all Dell Potter's idea, and unfortunately the man was now missing from the political arena.[16]

The week before the general election, the *Silver City Enterprise* published seven attack stories pounding the Democrats concerning the false affidavit scandal. In one piece, the *Silver City Enterprise* took the Silver City *Southwest Sentinel*'s editor Allan MacDonald to task for his misleading campaign rhetoric saying, "Out of the stygian darkness of the explanations arise fogs of democratic despair and odors of untruth." The Republican voice then asked voters a simple question: "Leaving out Mr. Baca's denial of accepting the bribe, can any one not blinded by political bigotry or personal hatred doubt where lies the weight of evidence?"[17] Interestingly, Grant County's Populist Party's campaign newspaper, the *People's Advocate*, did not concern itself with reporting any aspect of the Baca-Fox cesspool, a classic example of "see no evil, hear no evil, print no evil."

J.E. Sheridan, the *Silver City Enterprise*'s editor, wrote a few days before the election that in spite of the public knowledge concerning the false statements contained within the Fox document, the Democrats "still continue to insinuate, by low innuendo, all sorts of crimes against candidates of the republican party." Another editorial said, "Cipriano Baca has been sworn into office by the false affidavits of unscrupulous democratic candidates. He will make a good sheriff; there never was a better chief deputy." Finally, editor Sheridan suggested that since a Russian holy man had recently prayed for the good health of the Czar, wounded in an assassination attempt, and the monk seemed to be successful in his request, maybe "the Democratic party of Grant County should obtain his services to pray them out of their present dilemma."[18]

To help aid the Grant County Democrat get-out-the-vote-campaign, territorial governor William T. Thornton and the territory's congressional delegate Harvey B. Fergusson arrived in Silver City for a big rally on Thursday, November 1, and the "big guns" maneuver proved successful in the territory's southwestern section.

Election judges quickly tallied the ballot boxes from Silver City, Deming, and Lordsburg. Baca lost the county seat by 51 votes, but won Deming by 28 and Lordsburg by 22 votes. Baca was trailing by one vote. It took a couple of days before the rest of the precincts did their count and a week before officials received the totals from the last box in a remote part of the county. The Russian monk's prayers worked; Baylor Shannon garnered 878 votes to Baca's 785, a 143-vote margin. While Cipriano Baca lost his race, most of the county's other Republican candidates won their electios.[19]

6

A New Life in Mogollon

"Be strong and courageous. Do not be terrified; do not be discouraged, for the L-rd your G-d will be with you wherever you go."—Joshua 1:9

Cipriano Baca felt rejected by the populace of Silver City and the citizens of Grant County. The public record concerning Baca's life for two months following the election is void. At some point, he must have accepted his defeat, become aware of his wife's death, and begun to think about his future. To Baca it must have seemed that his world just collapsed when he suffered three back-to-back slaps from fate. His young wife's death, his political rejection, and dismissal from his deputy's job by the new sheriff must have had a disheartening effect upon Cipriano. Three personal losses and an uncertain future—this was the test of the mantle of a man on the verge of becoming a living legend. Did he cope alone or did he lean upon his friends?

One door had closed, but another soon opened, and Cipriano Baca walked through that new door. The need for a change and new adventure, plus the lure of mineral wealth, caused the recent widower to pack up and relocate to a mining camp in the remote mountains of western Socorro County. In late January 1895, the *Silver City Enterprise* told its readers that Grant County's former chief deputy sheriff "is now running a butcher shop at Mogollon."[1]

* * *

The Apostle Paul wrote in his *Letter to the Church at Ephesus* that in this life a person should always make wise use of each opportunity that comes his way. Upon his becoming settled in the booming mining camp of Mogollon, Baca became an active disciple of this biblical wisdom. He was soon a cornerstone of the social, political, and business life in western Socorro County.

Don Juan Ignacio de Flores y Mogollon served as governor of the Spanish Province of Nuevo Méjico from 1712 to 1715 and gave his name to the mountain range along the present-day New Mexico–Arizona border. Named for the mountains, the mining town had been formed in 1889 and gained a post office the next year. The Peacock, Little Fanny, Silver Queen, Last Chance, and Confidence mines had made millionaires out of their owners. Within a short time, miners dug holes into the steep slops and cliffs along Silver Creek, and men were working around the clock to extract the rich veins of gold, silver, and copper. The Mogollon Mining District would become one of the most

Mogollon, located in a canyon along Silver Creek, was an active multi-culture mining town first settled in the 1800s and today is a privately owned ghost town. During Mogollon's heyday, the settlement had large Italian, Hispanic and Anglo populations and they celebrated each other's festivals and holidays (Jim Stauder Photograph Collection).

productive mining regions in New Mexico Territory and eventually produced well over $15 million in high-grade ore.

A regular stage route soon connected the village of Mogollon with the railroad spur line from Silver City to Deming. In Deming, a person could take the Santa Fe train to Socorro via Rincon. This 300-mile trip to the Socorro County seat was expensive, grueling, and time consuming. "The very shortest route [from Mogollon] to the county seat by way of Magdalena is 150 miles," reported the *Mogollon Mines*, "and that distance must be covered by a good saddle animal, there being no roads which are practicable for heavy teams or light wagons."[2]

In the latter part of the 1890s, convict laborers used picks and shovels to chop an eight-mile trail from the trading center at Glenwood down into Frisco Valley along Silver Creek. From the treeless flat top of Whitewater Mesa, the convict road twisted down the steep mountainside through cactus and mesquite and rabbit brush. This labor-intensive single-lane trail still affords a magnificent panoramic view of the valley and its ghostly settlement along both sides of the creek. The tree line is marked by yellow pines and junipers, and even today the opening to the Pacific Mine and its outbuildings can be seen on the forested shelf far below. The first view of Mogollon is the white tailings of the dump from the Little Fanny Mine, and then the business section begins as the downhill road reaches the bottom of the valley.

When Cipriano first saw the mining camp, it was a pastiche. The hodgepodge settlement of Mogollon was still recovering from a fire that had whipped across the valley in June 1894. The *Silver City Enterprise* had described the rebirth in mystic terms: "The town of Mogollon is arising phoenix like from the ashes."[3] Six of the new structures were of stone construction. The rebuilt town still had more than enough saloons, a dozen brothels, a couple of major mercantile stores, and other assorted businesses located along Silver Creek. The post office, a small school, the Presbyterian Church and the Catholic Church were the only public buildings in the mining camp. Some of the larger mine operations had installed small gasoline generators to create a limited supply of electricity for their office complex and electric lighting in their mine shafts, replacing the candle and oil lamp. None of Mogollon's homes were equipped with incandescent lighting.[4]

Governor William T. Thornton discussed the condition of the territory's mining industry in his 1895 report to the secretary of the Interior. "The mining industry, which was suffering so seriously one year ago as the result of the depreciation in the price of silver and lead, the two minerals most generally produced, has very much revived during the past year. Especially is this the case with reference to the camps containing gold, and there are engaged in the business of mining almost as many miners as at any time in the previous history of the Territory of New Mexico."[5]

* * *

Holm Olaf Bursum, an Iowa-born orphan, had a few years of public school education before migrating to New Mexico in 1882. A.H. Hilton, Bursum's uncle, had invited the teenager to come to the Sunshine Territory to work as a clerk in his store in San Antonio; his cousin Conrad grew up to found the Hilton chain of hotels. Bursum was restless for adventure and to start his own fortune, so he begin hauling freight from Albuquerque to Fort Wingate on the Arizona line. Later, he became a subcontractor for the Atlantic and Pacific Railroad and amassed the capital he needed to found a livestock operation in western Socorro County. In this terrain, Bursum became a sheep and cattle raiser, invested in mining ventures and other business enterprises, became a master Mason and lifetime member of the Socorro Lodge and served as a member of the governing body of the Presbyterian Church at Socorro. He next entered the Socorro County political wars and started building a platform to launch his quest for political power.

In November 1894, the 27-year-old pipe-smoking Bursum was elected sheriff of Socorro County with over a 400-vote majority. On Tuesday, January 1, 1895, Baylor Shannon took office as sheriff in Grant County, and Bursum pinned on the sheriff's star in Socorro County. It is uncertain when and where Bursum first met Baca, but it may have been during the Bursum-Moore courtship. Bursum and Baca became not just political allies, but over the years, they also became friends.[6]

The *Socorro Chieftain* noted, in mid-July 1895, that the man who had served Sheriff Leopoldo Contreras, a Democrat, as deputy sheriff at Mogollon had resigned, so that Bursum, a Republican, could name his own man to the post. The newspaper pointed out that Bursum had received numerous petitions supporting candidates for the office.[7] No official record now survives to suggest that Baca had been one of the applicants, yet Sheriff H.O. Bursum offered Baca a deputy appointment, in the Mogollon mining district, with a $25 per month stipend. The local mine owners and other village businessmen had already agreed to support a funding pool to pay Cipriano an additional $100 per month if he also functioned as the precinct constable and ex-official marshal of Mogollon. Cipriano accepted the offer, and what was Grant County's loss now became Socorro County's gain. This "subscription lawman" arrangement began a long relationship between Baca, the denizens of Mogollon, and the law enforcement establishment operating within Socorro County.[8]

One of Cipriano Baca's first duties as the representative of the law in Mogollon was to take into custody a woman who had slipped over the edge into insanity due to her isolated existence. The unbalanced woman was almost beyond control by the time Sheriff Bursum arrived in Mogollon to escort her to the territorial asylum. The sheriff had to restrain his charge during the long and arduous trip to Las Vegas, via stagecoach to Silver City and then a railroad trip of hundreds of miles to the eastern side of the territory. Deputy Baca had made the arrest, but Sheriff Bursum collected the transport fee from the county commissioners. The woman lived the rest of her natural life in her fantasy world.

Winter was upon the mountain country, and residents were beginning to think about the season celebrating the birth of the Prince of Peace. Not all citizens were, however, in a peaceful mood, and Chloride's *Black Range* reported the misdeed.

> A shooting scrape happened between Tom Rice, who abused in no very decent language M.C. Logan. Rice had been making threats and flourishing a six-shooter going to Logan's house, and entering it. He was shot by Logan who is considered justified in doing so. The shot took effect in the neck, but it is not considered fatal.[9]

Baca received the incident report and went to the area to investigate and found enough reason to take the troublemakers in tow. Baca restored the peace of the season along Silver Creek.

Baca brought a strong law enforcement reputation with him to the Mogollon country, and the businessmen and mine owners of the area soon discovered that Baca's record was honestly earned. *Obsta principiis*, a Latin dictum, means a person should oppose "small bad things" before they grow into troublesome habits. Cipriano Baca understood this motto as it applied to a mining camp and law enforcement. He set a high standard, and citizens accepted his just application of the law. Baca proved to be a highly effective deputy sheriff and constable, but, even so, on a couple of occasions Sheriff Bursum reminded tardy mine operators of their commitment to contribute to Baca's salary fund each month. Each time, within a few days, payments were up to date.[10]

The acreage surrounding the Victorian courthouse on the south side of the business square in Socorro was rocky and almost void of vegetation. That picture changed in the early fall of 1895 when Sheriff Bursum had his jail prisoners level the grounds surrounding the courthouse, till the soil, plant grass seed, and construct flowerbeds. The *Socorro Chieftain* proclaimed, "The county property is a place of beauty."[11] In the fall of 1896, county jail inmates completed their beautification project by constructing a two-foot-high stone fence around the courthouse grounds. Now Bursum turned his attention toward Mogollon and western Socorro County.

Baca and Bursum teamed up again in the spring of 1896. Bursum was in Mogollon in April conducting a tax levy inventory and heard Mogollon's leading businessmen discuss a shortcut road between the camp and the county seat. The county's western residents were required to travel to Silver City to catch a train to Deming and then transfer to another train heading north to Socorro. Silver City and Grant County merchants were profiting off Socorro County taxpayer trade dollars. A direct route across the plains would drastically reduce travel time between the Mogollon minefields and the Socorro County business center. Bursum understood the necessity and agreed to spearhead the improvement project with the county commissioners.

By May, Bursum had convinced the Socorro County Commissioners' Court to allow the county surveyor to lay out a route for the proposed wagon road. The sheriff next set about collecting private funding to cover the ongoing maintenance cost of the road. Every local and territorial politician or wannabe public office seeker added his name to the conscription list. Mine owners saw the prospect of an easier route to get their ore to the railroad. W.W. Jones soon had a feasible trail surveyed, and work was under way by summer. Bursum asked Deputy Baca to oversee the county convicts assigned to the western end of the construction effort headed out of Mogollon down the mountainous slope and eastward across the plains.

The "Bursum Road" is still in use today. The gravel road leaves Mogollon as Forest Service Road 159 headed east between Spring Mountain and Willow Mountain then along the north bank of Gilita Creek to the Willow Creek Campgrounds in the Gila National Forest. Here the road goes north past Negrito Fire Base and over the Continental Divide to junction with Forest Service Roads 94 and 30 north of the 9,678-foot-high Elk Mountain range. At this point, the "Bursum Road" becomes FSR 30 and heads east through O Bar O Canyon where at the mouth of Railroad Canyon the road designation becomes New Mexico Highway 163. North of the 8,266-foot-high Rock Springs Peak, on the southern edge of the San Agustin Plains, NM 163 merges into NM 52 and heads due north to join U.S. 60 between Datil and Magdalena near the site of the Very Large Array project. This trip provides the modern-day traveler a firsthand leap back into the past. The natural scenic beauty and the remote loneliness of this vast region quickly engulf the pilgrim just as it did over a century ago.

Sheriff Bursum was a frequent visitor to the Mogollon area checking on the road's progress. The new route progressed as quickly as the sheriff's courting of a Silver City lady. The accomplished violinist-lawman often entertained friends with his versatile style.[12] Bursum married Lulu M. Moore, the daughter of a Grant County rancher, at her parent's Silver City home in August 1898.

* * *

Cipriano Baca was the law in Mogollon from the summer of 1895 until January 1897. During these eighteen months, he evenhandedly enforced the law and maintained a peaceful community while also engendering trust among the inhabitants of the mining camp. He was popular and respected. Cipriano had developed his people skills during his youth, and he learned quickly how to deal with Hispanic cultural issues like pride, politics, and ethics. Baca understood the frustration his Anglo counterparts felt when Hispanics refused to divulge the identity of an assailant. He knew that many times the victim was not shielding the criminal but was reserving his own right to settle the debt personally outside the court system. The idea of using a court of law to settle a personal or family matter of honor, a personal injury, or property damage was an alien concept, since many Hispanics considered personal revenge a birthright.

In Spanish, the word *robar* means robbery, burglary, or any form of taking something from someone. There is no distinction made concerning the use of force or a weapon or even if people were present when the crime was committed. This lack of difference in meaning sometimes made understanding the exact nature of a crime difficult to determine. Even the Hispanic concept of time and the nature of giving directions presented problems for Anglo officers. Cipriano became a master at seeing straight to the heart of an issue and knowing how to deal with the problem. His "street smart" talents worked in both cultural worlds, and Baca used his skill to gain knowledge concerning the murder of Albert Jennings Fountain and his eight-year-old son Henry in the vast White Sands region in February 1896. The posted reward remained active for years, and Baca was still pursuing leads over a decade later. The case remains one of New Mexico's premiere mysteries.

"We boast on our present deputy sheriff C. Baca, who keeps the camp in a most orderly manner and every good citizen receives protection, no bar room fights or street brawls here since he has been appointed [to preserve the peace]," wrote "An Old Timer" in a letter to the editor of the *Socorro Chieftain* in early August 1896.[13]

What is faith? Faith by definition must be personal in order for it to be "faith." Faith is a belief in that which man cannot prove, but for which one may be held accountable. Faith builds a moral code to live by in this world. Baca was a man of faith, but his actual attendance at religious services changed with the stages of his life and the encouragement of the woman in his life.

In the spring of 1896, Cipriano came face to face with a "legendary holy man" who is known as the Healer in Southwestern folklore. The faith healer's real name was Francis Schlatter. He was the son of German peasants who died leaving the boy an orphan. He immigrated to America in 1884, and in this new land, he learned the trade of a shoemaker, finally working his way west to Denver in 1892. It was in the Mile High City that Schlatter claimed he first heard the call of the Father to conduct a healing crusade. Countless Colorado and New Mexico newspapers recounted the Roman Catholic layman's four-year ministry. These contemporary accounts chronicle the witness of thousands of infirm individuals who flocked to touch the bearded wonderworker and walked away healed. These tales of fulfilled prayers for new health may sound like science fiction mythmaking to the twenty-first-century reader, but the truth of these believers' statements was never in doubt in the late 1890s. We may never know if Cipriano Baca had faith in Schlatter's spiritual relationship with the Father or his ability to act as a conduit for renewed health.[14]

Francis Schlatter spent three months over the 1895–96 winter boarding at the Morley Ranch near Datil in northwestern Socorro County. During these long cold evenings in the high country, the Healer sat around a warm fire and discussed his views concerning the Father, reincarnation, faith healing, the End of the Age, the coming of the New Jerusalem, and a thousand-year reign of peace. Mrs. Ada McPherson Morley, widow of the railroad engineer William Raymond Morley who plotted the Santa Fe's route into New Mexico Territory via Raton Pass, wrote these comments down and with Schlatter's grateful permission had them published in a small volume titled *The Life of the Harp in the Hand of the Harper*.

Decades later, Mrs. Morley's daughter, Agnes Morley Cleaveland, included a chapter about Francis Schlatter in her autobiography *No Life for a Lady*.[15]

One day Schlatter informed Mrs. Morley that the Father had told him it was time to move on. The next morning the Healer thanked Mrs. Morley for her kindness, blessed her family, mounted his big white horse Butte and left the ranch headed south. During the first few days of April, Schlatter made his way across the plains into the mountains while traveling the back trails to avoid settlements. There had been a heavy rain in the mountains a few days before so Cipriano Baca was in the backcountry searching for dislodged ore that might have washed down the streams. These wayward samples might lead him to a promising new gold or silver strike.

Baca had made camp along Gilita Creek, east of what would soon become the Bursum Road from Magdalena to Mogollon, and created a panning site. It was about dusk one evening when a tired horse and a weary rider stopped at the camp. Baca asked the man to stay for supper and the two talked into the night. Schlatter spent the next day fishing and helping Baca do some panning. They talked again the second night. The next morning the Healer and Butte continued their journey south.

The faith healer reportedly died in the spring of 1897 near Casas Grandes, about 70 miles south of La Ascencion, in Chihuahua, Mexico. Mrs. Morley never accepted any account of Schlatter's death: "He told me to expect this. He is not dead. He will return. I must wait for him." Agnes Morley Cleaveland wrote of her mother's faithful watch. "There after we walked in the presence of one who was with us but not of us. The home life went on around her but she was no longer interested in it." Today the copper "healing rod" that Schlatter used during his exercise routine, which was needed he claimed so he could maintain his ability to use The Father's power to heal those in need, is housed at the Museum of New Mexico in Santa Fe.

A few days after Schlatter left his camp, Baca returned to Mogollon and read a Silver City newspaper and discovered that someone spotted a man believed to be the long-sought-after faith healer of the Rocky Mountains west in the Silver City area. Baca told his friends, including Sheriff Holm Bursum, about his meeting the Healer. Baca said that the tall, bearded, ramrod-straight mystic had told him there would be a big war before the end of the century (the Spanish-American War took place in 1898) and that this war would change America forever. He also told Baca to be careful because if he "sowed the wind he would reap the whirlwind" because "that is the Law from on high." Cipriano Baca never saw Francis Schlatter again after they parted on Gilita Creek, but he never forgot their time together. Sixteen years after he received his prophecy, Cipriano kept his appointment with the whirlwind on the main street in Mogollon.[16]

* * *

In August 1896, Mogollon was a bustling town. The community boasted of three hotels, three general stores, seven saloons, a butcher shop, a bakery and confectionary shop, three barbershops, a blacksmith and wagon repair shop, a livery stable, a stage line, a large multi-grade school, a telegraph office, several churches, and daily mail delivery from Silver City, plus an active red-light district.

Deputy Sheriff/Constable Cipriano Baca became part of the community of characters that populated the Mogollon mining camp along with Frank Hitchcock who organized the development of the Mogollon Mines Company. William Childs, an eastern restaurateur, financed exploration on the Little Fanny Mine, and Ernest Craig, an Englishman, went broke on his first and second claims, but hit it big on his third effort. He later returned to England, and neighbors elected him a member of the House of Commons. William J. Weatherby, a very particular person in dress, discipline and purpose who created a conglomerate of mining claims, became wealthy in the process and kept a daily diary describing his adventure in the mining camp. Baca probably shared more then a few beers with Billy the Kid's older brother, "Uncle Joe" Antrim.

Baca's favorite old-timer was "Uncle Harry" who hit pay dirt with the first sawmill lumber business in the Mogollon country and furnished 90 percent of the timber used in the mine tunnels for shoring up the walls. Harry Herman had been born in Baden in 1843 in what later became Germany. The Jewish merchant donated mine timbers to build Mogollon's first jail and after an all-night drunk became its first guest. Herman and Baca became neighbors when Cipriano brought his family to the mining camp in the spring of 1911.

Deputy Sheriff Baca demonstrated his leadership in another arena in late August. The town had barely recovered from a devastating fire when a hard rain in the high mountains caused Silver Creek to overrun its natural boundaries. The *Black Range* of Chloride recorded the events saying,

> The big flood that occurred a few days ago was a hard blow to the camp. Some fifty families were well nigh rendered homeless; twenty-six houses were wrecked and the damage to mills and mines amounts to many thousands of dollars. John Knight and an unknown Mexican were drowned and their bodies found several miles below the camp, and it is reported that seven or eight persons are missing since the flood. The wagon road [from Silver City] leading to that camp was entirely destroyed and now all freight taken into that place is carried on pack animals.[17]

Baca quietly maintained order and his seeming omnipresence kept looters from raiding damaged business establishments. Residents and business owners quickly cleaned up the flood damage, and life returned to normal. The area mines never missed a day's production. Workers repaired the road to Silver City, and the road northeast to Magdalena was completed.

* * *

The 1896 Socorro County Republican Convention convened on Wednesday, October 14, to select their candidates for the November election. Severo M. Vigil received the nomination for tax assessor/collector, but within a week, Cipriano Baca replaced him on the ballot with no reason given for the change. It is unknown how much influence, if any, county political boss Holm O. Bursum had engineering a candidate change, but Baca's certificate of election is among Bursum's private papers housed at the University of New Mexico.[18]

The *Socorro Chieftain* told readers that Baca was "a resident of Mogollon where he is the efficient deputy sheriff. He is well known in that part of the territory to be a most capable man in any official capacity." The newspaper ended the item by saying, "He should be elected by a big majority."[19] Over in Grant County, the *Silver City Enterprise*, a Baca partisan, echoed the Socorro press in their appraisal of his candidacy,

> The choice is an excellent one. He is possessed of a first-class business education and a full understanding of the office to which he aspires. The citizens of Socorro county are to be con-

gratulated upon having the opportunity to acquire the services of so capable a man in the office of [property tax] assessor.[20]

The first results of the national election to reach Mogollon suggested that the Democrats were sweeping the popular vote, so the few local supporters of the Donkey party celebrated the occasion by decorating pictures of Republican presidential candidate William McKinley in black and hanging them across the main street. In their drunken celebration, this minority of elated Democrats also poked fun at the local Republican leaders. Longtime resident E.D. McIntosh later recalled how the revelry ended when "the stage came in that evening with word that McKinley had won, everyone went home and tried to sleep it off."[21]

With the official counting of the Socorro County ballots a few weeks later, Baca won the race for county property tax assessor by 180 votes, 1,418 to 1238, over the Democrat Party candidate. A Socorro reporter said that Baca "is a thorough gentleman and is well fitted for the office he will fill after January 1st next."[22] Cipriano's new job came with a $1,000-a-year salary.

7

Socorro, New Mexico Territory

"Cypriano Baca is making the best assessor Socorro county has ever had."—*Socorro Chieftain*, 09 July 1897

"The wisest and soundest method of solving our tax problem is through economy.... The collections of any taxes which are not absolutely required, which do not beyond reasonable doubt contribute to the public welfare, is only a species of legalized larceny," said Calvin Coolidge during his inaugural address as president of the United States in March 1925. "The wise and correct course to follow in taxation is not to destroy those who have already secured success, but to create conditions under which everyone will have a better chance to be successful. The verdict of the country has been given on this question. That verdict stands. We shall do well to heed it." Three decades before Calvin Coolidge became the nation's 30th chief executive, Tax Assessor Cipriano Baca implemented these same economic principles in Socorro County, New Mexico Territory.[1]

In mid–December 1896, Baca, at the time using the spelling "Cypriano" for his first name, came to Socorro to find a place to live and to post his duty performance bond. Baca's bondsmen were David Baca, G. Biavaschie, and J. Francisco Towle. The new assessor named William Smith, a Mogollon bookkeeper, as his office clerk and J.F. Towle, his friend and bondsman, as chief deputy assessor and office manager. "Assessor Baca is to be congratulated on the selection he has made for an assistant."[2] On Friday, January 1, 1897, Cipriano Baca replaced Nestor P. Eaton.

Eaton had held the tax assessor office in Socorro County for the previous four years. Eaton retired to his ranch and died in 1944 at age 83. His Socorro home is now a state historic house site. The Eaton family patriarch, Col. Ethan D. Eaton, had been a Union officer during the Civil War, a Socorro County rancher, farmer, mine owner and civic leader. In 1884, he headed the Socorro vigilantes that hung Joel Fowler and a few other hardcases. Eaton's great-granddaughter married the son of John F. Fullerton, first captain of the New Mexico Mounted Police. Fullerton had served 77 days as Socorro County assessor before accepting leadership of the territorial rangers.

* * *

In early February 1897, Bursum, Baca and Smith were in Santa Fe on a lobbying mission with members of the Territorial Legislative Assembly. Bursum was seeking an adjustment to the sheriff's fee schedule, while Baca and Smith sought to protect the commission and fee system of the assessor's office. A week later, the *Socorro Chieftain* reported that Baca "had been spending a few days in Silver City" visiting with the managers of the large mining ventures operating in western Socorro County. To the mine owners' dismay, Cipriano explained that he planned to adjust the tax rolls upward to reflect the true value of the property. A few weeks later, the newspaper confirmed that Baca was "very busy these times making the 1897 assessment for this county."[3]

"We are informed," said the *Socorro Chieftain*, "that a large list of names have been reported to Assessor Baca, who in past years have failed to make their [property ownership] returns and by so doing were omitted from the tax roll." Cipriano Baca had good reason to be diligent in his official duty. The new territorial law, which Baca had helped to lobby for, provided that a tax assessor received 4 percent of the tax collected in 1897 and 2 percent of the collected tax in 1898. The penalty for noncompliance with the tax law was a healthy 33 percent of the tax due.[4] The county had been suffering an acute fiscal depression since 1893, but now the economy was on the rebound so Baca was adding many new names to the county tax rolls, and his strict demand for prompt payment was enforced.

"The assessor's office is very busy these days," reported the *Socorro Chieftain*. Tax Assessor Baca was as good as his campaign promise. He had said that if Socorro County property owners did not voluntarily make a timely value statement then "he will make them [the statements] himself and add the penalty." Both William Smith and J.F. Towle earned their pay during the tax collection season. The men were in the Assessor's Office from 9 A.M. to 4 P.M. daily except on Sunday.[5] Towle collected the annual property owner's reports, Baca placed the annual assessment value upon all privately owned property, and Smith kept the billing records in order. They were a one, two, three punch for increased tax evaluation in Socorro County.

Robert E. Lee once told an assembly of college students, "Do your duty. That is all the pleasure, all the comfort, all the glory we can enjoy in this world." Tax Assessor Baca discovered how true the former general's words had been. Socorro County's funding base increased, but Cipriano Baca's political capital decreased expeditiously.

In the late 1890s, Congress implemented a tariff system that levied an import tax on galena, lead-sulfur ore, shipped into the United States. The import tax made it profitable for America's small galena-silver producing mines to make a profit in the decade before the twentieth century. County Assessor Baca made a trip to the western part of Socorro County "on official business" in late May 1897. The next month he was back in the Mogollon country to visit with old friends and investigate property values.[6] The *Socorro Chieftain* flatly stated, "Cipriano Baca is making the best assessor Socorro county has ever had."[7] Did this editorial comment mean that citizens perceived Baca as being both fair and equable with his new appraisals? A week later newspaper readers read, "Assessor Baca drove to Water Canon [in the foothills near Magdalena] last Sunday to observe what improvements were going on in the mines there."[8]

There is little doubt that Baca was committed to doing the best job he could do, for the better assessment job his office did the more bonus money Cipriano could make each year. Baca may have had more than a professional interest in the development of Socorro County's mining industry. His daughter Cipriana suggested another reason. It seems that her father was investing in Socorro County low-grade galena-silver mine operations along with his friend Holm Bursum, yet no one at the time questioned this action as a conflict of interest.

"Father must have had some dream of becoming wealthy in the mining business," recalled Cipriana Randolph. "We found some old stock certificates among his personal papers [after Baca's death], but none [of these stocks] were worth anything in the 1930s. Florentino [Cipriana's brother] burned them after Father's death. I don't think these ventures made much money, but I guess Father just hoped that some day they might have [some financial] value."[9]

The Mexican Province of Nuevo Méjico became a U.S. territory in 1850 by an act of Congress. Two years later the new territorial government created nine administrative districts. Socorro County was one of these original counties. The new state of California bounded New Mexico Territory on the west, and Texas served as the eastern boundary. Socorro County's massive east-west land mass was bordered by Valencia County on the north and had a vague southern boundary with the newly established Dona Ana County. Congress created the Arizona Territory in 1864, with the borders of the present-day state, thus reducing the width of Socorro County by half its former size. Five years later, in 1869, the New Mexico territorial lawmakers created Lincoln County from the eastern half of Socorro County. This action formed the county dimensions known to Cipriano Baca during the time he lived in the area.[10]

The world-renowned economist Adam Smith, in his monumental work *An Inquiry into the Nature and Causes of the Wealth of Nations*, makes the assertion that national rulers make a show of seeking to protect their nation's economy and restraining government expense. Smith then points out that lawmakers, or monarchs, have been, in fact, the greatest spendthrifts in any society in history. Later he purports that if people had more control over their own extravagance, without government interference there would be less government debt and less need for taxation. Baca seems to have subscribed to Smith's economic beliefs first published in 1776.[11]

The *Socorro Chieftain* made an interesting observation in October 1898: "Cypriano Baca, county assessor, returned from a business trip to the East the first of the week." In New Mexico during the territorial era, the term "the East" usually referred to the states east of the Mississippi River. However, in this case the reporter most likely meant the vast area of Socorro County that is located east of the Rio Grande. The newspaper published no follow-up as to the nature of Baca's business on the eastern trip. This excursion was most likely just an on-site assessment of local property values or another one of Baca's trips seeking potential investment property.[12] Cipriana Randolph recalled her father's travel dreams,

> If Father ever made a trip back East he never talked to us kids about it. Father always thought a visit to Washington [D.C.] would be wonderful and he and Mamma talked about it once. Father worked for some railroad and could get [free] passes for all of us. We never went because something changed the plan. I'm not sure but I think Father changed jobs. I almost forgot. Father did talk about how he always wanted to see New Orleans, but [he] never went. I don't remember now why he wanted to go there, but he said he did. Father worked very hard to make enough money to care for us kids and Mamma. Father was always a hard worker.[13]

* * *

Newspapers across the midwest, south and southwest sections of the nation reported numerous "airship" sightings during March and April 1897. Today these UFO style sightings are everyday fodder for supermarket tabloids, but in 1897, the concept of man being able to fly long distance via a heavier-than-air powered vehicle was still in the realm of fiction novels. One of the most believable sightings was an account first published in the *Dallas Morning News* and was the tale of an airship that crashed on a farm near the village of Aurora, in Wise County, Texas, about dawn on Saturday, April 17, 1897.

This report differed from other accounts of the era because the Aurora episode contained not just a sighting of an aircraft, but a crashed craft and a badly disfigured body. The story claimed that the flying object had hit a windmill or windless tower on the farm of a local judge, left a debris field of metal pieces, and a dead pilot wearing a "flight suit." Some accounts reported that an Army's Signal Corpsman, the 1897 equivalent of a present-day military intelligence officer, who just happened to live in the village at the time of the crash, identified the body as an "alien" being, before the miniature pilot received a "Christian burial" in the Aurora Cemetery. H.E. Hayden, a stringer reporter from Aurora, provided this detailed account to the *Dallas Morning News*. Some writers have claimed that long after the Aurora story had been published nationally, Hayden confessed that he had invented the tale to bring tourists to his dying Central Texas community. If Hayden's confession was real, he got his wish. However, it took a century before its fulfillment.[14]

It is unknown if Baca ever read an account of the Aurora incident, but among his papers was an old newspaper clipping describing a flying craft's crash in southwestern Nebraska. The *Nebraska Nugget*, published at Holdrege, did in fact print a story in June 1884 about four cowboys and a state brand inspector who witnessed a large "aerolite" crash near a roundup site about 35 miles northwest of Benkelman in Dundy County near the Nebraska-Colorado border. The report said that the wreckage of the flying machine contained metal objects with moving parts, but no body. The article described the "aerolite" debris area as remote, rugged, and unsettled range country. No follow-up account concerning the "aerolite crash" has been located. It is unclear if Cipriano Baca had a copy of the *Nebraska Nugget* story or a reprint account taken from another newspaper. He was very active in the livestock business during this time frame and could have had many opportunities to acquire the clipping from like-minded livestock dealers. Reason would dictate that Baca must have had some compelling reason for treasuring this newspaper clipping.

Mrs. Randolph said her father enjoyed flying kites and always wanted "to be like a bird." The 1920s and 1930s motion picture "spacemen" serial adventures interested Baca, and it is very likely that he witnessed the "fearless birdman" L. F. Nixon's flight over Deming in November 1913. "Father always believed that men from other worlds might have visited Earth."[15]

* * *

Baca not only ran the assessor's office; he also continued to serve Sheriff Holm O. Bursum as a deputy. In March and April 1897, Baca was the acting sheriff of Socorro County in the absence of Bursum, who was in the nation's capital on political business. In early April, Cipriano and deputy sheriff–jailer A.B. Baca took up the trail of a few reckless Cowboys who where suspected of killing a prominent Horse Springs rancher named George Smith. A.B. Baca was paid $50 per month as the county jailer and was eager to earn part of the $500 reward that area cattlemen had posted to encourage an exerted effort to locate the suspect Cow-boys. The two officers followed back trails for two weeks looking for these suspects, but to no avail.

On Wednesday morning, April 7, Cipriano and A.B. Baca rode up to Magdalena to attend the inquest for George Smith. They then headed west over the cattle trail toward Datil and the Baldwin Ranch to interview Frank Melville. The cowman was able to give Cipriano a description of the assailant and indicated that Smith had known his killer. The *Deming Headlight* published Melville's description of the murderers saying one suspect was "tall, dark complexion and about 25 years old. The other is about 35, heavy set, short and with a light complexion." On Thursday, the two officers rode to the Smith Ranch to examine the murder scene. They spent the next four days riding west in quest of their suspects. On Monday morning, April 12, the New Mexico lawmen reached the mining town of Clifton across the mountains in Arizona Territory. Here Baca consulted with Graham County deputy sheriff Ben Clark concerning the two men they hunted.

Clark identified one of the suspects as Sid Moore and knew the other by sight. Clark said both men had paramours in the area, and he believed they would show up in Clifton eventually. Acting Sheriff Baca assured Clark that if he could apprehend one or both of these men, he would provide the deputy with the necessary warrants covering his actions. Some present-day writers have asserted that Clark had named Tom "Black-Jack" Ketchum as one of Smith's killers. The evidence to prove this claim seems to be missing from the contemporary record.[16]

The Bacas returned to Socorro, and Cipriano arranged to have the local newspapers print that he was "satisfied the murderers went to Mexico." Baca had meant this misleading account for the outlaws and their friends in hopes that the wanted men might come out of hiding and make a run for the border. Baca made two more trips into western Socorro County in search of the wanted men. "We know that all law abiding citizens are with him in his efforts to hunt down the cowardly assassins of George Smith and their even more cowardly accomplices." Cipriano was like a bulldog in pursuit of his suspects, and he put relentless pressure on all the wanted men's known friends.[17]

In late June, one of these suspect ranchers, a man named George Belcher, sent a protest letter to Socorro's *Industrial Advertiser* accusing Cipriano of official misconduct when he visited the man's ranch. The rival *Socorro Chieftain* was quick to defend the officer by reprinting the letter Belcher had sent to the *Industrial Advertiser* and then adding Baca's rebuttal account of the events. "To start from the first, let me say that on the same day of receipt of the news of the murder of George Smith I started on the trail and have devoted nearly all my time since to the hunt for the murderers," wrote Acting Sheriff Cipriano Baca.

Baca went on to describe the trip he made to the Belcher place, accompanied by Deputy Sheriff Dan Higgins of Mogollon, and then described the altercation in question. Unknown to Baca or Higgins, James M. Shaw, a deputy sheriff from Graham County, Arizona, had concealed himself in the ranch house. Mrs. Belcher had told the deputy that Baca and Higgins were the outlaws and that he should hide. She and her cook then tried to prevent the Socorro County officers from discovering the Arizona officer. When the cook made a move to interfere with Baca, he was disarmed. When George Belcher returned home, Mrs. Belcher continued her deception and told her husband that Baca had insulted and threatened her. The incident ended when Shaw's traveling partner, Deputy U.S. Marshal Charles Fowler, returned to the ranch from his trip to the area post office to check on any communications, and Mrs. Belcher's tale was unmasked.

It is hard to determine a motive for why Mrs. Belcher perpetrated her hokum. Maybe at first she really believed that Baca and Higgins where outlaws, but once she discovered her mistake, why would she continue the drama? Maybe Baca got the reasoning right back in 1897.

> I would repeat, in conclusion, that the Belcher letter is a malicious and barefaced falsehood, and believe, from the best information I can obtain, that he [Belcher] is being nagged on by friends of the outlaws who wish to prevent their capture, and also by a few democrats who wish to cast reproach on any official who happens to be a republican in politics.[18]

The record supports the contention that Baca did all he knew how to do to effect capture of the Smith murder suspects. Nevertheless, in spite of Cipriano's diligent effort the murderous cowboys where able to escape into Old Mexico, and once again politics got in the way of justice.

* * *

Edward L. Hall, the United States Marshal for New Mexico Territory, and his brother-in-law and chief deputy H.W. "Will" Loomis made a trip into the southwestern section of the territory during the spring of 1897. The lawmen where taking personal assessment of the hunt for the marauding Black Jack outlaw gang; men like Bill and Bob Christian, Tom and Sam Ketchum, Daniel "Red" Pipkin, Cole Young, and George Musgrave. In a spirit of cooperation and the end of the reign of these troublemakers, Marshal Hall and his Arizona counterpart, each sent a posse into the field to capture or kill these outlaws. Deputy U.S. Marshal Fred Higgins, Marshal Hall's deputy stationed in eastern New Mexico had tracked the Black Jack Gang across New Mexico and into Arizona Territory, led the posse in Cole Creek Canyon near Clifton, Arizona on April 28, 1897. The posse claimed they killed William T. "Black Jack" Christian that day. They gave the body a hasty burial due to the hot weather, and over time, some have questioned the body's identity. Higgins would later serve as city marshal of Roswell, Chaves County sheriff, and as a New Mexico territorial ranger under Captain Fred Fornoff.

Within weeks of Black Jack's reported death, Christian's surviving band of raiders was calling themselves the High Five Gang. High Five is a card game similar to Seven-Up and was exceedingly popular at the turn of the century before Bridge became a commonly played home card game.[19]

In one of his two autobiographical books about his life on the New Mexico cattle range, William French, an Englishman, recounts a meeting he had with Cipriano Baca. "Our researches [seeking information about a horse thief named Black Jack] there [at Clifton, Arizona] met with no result until we ran across an acquaintance of mine named Cipriano Baca, whom I had known as a peace-officer in Silver City. Cipriano told us he was holding down the office of town marshal in Clifton, and asked if he could be of any assistance during our stay." It is possible that French's memory had played a trick on him. It is very likely that French had really encountered Baca from his years as a deputy at Silver City or later working out of the small jail at Mogollon.

A few pages later, French tells how the next time he met Baca, at some undisclosed location, the lawman "drew my attention to a new pair of boots that he was wearing and said they had belonged to Black Jack." He said that Black Jack and a companion were "called upon by Cipriano, in his capacity as a peace officer, to give themselves up, they had resisted arrest and were promptly put out of existence." French also erroneously wrote that Black Jack was a half-breed.[20]

It is possible that French had recalled reading about Black Jack's fancy boots in the *Silver City Independent*. The newspaper account said that deputy U.S. Marshals had killed William T. Christian, the desperado known as Black Jack, near Clifton, Arizona, but did not name any of the federal officers. The story did, however, say, "The boots were taken from the dead body of Black Jack by Cipriano Baca before the remains were buried, and given to R.G. Hanner, of Pleasonton, who brought them to Silver City where they created considerable curiosity." The boots described as "regular cowboy fashion, with high heels, ornamental stitching, etc." had the name "Williams" written along the inseam in purple ink, doubtless the boots stolen from J.C. Williams, a shopkeeper in Chloride, on January 30, 1897. The captured boots ended up on public display at Max Schutz's Club House Saloon. The *Enterprise*'s short tale reported, "The boots were taken off the corpse by deputy-sheriff Baca, of Socorro county and were given to Robert Hanna." It would seem from the contemporary sources that a man named Hanner or Hanna had possession of the Black Jack boots, not Baca. If he was even in the area, Cipriano Baca simply did the duty of removing the footwear from the dead outlaw.[21]

Cipriana Baca Randolph further cast doubt as to the truthfulness of Captain French's tale of Baca being the town marshal at Clifton, Arizona.

> I know nothing about Father being a lawman in Arizona, but Father was some kind of a policeman in most places that we lived. He had a collection of badges that the boys [her brothers] would play with, but that has been lost for years. I don't believe Father was a police officer before he came to New Mexico.[22]

Former territorial governor Miguel Otero agreed with Mrs. Randolph. "I know all about Captain William French who also wrote a book which I take no stock in." Each time someone asked Otero about a tale recounted in one of French's books he would remark, "This is another lie."[23]

* * *

Few details concerning Baca's personal life during his early years at Socorro exist, and only a few notations about his social calendar survive.[24] During the summer of 1897, Cipriano and his friend R.W. Monroe joined the growing community of Socorro County bicycle riders. Baca had first encountered a bicycle club three years earlier in Silver City. The Socorro newspaper dutifully reported that Baca and Monroe had each purchased a set of "first class wheels" for pleasure trips around the Socorro countryside.[25]

This healthful hobby was not inexpensive. A person could purchase a tube tire bicycle through the 1897 Sears, Roebuck & Company catalogue ranging from $24.95 to $56.50. The expense comes into focus when compared to other transportations needs. A single horse top buggy sold for $28.95 to $39.90, while a fine-quality work stock saddle could be had for about $18 plus shipping charges. A locally purchased set of wheels could have cost more, so Baca's ownership of a bicycle would seem to substantiate his upper-middle-class financial status in the late 1890s. A juvenile bicycle, a decade later, could be bought for about $14 in either a boy's or a girl's model.[26]

Cipriana Baca Randolph recalled her father's love of the bicycle, telling the author,

Father enjoyed riding bikes with us when we were kids. When we first lived in Socorro, Father would take me riding in the early evenings while Mother was making supper. We would ride down along the [Rio Grande] river. Later in El Paso, Father got us kids a bicycle and he would race with us up and down the street in front of the house. Father took a couple of our bikes with us to Mogollon and that was real fun to race down the side canyons and sometimes in nice weather [we would] ride to school. Father wouldn't allow us to ride in the main canyon along Silver Creek, because of all the traffic and saloons. I don't known what happened to the bikes because we left them at the house when we left Mogollon.[27]

Cipriano Baca was handsome, dashing, politically and financially secure, and very popular. He may have found relaxation in riding his bicycle, but he was also developing another social interest. Her name was Mary Ann, and she was the oldest child of the recently widowed Mary Berry. Little is known concerning their courtship, but the romance moved swiftly toward marriage.

* * *

William McKinley, during his first presidential campaign against William Jennings Bryan in 1896, used the metal political candidate button for the first time. The Republican campaign token featured McKinley and his running mate Garret Hobart on a two-seater bicycle riding to the White House surrounded by the slogan "Gold didn't get there July 7, but watch us take it Nov. 3." The button's reference was to the Democrat Party platform, adopted at their summer convention, which supported an economy based upon unlimited minting of silver coin, while McKinley was the candidate who supported a strong import tariff and the gold standard to support the nation's economy. These new metal pins, and the traditional campaign ribbons, were used to show party and candidate support.

In the summer of 1897, the newly inaugurated McKinley appointed one of his supporters as U.S. Marshal for New Mexico Territory. The new chief federal officer was Baca's friend, Grant County rancher Creighton M. Foraker, brother of the influential senator from Ohio and friend of the new chief executive. In August, he asked Baca to sign on as a special deputy marshal and take up the hunt for the remnants of the Black Jack Christian Gang that had survived the April 28 shootout. Baca accepted the request to get these men, and Foraker sought permission from the attorney general to pay Baca and his tracking partner James M. Shaw[28] $5 per day for this patrol. Marshal Foraker justified the extra $2 saying, "You can't get good men for three dollars." This manhunting job called for the best men Foraker could put in the field even if the standard fee for federal posse men was $3 per day in 1897.[29]

To put Marshal Foraker's hiring request into perspective, consider that 15 years earlier the commissioners of Cochise County, Arizona, paid Sheriff John Behan's 25-man posse $5 per day. These men also received an additional $3 a day for horse care, for 10 days, to chase a five-man federal posse led by Deputy U.S. Marshal Wyatt Earp around southeastern Arizona Territory in March 1882. The total bill was $2,070.70 to taxpayers, and the county posse never did "locate" the federal officers who rode around the county in plan view of anyone traveling the public roads. This incident is what Arizona historians call Earp's Vendetta Ride, as he killed Cow-boys that he believed had assassinated one of his brothers and seriously wounded another brother. Both of these Earp brothers were Tombstone city police officers.

During the first few days of the 1897 pursuit, Deputy Baca and Jim Shaw accompanied Sheriff Bursum and his posse; however, within a few days the sheriff gave up the hunt as too costly to Socorro County taxpayers, and he and his men returned to Socorro. The two-man federal posse now took up the manhunt in earnest and moved into the Mogollon Mountains. New Mexico's new U.S. Marshal, Creighton Foraker, sent Baca a memo telling him, "Keep out of Arizona unless it is absolutely necessary to go there." Foraker had no funds to pay Baca if he left the marshal's jurisdiction. Cipriano determined to follow the trail regardless of the cost.

Baca and Shaw continued to follow a cold trail to Patterson, near the Fullerton Ranch, and then rode west to Graham in the Arizona Territory before turning south to San Simon and then back into New Mexico for a straight line down the Animas Valley for the Mexican border. The trail sign now indicated that the outlaws were just a day ahead of the two lawmen, so Baca and Shaw tried to close the gap. In the process, Cipriano's horse died under the strain. Deputy Marshal Baca and Shaw finally had to admit that they lost the gang's trail in the wilds of northern Mexico, and the chase concluded after 23 days in the saddle. The two weary men returned to Socorro after a manhunt that had covered 1,500 miles and used up 25 horses.[30]

Marshal Foraker wrote the attorney general that "great credit is due this small posse, I had hard work to get men of nerve and grit to go out and am in a measure proud of their success [in driving the gang into Mexico]; had this gang remained in New Mexico I think this posse would have made short work of them."[31] A short time later, the marshal was again defending Baca. The Department of Justice was questioning Foraker's payment to Cipriano of a $1.50 rent for the time Baca used his own horse during the 23-day chase of the High Five Gang.[32]

Many believed the remaining High Five Gang members killed Jim Shaw in October 1897. Strangely, Deputy Sheriff Ben Clark, of Clifton, Arizona, who investigated the "murder site," could not locate Shaw's body, but he did find some of Shaw's clothing pierced with bullet holes. Clark's report stated that he did not believe that Shaw was dead, suggesting he had left the area before a real death bullet came his direction.[33]

New Mexico Territory's federal marshal was becoming disgusted dealing with the Justice Department's bureaucrats, and the frustration showed in a report to the attorney general.

> I will not in the future request or suggest another posse to go out after these parties [the High Five Gang] as I think that the Gov't has been to a great deal of unnecessary expense with posses in the past [trailing the old Black Jack Gang] and deem it high time that the Territorial officials done [sic] at least part in the removal of these pests.[34]

In 1899, a measure to create a company of territorial mounted police died in committee in the New Mexico Legislative Assembly, but the ranger bill finally passed during the 1905 session and the ranger force operated until March 1921.

On Thursday, November 25, 1897, the High Five Gang rode into Fronteras, Mexico, and got roaring drunk in a cantina and then shot up the town. The Mexican federal police arrested the men and lodged them in the local jail, then sent word to U.S. authorities of the gang's capture. History records that the bandit captives were able to act quicker than the American police and bribed the local police commander and his jailer and escaped before they could be extradited back to Arizona Territory. Cochise County sheriff Scott White reached Fronteras shortly after the High Five Gang's arrest and later claimed "there was not even convincing evidence that the outlaws had been arrested," but they may "have voluntarily paid a fine" and quietly left the area. The men had nearly $9,000 with them from their recent train robbery near Grants, New Mexico. The "jail break" was the High Five Gang's last known escapade, and after this misadventure most of these adventurers just vanished from western history.[35]

Marshal Foraker kept Cipriano posted about the known movements of the border bandits led by George Musgrave. Baca visited some of his Silver City friends for the Thanksgiving holidays, and in early December 1897, the Socorro newspapers began to refer to Baca as "assessor of this county and deputy United States marshal."[36] Within days of his regular appointment, Cipriano joined a joint Arizona–New Mexico federal posse on the trail of a gang who tried to hold-up the Southern Pacific's Sunset Limited in Stein's Pass and rob the Wells Fargo Express car on Thursday night December 9. Guards killed one bandit and wounded another during the bungled robbery attempt. The joint federal posse was composed of "bring-them-in-dead-or-alive" veteran manhunters like George Scarborough, Jeff Milton and Wells Fargo Express Company detective Jonathan Thacker.

Early on Sunday morning, December 12, 1897, the hard-riding posse men caught up with the men they had been trailing, later identified as W.H. Warderman, T.S. Kephart, Henry Marshall, Leonard Alverson, and Walter Hoffman, at the Cush Ranch in southeastern Cochise County, Arizona Territory, about 20 miles from Old Mexico. The five outlaws where captured without a fight, but some members of the posse wanted to take revenge for past crimes they believed these men had committed. Walter Hoffman (Hovey) would later claim, "There was never any doubt but that for one member of the posse, Cipriano Baca, we would have lost our lives then and there." Hovey said that Baca told his fellow officers that if any harm came to any of the arrested prisoners that he would "kill the officer who fired the shot."[37] His fellow officers knew Cipriano for the kind of man he was, a phlegmatic individual who kept his word and his oath to uphold the law. All five prisoners reached jail safely and were brought to trial in Silver City. It is unknown how much reward money, if any, Baca received for his part in the arrest.

Shortly after the arrests, the *Socorro Chieftain* carried a story claiming the posse had made a mistake because the five men were not holdup men of the Black Jack Gang, but hardworking local Cow-boys.[38] The posse arrested rancher Cush as an accessory to the would-be robbery. Baca was one of the people called to testify at the trial. The district court jury believed the defendant's story and set the men free. Deputy U.S. Marshal Baca earned a travel stipend for his trip to the Silver City court.

Dona Ana County officials now arrested the five men on new charges and they faced trial in Las Cruces. Baca testified at the second trial and again collected travel fees. Some historians have suggested that Sheriff Pat Garrett fixed this jury to convict some of the men and send them to the territorial prison. A few years later in 1901, while being held in jail for train robbery, convicted holdup artist Thomas "Black Jack" Ketchum wrote a letter to President William McKinley saying that Alverson, Warderman and Huffman (Hovey) where innocent of the 1897 Stein's Pass holdup. Ketchum claimed he and five other men, including his brother Sam, "Bronco Bill" Walters, Dave Atkin, Ed Cullin, and Will Curver had done the deed.[39] On the strength of the confession, the Stein's Pass "bandits" gained pardons and release from prison. Baca left no comments concerning his belief in the guilt or innocence of these five men.

The incident at Tex Canyon, in the Chiricahua Mountains of southeastern Arizona Territory, epitomized the hallmark of Cipriano Baca's character. He was a peace officer of the first order, and he felt his job was to capture suspected outlaws and to turn them over to a court of law, judge and jury, to determine their guilt or innocence. Unlike some of his peace officer contemporaries, Baca did not think he was the law unto himself.

* * *

While Cipriano Baca was visiting friends in Silver City, the people he left behind in Socorro where subjected to a distressing Thanksgiving Day. The *Socorro Chieftain* reported that the weather was "rather disagreeable owning to freezing temperatures and high winds that prevailed all day." A cold heavy rain joined the mix of wind and low temperatures over the next few days, and many people became sick with a prewinter cold. Some businesses in nearby San Marcial, the second largest town in the county, and San Antonio closed due to sickness of their populations. The streets of Socorro where very muddy and the rains exposed rocks and other debris that gave the county seat a dismal appearance. Within days of the secession of the rain, deputy sheriffs had county prisoners organized as work gangs and began the process of street repair.

Today, as in the 1890s, we know that smallpox is a virus that is moderately contagious and spread by direct face-to-face contact by droplets passed in the air or via contaminated objects. A rash of round skin lesions on the face, arms and legs, and around the mouth, along with high fever, fatigue, headache and backache characterize smallpox, but it is not contagious during the week to two weeks of the incubation period. The skin lesions first appear like chicken pox, but soon they become full of puss. At this stage, the victim experiences sever abdominal pain and delirium. Modern medicine has developed a vaccine to prevent smallpox and most people believe the disease eradicated, but smallpox is still fatal in about 30 percent of cases because there is no way to fight the disease once a victim becomes sick.

The first week of December saw the county's doctors reporting an outbreak of smallpox. A week later, the killer disease was rampant in Valverde, Paraje, La Joya, and Sabinal. The public was in an agitated state of alarm as news reached Socorro. A week later, town leaders gathered to discuss the health crisis and to develop a plan of action. In their next issue, published on Christmas Eve, the *Socorro Chieftain* announced a quarantine proclamation for the town. Mayor Elfego Baca appointed special police officers to enforce his order "with power and authority to prevent any person or persons from entering said town of Socorro."

It is uncertain what specific orders the mayor gave his special enforcers, but over a century's distance has not changed the impact of what still reads like a "shoot to kill" order. The mayoral directive even ordered the Santa Fe Railroad not to sell tickets to anyone wishing to enter Socorro, but citizens where free to leave the town. They just could not return during the duration of the declared emergency.[40] It is unclear how long the Socorro town quarantine was enforced or how many citizens of the county died from the smallpox epidemic of the winter of 1897–98 because the territory had no central health authority. The Socorro County records and local newspaper archives are no longer available. Other available records indicate that the crisis may have been short-lived.

Cipriano Baca returned to Socorro before the quarantine order was issued, but by mid-December he had left town again and was in Santa Fe attending to his duties as a new deputy U.S. Marshal while fellow federal marshal Fred Fornoff, from Albuquerque, was reported to be in Socorro for a trial. Historians can only guess at Cipriano's feelings during these weeks, but it seems logical that if Baca felt that his fiancée or her family were in the path of danger he would have moved mountains to make them safe. The indicators point toward little concern on Cipriano Baca's part as he continued his routine work habit.

Another handicap to historians' understanding of the situation in Socorro County during 1898 is that virtually no issues of that year's *Socorro Chieftain* remain. During the second weekend of 1898, the *Albuquerque Morning Journal* reported that County Tax Assessor Cipriano Baca took the Santa Fe Railroad north to the capital to attend a meeting of the Territorial Board of Equalization. On this trip, Cipriano also acted as a Socorro County deputy sheriff as he escorted Willis Jackson, a burglary convict, to the territorial penitentiary. Baca, always a sharp businessman, had collected a prisoner transport fee and expenses that paid for his assessor business trip to the City of Holy Faith.[41]

Miss Mary Ann Berry

"Entreat me not to leave you, or to turn back from following after you; For wherever you go, I will go; and wherever you lodge, I will lodge; Your people shall be my people, and your G-d, my G-d."

— Book of Ruth 1:16

Charles Malchus Gilberson had come to America from Ireland seeking work in the Pennsylvania farming country around the settlement of Avondale. The cluster of houses and a few businesses straddled the road between Willington and Lancaster about three miles northwest of the border with Delaware. Mary Ann Lord had been born in that hill country on September 15, 1830, and was educated in the customs of the era. Charles and Mary Ann ended their courtship on Thursday, July 20, 1854, when they where married in her hometown. The young couple soon moved west across the Pennsylvania commonwealth to settle along the southern banks of the Ohio River near the port town of Wheeling in the panhandle or western mountain section of the Virginia commonwealth. It was here that on September 17, 1856, Mary Ann gave birth to a baby girl that the couple named Sallie Bonham Gilberson.

After the majority of voters in the Commonwealth of Virginia elected to secede from the Federal Union in April 1861, the residents of the northwestern counties did not accept this verdict and organized a pro–Union provisional state government with Wheeling as their capital. The Federal Congress and President Abraham Lincoln recognized these breakaway counties as the separated state of West Virginia in June 1863. Charles Gilberson was one of these pro–Union men.[1]

The Gilberson family made the overland trek to the region around the Great Salt Lake in the heart of Mormon country. It was in Utah's Great Basin that a young Sallie Gilberson met the older flamboyant James Fielding Berry, late of the Commonwealth of Kentucky. Berry was a tumbleweed-mining engineer, a reputed gambler and the same age as her parents. In a service held in Saint Mark's Episcopal Church Cathedral on Monday evening, February 12, 1872, Jim and Sallie united in holy matrimony.

Bishop Daniel S. Tuttle, of New York State, had come to the Great Salt Lake Valley in 1867 to establish a Protestant Episcopal Church in the heart of the polygamist empire of Brigham Young's Latter Day Saints. The congregation laid the cornerstone for the 500-seat cathedral in July 1870, and consecrated the edifice in May 1874. The red sandstone and heavy timber structure still stands in the center of Salt Lake City as a testimony to Tuttle's determination and faith.

This summer-winter couple may seem like a strange combination, but their 23-year marriage proved to be a Heaven-made match. Sallie and James lost their first child as a baby. Then three daughters were born while the Berry family lived in the Salt Lake City area. These girls, Mary Ann, Ruby Hamilton, and May Lincoln, would each grow up and wed a law enforcement official in New Mexico Territory.[2]

James Berry brought his family of women to the Sunshine Territory in 1881 and settled first in the Socorro county-seat, then in the silver and zinc mining camp of Kelly, three miles southeast of the cattle-shipping center of Magdalena. In 1884, the *Las Vegas Daily Optic* described the mining camp as a settlement,

> lying in the foothills just below the Kelly and Juanita mines, is a camp containing about two hundred inhabitants, business being represented by the usual collection of frontier stores, saloons, boarding houses, etc. The general drift of politics is Democratic, therefore not too progressive. The townsite is partly taken up as mining claims....
> The climate is pleasant and healthy, there being little sickness other than the miners suffering from lead poisoning when working the mineral. The society of the place will not be too close to scrutiny. Cornishmen and Dagos [Italians] form the nucleus of the Kelly mine employees. Miners' wages are three dollars [a day]. Board cost is from twenty-six to thirty dollars a month.[3]

The wild frontier nature of the Kelly mining camp proved less than a wholesome environment for a family of young impressionable females, so James returned his brood to Socorro in the late 1880s.

James Berry experienced one last bout of wanderlust. In 1892, he boarded the northbound train and traveled to Creede in the high mountain silver mining country of south-central Colorado to investigate a job offer, but soon returned to Socorro saying that Creede was no place "for a poor working man." It was also still a violent frontier settlement. Saloon owner Bob Ford, killer of the infamous bandit Jesse James, was shotgunned to death in his tent establishment in downtown Creede in early June 1892, by Ed O'Kelley, an unhappy and excitable patron who wanted to be famous.

Sixty-five-year-old James Berry became ill in the winter of 1895. Socorro's doctors could do little to help him, so his wife took him to an El Paso hospital for treatment. The Texas doctors could do little to effect a cure, and Berry died on December 8. Sallie Berry returned her husband's body to Socorro for burial in the family plot in the cemetery on the west ridge overlooking the community.[4]

May Lincoln Berry was called "Maisie" by her family. She was the oldest Berry child, and following high school graduation she taught school at a Socorro suburb called Park City[5] before she married her childhood sweetheart Willard Homer Hill in November 1893. Hill was a Democrat, and when Edward L. Hall, a Missouri-born Grant County rancher, became the U.S. Marshal for New Mexico Territory, he appointed Homer one of his deputies and stationed him at Socorro. After four years of federal service, Will became active in silver mining. The couple had a son, Willard Berry Hill, who was born in March 1895, and a daughter, Dorothy Ardis Hill, who was born in May 1901. Twenty-one months later, the girl survived a high fever that almost became pneumonia.[6] By 1920, Maisie Hill was a widow living at the Barry House with her widowed mother, and another widowed sister, Ruby Griffith, and her 11-year-old son William. At this time, Grandma Sallie Berry was also acting as mother to her 16-year-old grandson Florentino Baca and her 13-year-old granddaughter Maisie Hill Baca (Berry).[7]

Ruby Hamilton Berry was born in March 1880. She completed her basic education attending the grade school component of the New Mexico School of Mines in Socorro and like her older sister also became a grade school teacher. The Berry home was located next door to the residence of Abram Abeyta, the Socorro County school superintendent.

The *Socorro Chieftain* reflected the community's support for Ruby Berry as a teacher. "Miss Ruby Berry has received a letter from the school board congratulating her in very warm terms on her successful year's work in the public schools. The letter is a high compliment to Miss Berry's ability as a teacher and the compliment is well deserved."[8] Ruby would sometimes substitute or serve as additional help in the district clerk's office during the summer months between school terms.[9] It was in this county office that she became acquainted with an attorney named John Ellsworth Griffith.

In the fall of 1900, Ruby Berry opened her own private school. She had 15 students on opening day, and a month later she had five more pupils. "Miss Berry is proving herself to be an excellent teacher," said the *Socorro Chieftain*.[10] Two months later, the Socorro school board elected Ruby to become a public school teacher with a "salary increased to $35 per month" starting in January 1901.[11] When the school term ended, Ruby "accepted the position of typewriter in the office of attorney Jas. G. Fitch." Later, Governor Miguel Otero appointed her a notary public.[12] The term "typewriter," in the 1890s and early 1900s, was the name used to describe a present day typist. Over time, the term came to mean the machine and not the person who used it.

The *Las Vegas Daily Optic*, on March 10, 1903, noted how important Miss Berry became to her employers. The newspaper said that she accompanied M.M. Veeder and Ellsworth Ingalls to San Marcial "to take testimony in an important case before the court [hearing] Indiana [*sic*] depredation claims." Socorro County would continue to have Indian "incidents" during rest of the decade.

Ruby kept her "typewriter" job until the fall of 1905 when at 24 she married John E. Griffith. This was a second marriage for the 41-year-old Ohio-born Griffith who served as the secretary of the Socorro Commercial Club before election as the district attorney for Socorro County. John and Ruby had a happy, but all too short, marriage. John died September 17, 1913, of liver disease. As a widow, Ruby Berry Griffith again taught school to support herself and her son.[13]

The Territorial Legislative Assembly of 1901 enacted a law requiring the certification of all public school teachers and passing a mandated tuberculosis test. The new health exam cost the $2 for the certificate plus the doctor's fee. The instructional examination, with a $3 test fee, covered skills in reading, writing, spelling, geography, arithmetic, English grammar, U.S. history, and hygiene. The final part of the proficiency test covered "methods of teaching" students. At the turn of the century, a public school teacher's post was a political plum and the appointee might have earned $25 to $35 per month and, if lucky, might have found work for a five or six-month teaching year. In many schools, the teacher was also required to provide, at their own expense, the daily supply of coal/wood for the school's heating stove and the drinking water for the students. Student disciple and use of the McGuffey's Reader as the main textbook were mandatory, but quality teaching was optional.[14]

The only Berry son, James Fielding, Jr., was born August 19, 1882, and six years later, he received baptism, along with his sister Effie Hunter, at Socorro's Episcopal Church of the Epiphany. He, like the other Berry children, attended the grade school offered to local students at the Territorial School of Mines. Jim was 13 years old when his father died, and he became the man of the house. The teenager helped his mother turn the family home into a boarding house. The future mining engineer continued his schooling while doing odd jobs to help with the family income.[15]

When he was 18, Jimmy Berry spent the summer working for the American Beet Sugar Company at Rocky Ford, Colorado, and in a letter to his family, the young man wrote that the work was "hard labor on hands and knees in the hot sun."[16] Jim returned to Socorro in the fall of 1900 and worked evenings as a miller at the Crown Mills, but a short time later, he was in Silver City, living with Cipriano and Mary Baca, working as a day laborer in the local mines. When the Baca family moved to Deming, in the spring of 1901, 19-year-old Jim joined a construction gang working its way toward California, but a year later, the young Mr. Berry was back in New Mexico.[17]

James F. Berry, Jr., married Mary Carman Cortesy, of Socorro, in November 1903. The next year he enrolled in the college program at the Territorial School of Mines in Socorro. Following his college graduation in 1907, Jim went to work as an assayer with the American Smelting and Refining Company, and the couple made their home in Aguas Calientes, Méjico. He had become the general superintendent before his death in 1947. The

A close examination of this 1890s James Berry family gathering reveals that the future Mrs. Cipriano Baca wore glasses. *From left:* Mary Ann, Ruby, Effie, Maisie, Mrs. James Berry, Sr., James, Jr., and Pearl leaning on her mother's leg. A studio photograph taken at Socorro (John Amos Collection).

family brought Jim "home" for burial in the Berry family plot in the Socorro Cemetery near his father and mother.[18]

Effie Hunter Berry was the first young woman to receive a diploma from the New Mexico School of Mines. "Miss Effie has set a good example which it is hoped will have many followers," said the *Socorro Chieftain* concerning the May 1900 event. Two years later Effie became the assistant postmaster and the press reported, "If Socorro's new postmaster acts as wisely in other matters as he has in the choice of his deputy the patrons of the office will have no reason to complain." Effie Berry enjoyed a whirlwind courtship with a son of Robert "Stuttering Bob" Lewis, a well-known Socorro County cattleman and lawman, which culminated with an engagement ring, but the marriage plans ended before the couple wed. The young brokenhearted Effie Berry lived with her social scandal until she met and married Clyde Eldon Stauder and moved to a sheep ranch, near Chama in Rio Arriba County, in November 1909.[19]

The last Berry child, Pearl Thompson, was born in September 1889, and like her older siblings, she attended the grade school at the School of Mines. Pearl was closest to her sister Mary Ann and spent as many school vacations as she could with the Baca family. She married Alexander Walter Edelen, a college professor at the School of Mines and later a mining engineer, in the fall of 1906. The couple had a son and two daughters.[20]

Mary Ann Berry, called Mamie by family and friends, was born Wednesday, January 7, 1874, on a bitter cold Wednesday in the Great Salt Lake Valley in Utah Territory. Over a decade later, Episcopal Bishop Kendrick confirmed the teenage Mary as a child of G-d baptized into the Christian faith during the morning worship service held on November 29, 1891, at the Episcopal Church of the Epiphany in Socorro.[21]

Mary was an above-average student, and among the few mementos that Cipriana Randolph inherited from her mother is "a silver pin in the shape of an 'L' that my mother got for achievement in Latin." The pin has "*Summa Cum Laude*," meaning with the highest distinction, engraved on the front and the initials "MB" engraved on the pin's back. Sadly, no year appears on the trophy.[22]

"Miss Mamie Berry" was the teacher of the "primary department" of the Socorro Public School for three years after her graduation from high school, and she had passed the territorial teacher certification test. The Socorro County board of education was very pleased with her work; the school's principal, Professor U. Francis Duff, found her delightful to work with; and parents and students loved her as "a compassionate teacher."[23]

* * *

It is uncertain when Cipriano Baca recognized he was ready to think about matrimony again. It is possible it was not a conscious realization. Cipriana Randolph lovingly recalled her parents,

> Mama was a good cook. I was ten when Mama died, so I became the cook for Father and the rest of the family. I tried, but it was Aunt Effie who really taught me how to cook. I remember that Mama made wonderful pies and we kids loved it when Mama was baking. She would let me help roll out the dough for the biscuits. You had to make them from flour and water with some shortening and such.
>
> Father was a big coffee drinker and he loved Mama's beans and cornbread but he could also

eat a good steak with potatoes. Mama had learned all the Mexican dishes and we [the Baca kids] had more fun with her chili peppers. We had eating contests with some of the Italian kids [children of the miners] we went to school with at Mogollon. We always won because they couldn't eat them.

The Baca house always smelled so good. Neighborhood kids loved to come over to our house because Mama always had cookies. I remember Mama would sprinkle the cutting board with powdered sugar instead of floor; too much floor made the dough heavy and Mama's cookies were never heavy, just always good.[24]

Mary Berry first met Cipriano Baca at a church social. The family tradition is that for the studious brown-haired girl in the wire-rimmed glasses it was love at first sight, and Mary told her mother that she was going to marry Mr. Baca. It is very possible that Cipriano lived at the Widow Berry's boarding house, located on the northwest corner of Eaton Avenue and its junction with McCutcheon Avenue, when he first moved to Socorro. This would have been a convenient residence since Baca would have had only a short walk east on McCutcheon to his office in the courthouse.

Like her mother, Mary Berry was a well-educated and headstrong woman, a quality cook and baker, and a good seamstress and housekeeper. These talents, as well as Mary's charm, wit and female figure, may have had a profound effect upon the popular, dashing, dapper widower who was the Socorro County assessor and a rising star of the Socorro County Republican Party.[25]

Cipriano Baca became very attracted to Grandma Berry's daughter, and in the fall of 1897 he decided maybe he was ready to once more stake wedded happiness against fate. Cipriano had learned hard lessons from his previous marriages.

The Baca Boys of Socorro County

"In his heart a man plans his life's course, but the Lord determines his steps."—Proverbs 16:09

Cipriano Baca, Elfego Baca, Leandro Baca, and a few other men surnamed Baca each served as a peace officer in Socorro County, New Mexico Territory. Some historians, including the author, have mistakenly recorded that Cipriano Baca was related to some of these other Baca boys. The truth is that there was no relationship between these battling leaders of Socorro's Hispanic community in the decades on both sides of the birth of the twentieth century.[1]

* * *

Leandro Baca was born at La Joya, New Mexico, on March 8, 1851, as the son of Tomas Baca and his wife Consicion Chaves. Baca became a rancher-farmer at his birthplace along the Rio Grande River north of Socorro where he bought eleven parcels of farm land between the spring of 1884 and the summer of 1894. Leandro used the letters "LB" as his livestock brand on his ranch property. He became an important wool dealer and organized an annual wagon caravan to take his wool to market. Early in the 1900s, Leandro bought a house in Socorro, speculation property in the mining camp at Alma, and fixtures and gaming equipment for his saloon in Socorro. Leandro Baca married Genoveba Jaramillo, and they had two sons and two daughters.[2]

Leandro had proven his mastery of agriculture and ranching, but he also appreciated the security of a regular paycheck. He ran for public office as a Democrat and won his first try for elective office in November 1886, and took office as the Socorro County tax assessor-collector on January 1, 1887. Two years later, the Magdalena *Mountain Mail* commented upon Leandro's chances of reelection for another two years by saying Leandro "will be given almost the solid vote of the west as any man who is acquainted with both candidates will not vote for Estevan Baca." Estevin was just another "Baca Boy" who wanted a public office and a government paycheck. He got both wishes later with an appointment as Socorro postmaster and five years as mayor of the town.[3]

Genoveba Jaramillo Baca died in January 1890, leaving her husband devastated. Her passing caused Leandro to refocus his life from public service and turned it toward the care of his children. He did not run for a third term as county tax assessor-collector. In July 1891, Leandro Baca married Mariana Padilla, and they had a daughter they named Domitila.

During his last two years as tax assessor, Leandro had become friends with Clarence A. Robinson, who took over the sheriff's office in January 1889 and became knowledgeable about jail management and the operation of the sheriff's office. Robinson served as sheriff for four years, but he chose not to continue in public office, moved east, and became an alligator farmer in the "new frontier" of the state of Florida. Leopoldo Contreras, Baca's La Joya neighbor and protégé, became the Democrat candidate for sheriff in the 1892 general election.

The *Socorro Chieftain* told readers that Contreras had promised to make Baca his chief deputy when elected. "Do you want Leandro Baca for sheriff [?]— if you do vote for young Contreras and you will get him." Because of Contreras' youth, he was nicknamed "the boy sheriff" after his 855-to-600-vote victory over Dr. Charles F. Blackington, the Republican candidate. Elfego Baca ran for county clerk in this same election and lost 988 to 678. Dr. Blackington finally won the sheriff's office in 1898 and held control of Socorro County law enforcement until Leandro Baca took over the sheriff's office in January 1903.

"Leandro Baca has taken charge of the jail under the new sheriff, and will dish up the feed to the boarders in the hotel," said the *Socorro Chieftain* a few days after Contreras took office. Five months later the *Socorro Chieftain* boasted, "The jail is a pink of neatness, and is as clean as a brand new pin. There is none of the stench coming from it of former days. Leandro Baca seems to be the right man in the right place this time." Another "Baca Boy" now moved onto the Socorro County political stage. Chief Deputy and Jailer Leandro Baca appointed his son-in-law Justiano Baca, husband of his eldest daughter Josepha, as the office deputy at the courthouse. Regardless of his age, Sheriff Contreras did work at his job. Just a few months into office, he and his chief deputy escorted some Socorro County prisoners to the territorial prison. Later, Chief Deputy Leandro Baca was required to attend court in Dona Ana County and became "thoroughly convinced that Las Cruces bed bugs are above the average in viciousness."[4]

Contreras lost his reelection bid in the 1894 national and territorial Republican Party landslide victory. Holm Bursum won the sheriff's office with a 1,446-to-1,064 victory. Leandro continued work as a deputy under Bursum until he turned the office over to C.F. Blackington in January 1899. In the November 1902 general election, Democrat candidate Leandro Baca

Leandro Baca was a native of Socorro County. His family had roots as farmers and small ranchers. Baca was sheriff of Socorro County and served as a territorial ranger under Captain Fornoff. He was appointed the first sheriff of Catron County following its creation in 1921 (*History of New Mexico: Its Resources and People*, 1907).

became the 23rd sheriff of Socorro County. Voters reelected him in 1904 while running jointly as an Independent Republican and as the Democrat candidate.[5]

Cipriano Baca, while serving as lieutenant of the territorial police, worked closely with Leandro on some horse-and cattle-stealing cases. The two men had a friendly working relationship. Leandro bought a house from Mounted Police Sergeant Bob Lewis which was located "opposite the courthouse coal room" for $120 in April 1906. Lewis had bought a larger house to accommodate his growing, rambunctious family.[6]

Leandro Baca made a highly publicized switch to the Republican Party in the spring of 1906 and, in the process, brought with him nearly a hundred of his fellow Democrats to his new political camp. Overnight, Leandro had become a powerful figure in the Socorro County GOP and a new political threat to another Hispanic Republican boss named Elfego Baca. This incident was the spark that lit the fuse for decades of infighting for control of the Socorro County GOP.[7]

In October 1906, Territorial Governor Herbert J. Hagerman took center stage in the struggle and held a public hearing concerning Leandro Baca's ability to manage the sheriff's office. District Attorney Elfego Baca, acting at the request of some Socorro County businessmen, had charged the sheriff with misconduct and mismanagement of his office. Oddly enough, Cipriano Baca was one of the prosecution witnesses during the formal hearing. A Progressive Republican, like Elfego, Governor Hagerman agreed with the complaint, disregarding the testimony given at Leandro Baca's hearing, and removed the sheriff from public office.[8]

In a strange twist of fate, a few months later President Theodore Roosevelt, who had appointed Hagerman governor, used the mismanagement of office charge to demand that he resign. Former governor M.A. Otero later wrote, "I thought that it [Hagerman's removal] was a great outrage and a disgraceful piece of injustice and absolutely unworthy of a fair and just man."[9] Otero's sentiment reflected the former governor's disdain for Theodore Roosevelt. Hagerman had replaced Otero as chief executive on January 22, 1906, and turned over his office to Secretary of the Territory–Acting Governor J. W. Raynolds on May 3, 1907.

Misais Baca, an Elfego Baca Republican, replaced Leandro Baca. Mounted Police Sgt. Bob Lewis had to separate the two unrelated "Baca Boys" during an altercation at the Socorro County at one point during the transition of authority. Governor Hagerman's interim sheriff was not popular enough with voters to hold the office in the November 1906 general election against the challenge of Aniceto C. Abeyta, a Democrat.

The newly elected sheriff, unlike the governor, was in tune with the feelings of the general populace of Socorro County. Abeyta quickly named Leandro Baca as one of his field deputies, and to add an additional insult to Hagerman's judgment, the leadership of the Territorial House of Representatives showed their support of Cipriano Baca by naming him to be the sergeant-at-arms for the 1907 legislative session.[10]

In the spring of 1908, the new governor, George Curry, appointed Leandro Baca to the territorial police to replaced Fred Murray who was suffering his own political troubles.[11] The governor and Baca had known each other since the 1890s when Curry served as the district court clerk at Socorro. Leandro Baca earned a good record with the Mounted Police and received reappointment as a ranger in April 1909, but Captain Fornoff requested his resignation in October due to his continued excessive drinking problem. Former San Juan

County Sheriff Boone Vaughn replaced him. In a strange twist of fate, Elfego Baca pleaded with Captain Fornoff to have his old political foe reinstated in the territorial police.[12] Fornoff, himself an excessive drinker, could not stand a public drunk, so even after Leandro Baca broke his alcohol dependence he was not welcome back into Fornoff's company of Mounted Police. In 1910, Governor William J. Mills refused Leandro's appointment as a special non-salaried territorial officer.[13]

Following New Mexico's admission into the union, voters elected Leandro, from the western district of the county, as a Socorro County commissioner. In 1919, Leandro was serving under newly elected Sheriff Elfego Baca as a deputy in western Socorro County when a new captain and a new state governor were willing to welcome him back into the Mounted Police Service as a special nonsalaried officer.[14]

Elfego Baca lost his reelection bid in 1920, and with the new year, Leandro Baca was also out of a job. Merritt C. Mechem, the newly elected governor, came to Leandro's rescue and appointed the 63-year-old veteran officer as the first sheriff of the newly created Catron County. The county, newly formed out of western Socorro County, located the courthouse at the village of Reserve. After leaving the sheriff's office, citizens elected Leandro the county's tax assessor.[15]

* * *

The "Legend of *El Gato*" has Elfego Baca being born on a Socorro softball field on February 27, 1865. His mother was playing in the outfield when Elfego decided to enter the world. Legend or fact, within the year Baca's parents moved the family to Topeka, Kansas, but five years later, Francisco Baca brought the remainder of his family back to Socorro. While in Kansas, he had lost his wife, a son, and a daughter to illness.[16]

Belen's mayor appointed the senior Baca town marshal, and a short time later he killed two Anglo Cow-boys who were hurrahing the village. The sheriff arrested Marshal Francisco Baca and placed him in his own jail. A young Elfego learned that a Cow-boy mob planned to lynch his father so the boy freed him, and they both headed for safety in El Paso, Texas.

In later years, Elfego's hyperactive imagination produced many fictional adventures that he had shared with his friend Billy the Kid and other western personalities. Many of these windbag tales are recorded in his 1928 semi-autobiography, *Law and Order, Ltd.; The Rousing Life of Elfego Baca of New Mexico*, written by Kyle S. Crichton.[17]

One legitimate exploit in Elfego's life may rank as the prototype of the classic Hollywood western gun battle. The real-life fight pitted Baca against as many as 80 Anglo Cow-boys bent upon killing him for his self-appointed arrest of one of their own. Halloween Day, 1884, is recorded in New Mexico history as the date of the shootout at Frisco Plaza, or Baca's Battle. Legends say that the Cow-boys fired over 4,000 bullets during a 33-hour siege of Baca's *jacal* (shack). On one attempt to kill Elfego Baca, the Cow-boys tried to dynamite him out of his below-ground hiding place.

Almost four days after the standoff had started, an Anglo officer from a neighboring village rode into the plaza and ended the fight. He arrested Elfego Baca, charged with two counts of murder in the deaths of the Cow-boys killed during the attacks upon his stronghold. Elfego arrived in Socorro under heavy guard and lodged in the Socorro County jail. He languished in his cell for four months before having a trial, on a change of venue, in Albuquerque. In the Duke City, a Bernalillo County jury believed Elfego's story that he had been acting as a special deputy sheriff and had only defended himself from an unruly mob. Acquitted on both counts of murder, Baca quickly became a regional Hispanic hero.[18] Today a life-size bronze statue of the young defiant gunfighter stands in the old Frisco Plaza in Reserve.

Twenty-year-old Elfego Baca married a sixteen-year-old girl in 1885, and despite his reported infidelities, the couple lived together for 60 years and raised six children. During his life, Elfego Baca survived two serious automobile accidents, stabbing by a maniac with an ice pick, and being shot in an assassination attempt on the streets of El Paso. Elfego killed his would-be murderer and was acquitted of the shooting. That is why Hispanics of his era called him *El Gato*—the cat with nine lives.

Shortly after his marriage, Elfego Baca changed his life from being a self-appointed deputy to reading some law books so he could be a lawyer. Years later, Elfego even earned the right to present cases before the U.S. Supreme Court. The *Socorro Chieftain* called Elfego Baca, "a silver tongued orator who can present a case to a jury in a clear and forcible manner."[19] Lawyer Baca soon became interested in politics and won election as Socorro County clerk in 1892 and reelection 1894. In 1895, he started a two-year term as the clerk of the Socorro County Probate Court. Two years later, citizens of Socorro elected him mayor of the village, but he lost his reelection bid. Next, Elfego won a two-year term as county school superintendent.[20]

In the spring of 1896, Elfego Baca tried to get Democrat governor William Thornton to appoint him as the lead investigator seeking evidence in the White Sands murder of A.J. Fountain and his young son. Fountain was a popular and effective prosecutor of livestock thieves. The Territorial Legislative Assembly authorized the governor funds to hire special detectives and pay a substantial reward to bring the murderer or murderers to justice. Thornton turned down Baca's offer to head the search and instead named Pat Garrett, the killer of Billy the Kid, and some Pinkerton men to find the fugitives. Elfego Baca claimed he knew the identity of the killers, but the Pinkertons marked Baca as just another "frontier confidence man."

During his years at the Socorro County courthouse, Elfego became acquainted with Cipriano Baca. The two men were not social friends, but they did attend many of the same public functions.[21] It is uncertain how they viewed each other professionally, but Elfego was not politically supportive of any measure that would allow a political rival to become sheriff of Socorro County. Governor Hagerman had entertained the idea of naming Cipriano Baca to replace Leandro Baca, but the idea had little support with the old-line Republican leadership in Socorro County.[22]

In 1905, the 40-year-old Elfego Baca, now overweight and wearing glasses, received appointment as district attorney for Socorro and Sierra counties. Elfego had hit the big time, but his questionable conduct caused him to resign the district attorney's office in April 1906.[23]

A few months later, Elfego moved his family to Albuquerque and headquartered in the Duke City for the next decade. Baca produced a Spanish-language newspaper, practiced law, and served as an agent of the rebel cause during Mexico's 1910 Revolution. In 1916, Elfego ran for the sheriff's office in Bernalillo County and lost. Baca relocated to Socorro County following this defeat, and here he finally realized his ambition and won election as a sheriff in November 1918. Many voters in Socorro County had forgiven him for the trouble he had caused years before, and younger voters believed Baca's self-promoting legend and supported his nomination. However, two years later he was the only Socorro County official to lose reelection.[24] Elfego Baca could not seem to stay out of political trouble with his fellow Socorro County Republicans; he was a *travieso*, a lovable naughty rascal.

"The cat with nine lives" next moved to Juarez, Mexico, and ran a gambling hall and saloon. The old opportunist did volume business due to the prohibition enforcement in the United States, but this venture ended when Elfego accepted a short-lived investigator's job with the Department of the Interior. Baca worked for a few weeks in Utah, got lonesome, and then headed back home.[25] The old warhorse returned to New Mexico and again practiced law in the Duke City. Baca became a perennial candidate for public office until his death in 1945. Elfego and his wife rest in Albuquerque's Sunset Memorial Park, just two sections over from Cipriano Baca's grave.[26]

In his own lifetime, Elfego Baca had effectively cast himself into a folk hero — a gunman, a politician, a lawyer, a district attorney, a sheriff, and a newspaperman. It was not, however, until a decade after his death that a new generation of admirers made Elfego's name known worldwide. This happened during the height of the craze over the western heroes that populated the new small-screen medium of television. These late-1950s fans were introduced to Elfego Baca by the same man who had created the rebirth of the Davy Crockett saga earlier in the decade.

Television viewers where able to relive Elfego's highly fictionalized life as a fast-shooting lawyer and later sheriff on *The Nine Lives of Elfego Baca* starring Robert Loggia as the intrepid Hispanic hero. The ABC-TV network broadcast the ten adventure shows on their Sunday-night *Walt Disney Presents* between 1958 and 1960. The ole faker would have loved his television persona.[27]

10

Baca Family Life

"A capable wife who can find? She is far more precious than jewels."—Proverbs 31:10

In February 1898, the *Silver City Enterprise* reported that Cipriano Baca "who served as principal deputy U.S. Marshal in the capture of the Stein's Pass train robbers is in attendance at [district] court here awaiting the trial of the prisoners mentioned."

Later, the *Silver City Independent* claimed that Cipriano Baca "was one of the most prominent and popular republicans of southern New Mexico." In this same story broke the news, published the week before in the *Socorro Chieftain*, that Baca "surprised his many friends in the territory on last Saturday by quietly slipping away [from Socorro] to Kelly and while there married Miss Mamie Berry, an estimable young lady of that place. So quiet was the happy event kept that Mr. Baca's most intimate friends did not learn of it." The *Silver City Enterprise* joined the celebration saying that Baca was "receiving congratulations upon the capture which he made of a charming wife."

Mary and Cipriano had repeated their vows before her family, close friends, and a preacher of the Methodist Episcopal Church-South. The Rev. S.L. Adams served as the pastor of the churches at Magdalena and Kelly. George A. Hasty was Baca's best man, and Mrs. James Thrope, a fellow schoolteacher, stood up for Miss Berry. Abraham Lincoln's birthday in 1898 became the wedding day for the 39-year-old Cipriano Baca and his 24-year-old bride.[1]

Three days later, while the newlyweds were on their honeymoon, the U.S. battleship *Maine* was rocked by a terrific explosion as it lay at anchor in the harbor of Havana, Cuba. Two hundred and sixty-six sailors and marines died that night, and the wreckage of the *Maine* was later dragged out to sea and sunk. An American naval commission claimed a Spanish torpedo struck the battleship, while the Spanish investigation suggested that the blast was internal from the ship's ammunition supply. A decade later a less partisan investigation supported the Spanish claim, but by that time Cuba was a self-governing nation and the United States had become a worldwide military power and a political and economic empire with oceanic territory.

* * *

On Thursday, March 4, 1897, in his first presidential inaugural address, William McKinley told the nation,

We want no wars of conquest; we must avoid the temptation of territorial aggression. War should never be entered upon until every agency of peace has failed; peace is preferable to war in almost every contingency. Arbitration is the true method of settlement of international as well as local or individual differences.[2]

Most Americans assumed that no matter what the new chief executive said their nation would soon go to war, and songwriters saw a market for new compositions. The words and music for Charles K. Harris' "Break the News to Mother" was one of these new songs. In the song, a young soldier saves his country's flag during battle and dies in the arms of his father. The song became so popular that a decade later musicians revived it for the nation's entrance into the World War in Europe.[3]

William McKinley was not a dynamic political leader, but he was an honest public servant who kept an ear to the ground concerning public opinion. He had labored long and earnestly to maintain peace for his country, but he finally relented to the tremendous public pressure, demands of Congress, and his own frayed nerves. After months of negotiations, continued peace between the United States and the Spanish Empire ended on April 23, 1898, when Spain declared war upon the United States. The war the American media had long demanded had come to the United States. President McKinley reluctantly requested that Congress reciprocate with its own war declaration. In the end, only a bloody sword could sever the Gordian knot binding Cuba's freedom.

During that spring of war, the Congress provided a special emergency war fund for the protection of the commander-in-chief. The legislation authorized the Treasury Department's Secret Service to establish a round-the-clock detail to guard the president on the grounds of the White House, at the main entrance on the first floor, and near the executive office on the second floor. This was the first authorized presidential protection detail, but the detail did not become official or permanent until the Sundry Civil Expenses Act of 1907 made protection duty a line item of the Treasury Department's Secret Service budget. By that time, McKinley had died from an assassin's bullet, and his successor Theodore Roosevelt was concluding his second term.

The new wartime commander-in-chief called for 125,000 volunteers to supplement the ranks of the regular army. These volunteers were asked to serve for two years or until the conflict was won. This was the first time since the concluding of the War Between the States that the federal government had called for volunteers to staff a national army. During most

Governor Otero appointed Cipriano Baca as the first sheriff of Luna County in 1901 and named him the first man appointed as lieutenant of the territorial rangers in 1905 (Irene Fullerton's Photograph Collection, NMMP/AC).

of the nineteenth century, citizens of the United States were more devoted to their state and local community than to a national identity. Only after the rebellion did people begin to speak in terms of a continental nation consisting of multiple nationalities blending in a melting pot of cultures. The war with the Spanish Empire provided the U.S. government its first opportunity to act on behalf of a united nation before the watchful eyes of the world. America had come of age.

The First Regiment of the U.S. Volunteer Cavalry, which became famous as Colonel Teddy Roosevelt's Rough Riders, was formed mostly with men from the southwestern territories of Arizona, Oklahoma, and New Mexico.[4] Three Rough Riders who served with the New Mexico squadron would later serve with the New Mexico Mounted Police: Fred Fornoff became captain, while William E. Griffin and George Fred Murray rode as rangers. President Theodore Roosevelt appointed Troop H captain George Curry as New Mexico's territorial governor in 1907.[5]

Governor Otero, as commander-in-chief of the New Mexico militia, made a second appeal for volunteers. The president requested that New Mexico provide a battalion for the Arizona-Oklahoma-New Mexico-Indian Territory United States Volunteer Infantry, nicknamed the Big Four, to be inducted into federal service, with 50 officers and 1,265 men, as part of the First Army commanded by Major-General James H. Wilson, as part of the Department of the Lakes. The Big Four Regiment was well trained while stationed at Whipple Barracks, later at Camp Hamilton at Lexington, Kentucky, and finally at Camp Churchman in Albany, Georgia. The United States had never fought a war off the North American continent and was unprepared to transport troops across a large body of water, thus the Big Four Regiment was never able to get into action before the 115-day Cuban Campaign concluded with an armistice on August 13. Each Big Four trooper was paid $77 for his military service, plus rail fare to their home when they mustered out of federal service in February 1899. Six troopers had died due to disease, and 29 other men deserted the regiment.

"Reports from New Mexico," editorialized the *New York Times* in August 1898, "are to the effect that, as a rule, the Spanish-speaking part of the population has given all its sympathy to Spain during the whole cause of the war ... and has demonstrated, as freely as its members dared, a deep hostility to American ideas and American policies." Even in old age, Miguel Otero denied any statement that implied that New Mexico's citizens of Spanish heritage were not as patriotic as the territory's Anglo residents. In his book about being governor, Otero devoted a chapter, "New Mexico Proves Her Loyalty," to the subject. He wrote, "When war came, our people were ready to do their share of the fighting, and more — even though many of them were proud of their Spanish blood."[6]

The facts show that in the spring of 1898, army and naval recruiters made a mass appeal across New Mexico Territory for volunteers to "Revenge the Maine" and to "Free Cuba" from their Spanish taskmaster, but the battle cry landed on deaf ears in Socorro County. The result was that only four of the 342 recruits of the New Mexico squadron of the First U.S. Volunteer Cavalry Regiment, popularly called the Rough Riders, enlisted from Socorro County, and these men came from middle-class Anglo families. During the Cuban campaign, 33 New Mexico Rough Riders where wounded, five where killed in combat, four troopers died of disease while in camp, and five men were listed as having deserted their post.[7]

President McKinley had reluctantly led the nation into a war to free Cuba from the colonial rule of the Spanish Empire and in the process divested the Spanish of the islands of Guam and Puerto Rico. The United States also forced Spain to sell the Philippine Islands for $20 million. With this acquisition and the annexation of the Hawaiian Islands, America had become a force in the Pacific region and a colonial overlord. The American nation was now a major world power. McKinley used the new American might to suppress rebellion in the Philippines and in China during the Boxer Revolt.

In 1902, Cubans established a civilian government to replace the U.S. military occupation, but remained a virtual U.S. protectorate until 1934. The Philippine Islands were an American colonial property until 1947. Hawaii became a state in the union, while natives of Guam and Puerto Rico gained commonwealth status and citizenship within the American republic. The last known American veteran of the Spanish-American War died in 1992 at the age of 106.[8]

The thirty-nine-year-old Cipriano Baca felt no burning desire to enlist in the military and leave his bride to fight a war thousands of miles from home. His family heritage had roots in Spain. He had traveled the western oceans and found seasickness unpleasant. Baca knew the zing of bullets flying overhead and did not like it, so he chose to live by the commandment in Deuteronomy 24:5, "When a man is newly married, he is not to be drafted into military service or any other public duty; he is to be excused from duty for one year, so that he can stay at home and make his wife happy." The year 1898 was very happy for the Baca newlyweds.

* * *

Anti-Spanish war fever had gripped the nation, even in remote regions of New Mexico Territory. This new patriotism, however, did not change everyone's method of earning a living. In the wee hours of Monday, May 23, 1898, the express passenger train from Albuquerque arrived at Belen's station. Right on time, just moments before 2:00 A.M., Santa Fe engine 21 moved off into the darkness with two nonpaying passengers on board; the men where William "Bronco Bill" Walters and his new criminal partner William "Kid" Johnson.

Later that day, Maximiliano Luna, a former Valencia County sheriff, led a posse from Belen and started after the two robbers. A month later, Luna was with the Rough Riders serving as captain of Troop F and headed for the Cuba campaign. Upon his return home, the popular Luna earned a seat in the Territorial Legislative Assembly where he served as the House speaker, but his Uncle Solomon Luna thwarted his infant political career. Maximiliano Luna returned to army life and died in the Philippines fighting the native insurrection in November 1899.

Sheriff Bursum received notification of the Belen robbery, and he made plans to join the search as quickly as Cipriano Baca could return to Socorro to ride with his posse. Baca was in El Paso on business for the federal court. The next day, the Socorro County posse left the county seat with hope of picking up volunteers along the trail. He was disappointed in his quest.

The nation was in a war mood, and army recruiters were actively seeking volunteers in every section of New Mexico. Many Hispanic men living in rural Socorro County were so embarrassed by not wanting to fight against their Spanish "brothers" they hid from authority figures who came to their villages. Sheriff Bursum witnessed this firsthand when

10. Baca Family Life

he stopped in a remote settlement in western Socorro County to resupply his posse while hunting for Walters and Johnson. The sheriff was mistaken for a military recruiter, and the 31-year-old sheriff found it difficult to locate any additional men to ride with him.

Three decades after his posse rode, Sheriff Holm Bursum recalled the hunt.

> A few hours ahead of me was another posse of the sheriff of Valencia County Carlos Baca — with some Indian trackers — they met the hold ups on Alamosa Creek — a pitched battle took place [with the] results Deputy Sheriff Vigil and one tracker killed — horses of outlaws killed — and Bronco Bill and Johnson struck out on foot before we could overtake them — they secured fresh horses in the Datils [mountains] and made for Arizona where the Arizona Rangers [an Arizona posse] had another battle with them — killing Kid Johnson and wounding Bronco Bill.[9]

Maybe it was a faulty memory, but Bursum was wrong on one point. The Arizona Rangers first rode in the late summer of 1901.

Eventually reality forced Sheriff Bursum to turn his men for home. He had run out of expense money to support his posse in the field. He had earlier explained to local businessmen how the lack of county funds hindered such extended action against roving outlaw bands.

> I am sure that I can get every man of them [marauding outlaws] if there was only some means to pay the expenses of keeping the search up, but the county has no available means that could be used for this purpose and I cannot personally afford to stand the expense any longer, in as much as the county is unable to do anything towards defraying the expense....[10]

Bursum again said he would continue the chase if he could find pledged underwriting for his proposed expanded manhunt. No one came forward to offer the financial support for the effort. Outlaw gangs continued to plague New Mexico until 1905 when territorial lawmakers finally authorized the creation of the New Mexico Territorial Mounted Police. Within a few years, these rangers had broken the back of organized outlaw gangs in the Sunshine Territory. We will discuss Cipriano Baca's key role in this task in a later chapter.

* * *

On Saturday, Christmas Eve, 1898, Mary and Cipriano received an early Christmas present in the form of a baby boy. A month and a half later, on Wednesday evening, February 15, 1899, in Socorro's Church of the Epiphany, the new parents christened their son Gilberson Briones Baca, honoring grandparents on both sides of their extended family. The boy quickly became Gil within the family, but as a young man, he Anglicized his name to George. The Bacas' first child grew up to become a radio salesman living in northern Illinois, marrying twice and raising two daughters before his death in April 1968. His World War I service in the U.S. Navy earned him the right of burial in the National Cemetery at Santa Fe.[11]

* * *

Cipriano Baca was not a real politician. He was happiest when he was upholding the law and protecting his fellow citizens. On Sunday, January 1, 1899, Cipriano turned over his desk as Socorro County assessor and became a full-time deputy federal marshal.[12] Baca had first been offered the post almost a year earlier when U.S. Marshal Creighton Foraker had written Cipriano, "I have received authority from [the] Attorney General to make the appointment of district deputies, about which I had a conversation with you some time ago." The marshal went on to explain to Baca that the "Salary to be paid is $900 per annum, with expenses, actual, while away from [your] official residence."[13] Baca knew that a job as deputy federal marshal would pay him less than he could possibly earn collecting tax assessor fees, but he also knew that he enjoyed working in law enforcement more than he did assigning and collecting tax obligations.

Deputy U.S. Marshal Cipriano Baca was on court duty in Las Cruces during the last half of January 1899. The local federal Chinese inspector had arrested five illegal farmhands and brought them before U.S. Commissioner Pino for a deportation hearing. During the hearing, the Chinese were declared guilty and ordered transported to San Francisco for deportation back to China. The U.S. Marshal's office is in charge of federal prisoner transports, so Deputy Marshal Baca received the assignment to convey the prisoners to the West Coast. Federal law permitted Baca one posse man to accompany him, so he took a deputy sheriff friend along to help guard the five Asians.[14]

The two officers were gone about a week on this duty and enjoyed some "down time" visiting with Baca's California family and friends, doing some fishing, and socializing. "Father loved his older sister [Jovita] and enjoyed very much being with her when she came to visit us," remembered Cipriana Randolph. "I don't recall that Father visited with other family members after us kids arrived, but maybe he did before we all entered the picture." One thing is certain, Baca returned from California with a five-pound block of Monterey Jack cheese made in Tillamook County, Oregon. Cipriano had learned to love the tasty cheese during his youth. A decade after Baca's purchase, the Oregon dairy farmers established a co-op to market their product outside their region. Today the Tillamook cheese Baca loved has a wide distribution.[15]

Six months later, Marshal Foraker was still trying to help Baca clear up his expense account from his San Francisco trip. The U.S. Customs Department would reimburse Marshal Foraker's field accounts only $10 towards Baca's $37.50 travel bill. Finally, Foraker asked Cipriano to repay the U.S. Marshal's office the over-reimbursed money he had advanced to Baca. Strict bureaucratic regulators won in the final accounting. Deputy U.S. Marshal Cipriano Baca was required to pay the federal government $27.50 for the honor of performing his sworn duty as a federal officer.[16]

The difficulty with the accounting for Baca's transport duty service is a typical example of how the eastern-based federal bureaucracy imposed their cosmopolitan price standards upon officers who had to deal with the extra costs of operating in the rural frontier west. Distance, limited means of transportation, weather, terrain, and limited local support services for long-distance travel caused the expense difference between western and eastern deputy marshals providing the same service, but the Department of Justice regulations made no distinction due to a deputy's locale.

A short time after Deputy Marshal Baca returned from California, he reported to Santa Fe. Marshal Foraker needed all his deputies to help with the move to a new headquarters building. Albuquerque had become the territory's central railroad junction, communications center, and commerce hub, so it had also become the logical home base for the small force of federal officers.[17] The marshal and all of his deputies would serve out of the new headquarters complex. It is uncertain where Baca settled his family during their short stay in the Duke City.

While Baca was in Santa Fe, he took the opportunity to visit with members of the

33rd Legislative Assembly and lobby for passage of the Council Bill 54 to create a territorial ranger force. Baca had firsthand knowledge of the troubled conditions in southern New Mexico, and he presented a strong endorsement for the ranger force proposal. One of the first-term councilmen was Baca's friend Holm Bursum, who had finished his four years as sheriff and was now representing Socorro and Sierra counties in the assembly's upper-chamber. The many upper chamber lawmakers understood the need for the rangers, but led by political boss T.B. Catron, of Santa Fe, and his henchman J.A. Ancheta, representing Grant and Dona Ana counties, the council tabled the ranger bill and it died in committee. Catron had not wished to give Governor Otero a territorial police body he could command and maybe use against his political ring, and he was unwilling to risk political power by passing the tax needed to fund the territorial police.

In late February 1899, Cipriano Baca wrote his "Friend Bursum" a letter, written on letterhead of the 33rd Legislative Assembly with Santa Fe crossed out and Socorro substituted, on behalf of a mutual friend who was seeking Holm Bursum's assistance with a political appointment. Baca ended his letter saying, "nothing new here."[18] It can be assumed that what Cipriano implied by these three words was that he had no news concerning events in Socorro or his family's possible relocation to Albuquerque. Bursum was unable at assist Abram Abeyta with his employment request, but in late March, Bursum was able to offer Baca the chance to work with him in Santa Fe.

11

Life in Santa Fe

"In the matter of crime and disorder the [New Mexico] territory presents a record that is by no means unfavorable, considering the circumstances of position on the Mexican Frontier, constant ravages of Indian foes, defective organization of the courts, lack of suitable jails, the ignorance and primitive character of the people, and the presence of miners, soldiers, and liquor-traders in remote parts of the country."

— Hubert Howe Bancroft, *History of Arizona and New Mexico, 1530–1888*, 1889

"There was so little restraint in frontier society," wrote Governor Miguel A. Otero in 1940. "It naturally followed that it [the penitentiary] was one of the most important institutions of the territory during my administration [1897–1906], and hence claimed the governor's attention frequently." Otero finally called on a man he had ultimate confidence in to take charge of the prison complex. "I gave considerable thought to the territorial penitentiary from time to time, but never again for such personal reasons as in the spring of 1899." Holm O. Bursum was appointed prison superintendent on March 14, and he oversaw the prison operation during the remainder of Otero's nine years as chief executive. "Mr. Bursum proved an able administrator, as well as a shrewd politician." Otero believed that Bursum "kept the institution going pretty well." In his autobiography the governor noted that he "kept an eye" upon the prison operation.[1]

Holm Bursum agreed to Governor Otero's request upon condition that he be able to name his two assistant wardens. The new superintendent sent word to Cipriano Baca seeking his interest in working as a guard captain at the prison if an opportunity opened up. Baca indicated he would consider such an offer favorably.

It was during Cipriano Baca's 20 months' service in Santa Fe that he became acquainted with the territory's chief executive. It is a reasonable assumption that these two men did not know that this budding acquaintanceship would have such an impact upon the future of law enforcement.

The 1900 census of Santa Fe County listed the Holm Bursum family as residing within the prison complex. The Socorro County census takers noted the couple as residing in their home in Socorro and listed them as the "superintendent" and "matron" of the territorial penitentiary. Who said that important government officials do not count more than ordinary citizens?

* * *

The original section of the New Mexico Penitentiary, completed during the summer of 1885, remained in use until 1956. The original territorial prison plans called for three buildings of quarried stone to consist of the main building that would house the warden's residence and guards' quarters, kitchen, dining rooms, chapel, hospital and armory, while the other two buildings were the engine house and laundry and the large cell-block. The cell block contained four tiers of cells that provided 104 cells, constructed 7 × 7.5 feet with a seven-foot-high ceiling, intended to house two inmates per cell. The design had no separate quarters for female prisoners. Convict labor completed some of the construction on the ten-acre site.

Thirteen months after the groundbreaking ceremony, the Territorial Prison Board held a dinner and dance to dedicate the new facility and to once more brag about Santa Fe's good fortune in being selected as the site of this grand enterprise of political and economic patronage. The Territorial Legislative Assembly granted the upstart community of Albuquerque the second-place prize as the home to what today is the massive University of New Mexico compound and medical school complex with its large state payroll and highly successful, not to mention lucrative, men's and women's Lobo's athletic program.

Two years after opening the prison, the facility was under legislative investigation. The walls of the main building were not plumb, and the structure was settling at an uneven rate because the foundation rested upon a base of small stones. Plaster was falling from the ceilings in the cell block, and the iron used in the grates, bars, and cell doors was of inferior quality and was already rusting. The prison was located on a mesa, with no natural water source, about three miles south of Santa Fe's plaza on the road 20 miles from the Cerrillos mining community. From the main road, a small side trail, called Pen Road, led the final few hundred yards to the lockup. The investigations of 1887 noted, "There has been about $70,000 of the people's money squandered in this item of building for the people a penitentiary, to say nothing about the loss by reason of the improper locality of the institution."[2]

At the turn of the 20th century, the penitentiary was still a place of hard work, strict rules, and quick punishment for any infraction. One prison reform investigation called New Mexico's prison guards the "most brutal" in the nation. The prison operated with almost inhumane prisoner overcrowding, primitive sanitation conditions, and the endless nightmare of prisoner-to-prisoner brutality. Future legislative investigations and court-ordered hearings would continue to plague the penitentiary operation until the bloody prison riot of February 1980 ended with 33 deaths and $20 million worth of destruction. Circumstances forced the state legislature to fund the construction of a new central prison at Santa Fe and multiple smaller lockups strategically located around the state. By the late 1990s, New Mexico's six prisons were "dismal compounds wrapped in razor wire and despair." According to the wishes of New Mexico voters, nothing has changed in the early years of the 21st century except the building of more prisons.[3]

In 1899, Santa Fe had a population of just over 5,600 people. The capital city had slowly grown a mile and a half southwest from the plaza until new homes surrounded the territorial prison, located on ten acres that formed the southwest corner of the new Cordova and St. Francis streets. By the time Baca brought his family to Santa Fe, little children were playing stickball under the watchful eye of the men in the main guard tower alongside the tall brick prison walls. The inmate population had grown to overflow the main cell block; so temporary buildings located in the center of the open-air penitentiary compound housed many prisoners.

A brick-making plant became part of the prison complex in 1893. This new source of income substantially increased the operational funds earned by the leasing of prison chain gangs to private businesses. Especially trusted inmates kept the territory's public buildings and lawns in shape while other mid-level trustees built and maintained New Mexico's infant public road system. Most of the more troublesome prisoners labored on the prison farm under the watchful eye of the prison guards.

The nature of these prison businesses led to some "loose bookkeeping," and political rivals lodged frequent charges of "misappropriation of funds" against prison officials. Management of the prison was a lucrative political appointment and held many side benefits including free housing and board because the 1889 territorial lawmakers had authorized the prison superintendent to draw his personal household supplies from the prison commissary. This unaccountable privilege led to misuse of public supplies and created a source of graft, but it took eight decades before the "larder law" saw repeal in 1969.

The individual prison cells had no commodes, so the prisoners' quarters were equipped with chamber pots. Unruly prisoners had daily assignment to the detail that collected, emptied, and cleaned these porcelain pots. This system of punishment was in use as late as 1950.[4]

A good example of how the territorial prison was operated at the time Holm Bursum took charge of the operation can be found in the status report made by his predecessor Col. E.H. Bergman. The German-born soldier had first served as the superintendent of the territorial prison from 1891 until John R. DeMier replaced him for a few months in 1892. Bergman was called back to serve in 1893 and held the post for the next six years. In his status report to Governor William T. Thornton, for use by the governor in his 1895 report to Washington, Bergman wrote that the prison discipline was "exemplarily good" and that "little punishment has been administered, and that only for trivial infractions of the prison rules." The old military man continued,

> The convicts labor well and cheerfully at the work assigned to them.... Moral and religious instructions have been steadily kept up every Sunday during the year. Divine service and the Bible class are eagerly attended, and the male choir has made marked progress.... The convicts in the New Mexico penitentiary did not only earn their maintenance [during fiscal year 1894–1895], but earned in Territorial work, over and above it 7.07 cents each per day. I beg to state that the cost of maintaining your convicts during the past year has been also reduced from 43 cents to 38.84 cents per man per day.[5]

From November 2, 1884, until January 1, 1912, the New Mexico Territorial Penitentiary staff assigned 2,932 inmate numbers to persons incarcerated at the facility; 83 of these prisoners were women. The old stone and brick complex saw service for another 44 years following statehood.

On Wednesday evening April 17, 1901, Mrs. Lulu Moore Bursum had begun the process of childbirth with Dr. Knapp in attendance as her husband, clad in his nightshirt, paced the floor of the family quarters in the prison compound. At that moment, three convicts made their attempt for freedom. A convicted murderer named George Stevenson shot Guard Felipe Armijo just before a slug from Bursum's Winchester brought him down. The wounded guard was able to drop William Simmons, another escapee, with a lode of buckshot. The third man, a trustee named Frank Carper, surrendered after he, too, was wounded. Carper survived his wound, but lost his position of trusteeship. The other two earned pine boxes and a plot of earth.[6] Mrs. Bursum gave birth to a healthy baby girl. The couple would raise four children.

11. Life in Santa Fe

A few years after Baca left the New Mexico prison system, some changes took place in the daily operation. The *Detroit Free Press* did a Sunday feature, with three line-drawing illustrations, concerning "Flowers and Criminals" in the Santa Fe prison. The article said, in part,

> Floriculture as a means of relining the nature of the hardest criminal, is being carried on at the territorial penitentiary of New Mexico, in Santa Fe. In a well-equipped, thoroughly modern conservatory, which has been constructed within the four grim walls of the prison, some of the most desperate men in American annals of crime are taking pathetic delight in caring for a profusion of flowers of many kinds. General interest is taken in the conservatory, among the 150 convicts in the penitentiary; and it is no uncommon thing to see a "lifer," with a record of blood and violence against his name, tenderly caring for a spotless lily or a delicately perfumed rose.

The *Free Press* had high praise for Superintendent Bursum, saying he "has been quick to recognize the good that the conservatory is doing among the inmates of the prison, hence every convict who desires to work among the flowers is given an opportunity to while away time in the greenhouse." Assistant Superintendent Garrett oversaw the pioneering project.

One of the program's star inmates was "Bronco Bill" Walters. The *Free Press* called Bill one of "the most desperate criminals ever brought to justice." The paper said that Walters now "handles a lily or a rose with the gentleness of a woman and his face is the picture of contentment when he is in the greenhouse." Garrett told the reporter that he believed that when inmates where granted some constructive personal time there "would be fewer tragedies in penitentiaries — fewer attempts to break out and fewer officials sacrificed in doing their duty."[7]

Governor Herbert J. Hagerman had his own ideas about how to operate a prison and they did not agree with the concepts of Bursum or the commissioners of the territorial prison board. The governor unceremoniously fired Bursum in late March 1906, and appointed Arthur Trelford, a career penologist, to administer the prison complex; he lasted until April 1907.

Herbert Hagerman, who had replaced Governor Otero in January 1906, hired an accountant to audit Bursum's prison account ledgers. Based upon faulty information from the accountant's report, Hagerman accused Bursum of pocketing about $4,000 rightfully

Bursum was a mentor for Cipriano Baca. As Socorro County sheriff, Bursum made Baca his deputy at Mogollon and superintendent at the territorial prison, Bursum made Baca captain of the prison-yard guards. Bursum later served as a U.S. senator from New Mexico (*New Mexico Blue Book*, 1919).

due the territorial fund. Bursum paid the claim, under protest, and then sued the territorial treasurer to recover his money. The territorial courts ultimately vindicated the former warden and refunded his money. Holm Bursum became a leader in the effort to replace the governor who had fired him. His many supporters openly rejoiced when President Theodore Roosevelt fired the misguided Hagerman and replaced him with one of his Rough Rider friends, Captain George Curry.

Holm Bursum was a successful stock grower, general supply merchant, and a multicultural financial investor, but the unwarranted smear job done by Hagerman and his followers stayed with Bursum the rest of his life. Bursum served as mayor of Socorro, 1906–1918, and as a delegate to the 1910 Constitutional Convention that wrote New Mexico's basic charter for a state government. Following statehood, Bursum twice ran for governor, but each time he was unable to carry the day. Hagerman's Progress Republicans joined forces with the Democrats to defeat the old warrior. Revenge is a deadly two-edged weapon. In the early 1920s, Bursum finally achieved high office when the governor selected him to fill a vacancy as one of New Mexico's U.S. senators. Miss Clara Olsen, private secretary to the governor, commented on Bursum's appointment, "Well, it looks as if we Norwegians were coming into out own."

Senator Bursum introduced many productive pieces of legislation in the Senate, but his Indian Land Bill is the most remembered. Many lawmakers viewed the Bursum Indian Land Bill as a land grab and defeated it because it was unfair to Native Americas. Bursum lost his 1922 bid for election to a full senatorial term because of this misguided legislation to reduce the size of the Pueblo Indian reservations in New Mexico. Bursum returned to private business and lived to be 86 years old before dying in August 1953 in a Colorado Springs sanitarium. Lulu Bursum died in 1965.[8] The Bursum family still lives in and is part of the political leadership of Socorro County

* * *

Duty at the territorial prison provided Baca standard work hours with little or no out-of-town travel, no court duty, and no extended criminal hunts with a posse. Cipriano accepted his friend's offer; a few weeks later, he headed north to begin his posting as yard master or captain of the prison guard day shift. The *Albuquerque Daily Citizen* had made the announcement of Baca's new assignment in conjunction with other prison news that it reported on May 3, 1899.[9]

From all accounts, it would seem Baca quickly adapted to his new responsibilities and enjoyed the opportunity to work outdoors. Nearly a year and a half after moving to Santa Fe, the *Socorro Chieftain* noted, "[Prison] Captain Cypriano Baca, who is well and favorably known in Socorro County, has proved to be a hardworking and efficient yard master at the penitentiary."[10] Baca knew many of the 188 prisoners admitted during his stay in Santa Fe. Among the group were veteran outlaws William "Bronco Bill" Walter and William McGinnis (Elzy Lay).

In May 1900, the *Socorro Chieftain* told its readers that Ruby Berry had finished her teaching assignment for the year and "took the north bound train" headed for Santa Fe. Ruby planned to "spend a month visiting relatives." The newspaper story concluded by saying Miss Berry hoped to "enjoy a period of well earned rest and recreation." It would seem that Ruby must have had an exciting school year from the tone of that report. She had a wonderful time in Santa Fe, and her visit must have seemed excessively short for her and her sister. After a month, however, Ruby returned to the Oasis on the Rio Grande and went to work as an assistant clerk in the Socorro County district clerk's office for the rest of the summer.[11]

Fifteen-year-old Effie was the next Berry sister to make the trip north. The *Socorro Chieftain* said that the teenager "will spend the summer with her sister, Mrs. Cypriano Baca, and family." The Bacas were "the proud and happy parents of two children." Effie enjoyed the hot months in the cool mountain air of Santa Fe where she helped her older sister care for the Bacas' children, "a bright boy and one of the prettiest of girls."[12] Gilberson Briones Baca was about 18 months old, while his sister Eva was just over her half-year mark. Mary appreciated Effie's assistance because she was pregnant again, with a due date near the end of the year, and lively active kids can take their toll on mothers.

Cipriano enjoyed the security of steady work and a monthly paycheck, but he grew to dislike the brutality that existed within the prison walls. He tried to make a difference, but could not change a punishment system ruled by force and fear that ended only after a bloody prison riot in 1980.

In his annual report to the secretary of the interior, concerning the condition of the territory from July 1, 1901, to June 30, 1902, Governor Otero included a short update on the territory's prison operation. Included in the financial data is a line item mentioning a "New dwelling [yardmaster's] ... $172.81." The money bought construction supplies so the inmates could build the yardmaster a residence on the prison grounds. "Cipriano left Santa Fe because he didn't want the [Baca] children to grow up near all that pain," Mrs. Louise Nazarine Baca told the author.[13]

12

Return to Silver City

"People will forget what you said. People will forget what you did. But people will never forget how you made them feel." — Anonymous

Baylor Shannon, the man who beat Cipriano Baca in the 1894 election, proved to be an inept and irresponsible sheriff and the cowardly killer of his own chief deputy. The sheriff had led a posse hunting for the Black Jack Gang and had stopped to make a cold camp. He assigned Chief Deputy Frank M. Galloway to the first watch. Later that night, Galloway made some noise while doing his sentry duty. Sheriff Baylor Shannon became excited and shot him as an intruder.

Back in Silver City, the sheriff claimed he had personally led the posse in the big fight with the William "Black Jack" Christian outlaw band and made light of Galloway's death. The boasting quickly ended as soon as Grant County voters learned federal marshals had actually done the fighting with the Christian Gang while Baylor and his deputies remained in hiding. In fairness, the sheriff was also a federal officer because Marshal Edward L. Hall, a Democrat, appointed Shannon a special nonpaid deputy U.S. Marshal in August 1895. The courtesy allowed the Grant County jail to continue housing federal prisoners and earn housing fees.

Some people remembered how Grant County could have had a first-class sheriff if only a few more people would have voted Republican at the last election. Baylor Shannon was not reelected sheriff because the Grant County voters recognized him as a coxcomb of the first order. In the words of the poet and playwright E.E. Cummings, Shannon became "a recent footprint in the sand of was."

A couple of years after Baca left Silver City, the *Enterprise* did an appraisal of his service as Grant County's chief deputy sheriff. The newspaper's glowing remembrance said,

> He filled the position to the entire satisfaction of the people of this county and with honor and credit to himself. Grant County has never had a more efficient officer. The garb of authority only brought into prominence the natural and instinctive politeness and courtesy of the gentleman, which traits are possessed in a high degree by Mr. Baca. With all his kindness and consideration for those with whom he was brought in contact in his official capacity, he yet in every instance proved himself a brave, determined and fearless official.[1]

In December 1900, the newly elected sheriff of Grant County offered prison guard captain Cipriano Baca a "desirable position" as his chief deputy if he would return to Grant County. Baca took the offer under advisement before accepting the offer made by Arthur

S. Goodell. Six years had passed since a Democratic smear campaign had engineered his narrow loss to Baylor Shannon. Baca was not sure he had recovered from his feelings of rejection by the voters. He was equally unsure about returning to the city where he had received the news of the tragic death of Marie. It took strong encouragement from remaining friends before he agreed to return to Grant County.

* * *

On Sunday morning, December 30, 1900, the new chief deputy sheriff of Grant County deposited his family in Socorro for a visit with Mary's mother and her brother and sisters. The baby named Sallie Baca had made her entrance into the world two weeks before Christmas, and the Widow Berry had not yet seen her namesake. After a couple of days visiting with his Socorro friends, Baca went on to Silver City, the little community sprawled over numerous hills on the site of an ancient Apache campground, to take his oath of office and to locate a suitable house for his growing family.[2] Baca quickly started to rebuild his old political base, and he just as quickly jump-started his law enforcement career.

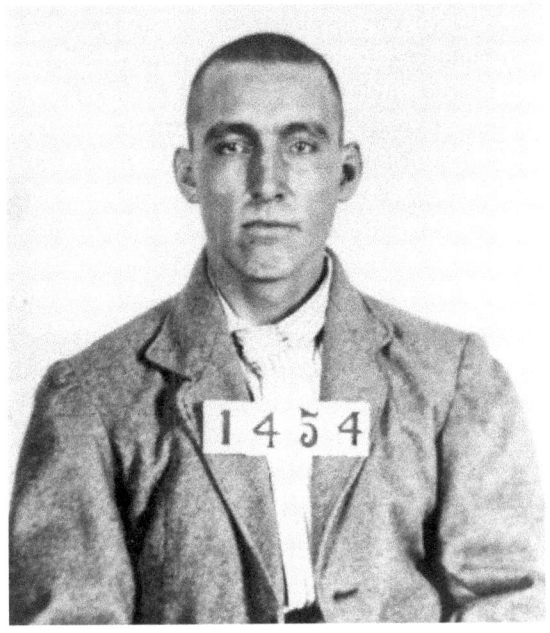

Calles was a youthful ore sorter when he killed a man in a fight. The 17-year-old received a life sentence in the New Mexico Territorial Penitentiary and became inmate #1454 in June 1901 (Fred Lambert Paper, NMMP/AC).

The *Socorro Chieftain* of January 12 crowed, "Cipriano Baca is quickly proving his efficiency as deputy sheriff of Grant County. Sunday he ran down a murderer and captured him within an hour after the commission of the crime."[3] Chief Deputy Sheriff Baca now seemed to be in the right place at the right time and may have developed visions of again seeking the sheriff's post in Grant County.

Andres Calles was 17 years old when Cipriano Baca encountered the youth in the Grant County jail. The local newspapers referred to Calles as "the boy" and seemed to be very concerned about his plight. Even Governor Otero took a special interest in the teenager during his trial.

Calles, who stood just over five feet tall and weighed less than a hundred pounds, had been arrested for murder. The youth's body was covered with numerous scars that testified to his dangerous work as an ore sorter in an area mine. Openly indifferent to local public opinion, the trial jury found Andres guilty and gave him a death sentence. Governor Otero, however, felt that the youth deserved a second chance, so he commuted the death sentence to life in prison.

On Wednesday, June 12, 1901, Calles was logged into the territorial penitentiary as prisoner number 1454. Eight years later the former ore sorter made a bid for freedom, but a day later Territorial Mounted Policeman J.B. Rusk recaptured him. In 1912, Calles again escaped and was loose for almost a year before he was caught in Arizona and returned to Santa Fe's prison by State Mounted Policeman Fred Lambert. Calles now became a model prisoner and learned the chief's trade. He was finally pardoned, and upon his release he just disappeared; but Calles left behind a trivia morsel for students of New Mexico Mounted Police history. He was the only criminal to be held in the custody of three different men who served as New Mexico rangers.[4]

Mary Baca, the three Baca children, and her brother James Berry made the extended railroad journey to join Cipriano in Silver City in late January 1901. Mary had spent three weeks visiting with Grandmother Berry and her siblings before joining her husband in their new rent cottage. Meanwhile back in Socorro, Ruby Berry spent her days teaching school, and afterward she helped Effie, Pearl, and her mother with the chores around the family boarding house.[5]

* * *

Miguel A. Otero, in the third volume of his autobiography concerning his nine years as New Mexico Territory's governor, wrote that there "was nothing especially outstanding about the thirty-fourth legislative assembly, which met [convened] in January, 1901."[6] Most people who made their homes in the southwestern corner of the territory would not have agreed with Governor Otero's sentiment because events that happened in Santa Fe that winter changed their lives and the political spectrum of the region.

About six weeks into the legislative session, in mid–February 1901, Cipriano Baca joined a delegation of prominent Silver City residents who caravanned up to Santa Fe to lobby the territorial lawmakers against the creation of a new county in the southwestern region of the territory.[7] Baca and Grant County Sheriff Arthur Goodell took this opportunity to present Silver City's case against a new county to their friend Governor Otero.

For a few days on both sides of their visit, Clara Olson, the governor's private secretary, wrote in the executive office appointment ledger, "Tony sick in bed." Otero had a winter cold, but the chief executive got up from his sick bed long enough to visit with Baca and Goodell.[8] They told the governor that Silver City residents were strongly opposed to splitting Grant County into two separate counties. The governor explained to the two men that he understood the sensitive political nature of the issue under debate in the territorial assembly and agreed not to openly push for passage of the new county bill. Otero, however, told them that if the lawmakers passed the legislation to create the new county he would sign the measure into law because he privately favored the concept.

A territorial newspaper story summarized the political and economic conflict by saying, "The Deming people are again working for such a measure [a new county] with the idea of making their town the county seat of a new county to be called Luna [in honor of Salomon Luna, the territory's dominant political figure]." Five years earlier the *Las Vegas Daily Optic* had prophesied, "Deming is destined to become one of the most important railroad centers in the southwest." In the spring of 1901, the population of Deming had reached 1,341 residents. The passenger promotion department of the Santa Fe Railroad published a small pamphlet in 1902 called *New Mexico Health Resorts*. The transportation company used public data to promote Deming and Luna County, saying,

> The cost of living is not exorbitant. An economical family can get along nicely on from $15 to $20 per month for provisions. Rent is from $10 to $25 per month, the latter securing the best houses in town and some of them furnished. Board is from $20 to $35 per month.

As new eastern settlers attracted to the area's economic expectations arrived, they brought with them new business ideas and social customs. The political climate slowly changed and Deming became more Democrat in its philosophy.[9]

Silver City citizens did not wish to have the Deming area separated from Grant County because the railroad junction was a strong growth section with an expanding tax base. The loss of Deming's developing financial base meant that the Silver City and Lordsburg area taxpayers would have to pay a higher tax rate to continue their present level of county services.

Some Silver City businessmen were opposed to the new county because they believed that Deming was not yet financially stable enough to support its own county government without Silver City. This same scenario held true for some of Deming's citizens because the area's residents would need to provide office space for their new county government and pay the full expense of county officials. The new county's voters would also need to pass a bond issue to build a courthouse. The would-be citizens of the new county said they were ready and willing to face the tax problem if it meant that they would have more local control of their own fate.

The 34th Territorial Legislative Assembly finally granted Deming's request by creating a new 2,957-square-mile county out of eastern Grant County and western Dona Ana County with 53 miles of open rangeland forming an international border with the Republic of Mexico. True to his word, Governor Otero signed the measure into law on Saturday, March 16, 1901. The new creation legislation also authorized the governor to select the first set of county officials.[10] These men would serve until Luna County voters had a chance to select, via their ballots, new officials at the 1902 general election.

Over a century after its creation, little has changed in mostly rural Luna County. Young people comprise about 60 percent of the county's 25,000 citizens and a majority of these are females of Hispanic heritage. The median family income is $25,000, and Deming and Columbus are the only incorporated communities. Ranching and growing Hatch-style chili peppers are the chief cash crops. The interstate highway that bisects the county has replaced the railroad as Deming's link to the rest of New Mexico, but the renovated brick courthouse, with its Victorian-era clock tower, continues to stand sentinel over Luna County. The relocated old railroad depot now is the hub of a beautiful family-centered park.[11] The past, the present, and the future seem to be one in this portion of the old Gadsden Purchase from Mexico.

13

Luna County Sheriff

"Deming morals are not to be discussed in a newspaper 'til she has some." — C.M. Chase, 27 Nov 1881

Within days of Governor Otero signing the enabling act to create Luna County, the leading Republicans in the new county held a few private caucuses to discuss possible candidates they would recommend for county offices. It is ironic, considering his public opposition to the creation of the new county, that Cipriano Baca became a top contender to become the first sheriff of Luna County.

On Friday, March 29, 1901, Governor Miguel A. Otero, the new county's namesake Solomon Luna, and other territorial officials visited Deming. During a public meeting "the leading citizens of Deming and many cadies [messengers]" met the governor and his entourage, who listened as numerous speakers engaged in a pro-and-con discussion concerning the qualifications of the candidates presented by the Republican caucus. Otero "listened to all that was said for and against each of the candidates, looked wise and said nothing."

An afternoon reception was held in Deming's Club Room for the town's ladies, so that they could meet the special guests from the capital. In the evening, a dinner was in the Fred Harvey Hotel and Restaurant complex, located between the railroad depot and the freight storage area just north of the present-day I-10. Toasts and speeches were the order of the event. Many Silver City residents were present to help the Deming folk party, and one of the celebrants was Grant County sheriff Arthur Goodell. Strange as it may seem, local newspapers did not mention Cipriano Baca as being one of the merrymakers present at Deming.

At nine o'clock, the northbound train was ready to take the out-of-town dignitaries back to Santa Fe, but the local party was not over yet. The dinner crowd divided itself into two groups. Some took the celebration to the Cabinet Saloon, and others went back to the Club Room. Everyone in Deming wanted to know who would be the new county officers, but the "governor had refused to take any Demingite into his confidence, and no one knew [who would serve the new county]."[1]

* * *

In the Hebrew Scriptures, or Christianity's Old Testament, is a list of the seven essential attributes of a good leader. They are wisdom, ability, understanding, experience, love of

G-d, trustworthiness and incorruptibility. It is unknown if Governor Otero consulted this biblical list while he was considering candidates for the leadership of Luna County, but this list would seem to be a blueprint of Cipriano Baca's character.

On Monday, April Fool's Day, 1901, the Luna County appointments were made public. "Even Governor Otero's enemies must admit that, in appointing [Cipriano Baca as the first sheriff] of Luna County, he made an excellent and discriminating choice." The *Santa Fe New Mexican* had captured the feeling of many Grant and Luna County citizens concerning Baca's appointment.[2]

The day after Governor Otero's office announced the Luna County appointments the *Deming Herald* reported the new officials under the heading, "Luna County Officers." The next column contained a story concerning a young man's attempt to kill his youthful bride by stabbing her. This was a powerful reminder why Luna County needed a strong law-and-order sheriff.

"The new officers appointed by Gov. Otero for the county of Luna are entirely satisfactory to the people, and they will assume their duties with full confidence of every taxpayer in the new county," stated the *Deming Herald*, the voice of local Republican Party. "No improvement whatever could be made in the governor's selections and satisfaction is expressed on all sides. It is a representative republican administration and much good is expected to be derived from it." The glowing spirit expressed by the *Deming Herald*'s editor may have reflected the initial euphoria concerning the fulfillment of a long-sought goal. However, reality and partisan politics would quickly begin seeking their place in the bright desert sun.[3]

"Last Wednesday morning those who the Governor decided to honor with appointments in this county, received their handsome lithographs and naturally were greatly elated thereby," reported the *Deming Headlight*. "All are now busy getting matters pertaining to the new county's government into shape and ere long everything will be running smoothly." Now the editorial writer, like his *Herald* counterpart became engulfed by the Luna County euphoria. "Universal satisfaction as to the governor's appointments is the only way to state it and all concede that Gov. Otero has again added to the friendly tie that binds him to the county of Luna."[4]

The *Socorro Chieftain*'s editor happily told his readers about Cipriano's new position. The notice ended by saying Baca's "many friends in Socorro county will feel like congratulating him very heartily over his good fortune." The pro–Otero administration *Silver City Enterprise* commented that the new sheriff "is probably better known throughout the county than any other appointee. Mr. Baca has always proved himself a competent and faithful servant and there is universal regret in this part of Grant county that he should leave."

The *Deming Herald* struck a different cord when Editor P.J. Bennett wrote,

> As a law officer at Santa Fe and Silver City he [Baca] was highly esteemed by the law abiding and sincerely feared by the criminal class and no doubt our county is fortunate in securing such a sheriff. Sheriff Baca has an excellent wife and three interesting children, who will be welcome to our family circles.[5]

By late April, four of the new county officials had opened their offices for business. Probate judge W.R. Merrill, and his clerk B.Y. McKeyes, shared the single office with county assessor Ed Pennington and Sheriff Baca. The *Deming Herald* said the combined office was located in "the Deckert block where they will be pleased to transact county business for any one desiring it."⁶ Baca used the hospitality of the Deming jail to house county prisoners until the new county government was able to locate and equip a proper lockup.

Baca did not have a clean break from the Grant County sheriff's office. By necessity, Cipriano held commissions in both Grant and Luna counties for a couple of months. The *Deming Herald* noted that one of Baca's last duties for the old county was "summoning jurors for the coming term of court." The *Lordsburg Western Liberal* expanded on the reason. "Cipriano Baca, sheriff of Luna county, and principal deputy of Grant county, was in the city Saturday summoning jurors to attend the next term of [district] court, which opens in Silver City next Monday."⁷ Some of the pending court cases, concerning crimes committed in the territory that then was Grant County but now formed part of Luna County, needed closure before Cipriano Baca could ethically divorce himself from all responsibility to his parent county.

A deputy sheriff earned mileage fees and service fees for delivering summons and performing court duty. Baca needed to make all the extra money he could earn before taking up his duties in Deming because the new county had no treasury with which to pay county salaries until property owners paid their tax bill.

In mid–May, Cipriano Baca was still earning money from Grant County: "Sheriff Baca of Luna county passed through this city [Socorro] Monday morning in charge of five Grant county prisoners sentenced to terms in the penitentiary."⁸ The prison records indicate that two of the five, each a Mexican, had been convicted of murder; one died in prison and the other was pardoned by Governor Otero in June 1906. An Anglo and a Mexican received sentences for burglary, while the fifth prisoner, a Mexican, earned a year because he unlawfully discharged a deadly weapon.⁹

Even the U.S. Marshal was seeking assistance from Luna County's new sheriff. Marshal Creighton M. Foraker asked Baca to assist a Kansas man "who will visit Deming upon an important mission." The federal officer added, "He may require your assistance and I assure you that any thing you can do to assist him will be appreciated by me."¹⁰ It is unknown what, if anything, Baca was able to do to assist the unidentified individual, but the request does point up a dominant character trait of Cipriano Baca. He was a people person, and people trusted him.

* * *

In the spring of 1901, Territorial Governor Miguel A. Otero appointed Cipriano Baca as the first sheriff of the newly formed Luna County, with Deming as the seat of government (Mary Baca Photograph Album/Cipriana Randolph).

J. Marvin Hunter, an itinerant newspaperman and later founder of the pioneering western history magazines *Frontier Times* and *True West*, wrote an autobiography in later years. In this work, Hunter wrote about his stay in Deming. Once he left his observations about a presidential visit.

> When President McKinley made his famous "swing around the circle," just a few weeks before he was assassinated, he passed through Deming, and the presidential train made a ten-minute stop there. Excursions were run from various parts of the Territory, and fully 10,000 people greeted the President in Deming.[11]

William McKinley had been a very popular and effective company commander in the Union Army during the War between the States and honored for gallant and meritorious action in three engagements. Following his wartime service, he became a teacher, a respected lawyer, a criminal prosecutor, a seven-term congressional representative, and a two-term Ohio governor before twice being elected to the presidency. McKinley, while a congressman, had been able to put his financial principles to the test and successfully sponsored a high import tariff to protect the nation's newly expanding manufacturing industry. McKinley published his economic treatise *The Tariff in the Days of Henry Clay and Since* in 1896 and used this work to launch his presidential campaign. "I am a tariff man, standing on a tariff platform," McKinley would say, and he used the slogan "A Full Dinner Pail" to signify his promise to voters to continue the nation's economic expansion.

Inauguration Day, 1897, was mild and sunny in the nation's capital, and the District of Columbia was overflowing with visitors in town for the festivities connected with making William McKinley the 25th president of the United States of America. "If good weather for so important an event may be accepted as a favorable augury," said the *New York Times*, "President McKinley has begun an administrative career that should be full of sunshine, good order, good humor, and general satisfaction. Not a cloud cast its shadow over any of the inaugural proceedings."

Then the newspaper alluded to McKinley's campaign to make gold the monetary standard for the nation; his major opponent had championed silver as the chief value standard. "The sun looked all day like a great disk of burnished gold. It was weather truly emblematical of the victory, which resulted in the ceremonies of today. In more senses than one it was a golden inaugural." The Gold Standard Act of 1900 backed U.S. paper currency with the precious gleaming metal and set the base price at $20.67 an ounce.

McKinley was an astute politician and a practitioner of the, yet unnamed, art of public relations and media manipulation. He was the first presidential candidate to utilize the telephone to stay in quick contact with his regional campaign coordinators. He was a heavy cigar smoker to the point that his doctor once ordered him to stop smoking to save his health. McKinley understood the negative image his vice projected in the age of moral revolution, so he never allowed photographs of himself with a cigar. "The children of America must not see their President smoking."[12]

The president was a strong exponent of big business, and Cipriano Baca was one of his disciples. McKinley defended his ideas, saying,

> Business life, whether among ourselves or with other people, is ever a sharp struggle for success. It will be none the less so in the future. Without competition we would be clinging to the clumsy antiquated processes of farming and manufacture and the methods of business of long ago, and the twentieth would be no further advanced than the eighteenth century.

The weather at McKinley's second inaugural ceremony in 1901 was overcast, but the rain held off until that afternoon and only ruined the inaugural parade and the late-night fireworks display. Was this a sign of possible troubles to come? Among his plans for a second administration McKinley wanted to take an extended "get acquainted" visit through the western United States early in the term. This presidential excursion began on April 20, 1901, as the Ohio-born president and his wife left the District of Columbia on board the presidential train accompanied by several members of his cabinet. John E. Wilkie, chief of the Treasury Department's Secret Service Bureau, sent a small detachment of special agents to accompany the chief executive and First Lady on their cross-country visit. Wilkie had been appointed to his post because he was a polished civil servant, a former *Chicago Tribune* reporter, and, most importantly, a friend of the president. A highlight of McKinley's West Coast trip was the president's planned ceremonial launch of a battleship, at San Francisco, named in honor of his home state of Ohio.[13]

On Monday, May 6, the presidential train reached New Mexico Territory's newest county seat. "Deming was a great, swelling balloon of red, white and blue" to greet the presidential train. Over 2,500 people were present, including about 200 schoolchildren, when the special train pulled up in front of Deming's 350-foot-long train station-hotel-restaurant-freight storage complex. The engine was "beautifully decorated and bearing a picture of the President at its head."

Luna County commissioner William M. Taylor greeted the president with a sign saying, "McKinley and Prosperity," and told the chief executive he meant every word of the sentiment. McKinley said, "Thank you," and Taylor replied, "I mean it." McKinley shook Taylor's hand and replied, "I know you do." A national newspaper correspondent who covered President McKinley wrote in his autobiography that the President "shook hands with exactly the amount of cordiality and with precisely the lack of intimacy that deceived men into thinking well of him, too well of him." Four years after the McKinley visit, Taylor turned down an appointment by Governor Otero to become a member of the first company of New Mexico Territorial Mounted Police, only to regret the decision the rest of his life.

The *Washington Post* once commented upon what they referred to as McKinley's "usual costume" by saying, "Spring, summer, autumn, and winter come and go, but McKinley's attire never changes as to style." This evaluation seems to have been true because the president appeared before the folks at Deming dressed in his dignified trademark dark suit, with a white vest, and a red carnation in his buttonhole. During the 10-minute welcoming ceremony, the five-foot-six-inch stoutly built president was presented with a basket of locally grown apples and a Navajo blanket, while Mrs. Ida Saxton McKinley was given some flowers and a packet of turquoise stones. One local newspaper commented, "President McKinley was kindly and sociable in demeanor, but looked much fatigued by his trip." Hundreds of schoolchildren attended, and many where carrying flags bearing the message "We Want Statehood" emblazoned upon them. Photographs memorialized the occasion and sold in the shops of Deming for weeks after the visit.[14]

Before McKinley made his visit, two other presidents had stopped in Deming during its pre-railroad days. Both Ulysses S. Grant and Rutherford B. Hayes had reached the village via a rocking and dusty stagecoach ride. Grant had been out of office nearly four years at the time of his visit. His wife, Secretary of War Alexander Ramsey, General William T. Sherman and a support staff accompanied President Hayes on his trip, during the final months of his self-imposed one term. Deming's old-timers told a tale about how some would-be bad men had planned to kidnap President Hayes during his October visit and hold the chief executive for ransom, but they were unable to pull off the caper. Baca was never sure if the tale was fact or fiction, but he was determined that nothing was going to happen to President McKinley while he was visiting in Luna County.

During his short stop in Deming, President McKinley held an open house and received many of the leading citizens of the area. Territorial Governor Otero and other Santa Fe officials headed the guest delegation. It is doubtful that Cipriano was present for the visit of either Grant or Hayes, but one of the men in the McKinley receiving line was the new sheriff of Luna County.[15]

Cipriana Randolph recalled President and Mrs. McKinley's visit to Deming, saying,

> Father had a picture of President McKinley that he kept with his personal papers. I vaguely remember Aunt Effie and Uncle Clyde [Stauder] talking about the McKinley visit. Mama was very proud that her husband had been in that reception line for the President. Mrs. McKinley got real sick on the trip and almost died. Everyone prayed for her. She got all right and the President and First Lady returned east. I think he was killed a few months later. Father prized his book about the President's funeral and such.[16]

While in California, Ida McKinley suddenly became very ill. This caused the president to cancel the remainder of his western trip and rush the First Lady to a San Francisco hospital. For days Mrs. McKinley lingered near death's door while the president sat at her bedside, and the American people watched as he showed his love and concern for her. Upon Ida's recovery, the First Family returned to Ohio for a restful vacation before returning to Washington. His wife was all the family that McKinley had; together they had mourned the loss of their two infant daughters, and strangely she survived him by almost six years. Mrs. McKinley suffered from epilepsy.

President William McKinley, a Republican, attended his second inauguration in March 1901 and took his oath of office with the Holy Bible opened to the 16th chapter of Proverbs. Four years earlier McKinley had used the Bible, opened to II Chronicles 1:10, given to him by fellow members of the Methodist Church where he taught Sunday school in Canton, Ohio. In the Executive Mansion, the president often held hymn-signing sessions in the Blue Room.[17] While doctors prepped the President for surgery following his attempted assassination, a doctor overheard McKinley softly reciting the Lord's Prayer. At first McKinley seemed to be recovering, but he relapsed and quickly slid toward death. The president's final words were, "It is God's way. His will, not ours be done."

* * *

The Socorro press told its readers that "Sheriff Cipriano Baca, and family, of Luna county have taken up their abode in Deming," and the *Deming Herald* said Cipriano had "rented one of the [Frank] McGlinchy cottages and will remove his interesting family here from Silver City." This rent house was only a temporary residence until Sheriff Baca could find a lot upon which to build a house. A territorial statute required public office holders to own property of a certain value within the county that they served. If Baca was going to seek election as sheriff in November 1902, he had to own some property in Luna County.[18]

The *Deming Herald* reported in August 1901, "Sheriff Baca has bought the property between the jail and the site of the burned Deming ice works, and will build a residence thereon as soon as convenient." It is uncertain if Baca built on this land because in late

April 1902, he invested $300 in two lots in the Boles Addition, a new housing area north of the downtown business section, under development by Michael Burk. In mid–September it was reported that "Sheriff Baca is pushing the work on his residence [on] Platinum street and in due time Mr. Baca will have a comfortable and commodious home." Cipriano sold the Platinum Street property to John Corbett for $700 in August 1903. Today the pavement of Interstate 10 covers these two house lots as it cuts east and west across the northern section of Deming.

In August 1901, a few months after Cipriano Baca moved his family to the new county seat, he joined the movement to profit from the town's new status by buying a lot for $40 in the developing business section of Deming. Seventeen months later Cipriano sold this property for the same amount, but in the meantime, Baca had rented the property and made his investment back plus a profit.[19]

A month later, Baca again ventured into land speculation by purchasing the four adjoining lots to his original town lot holdings. He bought these lots, on time payment, from the Old and New Mexico Improvement Company for $150, paying $50 down on September 1 and an additional $25 a week later. The sheriff did not pay any more on his account until May 1902 when he paid $10 and another $20 in June and July along with $10 in August. The final $15 was unpaid until November 3, a week before Election Day. It is unclear if Cipriano made a profit on this land transaction because the trust company records indicate that they issued title deeds in the name of Pedro Chavez and Antonio Gonzales for two lots each on the day Baca cleared his debt to the land company. The erratic nature of this payment process correctly reflects Cipriano Baca's cash flow problems due to the county's inability to pay his salary, earned fees, and expense reimbursements in a timely manner.[20]

Baca seems to have been on the right track to becoming a successful provider for his growing family. Early in the summer of 1901, Baca took another gamble and invested in a new kind of moneymaking proposition headed by William Greer. The civic leader had formed an investment company to drill for oil in Luna County, and the *Deming Herald* told readers that the "company was in good shape for systematic work in the Deming oil fields." The venture would prove unsuccessful for Baca, but he had made a positive impression upon Greer and his father-in-law that would pay big dividends a few years later.[21]

* * *

The *Deming Herald* editorialized about the territory's lawless past in May 1901, saying,

> New Mexico is no longer on the frontier—it does not mark the dividing line between civilization and barbaric wilds. It [New Mexico Territory] is a peaceful community. The day of the bad man has gone by. The fellow, who walks around with a chip on his shoulder and a revolver in his pocket, will get the trouble he is seeking and get it quick. He may terrorize one man, or drive a few people away from him, but the law is greater than the desperado and he will be searched out. He has only his life to lose and then his wickedness in the world ends.[22]

The new Luna County government understood the mission. They made every effort to help Sheriff Baca keep their infant county safe. The *Socorro Chieftain* reported, "The county authorities have furnished him [authorized the funding so Baca could have made] some chilled steel cages which he declared would make the Luna county jail the safest retreat for prisoners in New Mexico, not barring the penitentiary."[23]

The *Deming Headlight* covered the arrival of the jail cells in town. "The steel cages for the county jail arrived last Wednesday morning and were unloaded by Sheriff Baca the same day. Mr. Baca is now busy with the prisoners in the jail, putting the cages in place, and when they are done Luna County will have one of the safest 'holdovers' in the west; there are four of the cages and their combined weight was over 12,000 pounds." Six months later a prisoner managed to escape from one of the steel cages.

In that same July 20 edition, the *Headlight* reported a "Keystone Cops" style prison break during the unloading of the jail cages. Deputy Jim Hughes was supervising two county inmates when one of them made a run around the depot and headed up the tracks. "Hughes let out after him and the partner of the fellow, knowing a good thing when he sees it lit out the other way. Jim caught his man and returned to find the other one gone." Baca learned of the escape and went in pursuit only to run out of daylight. The next morning Baca sent two Mexicans in search of the prisoner, and by mid-afternoon the man was back in custody. Sheriff Baca chained him to the jail wall until a judge heard his escape trial. "Our officials in this county are altogether too swift for the ordinary man to escape from them." One can assume that Baca and Jailer Hughes held a pow wow concerning the proper methods to use when working prisoners upon the streets of the county seat because there where no more escapes from the Deming street gang during Cipriano's tenure as sheriff.[24]

The U.S. Marshal is the chief custodian of federal prisoners held within his jurisdiction. Since the federal prison located closest to New Mexico Territory was hundreds of miles away in the state of Kansas, the Sunshine Territory's United States marshal contracted with dependable sheriffs within the territory to house his short-term detainees at an established per diem. Marshal Foraker quickly selected Luna County's new jail for such use. A one-dollar-per-day-fee per inmate was the standard amount that Foraker paid for a prisoner's bed and board. For a county jail to be used to house federal prisoners, the sheriff in charge of the county lockup had to hold a commission as a special deputy U.S. Marshal so he could act as a federal jailer. Baca once again carried a deputy marshal's badge under his friend Creighton Foraker.

On one occasion, Foraker sent an urgent message to Sheriff Baca. "I write to you to ask you to be extra vigilant with those two Mexican prisoners [that Deputy Fred] Fornoff left with you yesterday. We are anxious to get a conviction in [their] smuggling cases and don't want the hombres to beat the jail, keep an eye on them." This was not a difficult task for Baca because he kept "an eye" on all his prisoners and was proud of the fact he never lost a man he held in federal custody.[25]

In the late summer of 1901, Foraker asked Sheriff Baca to house four more federal offenders. Weeks later Deputy U.S. Marshal Fred Fornoff arrived in Deming to transport the illegal Chinese to immigration authorities in San Francisco. This episode could cause one to wonder if Baca had any thoughts about his prisoner transport trip to the Bay City a few years earlier. This time Washington paid its bill in full, and Sheriff Baca received $105 for his expenses in hosting the Chinese prisoners for the federal government.[26]

* * *

Life always seemed to be exciting around the Baca house. On a Friday afternoon in June 1901, Mary Baca was looking for five-year-old Gilberson and could not find him. The boy had mysteriously disappeared. Mary sent for Cipriano, and the "anxious parents instituted a diligent search for him around town but without success." By early evening, Mary began to despair over the safety of her son as Cipriano continued the neighborhood search.

The Bacas' Deming home sat off the ground using a pier-and-beam construction method to create an air space under the dwelling. "When the hot sun finally began to set in the west, Gil crawled out from his shady playground and was found. Mama would tell this tale on him when we all got older. Gillie was always the adventuresome one," remembered Cipriana Randolph. "He was the oldest and the boss of us younger kids."[27]

* * *

It was a sunny June morning, and a storekeeper named Wallise and his customer Henry Coleman were settling a lumber bill when a young, dark-complexioned Anglo with a heavy black mustache pulled a pistol on both men. He told the merchant to give him the money from the store's safe. The man received about $50, and he put it in a flour sack. The bandit then took both men outside while he quickly mounted his horse and rode north toward the railroad tracks. Near the train station and Harvey House, a railroad workman watched as the rider turned his horse and headed southeast toward the Florida Mountains. "He [the bandit] was standing in his stirrups and his little Spanish pony was fairly flying," said the *Deming Herald*; however, the *Deming Headlight* reported that the bandit's horse was a large sorrel. On the frontier, most people learned to distinguish different horse breeds early in life, so this contradiction concerning the means of the robber's escape jumps from the printed page and causes the reader to ask the question, how could that confusion have happened? Was it sloppy reporting or an honest mistake?

The merchant ran back into his store to get a weapon, while Coleman ran to the sheriff's office. "Sheriff Baca, securing a Winchester, joined in the chase." A six-man posse trailed the robber until nightfall. "Nearly 70 miles were traversed, when the trail was lost and all were obliged to return to the city without having caught a glimpse of the robber horseman and his flying steed." The man they chased impressed even the posse members. "He was a wonderful robber, a wonderful rider and had a wonderful pony." No one in Deming ever again saw either the daring bandit or the stolen money.[28]

The first session of the Luna County District Court, held in the Knights of Pythias Lodge Hall on the second floor of the Clark and Company Store, convened on Tuesday, June 11. The *Deming Herald* was happy to brag, "Judge Frank W. Parker and his officials were highly pleased with their quarters, which had been nicely arranged by Sheriff Baca."

The district attorney, the jurors, and the judge proved to be diligent in performing their duty because Sheriff Baca and his deputies were required to transport several prisoners to the territorial penitentiary following the close of the district court session. Baca was a one-man Deming chamber of commerce while he was in Santa Fe as he "spoke enthusiastically of the conditions and prospects of the new county of Luna" to anyone within the sound of his voice.

While Sheriff Baca was in Santa Fe, a "holdup man" struck in a residential area. A local carpenter reported that he was walking home from his job when a man walked up and pointed a pistol at him. The robber got $16 and made good his getaway. This incident was just one more reason why Deming needed a town government and its own police force.[29]

* * *

President William McKinley reappointed his friend Miguel A. Otero as territorial governor, and Otero scheduled Saturday, June 22, 1901, for his second inauguration ceremony in Santa Fe. Sheriff Baca, J.A. Mahoney, and W.H. Greer had planned to take the train north on Friday night and be present for the occasion. Cipriano Baca's personal excitement about the trip was quickly dampened "owing to the sickness of his infant daughter." The sheriff's political duty was clear, but his personal duty was clearer; he decided to stay home with his family.

Within days, the tragedy that Baca feared most struck his family when death's angel visited his home and claimed the life of his second daughter, six-month-old Sallie. Her sister Eva, just a year older, was also very ill, but during the sadness surrounding Sallie's death she stubbornly clung to life. George L. Shakespeare, editor of the *Deming Headlight,* caught the spirit of his fellow Demingites when he wrote, "The bereaved parents have the sympathy of the community." Friends across the territory felt Cipriano and Mary's grief and the *Socorro Chieftain* expressed the loss thus: "Mr. and Mrs. Baca will have the heartfelt sympathy of their many Socorro friends in their sad bereavement." Governor Otero sent personal condolences to the Baca family.

The *Deming Herald* reported, "The funeral of little Sallie, the infant daughter of Sheriff Baca and his wife, was largely attended and the grave liberally strewn with flowers." There is no record how Mrs. Berry took the news about the death of her namesake. In the wake of all the sickness and sorrow, Mary Baca now became ill, but within a few days, she had recovered enough so that Cipriano was able to return to his official duties.

During the early stages of research for this work, in the fall of 1984, the author located the above newspaper accounts concerning Sallie Baca and sent a copy to Cipriana Randolph. She wrote back saying, "I am at a loss to understand where you look to find all this information. I had thought all the time that Sallie was older than Eva but I can [see] that I was wrong." Cipriana's additional loving expression of personal loss for an older sister she never knew seemed to be heartfelt. Mrs. Randolph soon embarked upon a mission to discover her family's lost heritage and followed that quest until her own death joined her with her lost family.[30]

* * *

On a Friday night in late June 1901, a carpenter named Thomas McMahan was headed home following a hard day working in Deming's building boom. A man appeared and robbed him of $16 at gunpoint. Eight months later, the *Deming Herald* reported another crime involving McMahan. The paper identified him as the man "who forged the names of Judge Field and Lou H. Brown, to a real estate deal and obtained money under false pretenses from one of the Baker Brothers" and continued by reporting that McMahan had "escaped from the Luna County jail Friday morning [January 31, 1902]."

Early in July, the *Deming Herald* told readers, "Sheriff Baca and Jailor Jim Hughes have the chain gang working on the streets. The gang consists of three Chinamen and two Mexicans." A few days later, the *Deming Headlight* expanded the street cleanup story. "The Luna County sheriff is using the prisoners to clean up the streets and alleys of the county seat and they show such a marked improvement already that it is noticed by all. Mr. Baca is the right man in the right place, without a doubt. Some one who can should now offer the use of their teams in spare moments and have the trash hauled away."

Deputy Sheriff-Jailer Hughes kept a watchful eye on his charges, and no one missed supper back at the jail.

A week later, Sheriff Baca arrested a man visiting Deming from Globe, Arizona. The drunken tourist was conducting himself in a disorderly manner, but the larger sin was that he was carrying a pistol. Baca took offense that a guest in his community did not feel safe enough to visit without arming himself, so the sheriff invited the man to visit his "hotel" for safety. The judge agreed with Baca and fined the man $50 and court costs the next morning. Later that day the visitor took the westbound train out of Deming.

In July 1901, the Luna County Commissioner's Court authorized payment to J.A. Mahoney of $99.18 for "office and jail supplies," and the company of Rosch and Leopold was paid $75 for "carpenter work at jail." Julius Rosch was the county surveyor. Sheriff Baca received a county warrant for $50.87 for fee collection and mileage earned while serving court processes. The court also reimbursed Baca $19.00 for feeding county prisoners. Old deposit slips in the archives collection at the museum in Deming testify that Baca used his county warrants to repay outstanding credit to local merchants. The Baca family bank account needed this timely infusion of cash to help pay medical and funeral bills.[31]

The "Bisbee Road" was laying railroad track southwest from Deming about 35 miles to the site of Hermanas. From that village, now a ghost town, the railroad company planned to extend on west to Hachita and Rodeo before entering Arizona Territory. The track crew began their labor in the fall of 1901, and the system was in operation by late February 1902. This railway line would later become part of the El Paso and Southwestern Railroad system, which Cipriano Baca would one day serve as a special agent.

"Jack Finley Slain; Stabbed to Death" was the headline of the August 3, 1901, edition of the *Deming Headlight*. Luna County had recorded its first murder late on Sunday evening, July 28, when John Finley, foreman for the Orman and Crook Company contractors who were grading a section of roadbed southwest of Deming for the El Paso and Southwestern Railroad, was stabbed to death. Finley and another man had been social drinking in the Cabinet Saloon when they began to argue and blows where struck. Finley was a big powerful man; his assailant was also strong. Witnesses said that the workman stabbed Finley twice before Finley knocked the man to the floor and "stomped his face." The attacker gained his feet and ran out of the bar while Finley collapsed in a bloody heap.

Finley's friends transported him to Deming for treatment by Doctors McLellan and Rexford at their hospital, but in spite of their effort to save him the man's wounds were too serious. He died mid-morning on Tuesday and was buried in the Deming Cemetery on Wednesday afternoon. "Sheriff Baca is going to great expense and working hard to capture the murderer and it is to be hoped that ere long his efforts will be crowned with success." The *Deming Headlight* reported that Finley's killer was a Texas laborer named Granger, while the Lordsburg newspaper said the man who used the deadly knife had been John Milton. Whatever the killer's real name was does not matter now, because he was able to effect his escape and reinvent himself in another place.

In mid–August 1901, Luna County had another railroad construction incident. Sheriff Baca drove a buggy out to the grading site near Carrizalillo Springs, a few miles west of Hermanas, to investigate a shooting incident and arrested a worker who had shot a young Mexican camp boy. "In Judge Marshall's court Monday it was clearly shown that the Mexican boy had been hit in the leg by a stray shot while [Charles] Anderson was shooting at birds, as he alleged." This carelessness with a shotgun cost Anderson $26.60 in court expense, but the man was not ordered to pay damages to the boy for his birdshot injury or to cover the medical cost for the boy's medical care.

Later that month, some boys found a body in the desert, and the *Deming Herald* called it "A Startling Discovery." On Saturday afternoon, August 31, two Mexican boys were riding in the Florida Mountains southeast of Deming, "remote from any stock trail," when they discovered the "emaciated remains of an American woman." Coyotes had eaten away parts of her body. "The Mexican kids were alarmed and galloped into town and informed Sheriff Baca of their horrible discovery." On Sunday morning, Baca and the boys rode out to the site and made a search of the area. When they returned to Deming, Sheriff Baca notified Judge Marshall of the death, and the judge impaneled an inquest jury. The group traveled to the death scene to examine the body. "The dried flesh and bones were buried on the spot at county expense and the question of identity may not be satisfactorily answered before the Florida mountains give up its dead." The cause of the woman's death was unknown, and the gruesome find was a topic of discussion for weeks as people tried to determine whom the victim might have been. Sadly, the mystery remains unsolved.[32]

* * *

On Friday, September 6, 1901, a self-avowed anarchist shot President McKinley while he attended a public function in Buffalo, New York. Eight days later, Ida McKinley led the national mourning for her assassinated husband while Theodore Roosevelt became "that damn cowboy in the White House."[33] Agents captured President McKinley's assassin at the scene of the shooting. He was tried and convicted of murder and was electrocuted in the state prison at Auburn, New York, on October 29, 1901.

The true character of the president had come to the fore when he was lying wounded. He asked his aide to keep the mob from hurting his assailant because he felt the man deserved a fair hearing in a court of law. The wounded chief executive then asked his secretary to be careful how he notified Mrs. McKinley about the attack because he was concerned about his wife's health and how she might react to news of his injury.

Ike Hoover, the chief usher at the White House during the Gilded Age, summed up the dichotomy of the man he knew when he wrote, "That kind, gentle, fatherly way of Mr. McKinley's made all comers feel that he was their friend, but left doubt in their minds as to the substantial result they had come to accomplish." During surgery prep following his attempted assassination, a doctor overheard President McKinley softly reciting the Lord's Prayer. Later, when the anarchist bullet finally claimed McKinley's life, that attending physician lamented, "Up to this time, I'd never really believed that a man could be a good Christian and a good politician."[34]

Leaders around the globe condemned the senseless killing of McKinley, and the cause of anarchy was equally condemned. Cipriano joined with Deming's leading citizens in wearing a black armband during a month of national mourning. Much of Deming wore black bunting, as did the new county's makeshift county courthouse, including the jail. Cipriano Baca never forgot his moment in the spotlight near a powerful world leader and always spoke highly of the man from Ohio. "Father had a book about the McKinley murder and we children would sometimes look at all the pictures," recalled Cipriana Randolph.[35]

Many New Mexicans mourned the death of William McKinley as if it had been the loss of a family member, but at the same time rejoiced that a new "old friend" had moved into the Executive Mansion. Time, however, would test that belief as "TR" quickly adjusted to the power of the office, the $50,000 annual salary, and the office expense account.[36]

President Roosevelt "has been clearing up the work that McKinley left unfinished," wrote William Allen White in his *Saturday Evening Post* review of TR's first year as chief executive. "There is no doubt that he sees the need in America for the return, in so far as civilization today allows it, to the simple life which made America sturdy and sane and brave a generation ago." White continued his analysis saying, "The difference between the two Presidents is in their attitude toward the people. McKinley went to the people. He was a great follower. The people influenced him. Roosevelt influences the people. They follow him. He is a leader."[37]

Like many New Mexicans, Baca had held McKinley in high esteem. It is uncertain what he felt about Theodore Roosevelt because he left no record concerning the Cowboy President.

* * *

On a Wednesday night in late September 1901, Sheriff Baca met his friend Fred Fornoff at the Luna County jail so Fornoff could house a federal prisoner overnight. The two men then went to Baca's house for supper and conversation. The deputy federal marshal was escorting a prisoner from Silver City to Albuquerque. Later, a deputy took the man to Las Cruces for a hearing before the federal grand jury, charged with "being implicated in the death of President McKinley." The nation was still reeling from the misguided deed of a single anarchist, so now all professed anarchists were conspirator suspects in an unspecified massive anti-government plot. Baca and Fornoff parted company at the railroad depot the next morning.

During the October session of the Luna County Commissioner's Court, the county trustees authorized payment to Sheriff Baca of $269.50 as reimbursement for the cost of feeding the county's prisoners. During that month Cipriano had turned over to the county treasurer $211 in fees that his three deputies had collected for the county court.

Cipriano Baca was way ahead of his time with political correctness in his deputy appointments. Baca, a Hispanic sheriff, had an all–Anglo force of field deputies. Okie Cox, David Colson, and a man named Johnson, as the above fees report testifies, were all hard-working officers dedicated to keeping the peace and serving legal papers in the rural sections of Luna County. Jim Hughes was the county jailer and cook.

A nonpartisan assessment of Baca's law enforcement team indicates he was a competent manager of men and finances. However, to some of the county's new settlers, he was that "Mexican" sheriff, and they had no appreciation of Baca's contributions to the development of the county. More importantly, they did not care. He was not an Anglo or a populist Democrat.[38]

* * *

"Miss Ruby Berry is here from Socorro, visiting her sister Mrs. Sheriff Baca," reported the *Deming Herald* in early October, and the *Socorro Chieftain* added that she was "summoned thither by the serious illness of her little niece." Neither story mentioned that Mary Baca was seven months pregnant and the round-the-clock nursing of Eva, caring for three-year-old Gil, and maintaining a household had sapped her energy. Mary needed a rest and asked her younger sister to come for a short visit. Ruby was able to take a short leave from her teaching job and go south to visit Mary and her family. A week later, Mary was feeling rested, so Ruby returned home and the Socorro newspaper reported that Eva Baca "has been sick almost three months [but] is improving slowly."[39]

It had been a long hot sad summer, but with the beginning of fall, the Baca family doctor hoped that Eva would improve with the cooler weather. The family's daily routine regained a sense of normal as Mary did her household duties, cared for little Eva, played with her son, and counted the days until the birth of her new baby. Cipriano concealed his grief over Sallie's death and his concern over Eva's declining health by submerging himself in his investment plans and his law enforcement duties. Baca felt optimistic enough about conditions at home that he agreed to attended a political convention in Albuquerque the second weekend in October.

* * *

Theodore Roosevelt's unexpected ascension to the White House gave new hope to New Mexico's 50-year-long quest for statehood. The young president had commanded the Rough Rider regiment of volunteer cavalry, composed of many troopers from New Mexico Territory, just a few years before. Three New Mexico troops were among the men who fought with Roosevelt to capture Kettle Hill and then made the famous charge up the San Juan heights overlooking Santiago, Cuba. Many of New Mexico's leading business and political leaders counted Roosevelt, known worldwide as TR, among their Washington friends.

The new chief executive had attended the Rough Riders' first reunion, held during the summer of 1899, in Las Vegas. During the reunion festivities, Roosevelt, then governor of New York, had pledged his full support of statehood for all the western territories. Now that he was president, many New Mexicans felt that the Sunshine Territory would quickly achieve the promised admission into the union. Statehood supporters hastily organized a convention in Albuquerque for early October 1901, so that delegates could draft a formal statehood request for the Congress and the president. The Luna County Commissioner's Court selected Sheriff Baca and W.H. Greer, a large ranch manager, to represent the county. Baca knew John F. Fullerton, one of the other statehood delegates, as a sheep raiser from his days as the Socorro County assessor. Unknown is if the three men had an occasion to meet during this convention, but four years later, each man would play an important part in the other man's life and the creation of the New Mexico Mounted Police.

Territorial Governor Otero addressed the Albuquerque convention in favor of the statehood movement. He also told delegates that the assessed value of New Mexico wealth was less than $40 million, yet in fact the real property value was closer to $120 million. Otero said, "You must see to it that proper men are elected to assess the property and equalize its value, so that we may appear to the world that we are in fact, as to our wealth and ability to pay our obligations." Otero prophesied that this measure was the key to any future statehood plan.[40]

A minority of New Mexicans had some doubt about TR and his political trustworthiness. He was the man who, in 1899, had pledged to support statehood for New Mexico. He was also the man who, while serving as governor of New York in 1900, had said that under no circumstance would he leave Albany and accept the nomination for the vice presidency; but he did. The doubters were right about Theodore Roosevelt and his New Mexico statehood plan. He did not keep that pledge either.

President Roosevelt tried, halfheartedly, to help all the southwestern territories become states. Political battles in Washington and Phoenix dashed high hopes for New Mexico's quick advancement to statehood. The president pushed a plan for Arizona and New Mexico Territories to become a single Anglo-dominated state called Arizona. When the bill passed Congress, the juncture measure provided that both territories had to approve the measure. On Election Day 1906, Arizona voters turned down the opportunity, so the Sunshine Territory's dream of full partnership in the federal union was unfulfilled until four years after the Rough Rider colonel left the oval office and retired to his New York estate. During his seven-and-one-half-year administration, Roosevelt only accomplished the Indian Territory–Oklahoma Territory statehood merger.

* * *

One October night in 1901, during a routine check of the railroad yards, Deputy Sheriff Johnson discovered six hobos and arrested them for "trespassing' and took them to the county jail for future investigation. Johnson and Jailer Hughes did an intake search of the men before they where locked up. "They had several stone hammers, believed to be stolen, in their possession, which the owners can recover by calling on Sheriff Baca."

Later that same October week, a reporter for the *Deming Herald* visited the jail to do a feature on the new lockup's condition. "When we visited the county jail Saturday Jailor Jim Hughes was feeding his prisoners. They get two meals a day, and this was their second meal and consisted of good beef and vegetable broth, meat, bread, etc." The reporter was impressed. "An excellent system of order prevails in and around the prison, commendable alike to James Hughes, the jailor, and his superior officer, Sheriff C. Baca." This was high praise for the housekeeping and cooking skills preformed by the bachelor jailer who lived with his sister. During the reporter's visit, the Luna County jail was host to eight male prisoners. Four of the men were charged with drunk and disorderly, one with vagrancy, one with forgery, and one with breaking into a railroad car. The eighth man was held on a rape charge. No charge was listed for the jail's single woman inmate.[41]

* * *

Even in the impersonal newspaper type, the sadness is evident. "Died, in this town Monday evening Nov 11, 1901, little Eva, only daughter of Sheriff and Mrs. C. Baca, aged 2 years. She was sick for a long time and a great little sufferer. This is the second child these parents have lost this summer [year], and only a little boy is left them," recorded the *Deming Herald*. "Little Eva was a pretty, bright child," said the *Socorro Chieftain*. "Such affliction arouses the keenest sympathy." Cipriano and Mary Baca had lost two small children within a six-month period. Eva joined her younger sister in the Deming Cemetery. Mary's grief was public, and her family and friends gave her comfort. Cipriano's hurt was carried inside him, so he maintained a stoic exterior that gave some people that did not know him well the impression he was an uncaring husband and father. It was a mask to cover Baca's grief as he buried himself in his official duties.

Following the close of the fall court session, Sheriff Baca spent Thanksgiving Day with his family, and then the *Deming Herald* noted that Baca delivered the county's newly sentenced prisoners to Santa Fe. Cipriano stopped off in Socorro for a short visit with his in-laws and some old friends on the return trip. "Sheriff Cipriano Baca of Luna county was a welcome visitor in town Wednesday [November 27]," reported the *Socorro Chieftain*. "Mr. Baca is always heartily greeted by his host of Socorro county friends." Baca's old friends always seemed to lift his spirits and in later years, there were rumors that the consumption of "spirits," played a vital part in helping the fellowship. Benjamin Franklin wrote an appreciation of social drinking in his *Poor Richard's Almanac*: "Beer is proof that God loves us and wants us to be happy." It can only be assumed that Cipriano Baca would have agreed with this Founding Fathers' opinion about beer because he was an unapologetic social drinker.

Deming had not changed during Cipriano's absence. Maybe it was the holiday spirit that caused all the over-zealous merriment, but whatever the reason it was still illegal and required Sheriff Baca's attention. "A couple of individuals are under arrest for kicking in the doors of a couple of fancy houses. Out of respect for their friends we will not mention names," said the Christmas Eve issue of the *Deming Herald*. In a different incident, reported in the same account as the whorehouse raids, the newspaper also said that Sheriff Baca "had captured the tough, at Santa Rita, who assaulted the Deming Restaurant proprietors." Happy Holidays, Luna County voters![42]

In January 1902, Luna County once again owed Sheriff Baca reimbursement money. This time the mileage and service fees amounted to $163.62, and Luna County was in a financial catch 22. The county had no money to pay the expense to hold the spring session of district court. This was Luna County's circle problem; if Judge Frank Parker could not hold district court, he could not approve Luna County's delinquent tax list. If the county tax collector had no official delinquent tax list, he could not force collection of past-due taxes. If past due taxes remained uncollected, then the Luna County government must borrow operating funds or default on payment of its current due bills.

Luna County's inability to pay county employees had caused Deming's business owners money problems also, and this mood had made for a less-than-enjoyable holiday session. The county commissioners were finally able to work out an arrangement with the local banks to borrow the needed funds until Baca's men could collect all the past due county taxes.[43] During these financially troubled times, Jailer Hughes left the Sheriff's Office to take a job with a reliable income working for the railroad building out of Deming. The construction company paid Mexican laborers $1.50 to $1.75 per day, while "American" workers earned $1.75 to $2.00 a day. Forty-five dollars a month was better pay than a jailer received with the discounted scrip issued by Luna County.[44]

During these weeks of uncertainty, Sheriff Baca had one of his infrequent moments of being sick, and the doctor finally sent him to bed with a case of pneumonia. Like many men, Baca proved to be a difficult homebound patient, but the due-any-day pregnant "Nurse Mamie" knew how to handle her husband. Following a week battling the life-threatening illness and giving Mary a hard time, Baca was able to return to the sheriff's office and get out of the house.[45]

Cipriano returned to work just in time. "Burglars forced an entrance into J.H. Hodgon's store Sunday night by raising one of the back windows. They secured $6 in money and about $100 worth of kid gloves, silk handkerchiefs, hats, corduroy suits, etc. They left a clue and Sheriff Baca and his men are working on it."[46] Neither of the two local newspapers reported a follow-up story on the success or failure of Sheriff Baca's Sherlock Holmes detective adventure, but Ed Morris, J.H. Green, Harry Quick, and Dolores Serna were convicted of burglary at the fall session of the Luna County District Court and each given three years at the Territorial Prison in Santa Fe.

* * *

A French proverb says that books, cats, and fair-haired little girls make the best furnishings for a happy room. The Baca family already had books and a cat in their home. In the new year, they received the third ingredient of the proverb's requirement for joy in the home. On Tuesday morning, January 28, 1902, Cipriano and Mary rejoiced after months of sadness, as their hearts "were made glad by the birth of a fine girl baby."

"I was named Cipriana for my Father. Aunt Effie told me that Father was a proud papa. He showed me off to everyone he could find. Aunt Effie said the loss of Eva and Sallie had been very hard on Mama, but especially hard on Father. I guess I was special to him so he gave me his name," recalled the baby in her twilight years.[47]

* * *

Cipriano Baca had been an officer for many years and had seen or experienced a wide range of criminal activities. "He had one this week that must have been an absolute novelty to him," commented a Socorro newspaperman. The criminal that Sheriff Baca arrested was a woman who "was going about in male attire." In the 21st century, this event seems like a joke, but in New Mexico Territory of 1902, it was a crime. "The woman was fined $11, which she paid, and departed for fairer fields with her young man traveling companion."[48] The local newspapers made no comment concerning what the women of Deming thought of this event, but it would have been interesting to know Mrs. Frank Thurmond's opinion concerning this woman.

A couple of early settlers in Deming were Frank and Charlotte Thurmond. The couple arrived in what then was only a tent city in 1882. Cipriano Baca first knew Frank as a wholesale liquor dealer when he was a meat contractor for the railroad and later when Baca was Deming's constable. Thurmond became the vice president of the Deming National Bank, capitalized at $50,000. Frank Thurmond also owned a ranch east of town. One of the directors for the new bank was William H. Greer. Thurmond, Greer, and Baca were each trying to make their fortunes by investing in area mining claims and each man had varying degrees of success. Even the wives knew each other. Mary Baca attended St. Luke's Episcopal Church where Charlotte Thurmond taught a Bible study. Mrs. Greer spent extended periods at the family compound in California. The three couples may not have been social friends, but they did know each other and shared common political and business interests.

Few people in Deming knew that Charlotte Thompkins Thurmond was in fact the legendary frontier woman gambler known as Lottie Deno. Even in her youth, she acted like a lady. In the 1890s, she became the model for "Faro Nell" and her husband Frank became the "Cherokee Hall" character in the *Wolfville* tales written by their old friend Alfred Henry Lewis. The *Wolfville* characters were first immortalized as serialized tales in *Cosmopolitan* magazine and then later collected in book form. William Randolph Hearst at that time published *Cosmopolitan*. He was very familiar with the people and places of Luna County,

New Mexico Territory, because his parents, George and Phoebe Hearst, operated a cattle ranch near Cow Springs in the northwestern section of the county. The ranch site had served as a watering stop on the Butterfield Overland Stage route crossing the Santa Rita to Deming.

Lewis also wrote a 1905 novel, *The Sunset Trail*, featuring another friend of his, a New York newspaper sports columnist named W.B. "Bat" Masterson, who was a former Kansas lawman associate of Wyatt Earp. In 1907 and 1908, Lewis edited a short-lived magazine titled *Human Life: The Magazine about People* and published a six-part series titled "Famous Gun Fighters of the Western Frontier" written by Masterson. Three of these short Old West biographies, Wyatt Earp, Buffalo Bill, and Doc Holliday, concerned men who had been tourist visitors to Deming. In his story about Doc Holliday, Masterson published for the first time the tale about a youthful Holliday having an encounter with some Negro youths swimming in a pond on his family's property and the shooting incident that followed the discovery. Masterson claimed that he had not heard the story from Doc, so it is possible that Holliday's fellow southerner Lottie Deno conveyed the story she learned from Doc to Lewis who added it to the Masterson article during the editing process. We may never know the correct sequence of who told whom or how much truth is contained in the episode.

The connection chain continues. Mrs. Thurmond had known Wyatt Earp and his dentist friend John Henry Holliday while they were gamblers at Fort Griffin, Texas. In fact some legend makers claim that Lottie won over $3,000 from Doc Holliday in an 1876 poker game.

The gambling fraternity circle continued with Frank Thurmond's friend Lou Blonger, who worked at Thurmond's ranch and mining claims from 1883 to around 1887. Sam Blonger was marshal of New Albuquerque in the spring of 1882 when Deputy U.S. Marshal Wyatt Earp and his fugitive federal posse, including Doc Holliday, sought refuge in the Duke City. Marshal Blonger was out of town on a business trip, so his younger brother Lou, who was his chief deputy, was New Albuquerque's acting marshal during the posse's clandestine stay in the community by the Rio Grande. Lou Blonger later moved to Denver where he became the city's crime boss in the 1890s.[49]

* * *

During the predawn of Friday morning, January 31, 1902, Luna County had a jailbreak, and Baca wanted his ungrateful guests back. He offered a $50 reward for the capture of Frank McMahan, an accused confidence man, and a $25 reward each for Elzie Brown, charged with assault to kill on the bartender at the Deming Saloon, and Walter St. John who held up the Cabinet Saloon. "The prisoners sawed the bars of their cells and getting out into the jail corridor, tunneled out under the doorway," said the *Deming Herald*. Then the editor made some value judgments. "In one sense it is probably a good thing for the county that it is rid of them. In another sense, however, Luna county should hold her prisoners more securely. As a piece of foolish economy, the jail has been without a regular jailer for several weeks." The newspaperman now added the coup de grace. "From the taxes of 1901 the county will secure sufficient money to pay its current expenses during 1902, and it should see to it hereafter that the county jail is in control of a regular jailer." Two weeks later, the *Deming Herald* announced, "S. Gallegos has been appointed jailor at the county bastille."

Walter St. John had headed south for Old Mexico, but he stopped for the night at a cowboy camp. "When St John got to the line he told a cock and bull story about how he put a head on [kicked out] Sheriff Baca and locked the guards in the jail and then took French leave, and put himself up for an all around bad man," said the *Deming Headlight*. St John was a "bad man" all the way back to Sheriff Baca's jail. The other two made good their escape and vanished into the vast desert of northern Chihuahua.

Sheriff Baca had the jail repaired, and in February, U.S. Marshal Creighton Foraker lodged three Chinese nationals in the Luna County lockup. A week later, Sheriff Baca added eight more illegal Orientals to that list. The vast open rangelands of Luna County had become a border crossing point for those trafficking in transporting of illegal aliens into the United States. Little has changed in 100 years; the Luna County sheriff's department still faces illegal immigrants, now also plagued by illegal drug smugglers and human traffickers armed with modern high-powered automatic weapons and muscle-engine vehicles.

Life was never simple for Cipriano Baca. "A Chinaman arrested in this city [Deming] one day last week for being unlawfully in this country, was broken out with small pox. The officer who arrested him sent him [the prisoner] to the pest house and then went and thoroughly fumigated himself. He was Sheriff Baca." There is no evidence to suggest that Baca caught the small pox bug, so once again Cipriano's guardian angel must have been working overtime.

In April, the Luna County Commissioners' Court was able to pay Baca an outstanding bounty. The board authorized and paid him $2 for "1 coyote killed." The commissioners, however, were unable to pay the sheriff the $345 due him for care and feeding of the county jail prisoners. Some of this jail expense was due to the arrest of army deserters from the camp near Columbus. Sheriff Baca held these men until military authorities came to take custody of their runaway troopers. The War Department finally paid Luna County feeding fees and the capture reward for the deserters.

By the summer of 1902, Luna County was past due in paying an additional $10.40 for water used in the jail, $9.50 for jail supplies, and $91.56 in sheriff's fees. Some of these debts carried forward from the last quarter of 1901. The 1902 third-quarter statement for the sheriff's department expenses was $193. This was $20.50 due in mileage fees, $6 due in sheriff's fees, and $166.50 for prisoner care. At the end of September, Luna County owed Sheriff Cipriano Baca $813.18, a princely sum by 1902 standards.[50]

* * *

The territorial secretary granted Deming a charter as an incorporated city in April 1902, and the citizens soon elected local officials and set up a city government. One of the offices established was city marshal, and T.L. Oglesby took over the police duties for the county seat. Sheriff Baca and his deputies were now free to concentrate on law enforcement duties in Luna County's rural sections.

A few weeks later in May, the citizens of Luna County learned that "Sheriff Baca is out summoning jurors for the coming term of [district] court." It was the same song, just a new verse, as the district court convened promptly at ten o'clock on Tuesday, June 9, with Judge Frank W. Parker presiding. Cipriano attended all district court sessions, and when the term ended, he headed to Santa Fe. "Sheriff Baca left Tuesday for the pen with prisoners in his charge that were sentenced at the term of court just closed in this county," commented the *Deming Headlight*. A few days later, the *Deming Herald* said that Deputies Gallegos and Smith accompanied Sheriff Baca to help escort the five prisoners to the penitentiary. The Luna County inmates made "the total number of convicts, at that instruction to 256, the largest number in the history of the institution." This fact must have excited Baca's friend Superintendent Bursum. The two men had a nice visit before Baca and his deputies took the morning train south. Baca had no way of knowing, but these were the last prisoners that he would transport to Santa Fe as a Luna County officer.

Baca relatives visited in Deming during June. Aunt Maisie Hill came to see her new niece and brought along her son Will to play with his cousin Gil. Maisie and Cipriano had passed each other at the Socorro train station. The *Socorro Chieftain* reported, "Sheriff Cipriano Baca of Deming was in the city Thursday just long enough to make his friends wish he would stay longer." When Maisie returned to the Oasis on the Rio Grande, she bragged to the neighbors about her niece and her sister's new home and Cipriano's prestigious job.

A few weeks after Maisie and Will had returned home, the *Socorro Chieftain* informed the hometown folks that Mary's youngest sister had gone to Deming for a short visit. Pearl told Mary that their sister Effie received an appointment as the assistant postmaster in Socorro. One day Cipriano drove the sisters and the children to Florida Lake, seven miles east of Deming, for a summer picnic. The sisters had a wonderful visit, and Pearl returned to Socorro with lively tales about the newest addition to the Baca clan.[51]

* * *

Sometimes Sheriff Baca was able to perform a "humane act of kindness." Even across the age as one reads the story in the *Deming Herald*, one can still feel the emotion, the pain, the understanding, and the compassion.

> Sheriff Baca took "Crazy Molly" to the insane asylum at Las Vegas this week. About twelve years ago 'Crazy Molly' was a beautiful young girl brought to Grant county under promise of marriage and ruined. She has a son living with relatives in the east — a bright, intelligent lad, whose photograph the demented mother has and pathetically fondles. "The Luna County jail was no place for 'Crazy Molly,'" said Sheriff Baca to the reporter, "and I am glad we have secured her quarters in the asylum."

Baca made the same trip two months later. The constant blowing wind, the dry desert heat, the vast landscape, long separations from loved ones, or the endless loneliness from human contact caused many people living in remote rural sections of the frontier to lose a grip on reality. The job Baca disliked most about being a county sheriff was the duty to take into custody this type of person. The cold type of the *Deming Herald* recorded the incident.

> Sheriff Baca has brought in from Hermanas and has confined in jail Manuel Sanchez, a crazy man. Sanchez worked on the Bisbee Railroad. He went crazy in two days. He is single and his relatives live in Old Mexico. He is not violently insane.[52]

Sheriff Baca went to Albuquerque in early August to attend the party given to honor Bernard S. Rodey. The celebration was to show physical and financial support for New Mexico's nonvoting territorial delegate to Congress. Rodey was a popular Republican, and Baca wanted to keep on good terms with his party's territorial leadership. Baca needed full party support in November when he faced the voters of Luna County for election to a full term as sheriff. Upon his return home, Baca made his public declaration that he intended to seek nomination as the Republican Party candidate for sheriff of Luna County, pending the action of the county convention.

Before the nominating convention could convene, Baca was required to make a trip to California to pick up a fugitive held by the Los Angeles city police and return her to Deming. Cipriano left no written account of this trip so it is unknown if he took an extra day to visit Golden State relatives, but it is very probable that he managed to visit his favorite sister Jovita Walker who lived in the City of Angels. She died four days short of her 99th birthday in 1955.

Baca's prisoner was the errant wife of a wealthy Luna County cattleman who wished to have her back home. "Rumor says the lady skipped some time ago with a neat bunch of her lord and master's dinero." There is no public record concerning the rancher's welcome-home words to his long-absent wife, and one can only wonder if he cooked the "fatted calf" for her return party. One fact is not in dispute: Baca disliked being a part of this type of domestic incident.

It was no surprise to anyone in Luna County when local Republicans nominated Cipriano Baca as the party's standard bearer for sheriff at the county's first general election. The *Deming Herald* editorialized, "Mr. Baca has made a safe, conservative and business-like officer and has a just claim for recognition on the business and industrial elements of the county." Meanwhile up in Socorro, a newspaper said that they would "guarantee that he [Baca] will continue to be an excellent officer if elected."[53]

* * *

One old-timer said that William Frederick Cody was the handsomest American of his time. Cody was also called the symbol of adventure in the frontier era. Men envied him, women wanted to spoil him, and little boys emulated his actions. Children of all ages read about his "adventures" in over 700 dime novel stories. The Native Americans called him *Pahaska* (Long Hair), while world leaders addressed him as Colonel Cody. He was America's living legend known around the world as Buffalo Bill.

Miguel Otero claimed to have known both Wild Bill Hickok and Buffalo Bill when he was a young man on the Kansas plains and during his golden years recalled the men in his autobiography. The former governor felt Cody was "a fine horseman and a commanding figure in the saddle," but

> was rather selfish and wanted all the pomp and grandeur for himself. He was always spectacular and in the first row on parade day. Buffalo Bill was in no sense a bad man; he was a perfect gentleman and a good businessman [Cody's business empire went broke twice]. He believed long hair and buckskin garments attracted attention and brought in the dollars.

Otero's comments contain a certain irony when it is considered that some people viewed the former governor as "rather selfish" and a man who "wanted all the pomp and grandeur for himself" even at the detriment of his own family.

In the early years of his arena show, one of Cody's chief headliners was a young woman from the Ohio countryside named Phoebe Ann Mosey, later Mrs. Frank Butler, who used the stage name Annie Oakley. "Little Miss Sure Shot" is what the Sioux medicine man

Sitting Bull called her. In 1897, Miss Oakley wrote President McKinley to tell him that she believed he could keep the nation out of war with the Spanish Empire over the fate of Cuba; then she added a second statement saying that if war could not be avoided, "I am ready to place a company of fifty lady sharpshooters at your disposal. Every one of them will be an American and as they will furnish their own arms and ammunition and will be little if any expense to the government." The short decisive war was over before there was a need for Oakley's Lady Sharpshooters, and the American military missed a historic footnote to the "Splendid Little War" with Spain.

In the decades on both sides of the turn of the 20th century, every child's dream was to see Buffalo Bill. This wish came true for the Baca family and the other Luna County "youth of all ages" on Wednesday, October 1, 1902, when Buffalo Bill's Wild West & Congress of Rough Riders of the World thundered into Deming. Cody's famous headliner Miss Oakley was not with the show; she had been badly injured in a train wreck almost a year before outside of Lexington, Kentucky, and was not yet able to walk on her own. She would recover but never again was a performer with Cody.

The Wild West Show's special train arrived at Deming late Tuesday evening. The next morning the performing troop held a parade from the train yards through the downtown business district to the show grounds where the show crew had already started assembling the large outdoor arena. School started late that morning so all the children could see the prologue to that evening's excitement. At 6:30, while the sun was still setting in the west, Cody began the festivities. The cost for the performance was $1 for adults and 50 cents for children under nine years old. The show's concessionaires made a profit during this super time performance.

Cipriana Randolph recalled the event. "I was just a baby, but my brother Gil remembered seeing Buffalo Bill lead the grand parade from the train depot. Gillie said he looked like his pictures and rode on a big white horse. Mother and Father took Gil and a neighbor boy to see the show. For years the boys played with one of those little lead Buffalo Bill horse and rider toys that Father had gotten for Gil."

In later years, the Baca kids also played with a silver-plated shield with three lines of black lettering on the front. The badge said, "Buffalo Bill, Police, Wild West Show" and was used by the show's security force. "Father must have done some work for the show, because he had a picture of himself with Buffalo Bill. I remember seeing it when I was a girl, but it's gone now. He also had that book Cody's sister wrote about him. So many things were lost when the family was split up and later after he died," recalled Cipriana Baca Randolph.

On the day after Christmas 1902, the Buffalo Bill's Wild West & Congress of Rough Riders of the World arena show opened a two-year final tour of England and Wales. Upon his return to the United States, Cody made many visits to Deming to see his friend, county commissioner and successful farmer John Hund. In 1912, the *Deming Graphic* reported on one of those visits and said, "The gallant old colonel has for a long time been a booster for Deming country, and now his enthusiasm is greater than ever." Fate, however, was about to turn on Buffalo Bill.

Cody had once been a millionaire, but poor investments coupled with an excessive drinking habit, and the deaths of his business partner Nat Salsbury and his daughter Arta, had brought the aging buffalo hunter and army-scout-turned-arena-showman to the point that he may not have realized he was on a downhill financial slide. Cody was forced to merge his show with rival Gordon "Pawnee Bill" Lillie's traveling show just to stave off creditors. This joint show appeared in Deming on Friday afternoon, October 28, 1910, where school was dismissed for the day so that young, and "older," kids could attend the arena show. However, this joint enterprise failed in 1913. Now Cody was totally dependent upon the goodwill of the owners of the *Denver Post*, who had bought up his overdue debt. In old age and deteriorating health, Cody performed in the company owned circus until two months before death freed him of debt on Wednesday, January 10, 1917.

William F. "Buffalo Bill" Cody, a role model to 30 years of children, lies in a crypt on top of Lookout Mountain west of Denver. Six months after his death the newly established 2,000-acre military training facility northwest of Deming was named Camp Cody in his honor. The military discontinued operations at Camp Cody in June 1919, but the Catholic Sisters of the Holy Cross operated the former training camp as a tuberculosis sanitarium for the next 20 years.[54]

* * *

A week after meeting the legendary Buffalo Bill, Sheriff Baca and Will Greer attended the Republican Territorial Convention held at Raton. The two men spent their nondelegate time promoting Luna County and making political contacts for the future. Cipriano Baca was a rising star in the party, and it is possible that he will have harbored a desire for higher elective office. On the return trip to Deming, Baca stopped off in Socorro to pick up his family who had spent a few days with Grandmother Berry. Cipriano also took the occasion to visit with his friends who wished him success in the election. Upon later reflection, Baca may have wished that he had spent these "fellowship days" seeking votes in Luna County.

Just a few days before the November general election, Sheriff Baca personally arrested a man for carrying a pistol on the street in Deming. The Saturday-night would-be badman was sensible enough to plead guilty before Judge Marshall on Monday morning, and the *Deming Herald* reported that the man was "taxed $50 and [justice court] costs."[55]

Upon his first ceremonial visit to the newly formed Luna County, Territorial Governor Otero candidly shared his trepidations, saying,

> I, as a Republican executive, had only one misgiving in signing the Act establishing the County [of Luna], and that was, that there would not be found enough Republicans within its limits to fill the various offices, but from the number of applications, and recommendations I have received for appointments I no longer have any such fears. In fact I am convinced that there are a great number of Republicans in this new county who are in full accord and sympathy with that great patriot and statesman William McKinley"[56]

In the spring of 1901, when Governor Otero appointed only Republicans to lead the new Luna County government, the *Lordsburg Western Liberal*, a Republican-leaning newspaper, had made a prediction about these men. "It will probably be a long time before all the officers of Luna county are again republican." In the November 1902 election, the newspaper's prophecy proved correct, and Governor Otero's assessment was wrong. Luna County is still a Democratic stronghold.

"It is probable that Cipriano Baca has been beaten in his race for sheriff of the Democratic county of Luna," said the *Socorro Chieftain* a few days after the election. "He was appointed sheriff of the county on its organization and has been without doubt one of the best officers in New Mexico. He will have a word of sympathy from his host of friends in Socorro county." A glass of beer would most likely accompany that "word of sympathy" from his pals.

Most people in southwestern New Mexico liked Cipriano Baca personally, but politically Luna County was a stronghold of the Democrat Party, and party loyalty was paramount. When election officials counted the votes, the popular sheriff had lost his bid to retain his badge. The Luna County Commissioners' Court canvassed the general election votes on November 10 and certified 504 votes cast in the sheriff's race. W.H. Foster received 281, 58 more votes than the 223 votes that Cipriano earned. Baca lost the Deming precinct by only five votes, but he also lost the tally in four other precincts: Mimbres 8–20, Cook's Peak 17–31, Columbus 3–23, and he did not earn one vote in the Cambray Precinct. All 19 votes at the railroad-watering stop went to the Democrats. Baca won only the Hermanas box, 14 to 2. All the Republican Party candidates went down in defeat except for Probate Court Clerk B.Y. McKeyes. Baca may have lost his 1902 election and felt rejection by the people he had so faithfully served, but the campaign held none of the bitter memories of the mud-slinging ranker of his 1894 defeat.[57]

Cipriano Baca had been an even handed law enforcement officer and an excellent administrator of the county jail. Even so, he was a Hispanic, and, more important, he was a Republican. Baca was disappointed with his loss, but life went on in the Baca household. Cipriano continued faithfully performing his duties as sheriff. Meanwhile, his successor, William H. Foster, made plans for his administration. One of his first public acts was to tell a newspaper reporter that he would retain "no deputies that he knows of now." To many Deming residents this comment demonstrated a purely political action because Sheriff Baca had appointed quality jail staff and field deputies. Foster and some of his victorious Democrat friends believed that to the victor go the patronage spoils. Sheriff-elect Foster named James Jones, of Cambray, as his jailer. Billy Foster had brought hostile partisan politics to the Luna County sheriff's office, but he would only serve one term in that office to enjoy his spoils.

* * *

Cipriano Baca, like his friend Fred Fornoff, had no respect for Patrick Floyd Garrett as a poker player, as a man or as a law enforcement officer, so it is uncertain if Sheriff Baca was at the train depot on November 16 when Pat Garrett came over to Deming on the Sunday train from El Paso. This was not just a pleasure trip so Garrett could stretch his long legs. Garrett, as Collector of Customs for the El Paso District, was gathering data about the affairs at the Deming Customs House. Garrett's office oversaw all the ports of entry along the border between New Mexico Territory and *el Estado de Chihuahua un el Republica de México*.

In December 1901, President Roosevelt had nominated the former sheriff to the lucrative collector's post based solely upon his frontier reputation as the killer of Billy the Kid. The Senate quickly confirmed Garrett, and his commission issued the same day. The old political hack was still riding his crest of good favor, but his luck did not hold. In 1905, Roosevelt did not reappoint Garrett. Pat had not adequately performed his Treasury Department duties.

* * *

One of Cipriano Baca's last duties as Luna County sheriff was to execute a writ of attachment. The district court ordered Baca to take control of the stock inventory at the Sam Robinson Store because creditors wanted overdue debt settlement from the man's estate. Robinson's widow was now living in California. Two days before Christmas, Baca made a property inventory for the court. The estate sale, however, took place early in the new year under the watchful eye of the new Luna County sheriff.

On January 1, 1903, Billy Foster became the second sheriff of Luna County. The *Deming Herald* editorialized about Baca's tenure by saying, "His has not been a flashy or brilliant reign perhaps, but it has been what is better — modest, safe and substantial." A few months after Baca's death, former governor Miguel A. Otero bragged about Cipriano's outstanding public service record and proudly stated, "I appointed him the first sheriff of Luna County."[58]

* * *

Cipriano was unemployed for only a few days. On the second Tuesday in January 1903, he won the election to the post of constable of the Deming Precinct. The former sheriff garnered 103 of the 289 votes cast in the race. This fee-based job was to function as the law enforcement arm for the justice of the peace court. Ed Pennington, also a Republican and the former county assessor, won the justice of the peace post by two votes less than his friend Baca. The *Albuquerque Daily Citizen* congratulated Cipriano upon his election: "Mr. Baca is a good man and will undoubtedly give us a good administration."

On a pretty April day, Baca located a stolen horse and buggy belonging to W.R. Hutchinson of Central. The man had rented the team to a couple of young men who had brought the rig to Deming and left it at the Deming livery stable. The two army deserters were lucky because they were able to skip town on the eastbound railroad before Baca knew of their crime. "Mr. Hutchinson was notified to come after the rig, which he was glad to do," reported the *Deming Graphic*. Baca earned a small processing fee as he kept his finger in law enforcement.[59]

Baca had given many years to upholding the law by tracking down criminal suspects, arresting them, and taking them before a court of law. In June 1903, he had the opportunity to witness the legal process from the judgment side by serving on a Luna County petit jury. A decade later, he would come full circle in the legal process by being a criminal defendant.

On Monday, January 5, 1903, the Luna County Commissioners' Court was finally able to pay Cipriano the money the county owed him for his outstanding accounts. The former sheriff took some of this $632 and used it to invest in his mining business. The remainder he used to buy a livery stable business in downtown Deming.

The Deming-Mimbres Museum's archive collection houses some primary records covering the development of Deming's business community. Among these documents is an account ledger that contains some transactions between Cipriano Baca and the merchant who kept the journal. The book's front cover and company identification pages are missing, so it is difficult to identify the business or the merchandiser involved in Baca's transactions. Some of the ledger's entries are in small print and some style of business shorthand, but the record does preserve a protracted relationship between Cipriano and the unknown business. The 1902 notations appear to be routine affairs of a county sheriff collecting service fees, but after he left office in 1903, Baca started a new business relationship.

On Saturday, January 17, 1903, Cipriano sold some livestock for $55 to this merchant and on the same day accepted a private loan for $200. In April, Baca sold the same man a quantity of eggs, butter, and some "Baker" for $10.55 while the May entry indicates that Cipriano borrowed an additional $35. In July, the merchant paid Baca $15 for some service rendered. On February 19, 1904, weeks after Baca left Deming, the unknown merchant's notation suggest that he "bought" or accepted Cipriano's Luna County warrant for $18.60 as payment of outstanding debt. The last Baca entry in the ledger is in April 1904, and seems to be the credit of $23.60 for a county warrant. These business journal entries present more questions than they seem to answer concerning the scope of Cipriano Baca's business deals.

Cipriano, however, found little time to be a good livery stable owner. It seems like Cipriano was always out of town looking after his mining interests and, in fact, his livery stable operation may even have lost Baca money. Deming's water company charged livery stable owners 25 cents a month for each horse stall located at their business. This user fee was due regardless of the actual amount of water consumed by the business. This was the same user fee structure the water company charged a barbershop.[60]

"The thirty-fifth legislative assembly, which convened in January, 1903, stands out conspicuously in my memory," wrote Governor Otero some 37 years after the session concluded their business. Cipriano Baca also remembered the session because the former sheriff held enough popular support to become sergeant-at-arms of the Territorial Council. The legislative assembly's upper chamber was composed of some of the most successful business and professional men from across the territory. Their daily political gatherings provided Baca with some influential contacts.

Among these powerful men were lobbyists for the territory's mining, banking, livestock, and railroad interests. House member R.L. Baca, a Santa Fe County sheep rancher, became one of Cipriano's mining partners along with men from El Paso and Los Angeles. After the close of the legislative session, the partners became very interested in developing some Socorro County and Luna County mining claims. The *Deming Graphic* said, "We hope that the mine may prove a bonanza and that Mr. Baca will soon be a rich man."

Congress enacted a statute dealing with prospect mining, and President U.S. Grant signed it into law in 1872. The law established a "homestead" style way for a person to claim public lands, with no obligation to do any mining, virtually free from the federal government. This legislation was to encourage development of the west's vast mineral wealth. The law served its original purpose, but has become antiquated and is in need of revision or repeal. This 1872 law now allows present-day mining companies, domestic or foreign owned, the ability to recover massive mineral wealth from public lands without paying any royalties like the oil, gas, and coal companies are required to pay.

Cipriano Baca became the legman, and during the summer of 1903, he made a trip to Douglas, Arizona, to examine some new mining claims, but the partners did not invest in this venture. In early September, Baca spent a few days back in Deming looking after business interests and spending some time with Mary and Gil and Cipriana. A week later, on a Tuesday evening, Baca was back in Socorro County and the *Deming Graphic* commented, Cipriano "bids fair to be a great mining magnate." Available public records, however, shed little light upon how profitable all these mining ventures were for Baca or his financial supporters.

Even Governor Otero participated in the search for mining wealth. He tried for years to interest eastern investors to put capital into his tungsten, hematite, and wolframite properties. When Otero had been a young lawyer, one of his clients paid him with ore samples from a copper-gold-silver deposit. Otero spent years grubstaking miners to search for this mystery ledge in the Sangre de Cristo Range between Abiquiu and Mora. He never did locate the area.

In another venture, Otero was president of the B.O.B. Mining Company at Mogollon. H.O. Bursum was the company's secretary treasurer, and the third partner was A.R. Burkdoll. The men operated the Deep Down Mine whose four- to eight-foot-wide vein of surface digging had produced about $100,000 worth of gold and silver by 1905. The company also owned a stamp mill.[61]

* * *

In May 1903, a new baby increased the Baca family. The *Deming Graphic* reported the news: "Born to Mr. and Mrs. C. Baca, last Friday [May 29], a boy." Cipriano named the infant Florentino Berry in honor of his oldest brother and Mary's family name. Baca had been in El Paso for two weeks, on a business trip, prior to the boy's birth.

The father-son relationship began as a close and loving one, but became strained after Mary Baca's death. Twenty-four years after her husband's death, Louise Baca talked about Florentino's estrangement from his father. "My husband, Florentino, resented his father all his adult life for having abandoned him. Mr. Baca was not around when Florentino was a teenager and needed him the most. He would never forgive him for that." In a strange twist of fate, it was Florentino who checked on his father during his last days, signed his death certificate and made the funeral arrangements, but he didn't attend the funeral service.[62]

* * *

Slowly, over a period, Cipriano Baca came to believe that he could not win back the sheriff's office in a Democrat-controlled area like Luna County. Quietly Baca began to search for a job that would gave him the freedom of movement he desired so he could continue to develop his new mining interests, yet offered a standard means to earn a paycheck. The answer was simple. Baca needed a federal government appointment. In mid–November 1903, the Spanish-language section of the *Deming Graphic* contained this simple item, "*El Senor Cipriano Baca ha vendido su residencia en Deming y es ahora ciudadano de Albuquerque.* [Mr. Cipriano Baca has sold his residence in Deming and is now a citizen of Albuquerque.]"

In late January 1904, Fred Fornoff resigned his post as a federal deputy marshal to become a special agent of the Treasury Department, assigned to the U.S. Secret Service branch office in Denver, to work with the forgery and counterfeit currency unit. Fornoff's timely resignation and Marshal Foraker's job offer made it possible for Baca's graceful departure from Luna County before he had to face the challenge to run for sheriff in the fall election.

Cipriano and Mary Baca had moved to Deming in 1901 with three small children, a son and two daughters. Three years later, the Bacas left two small graves in Deming as they departed Luna County with three small children, two sons and a daughter. The 1904 city directory of Albuquerque listed the Baca family as residents and Cipriano's occupation as a deputy U.S. Marshal.

Had Cipriano Baca been able to peer into the future, he might have had quite a chuckle. Nine decades after he resigned as constable and left Luna County, area officers investigated the "Great Nut Rustling Caper." The criminal nature had not changed, but his modus operandi had. Thousands of pounds of nuts, worth over $40,000 wholesale, had been "rustled" from area pecan farms due to the high value of the cash crop that fall and an open market for sellers. The "Nut Rustlers" escaped capture.[63]

14

Deputy U.S. Marshal Cipriano Baca

> A U.S. Marshal shall "execute throughout the District, all lawful precepts directed to him, and issued under authority of the United States" and is authorized "to command all necessary assistance in the execution of his Duty."
> — The Federal Judiciary Act of 1789

The U.S. Marshal's Office, District of New Mexico, made disbursements of $37,444.40 during the 1904 fiscal year. Deputy salaries, fees, and other office expenses accounted for $7,589.27, while fees paid to federal jurors were $16,785.50. Federal court witnesses earned $8,230.05, and court bailiffs collected $1,138.53 for their service during court sessions. The care and feeding of federal prisoners cost the marshal's office $2,786.85, and miscellaneous expenses added an additional $914.20 to the budget.[1]

Creighton M. Foraker began to reorganize the pay system for his field deputies shortly after first taking office in 1897. Congress had recently passed a law that established a set salary for the marshal and his chief deputy but continued the field deputies and special deputies on the old fee system. Marshal Foraker persuaded the attorney general to allow him to appoint all his staff as office deputies and assign them a district court to service. The plan was approved, and within a year all the backlog of court writ had been served. Marshal Foraker was rewarded for his management and fiscal efficiency by having his field deputy force reduced by two officers.[2]

Marshal Foraker earned $4,000 a year in 1897, while his chief deputy was given $1,800 and the office deputies earned $600. Two years later the office deputy earned $900 per year, and by 1906 they were paid $100 per month. Regulations allowed a deputy working in the field up to $2 a day for his meals and lodging and a set allowance for authorized transportation expenses.[3] At the turn of the 20th century, a deputy U.S. Marshal received his appointment to office from the U.S. attorney general upon recommendation of the federal marshal for the district he would serve, and federal civil service regulations did not apply to a deputy U.S. Marshal's job. Unlike his contemporaries, Creighton M. Foraker set high standards for his deputies. He had three standard qualifications. A deputy should speak, read, and write both English and Spanish, have some clerical experience and a background in some aspect of law enforcement.

Early in 1899, Marshal Foraker established his headquarters in an office on the second floor of the Golden Rule Saloon, at Third and Central, in the heart of Albuquerque's new town business section. The office furniture was on loan from Bernalillo County. Later, the headquarters relocated to the new post office building, and the command center received secondhand furniture from the recently disbanded federal Court of Private Land Claims. The new office was also equipped with special features like an ice-water cooler, an electric fan, and two typewriters.[4]

When Theodore Roosevelt became chief executive following the assassination of President McKinley, he retained Foraker in office. By the spring of 1904, his force of federal officers consisted of Chief Deputy George A. Kaseman, William R. Forbes, John M. Wiley, the marshal's brother Charles, and Cipriano Baca, appointed to the force on February 1.

One of Deputy U.S. Marshal Baca's first out-of-Albuquerque trips was to return to Deming. The Spanish language section of the *Deming Graphic* covered the visit. The newspaper said that the former resident was "*estuvo en nuestra plaza*" on Friday, February 19, to testify in the murder trial of Lang Gee, a Chinese worker accused of killing a fellow compatriot named Sam Fong. Deputy Marshal Baca must have felt redeemed to return to the area that had recently rejected him as their sheriff proudly wearing the silver-engraved badge of a federal peace officer. There is a Sherlock Holmes maxim that describes this phenomenon: "Now having secured the future, we can afford to be more lenient with the past."[5]

Another case was just as frustrating, but a little more challenging for Deputy Marshal Baca. He received a federal fugitive warrant for a man named Childress, wanted in Deming for an aggravated assault and believed by Luna County authorities to have relocated to Mexico. Cipriano was able to work his manhunter magic tracking down the fugitive and made an arrest based upon the Luna County warrant, but circumstances forced Baca to leave his prisoner in Mexico as a free man. It seems the Mexican government refused Mr. Childress' extradition document due to a technical irregularity. Baca returned home, and Childress remained free south of the border until he voluntarily returned to the United States in 1908. Childress quickly got into trouble, and Dalhart, Texas, officers arrested him.

While the Baca family lived in Albuquerque, Cipriano did not spend all his time doing police work. The federal officers and the Bernalillo county officials had played an annual baseball game since 1895 with the county team called the Fats and the federal team known as the Leans. It is not certain why these team names, but the yearly event always proved a hard-fought game full of "good clean fun." Cipriano Baca was not an accomplished baseball player, but he did play the game and especially enjoyed the beer and fellowship that followed the match. Cipriana Randolph fondly remembered her father playing baseball with her school friends when the family lived in Mogollon.[6]

Creighton Foraker's daughter, Mary, also had fond memories of Cipriano Baca. Even as an elderly lady she happily recalled how she and the neighborhood children were all "agog" looking forward to one of Baca's visits to her Albuquerque house on Menaul Boulevard.[7] It is a G-d-given blessing when children become excited and full of expectation, even curiosity, over the visit of a non-relative adult. Children loved to be near Baca, and he reciprocated their love. The tragedy of this blessing was that in later years some of Cipriano's own children turned their backs on him when he desperately needed their love and understanding.

* * *

During the late spring of 1904, Baca and George Kaseman made the 13-mile buggy ride south to the Isleta Pueblo to serve court papers on the tribal governor. Isleta translates to "little island." The name defines the settlement's earliest history when the pueblo was founded on an island in the Rio Grande before the community would relocate along both banks of the river. Kaseman had heard some of his Jewish friends discuss a place called *Cerro Los Moqujino*. He asked a tribal elder about the place that contained some ancient rock inscriptions and ancient village ruins. The old man said he knew of the place and would gladly take the two officers to the holy site, located a day's ride west from the main pueblo. A state road and a railroad track now cross the landscape nearby the glyph site, and the old Niclas Duran de Chavez Land Grant is now a family-operated ranch.

The *Cerro Los Moqujino* is a nearly flat uplift, rising about 400 feet above the desert plains, surrounded on all sides by steep cliffs, with the Rio Puerco along the east side about 1,500 feet in the distance. This stream flows into the Rio Grande a few miles to the south of the historic site. A natural drainage near the northeast corner of the small mountain acts as a passageway to the top. Near the entryway into this deep ravine is the face rock containing a carving of ancient Hebrew words from Deuteronomy 6:4. This carving contains the message normally found in a *mezuzah* on the "gateway" into a Jewish person's home. A few yards north along the trail to the mountaintop is a large brown and tan boulder inscribed with 216 characters that seem to record the Mount Sinai Commandments. On the hilltop are the remains of what has been identified as remains of an Anasazi settlement.

Isleta cultural traditions, and some modern archeologists and linguists, suggest that the glyph was "ancient" when Indians built the pueblo in the 1400s. It is interesting, however, that Adolph Bandelier, an early archaeologist of New Mexico's Indian culture, made no mention of the inscription rock in his massive *Journals*. Bandelier had visited Hidden Mountain and mapped the sight in 1883. It should be note that the archaeologist's focus seems to have been more on the dwellings and lifestyle facilities ruins than upon cryptic rock writings. It is worth noting that the area contains some rock graffiti contemporary with the Kaseman and Baca visit of 1904. Two of these "signatures" are of interest: one is dated "1898 M. Hannet," while the other says "E.R. Hratti 1907."

In Kaseman's account of his visit to the hilltop ruins and its strange monuments, he described an almost spiritual experience while sitting on a pinnacle listening to the stillness that surrounded them. If Baca left a written account of his visit to Mystery Mountain, it has not been located.

Scholars continue to debate the glyph's authenticity and possible meaning to the history and cultural development of ancient peoples living near the Rio Grande in the era before recorded time. The "Phoenician Inscription Rock" name appears on some present-day New Mexico wilderness area maps. The saga of the mountain of mystery continues.[8]

* * *

It was while he served as a federal marshal that Cipriano Baca developed his skill for the still hunt. This type of criminal pursuit demanded cunning, nerve, patience, and the ability to go unnoticed in a town or on a backcountry road. Cipriano was like a mountain lion hunter when he was searching for a wanted man and left no paper trail by asking for expense vouchers, and he kept his badge and gun concealed. He often traveled alone until he located his quarry and only then might he gather a posse to help him make an arrest.

In mid–April 1904, Deputy U.S. Marshal Baca transported two federal prisoners housed in the Dona Anna County jail at Las Cruces up-river to Santa Fe for their trial. A Chinese man had forged citizenship papers so he could live and work in America, but what he achieved was 17 months of hard labor for his trouble. A jury found the second prisoner guilty of violating federal postal laws, and the judge give him three months free lodging at Uncle Sam's expense. Baca returned the convicts to Las Cruces to begin their restitution to society.

Ten days later, Deputy Marshal Baca escorted two different Chinese men to San Francisco for deportation back to China. Following a daylong ride from Santa Fe, Baca lodged his prisoners in the Luna County jail for the night. One would suspect that Baca visited with some old friends over a cold glass of beer, but the *Deming Graphic* made a noncommittal comment, saying simply, "He spent the night here, leaving for the west on the S.P. train Saturday morning." Baca spent a few extra days on the coast visiting with relatives.[9]

On more than one occasion, Cipriano Baca displayed his keen judgment of the human character and his legendary fearlessness and determination. One such incident happened in the fall of 1904. Federal Judge John R. McFle had ordered that a federal marshal bring two Taos Pueblo Indians and a half-breed, who also lived at the pueblo, into his court to face a charge of refusal to honor a subpoena to appear before the federal court at Santa Fe. Baca found his visit to this northern pueblo much less friendly then his sojourn at Isleta.

Deputy U.S. Marshal Baca left Albuquerque on the morning AT&SF railway passenger train for Santa Fe. At the capital city's Union Depot, Baca switched to the Denver & Rio Grande's narrow gauge rail line. The "Chili Line," or Santa Fe Branch system, ran north to Espanola, then on up the Rio Grande to Embudo before moving into Colorado. The D&RG crew made the 125-mile trip along the riverbank in the scenic Rio Grande gorge daily, except Sunday, and took about seven and a half hours to complete the full journey.

A passenger on the Chili Line began their "eastward" journey at 11:00 A.M. and reached Embudo, 53 miles north of Santa Fe, at about 1:50 P.M.. Here passengers had a 20-minute rest stop for personal needs and a quick lunch. The railroad station at Barranca or Caliente (after 1915 it was renamed Taos Junction) was about eight miles north of Embudo. It took the slow-moving locomotive about 50 minutes to pull its cargo northward from Embudo, up the 4 percent grade through Comanche Canyon, to Barranca/Caliente. This trading post was the transfer point for travelers headed the 20 miles east to the three Taos settlements. Glen Woody owned a four-horse hitch, nine-passenger stagecoach that made the daily run from Barranca/Caliente to the town of Taos. Laucrino Hidalgo, who drove the contrivance, left Barranca/Caliente station at about 3:30 P.M. and reached the Taos Plaza at about 6:30 the same evening, barring any sudden thunderstorm.[10]

Baca sent Marshal Foraker a status report of his Taos mission. "I could not get to Taos from Embudo [via a hired team or horse] ... so had to go to Tres Piedras and higher [*sic*] a team. We started yesterday at 5 [A.M.] & [it] rained like hell all the way to this place [Arroyo Hondo]. Stayed here & leave this morning for Taos at 5 o'clock." Two days of rain later, Baca finally reached Taos. "I don't know if I will be able to get away tomorrow from Taos but will if I get Indians today."[11]

It is unclear from Baca's letter why he had tried to reach Taos from Embudo and not the commonly used jumping-off spot at Barranca/Caliente. Maybe Baca did not know that the station had a stagecoach connection to Taos, or maybe Baca had confused

Barranca/Caliente and Embudo. Maybe for some reason Woody's coach was not running on the day Baca needed the service. We may never know the answer to this mix-up, but the confusion cost Baca both time and money.

Taos Pueblo is one of the most imposing Indian settlements in New Mexico, consisting of two six-storied pyramidal tenements, separated by the Rio Pueblo de Taos, housing about 450 Indians. Baca rented a horse, rode the few miles north of the plaza to the pueblo, and arrived during the Indians' annual San Geronimo Festival. Cipriano had little trouble finding his quarry, but at this point, he had a protocol lapse and forgot the key element in the survival of a peace officer; always assess the situation, not just the individual of your concern. An effective peace officer knows that following their intuition is a major factor when attempting any arrest, and there are seven "must-do" cardinal rules. These rules, real or imaginary, are listening to your natural fear, apprehension, suspicion, doubt, hesitation, curiosity, or simple hunch. Interestingly, the human animal is the only creature that will override these warnings of nature. To disregard nature's warning system most often ends with the individual dancing on peanut butter and paying the consequence of their misjudgment.

The *Santa Fe New Mexican* reported the outcome of Baca's attempted arrest, saying, "The scene was typical of old time frontier days when the deputy pushed his way through a band of painted, naked warriors and requested that his men accompany him to jail." Two of the men started to leave with Baca when fellow dancers quickly became an inflamed mob and made a rush to free their friends from the "Greaser lawman." Cipriano's courage and determination saved him from what the *Santa Fe New Mexican* called "harsh treatment and probably death" at the hands of the enraged Indian mob.

Some of the Indians had grabbed Baca's right arm and pinned it to his side, but they didn't know that Baca wore his pistol for a cross-draw on his left hip. Cipriano, using his left hand, drew his pistol and "was showing the muzzle of a .45 Colt within a second." The Indians backed off, and Baca started to take his prisoners away. Within minutes, the dancers regained their whiskey nerve and again started toward Baca. When the pueblo's governor reached the scene, he quickly restored order and then later supported the legality of Baca's arrest effort before the pueblo's council. Deputy U.S. Marshal Baca took his prisoners to the Taos County jail.

The Taos County courthouse occupied a long, single-story adobe building facing the south side of the town's plaza in 1904. The back two-thirds of the county government's property faced south onto a narrow thoroughfare then called H Street, across from a grocery market. The county jail's centered location was to allow open space on all sides of the lockup for security. An outhouse shack sat on the east side of the lockup. A back door in the courthouse provided the jail an entrance into the court chambers. The adobe jail had an office for the sheriff, quarters for a night jailer, and a prisoner cell block.

Friends of the prisoners spent the evening making plans to rush the jail at first light and free their friends. Someone warned Cipriano about the jailbreak plan. He believed the threat of bloodshed was real and prepared to hold his captives at all costs. In the "Adventure of the Speckled Band," Sherlock Holmes seems to have caught Baca's situation when he told Dr. Watson, "Do not go asleep, your very life may depend upon it. Have your pistol ready in case we should need it." Cipriano Baca had a very restless night.

Fortunately R.R. Green, a local doctor who spoke Tawa, had also heard about the trouble at the pueblo, went to visit the Indians governor, and persuaded him to calm his people before someone died. Green and the governor arrived at the jail as about 50 Indians, dressed in their war robes, were preparing for an assault. The martinet governor quickly quieted his neighbors, then told the mob about Baca's mission and ordered the Indian insurgents to allow the Hispanic federal marshal to take their brothers to Santa Fe. The old warriors silently disappeared from H Street and returned to their homes for breakfast.

Dr. Green helped the Indians compose an affidavit saying they had not understood Baca's mission and were sorry for their misguided interference with his actions. The former hostiles said that they would give Baca no more trouble while he was in Taos. Baca learned later that political rivals of the sitting tribal government incited the jailbreak attempt to cause trouble.

The incident caused Baca to remain in Taos for a few extra days because the rains had caused some washouts that made travel difficult. "It is easily seen why the deputy marshal gave vent to a sigh of relief when the big doors of the penitentiary closed behind the red men," said the *New Mexican* account. In the capital city, the Native Americans appeared before Judge McFle and the judge ordered the lightest sentence he could issue because he believed the men had been political pawns. The four Indians each received 30 days in jail. Deputy U.S. Marshal Baca took no further legal action against the Indian dancers who had tried to harm him during the performance of his official duty.[12]

The arrest scene incident or the jail confrontation could have exploded into a full-blown riot because the Indians where "clad in what old-timers knew to be their war robes." Baca may have had to kill someone in an attempt to hold his prisoners, or at worst he might have been killed or wounded during an attempted jailbreak. Judge McFle did not appreciate the difficulties his deputy endured at the hands of the Indians and the almost total lack of support from the local authorities. The judge expressed that negative sentiment very bluntly.

It should cause one to wonder what the Taos County authorities were doing while this hostile, and potentially lethal, confrontation took place outside of their courthouse and jail. Where was Sheriff Faustin Trujillo during the confrontation? Where was Sheriff Trujillo's force of deputies? The citizens of Taos County seem to have wanted to know the answers to these same questions as they did not reelect Trujillo, a six-year veteran sheriff, that fall and a new sheriff took office in January 1905.

Now Deputy U.S. Marshal Baca had to deal with the paperwork: arrest reports and an expense account form. Cipriano had experienced difficulty getting a receipt from the "hack driver" that drove him from Tres Piedras to Taos. "Mex could not or would not sign [the receipt for the fare]," wrote Baca at the bottom of the field report he sent to Marshal Foraker.[13] This occasion was Baca's only visit to the Taos countryside. He had seen the plaza in the town of Taos and the pueblo village located at the base of the Sangre de Cristo Mountains, but he had missed the quaint and picturesque Ranchos de Taos and the classic adobe church built in the center of that farm community. This edifice is one of the most photographed and painted scenes in New Mexico.

Federal justice never slept or took a holiday while Cipriano Baca wore a deputy U.S. Marshal's badge. On New Year's Day, 1905, Baca was at Portales in eastern New Mexico serving a warrant on a man wanted by federal authorities in the Indian Territory. It was a peaceful arrest, and a few days later the marshal was back in the Duke City.

Deputy U.S. Marshal Cipriano Baca attended the session of federal court held at Santa Fe, during late February 1905, and he "incidentally took in the legislature" which was in session at the same time. Cipriano had many friends among the territorial lawmakers and a special friend in the chief executive's office.

Just before noon on March 1, Baca paid a visit to the territorial governor. The two men had a friendly visit before they discussed a new job that the governor wanted Baca to undertake, and in the end, Cipriano agreed to his friend's request. In mid–March 1905, Marshal Foraker wrote the attorney general, "Office Deputy Cipriano Baca has handed me his resignation to take effect Apr 1st next, for the purpose of accepting another position." The marshal did not state, if he even knew, what Baca planned to do when he left the federal service.

Deputy U.S. Marshal Cipriano Baca was in Socorro County, serving federal summonses for the grand and petit jury, when the public learned about his new job. Baca wrote Foraker, "I am getting along O.K., but think it will take me 3 or 4 days more [to locate everyone and serve all the papers]. I am getting anxious to get away from here and come home, but don't dare yet [because of the summonses not yet served]." Cipriano added a request to his official report. "I wish you [would] send me $5.00 but don't send them so the Post Office here knows that it comes from you for they will tell my wife I got money from you." Baca then thanked his boss for "the kindness."

It is not clear why Baca needed the extra money. His social functions with his Socorro friends or his travel expenses may have used up his pocket money. Mary Baca seemed to cast a dim eye upon Cipriano's "social" nights out with the boys.

Baca ended his letter to Marshal Foraker by saying, "I see by the papers I have been appointed Lieut." Baca's reference was to the public announcement of his appointment, by Governor Otero, as second-in-command of the newly authorized New Mexico Territorial Mounted Police force.[14]

15

The New Mexico Territorial Mounted Police

"A rather unusual institution within New Mexico is the mounted police, who numbered 11 [men] in 1907, whose work was almost entirely in the cattle country, and who had authority to patrol the entire Territory and to make arrests or to preserve order wherever their presence was needed, unhampered by the restrictions limiting the jurisdiction of the local police."
—*The Encyclopedia Britannica*, 1911 Edition

The New Mexico Territorial Mounted Police were born in a forge of frontier civil crisis and hammered to life upon the anvil of necessity. The war with the Spanish Empire had ended, and the rough-riding western volunteers had returned to the southwest range country hoping to begin anew, but many became just another disappointed adventurer. Some of these men chose illegal means to gain a living. In the early months of 1899, New Mexico lawmakers debated the need for a territorial police force to assist local officers in combating this renewed menace to peace, safety, and economic development.

A territorial police force would require money, and few legislators wanted to defend a tax increase, so lawmakers tabled the legislation. The lawmakers reasoned that the job of catching criminals was the chief responsibility of the county sheriff, so they increased the governor's ability to offer rewards for the capture of lawbreakers. The lawmakers' gamble failed; peaceful conditions did not improve with the dawn of the new century and economic growth also suffered in the Sunshine Territory.

In the spring of 1901, the legislative bodies in the State of Texas and the Arizona Territory each created a ranger force to deal with roving outlaw bands in their frontier regions. Within four years of their formation, these rangers had arrested, killed off, or driven these gangs from their jurisdiction. This aggressive action on New Mexico's eastern and western borders had caused the territory to become the central outlaw haven in the southwest. This unwelcome distinction was a strange twist of fate because the Arizona lawmakers had prudently adopted the territorial police plan proposed and rejected in New Mexico just two years earlier.

In 1903, some lawmakers made a second attempt to pass the needed legislation to create a force of New Mexico rangers. Special interests won again, but 24 months later, the political climate had changed. In the years since the freshman councilman from Roswell, Granville Richardson, first proposed the territorial police concept, New Mexico stock growers had organized a system of semi-official detectives or range riding bounty hunters. These manhunters freely roamed across the southern tier of counties empowered by deputy sheriff commissions issued in each county they served. The local stock associations paid the men a fee per case they handled, and the governor would from time to time offer a reward for some special criminal, but this reward or bounty system was only partly successful as the Sunshine Territory continued to witness a steady increase in all levels of criminal activity.

America's touch with the past became dimmer with the death of the nation's last living soldier of the War of 1812 in 1905. The honored veteran was 105 years old. The victory of this second encounter with the British Empire had set the young nation on the road toward Manifest Destiny and the conquest of the Spanish southwest. New Mexico became an American territory and part of this westward movement, but fate made the territory a haven for outlawry and a final bastion against the advent of civilization and statehood.

The 36th Territorial Legislative Assembly convened in Santa Fe in January 1905. Council Bill 36, a new enabling act to create a territorial police, was introduced by another freshman councilman and was endorsed by Governor Otero and the major economic forces in the territory. Baca's Deming friend William H. Greer introduced a Mounted Police bill that was a revised version of the Richardson Bill of 1899. Bipartisan support, in all sections of the territory, had grown for a central police force that would, without favor, justly enforce the law in all localities. The Greer Mounted Police Bill quickly passed both houses of the assembly and was just as quickly signed into law by Territorial Governor Miguel A. Otero.

The New Mexico Mounted Police Act authorized a single company of rangers composed of a captain, a lieutenant, a sergeant, and eight privates who were to be paid $60 per month for their service. The territory furnished each of the 11 men with a Winchester 95 rifle, a gray military-style uniform, a badge, a commission of office, and rifle and pistol ammunition. A mounted policeman or ranger was required to supply his own army-size Colt .45, a horse and saddle, along with packhorse and camp equipment. Each man paid his own personal expenses while on scout duty, including the care and feeding of his horses. The territory would replace a policeman's horse if it was killed or injured while on patrol, but a policeman had to pay his own medical expenses if he was hurt while performing his duty. When all the job's pluses and minuses where added up, most of the new territorial police felt the positives won. Albuquerque's *Morning Journal* caught the spirit of the new rangers when it reported that the "members of the territorial mounted police are as tickled over their jobs as a boy with an all day sucker."[1]

The drawing is Cirpirana Randolph's first description of the badge worn by her father when he served as lieutenant of the New Mexico Mounted Police in 1905. Years later, when her brothers would dress up and play "cowboys and Indians," they would wear their father's old badges. None of the original 1905 badges survive (NMMP/AC).

Governor Otero established a special two-man selection committee to review the over 200 applications from men seeking to serve with the new rangers company, and to make a list of recommendations for appointment. This two-man clearinghouse finally selected Socorro County stockman John Ferguson Fullerton to be the first captain at a $2,000-a-year salary. Fullerton had no law enforcement background, but he was popular among the territory's stock growers. Baca became the rangers' second-in-command, and Cipriano was to earn $1,500 per year as the company's lieutenant. The sergeant was to earn $900 annually, and like Fullerton and Baca, the committee's choice had Socorro County connections. He was former chief deputy sheriff Robert W. Lewis, nicknamed "Stuttering Bob" because of a speech impediment. Captain Fullerton selected the Socorro County seat as the location of his office and Mounted Police's primary base of operations for his two officers and a private. The other seven rangers maintained their "office" in their homes or on the back of a horse.

This first company of Mounted Police, commonly referred to as Fullerton's Rangers, was New Mexico's premier police agency with authority to enforce all level of laws in all sections of the territory, and the ranger's silver shield was their badge of authority. Cipriana Randolph had a "faint recollection" of having once seen her father's gray uniform, "but cannot for the life of me recall where or when. One of the boys [her two brothers] may have had it." Baca's uniform has not been located, and to date no one has located an authentic New Mexico Mounted Police uniform used by one of Fullerton's men.[2]

L.F. "Fate" Avant was the first Mounted Policeman forced to kill a criminal in the line of duty. On Thursday evening, August 24, 1905, Avant engaged in a shootout with a store robber in the village of Capitan. The results were deadly. A coroner's jury found that Fate Avant's lethal action was justified and he faced no criminal charges; henceforth no Mounted Police would back down in the face of danger. Sergeant Lewis became the model for the Mounted Police's determination to get their man. Lewis spent 71 days during the first months of 1906 trailing a murderer across snow-covered mountains deep into the Republic of Mexico, finally arresting a fugitive and returning him to the Sunshine Territory. During his absence, Bob Lewis' little daughter died in a tragic accident.

Lt. Cipriano Baca became the example of faithfulness to duty, and the Mounted Police mission to protect and serve came before personal needs or family. He spent more days on scout duty than any other member of Fullerton's Rangers. He continued that dedication under Captain Fred Fornoff. The professional relationship between New Mexico's county sheriffs and the Mounted Police was a stormy one from the inception. Sheriffs were elected officials and often supported local values and the judgment of the voters over unpopular laws like gambling and alcohol sales. Without local favoritism the Mounted Police were able to capture suspects that local officers could not or would not attempt to apprehend. The police earned an annual salary regardless of their job performance, while county sheriffs earned compensation in the form of fees for each warrant or subpoena he or his deputies served. Mileage and prisoner fees were another source of income.

Some of these officers felt the rangers' activities cut into their pocketbook, while other county officers were happy to let the territorial police do the fieldwork and then collect the prisoner transport fees. Mounted Police could not transport prisoners for mileage fees, nor could they collect fugitive reward postings.[3]

16

Lieutenant Cipriano Baca

"[Cipriano] Baca is said to be a fearless and capable officer, speaks both languages fluently and has a natural instinct to hunt criminals." — The *Tucumcari News*, 23 June 1906

One of Captain John Fullerton's first functions was to create an organizational structure for the new territorial rangers. Captain Tom Rynning of the Arizona Rangers had his 26-man command divided into a northern and southern detachment. The Texas Rangers operated under a plan where small detachments of the main company serviced assigned patrol areas. Looking back over so many years, it is hard to understand the reasoning that caused John Fullerton to develop his unique squad composition and duty assignment procedure.

Fullerton's organizational chart provided for two four-man Mounted Police squads each under the direct command of one of his officers. It is possible that Fullerton may have felt this arrangement would give each command the ability to function across the territory, but when put into operation during the first few months, this system seemed doomed to failure. In reality what John Fullerton's concept produced was an overlap of effort as one squad would retrace the same ground right behind the other squad. Both squads were seeking the same information or searching for the same suspects while causing confusion in the ranks. The structure lacked an effective communication system.

A review of Fullerton's original squad assignments and an examination of a New Mexico map quickly reveal the problem. Lieutenant Baca, headquartered at Socorro on the Rio Grande, had a squad that consisted of George Elkins from Hachita in the bootheel of southwestern Grant County; Julius Meyer from Estancia, the county seat of north central Torrance County; John Brophy from Clayton, the county seat of far northeastern Union County; and Will Dudley from Alamogordo, the county seat of Otero County, located along the eastern edge of the White Sands and the eastern mountain ranges and the Texas border. Sergeant Lewis, also headquartered at Socorro, was assigned Herb McGrath from Lordsburg located just a few miles north of Hachita and George Elkins; Octaviano Perea, like Will Dudley, from Alamogordo; and the two no-shows to the swearing in ceremony, Francisco Apodaca and William Taylor. L.F. "Fate" Avant of Capitan, a Lincoln County rancher, and Charles R. "Windy Dick" Huber of Santa Fe, a former stagecoach driver and territorial prison convict from Silver City, now turned lawman, eventually replaced Apodaca and Taylor.

New Mexico is geographically divided east and west by the Rio Grande and the central mountain ranges running north and south. Hindsight would suggest that Captain Fullerton should have formed an eastern sector patrol area and a western sector patrol area, with each squad having primary responsibility for its section and support function for the other detachment's area. This would have eliminated the endless overlap of patrol areas and the embarrassing lack of communication between the rangers living in the same general area but serving in different scout squads. Within months, Fullerton's squad system fell apart from nonuse as the men devised their own single-man or two-man team approach.[1]

* * *

The Mounted Police enabling act required the governor to organize the rangers within 60 days after the act became law. It is possible that during scheduling of the swearing-in ceremony no one realized that the chosen date was April Fool's Day, but as history would later prove, the Mounted Police would be no joke.

John Brophy, Will Dudley, Julius Meyer, George Elkins, Octaviano Perea, and Herb McGrath joined Captain Fullerton, Lieutenant Baca, and Sergeant Lewis in the governor's paneled office at three o'clock that sunny Saturday afternoon. Governor Miguel Otero missed the occasion because he was in California on a business/vacation trip, so Acting Governor J. W. Raynolds presided at the half-hour ceremony. Fullerton had already signed the standard territorial oath form on March 18 during a personal planning session with Governor Otero. Baca, Lewis and each of the six ranger privates present signed a crossed over National Guard Oath of Office form with its long-worded promise that the signer would serve the territory "honestly and faithfully." The half-page-size oath form closed with the entreaty of "So help me God."

"Captain Fullerton quoted his men two verses from the Book of Proverbs. One was about riding the path of justice [8:20] and the other one was something about defending the rights of the poor [31:9]. It seems funny now, but I remember the Ranger's motto best. It was the same as the Canadian Mounties. Maintain the Right. Father would sometimes quote one of those Bible verses or the motto, especially the motto, when we kids needed some attention paid to our backsides. Captain Fullerton must have been a closet romantic," remembered Cipriana Baca Randolph.[2]

The "Certificate of Mustering Officer" document, used by Captain Fullerton, was another converted New Mexico National Guard form. He crossed out the military term and wrote "Mounted Police." This roll was required under Section 2 of the Mounted Police Act. Fullerton's successor disregarded this provision as he did other details of the ranger's enabling legislation.[3]

Captain Fullerton informed his men that they would be governed by the rules and regulations of the U.S. Army "as far as the same may be applicable" because Section 9 of the Mounted Police Act prescribed that the territorial police would function under these guidelines. A year later, when Fred Fornoff assumed command of the rangers, he chose to abandon this paramilitary style and reorganized the rangers into the district system used successfully by New Mexico's deputy U.S. Marshals. No one seemed to have questioned the legality of this action or his removal of the ranger headquarters from "the most unprotected and exposed settlement of the territory" to Santa Fe.

The *Santa Fe New Mexican* printed the run-on sentence below as the lead to a page-one feature on the muster of the Territorial Mounted Police. The reporter wrote,

> There was noticeable about the streets of Santa Fe today several strangers who attracted a good deal of attention by their manly and independent bearing, and by their general appearance which indicated that they were men of strong character and nerve and of the true western stripe — men who were used to outdoor life, could ride and manage a bucking bronco, as well as a gentle gelding and handle a Winchester or a Colt's six-shooter with the greatest of ease and accuracy should occasion require.

Further into the account the territorial police were described as "men in the prime of life, strong of feature and build, active and energetic selected for their peculiar fitness and experience which will be required of them and which will be not only not easy and light but on the contrary will be arduous, dangerous, and strenuous." The *New Mexican* inserted an editorial comment, near the end of the feature, which predicted that the rangers "will prove, within a year, a great factor for the preservation of the peace and the protection of the lives and property of the people in the isolated and stock-growing sections of the Territory."[4]

* * *

Shortly after Cipriano Baca took his oath of office as lieutenant of Fullerton's Rangers, he returned to Albuquerque and packed up his family for the move to back to Socorro. By this time in her married life, Mary Baca had become an expert at packing up and moving a family. Once again, Cipriano brought Mary and the children to stay at Grandma Berry's boarding house, but a week later, they moved again. Baca had "bought the McCabe property in the western part of the city and he and his family are now home there," reported the *Socorro Chieftain*. "This is one of the desirable results of the location of the headquarters of the territorial mounted police force in Socorro." John McCabe became "a prominent cattleman of Lordsburg."[5]

John Ferguson Fullerton was a Socorro County rancher at the time of this picture, taken on a visit to Socorro, in about 1904. His daughter-in-law treasured this photograph as her favorite likeness of her father-in-law (Irene Fullerton's Photograph Album).

A very pregnant Mary Baca was extremely happy to be back in Socorro. She was now able to devote some time to assisting her younger sister Ruby plan for her fall wedding to John E. Griffith, a lawyer and rising figure in Socorro County's political wars. In June, another girl arrived to bless the Baca household, and Mary named the baby Ruby Hamilton, in honor of the young bride-to-be Berry sister. A newly engaged couple, a new baby, and a new job opportunity brought much joy and excitement to the tight-knit extended family of the Berry clan.

Much of the Sunshine Territory remained blanketed in white in the early spring of 1905, and a final cold snap almost wiped out the Mesilla Valley fruit crop. The bad farming weather soon caused many of central New Mexico's small homesteaders to seek backbreaking work in the rock quarries near Watrous. The need for hard cash drove other settlers to seek day work as harvest pickers in the southern Colorado beet fields. Some of these luckless homesteaders became livestock thieves, and this became the business of the New Mexico Mounted Police.[6]

The author and Fred Lambert, the last living member of the New Mexico Territorial Mounted Police, held a long discussion about how he would prepare for a ranger scout. One of the first chores Lambert would undertake was to study a Rand McNally map and a Post Office Department route map of the area he expected to cover so that he was familiar with the topography, settlement locations, telegraph and long-distance telephone connections, railroad lines, ranch boundaries and local water sources. He next estimated the distances to travel and the amount of time this might take barring no major mishaps. Lambert would double his estimate and use this measurement to determine the quantity of supplies he needed to conduct a successful extended scout and ensure the comfort of himself, his horse, and his pack animal.

Fred Lambert always believed that he would catch his man, so he planned for the extra supplies needed for his prisoner. If he felt that a resupply stop along his projected travel route was possible, then Lambert would plan to utilize the establishment as a checkpoint for communications with Mounted Police headquarters. The fewer trip supplies the ranger's pack animal carried the longer the animal could travel before it needed rest or replacement. Animal feed was the largest single supply item the ranger needed for an extended search; if bought on the trail, a full feed of oaks could cost as much as 30 cents a bag. The success of a mission often hung upon the health of the ranger's horse and pack animal, so they received priority care each evening and morning: feed, water and a rubdown.

The nature of his mission determined how open a ranger was about his presence in an area. Often area ranchers were willing to help the Mounted Police by providing fresh mounts and food supplies. Sometimes the rangers were able to spend the night as a guest at a ranch bunkhouse or at a line camp, and in the morning they and their animals might even get a free breakfast. A Mounted Policeman was always thankful for these small acts of kindness because lodging and breakfast could cost the lawman a dollar or more at a hotel or restaurant.

On a typical scout, Mounted Policeman Lambert would pack a floor sack he called a "greasy bag" with a five-pound slab of smoked beef and some bacon, thus the name for the bag. A tin of Arbuckale coffee and a tin of Luzianne tea with a small brew pot, a small iron Dutch oven, a pound of potatoes, a small sack of yellow onions, and some well-packed eggs. He also took two loafs of German rye bread, and three or four cans of Campbell's Condensed Tomato Soup to complete his food store for a short scout.

Lambert's warbag, which was used as a pillow at night, contained two suits of underwear, a spare shirt and trousers, two bandanas, a couple of pairs of socks, leather gloves, and an extra pair of boots. He also had a sack coat; in cool weather, he packed a cardigan sweater and a muskrat cap. His normal dress might include a vest, neckerchief, riding spurs, pocketknife, Stetson hat, and leather shirt cuffs. The new Gillette safety razor was one of the items in Fred's personal hygiene kit.[7] His pack animal also carried a rain slicker, two full water canteens, a folding water bag, a rope coil, a half side of a military camp tent, a camp ax, cook gear, and his own designed oversized sleeping bag. Fred Lambert was a man who enjoyed a restful night's sleep, so his bag was made of a folded waterproof tarp with ring holes down one side and the bottom so he could use a leather strip to sew up the side to keep it closed. Inside the tarp, Lambert used two soogans, a light cotton quilt, and depending upon the weather, one or two Navajo blankets.[8] Brown-tar soap lathers with a white foam as a body cleaner, hair shampoo, and is a natural insect repellent.[9]

The ranger found that living away from home was expensive. Even camping out in the summertime required portable food supplies for both man and horses. The outdoor menu was not always first class due to the time it took for the camp chores or the Dutch-oven cooking. Good drinking water for horse and man was always a problem, especially during the dry season or during a drought. Laundry needs and personal hygiene were other challenges of an extended patrol. A few examples should illustrate the expense of trail camping in 1905. A person could buy a pound of coffee for about seven cents, a dozen eggs for 14 cents, a pound of sugar for four cents, a pound of butter for 24 cents, and a pound slab of beef for about seven cents. These five items would have cost the ranger about 56 cents with no sales tax. If this cost is adjusted for a century of inflation to the 2005 rate, the 1905 costs of 56 cents would be $10.97 compared to the 2005 cost-of-living price of $14.11, plus state and local sales tax, for the same set of supplies.[10]

A New Mexico Mounted Policeman, in 1905, was paid $60 a month, or about $20 per month, more than the average range hand. The ranger had to pay all his patrol expenses from his salary while a range hand received free horse care, plus room and board from his employer. The question might well be asked as to who had the better economic deal.

The *Deming Graphic* was right when it prophesied quick action by the territorial police: "Capt. John Fullerton's mounted police are now mustered in and the New Mexico cattle thieves will soon hear something drop."[11] Two weeks after the muster, Fullerton reassembled his rangers on Saturday, April 15, at headquarters to discuss his plan of action. A short time later, Cipriano Baca, operating under sealed orders, led his ranger squad out of Socorro and headed up the road northwest into the mountain country. Baca's men were followed a day later by Sergeant Lewis and his two-man unit who crossed the Rio Grande and struck out for the east central range country. Other single-man ranger patrols also took the field, and the sudden presence of a Mounted Policeman or a Mounted Police squad in the remote sections of the territory surprised residents. Fullerton's Rangers quickly became the subject of conversation in every hamlet, settlement, village, town, and city in the territory.

The *Socorro Chieftain* was still leading the cheers for the Mounted Police. "It is safe to predict that the wisdom of the legislative assembly in providing for this force will be amply vindicated shortly after the force begins active operations." The newspaper continued, "Lawless characters will be suppressed or driven from the territory, crime will be diminished in number, the heavy expense heretofore borne for the trial of criminal cases will be reduced. New Mexico's reputation for law and order will be enhanced, and the business and social life of the territory will feel a new impulse." The newspaper report ended, saying, "These results are greatly to be desired and the territorial police force will therefore enter upon active service backed by the hearty approval and best wishes of all good citizens."[12]

The *Santa Fe New Mexican* correctly reported that Captain Fullerton had called the rangers to Socorro to give them their orders. "The Mounted Police of the Territory which was assigned to duty Saturday [April 15] will immediately proceed to take steps looking to the driving out of the numerous 'badmen' who have infested this Territory." The short report concluded on an optimistic note. "When the New Mexico force begins to drive them [bad men] from the north it is expected that a number of important arrests will be made as there will be the Mexican Rurales on the south and the Arizona Rangers on the west to hem in the outlaws and effect their capture."[13]

The Mounted Police directive was to apprehend "any outlaws, law breakers, marauding Indians or bands of hostile Indians or for the purpose of carrying out any measure that may contribute to the better security of the frontier." All the territorial rangers were exempt from military duty or jury service and had "full power to make [an] arrest of criminals in any part of the territory."[14]

The creator of the Mounted Police Act, Col. William H. Greer, believed that the Animas Mountains, in the Bootheel section of Grant County, was the central hideout of the border bandits. "The mountains are literally full of the worst class of desperados in the country, men who have found that there is no other section of the West so safe. In that neck of land there are gathered now a few of the most notorious outlaws of the time."[15] Greer pressured Fullerton to take some action in that area, but twice, severe weather conditions caused a postponement of the mass raid into the Bootheel.

In spite of George Elkins' field reports to the contrary, Lieutenant Baca held firm to the belief that there must be some kind of trouble in the "outlaw country" of the Bootheel. Captain Fullerton agreed with Baca, and he wrote Elkins that the lieutenant "thinks there is quite a goodeal [sic] of work down on the line." Unsaid, but understood, was the question, why have you not shown some results? Captain Fullerton underscored his meaning by telling Elkins that he was "very anxious to make a trip down in your country and will do so as soon as I can get transportation over the A.T.&S.F." Later in the letter the captain softened his tone: "Use your own judgment about the work that is necessary until I can come down." Fullerton signed off by saying he was still having trouble finding the right quality of uniform for the rangers.[16]

George Elkins was not overly concerned about having a Mounted Police uniform because no one was going to see him wear it in an area with few settlements and range camps that were days apart by horseback ride. The region is more sparsely populated a century after Elkins rode the Bootheel country and is still accessible mostly by unpaved dirt and gravel roads or horseback trails. One thing has not changed: the ruggedness of the Bootheel is still an outlaw paradise. Now the bad guys are drug runners, transient illegal aliens, and other border riffraff.[17]

With the perspective of time, it would seem that the Bootheel's outlaw menace of the spring of 1905 was more psychological than real. This fact may have been due to the territory-wide publicity campaign concerning an impending ranger strike force moving into the region. "The moral effect of the word 'ranger' is great. Outlaws do not care to meet a well armed body of that kind," Col. Greer had said.[18] The image of a massive, well-armed and determined police incursion may have had the desired effect of driving the gangs from the Bootheel, thus making the need for a full-scale Mounted Police raid unnecessary.

George Elkins endured three months of frustration over his inability to locate any longropers in the Bootheel and felt like a failure compared to the service rendered by his fellow rangers. Elkins gave up the hunt and became the first ranger to resign from the Mounted Police. Bob Putman, a Sierra County officer, who would become a ranger legend, replaced him.

* * *

A summer crop bulletin printed in regional weeklies reported that a semi-drought reigned on New Mexico's eastern plains, but "generally moisture is abundant elsewhere and streams are running high. The growth of crops has been rapid." The notice continued, "Range grass especially shows fine growth and stock of all kinds is improving steadily." The bulletin also told about the territory's major industries: "The calf crop is light thus far, but cattlemen expect a good increase later. Sheepmen are complaining of the loss of large numbers of sheep from poisoning from a new weed that is appearing on the range." Finally, readers learned about the territory's farmers. "Frost has thinned fruit somewhat in the northern counties, especially in Union and San Juan counties." Lt. Cipriano Baca headed for the San Juan Basin.

The Bootheel may not have had much action, but the northwestern section of the territory seems to have had some active livestock thieves. Captain Fullerton sent a ranger detachment to investigate. He agreed to the request. "providing the stockmen will furnish them [the rangers] with extra good horses, as it is too far to ride [horseback from headquarters] and would take too much valuable time." The area ranchers quickly agreed to furnish the Mounted Police the needed horses and pack animals, so Fullerton assured the cattlemen that if he "can possibly get away, [I] will go up with them."[19]

Lieutenant Baca was still making plans for a big Bootheel raid when fate took a hand. First, he became sick and was confined to bed for a few days; then Mary became ill and Cipriano was needed to care for her and the kids. Fullerton asked Baca to abandon the Bootheel campaign and instead spearhead the advance into the Four Corners region when he was able to take the field. Baca arranged for Julius Meyer and Octaviano Perea to rendezvous with him in Albuquerque. Here the three territorial police gathered their scouting supplies and took the Santa Fe Railway west toward Gallup, their jumping-off post to begin the hunt for the fast-moving rustlers.

Captain Fullerton anticipated that his men might run into trouble, so he requested that an Albuquerque mercantile store "ship by [railroad] express 100 rounds of 30–40 soft-nose cartridges, 100 rounds of 30–40 steal jackets, also two boxes of Colts .45 to Cipriano Baca [at] Ft. Wingate N. M." The captain knew his rangers would need all their cash for personal supplies so he added a second request: "Please prepay the express and send [the] bill to me." Fullerton issued Mounted Police Voucher #38 for $18 to cover the cost of the ammunition he had sent to McKinley County.[20]

Cipriano Baca always seemed to have a book with him. On this scout, he carried Owen Wister's novel *The Virginian*. One can almost envision Baca reading the book to Meyer and Perea and the trio discussing the tale over a stream-cooled beer. For weeks, Meyer would end his conversations with, "Smile when you call me that." Perea tried to liven up the evening campfire by teaching his partners to sing "In the Shade of the Old Apple Tree" like a barbershop trio, but Baca couldn't stay in tune. While they were on this long stakeout duty, Meyer taught Perea the fine art of shooting marbles and finally won back his poker losses. Fullerton sent Baca a reply to the lieutenant's letter concerning Perea's IOUs to cover his gambling losses. "Private Perea hasn't any money coming until the first of August. You had better keep a strict account of all the expenses and settle up the first or as soon as the money [Perea's paycheck] is received."[21]

Day after day and week after week, the three range riders continued to move north seeking the cattle thieves that were always just over the horizon as the trio moved north through the Navajo Nation. These Indian lands stretch from Gallup north along the New Mexico–Arizona border toward the Four Corners region. At the Tec Nos Pos trading post, Cipriano bought his wife an intricately designed rug made by the Indians, himself a bedroll blanket, and some trinkets for the children before pushing on into the agricultural oasis of the Mormon country.[22]

On Saturday, July 8, Lieutenant Baca took time to write a field report to Captain Fullerton. "I did not keep data since we left Socorro June 26th as we were detailed principally on a scouting trip with no definite clue of any particular matter, but only one day up to [the] 8th of July that we failed to ride and that was on account of our horses being rode down."[23]

Baca's ranger squad spent their days searching the backcountry seeking evidences, and many nights in range camps visiting with area cowhands. Weeks became months, and the hound and rabbit chase continued deep into the Nacimiento Badlands with its grotesquely shaped terrain of mesas, steep cliffs and rocky plateaus, low hills and open range country leveled along the San Juan, Animas, and La Plata river basins. Angel Peak is the sentinel within the wastelands created millions of years ago by a now vanished inland sea. The ancient Anasazi Indian ruins at Aztec, Chaco Canyon, and Salmon provided excellent hiding places for rustled cattle, and the rangers rode the timeless trails. It is likely that the rangers heard the winds sound like the chant of the Ancient Ones as it captures the spirit of the ages. "Now sleep Anasazi, the waters run quietly by so not to wake you, the sun climbs high in the sky to warm you, the wind and rain come to clean you, the time of your working is past, now sleep Anasazi, sleep." Baca and his men did not disturb the Anasazi.[24]

Finally, the rangers' persistence paid off. "Lieutenant Cipriano Baca of the New Mexico Mounted Police earns his salary," reported the *Socorro Chieftain*'s account. The *Albuquerque Evening Citizen* printed a dispatch detailing Baca's actions by saying that the police "had trailed the Magnum brothers, with 100 head of stolen stock, from Ramah [in southern McKinley County] to Bloomfield [in northern San Juan County] and had corralled the stock and captured the Magnums. If the report is correct, this is a very important capture, as the Magnums are known as desperate cattle rustlers." The report proved accurate. The *Silver City Independent* called the Magnums "a terror to the neighborhood in which they operated and have for some time past been running off stock and terrorizing ranchers."[25]

This Mounted Police scout proved interesting on two levels. Cipriano brought along a Kodak box camera and took some pictures as the rangers escorted the rustlers when they were in custody. These photographs are the only known pictures of the Mounted Police operating in the field. Secondly, on this protracted sojourn into the Four Corners region, the territorial police worked in conjunction with San Juan County sheriff Boone Vaughn and Territorial Cattle Inspector Rhea Stewart, men that Lt. Baca would later recommended as prospects for the Mounted Police.

Baca, Perea, and Meyer had been in the saddle for three months trailing these outlaw brothers. "Captain Fullerton is to be congratulated upon having in his service such men as Baca [and his squad]," commented Aztec's *San Juan County Index*. Rangers Julius Meyer and Octaviano Perea were not listed in many of the New Mexico newspaper stories concerning the Magnum brothers' arrests, but Perea's actions impressed a reporter for the *Evening Herald* of Durango, Colorado, enough to garner him his own headline: "Mounted Policeman Perea Makes Arrest." The story added this praise: "Mr. Perea appears to be a man well

This small 2 × 3 photograph features the prisoner (foreground), with Lt. Baca (in background), with Rangers Perea (at left) and Meyer as they bring in one of the Magnum brothers (Fred Lambert Papers, NMMP/AC).

chosen for this work, that of a mounted policeman or range rider."[26] Julius Meyer also did quality undercover work and was an important part of the successful San Juan County operation against stock thieves, but he did not like reporters.

During the extended absence of his three rangers, Captain Fullerton kept a watchful eye on the families of Baca, Meyer and Perea. Fullerton gave Mrs. Perea $25 to help her and her children with family needs, while he also deposited $55 at Price Brothers Store in Socorro so that Mary Baca could feed her family. He once wrote Libby Meyer just to reassure her that Julius was "all O.K." The captain would forward personal mail that he had received from his men to their wives and he often enclosed family letters along with his official communiqués to Lieutenant Baca. The captain was especially careful to reassure Cipriano that his family was safe in the aftermath of a devastating fire that destroyed Socorro's Windsor Hotel and almost took the whole town square business section with it that frightful night in mid-July 1905.[27]

Captain Fullerton had been unable to join his rangers in the San Juan basin during their hunt for the Magnum brothers, but he was present in spirit with his supplies and encouragement. Fullerton and the rustlers never met, but the shadow of their misdeeds cast an evil cloud over the captain that caused the new governor, Herbert J. Hagerman, to question his integrity. San Juan County Sheriff Boone Vaughn sold one of the recovered head of cattle to cover his posse's travel expenses during the roundup of the stolen animals. Vaughn charged the steer's owner, a Socorro County rancher, the difference between the funds received for the sale of the beef and hide and the sheriff's recovery fees. Governor Hagerman somehow believed that Fullerton illegally profited from this action and used that incident to remove the captain from office.[28]

The Magnum brothers posted bail, but Tom had not yet learned to obey the law. In May 1906, Sheriff Vaughn telegraphed Mounted Police headquarters at Santa Fe to inform Captain Fred Fornoff about Tom Magnum's latest crime. "Arrest and hold Tom Mangum [*sic*] left here [Aztec] sixteenth with cattle for Arizona or Socorro, charge wife decertion [*sic*]." At this point, the Magnum brothers made their escape and slipped into history's shadows.²⁹

* * *

In August 1905, the *Denver Republican* and the *Albuquerque Morning Journal* each carried accounts of night raids upon isolated ranches located in the western mountain ranges of Socorro County. These stories recounted the misadventures of Zenogalache, "Crazy One," a former Apache Indian scout gone "buck" known as the Apache Kid, and his squaw. Ranchers demanded help from Fullerton's Rangers, so the captain ordered Baca to take his squad into the Mogollon Mountains and investigate the cattle killing.

An attack of rheumatism kept Fate Avant from accompanying Baca on this scout, so Herb McGrath came up from Lordsburg and joined the lieutenant and Julius Meyer on the hunt. The trio spent days riding the backcountry, but the police were unable to locate any sign of the elusive renegade and his woman. Meanwhile, Sergeant Lewis who was tracking some suspected cattle rustlers in the Mogollon Mountains stumbled across Zenogalache's trail only to lose it again. Twice the rangers had missed the Crazy One and his woman. A few years later, a miner named Billy Keene claimed he shot and killed the Apache Kid in the mountains near Chloride. No one claimed to have seen the Indian again, and the legend of the Apache Kid lives today with a San Mateo Mountains wilderness area named in his honor.

President Roosevelt threatened to ban intercollegiate football in the United States due to the massive number of injuries and some deaths of players in the fall of 1905. A select committee of college representatives devised a new set of game rules and guidelines for player protection and presented them to the president for his review. He agreed to the improvements, and the gridiron competitions continued. No one knows if Baca, McGrath, and Meyer discussed this controversy around an evening campfire in the Mogollons. This is no idle speculation because Herb McGrath had firsthand knowledge of the college football problems; as a freshman quarterback at New Mexico Agriculture and Mechanical College (New Mexico State University) in 1895, he suffered injury in the big game against their rival, "the University" played in Albuquerque before a rumpus crowd of University of New Mexico fans. Doctors benched McGrath's football career, so he took up the sport of tennis and won two major tournaments during his only season on the court. Ten years after his college days, this tennis player was no dandy; he was a hard-as-nails seasoned peace officer that shot to kill if a man resisted arrest.³⁰

* * *

The 1905 New Mexico Territorial Fair was the largest show to that date, and the main attraction was Fullerton's Rangers. This appearance had taken a personal request from Councilman W.H. Greer, the governor's friend who had spearheaded the Mounted Police Bill through the territorial assembly, and a personal pledge from the chairmen of the two fair committees to pay the police's travel expenses. Only then did Governor Otero order Fullerton to muster the Mounted Police at Albuquerque and later at Las Vegas.

Captain Fullerton saw merit in appearing at the fairs because it gave the public two opportunities to see the new territorial rangers in their "battle gear" as they projected a tough police image. He also felt that two weeks of fair duty would be a great "change for all the boys" from the hard-riding scouts the men had been undertaking. Captain Fullerton planned a public relations show for the occasion. He ordered all the Mounted Police to gather at headquarters on Tuesday, September 19, so the company would travel as a team and arrive at the Albuquerque depot with military precision. The fair organizers placed the Mounted Police corps at the head of the 25th Annual Territorial Parade. The *Albuquerque Evening Citizen* told readers that the appearance of Fullerton's Rangers would "afford fair visitors an opportunity of judging for themselves whether this branch of the law is formidable or not." The paper concluded that the "verdict will most likely be in the affirmative."[31]

Dick Huber was, as usual, the odd man out. He chose not to go to Socorro as ordered but went directly from his Santa Fe home to the Duke City and made a personal show of arriving, thus undermining Fullerton's press plans. Huber, as a friend of Governor Otero and his personal policeman, took advantage of every opportunity to demonstrate his special status to Captain Fullerton. Captain Fullerton wanted his men to present a positive image in their new gray uniforms, so he bought for each of the rangers a new gray hat from the Simon Stern Mercantile Company.[32]

Captain Fullerton led the Mounted Police Company followed by Lieutenant Baca and Sergeant Lewis in the fair parades. The maverick Dick Huber carried the company's guidon.[33] Baca must have had trouble reconciling the prison escapee "bad boy" of Grant County ill fame serving as a territorial ranger. Within the year, Baca disciplined Huber for on-duty misconduct, and Captain Fullerton would suspend this free spirit for disobeying a direct order. Huber resigned. A few months later, the new governor returned Huber to the rangers at the request of the new Mounted Police captain, Huber's whiskey-drinking pal Fred Fornoff.

Ranger John Brophy was a standout with his bandaged face. He looked like a hard-fighting ranger showing the results of facial wounds he received while subduing a prisoner who was trying to escape from his custody. The man had hit Brophy during the struggle, breaking his glasses and cutting the ranger's face. The man went to jail, and John bought new glasses.

Albuquerque's police department was under investigation during the summer of 1905 for the "bad conduct" of its officers and the association with the town's brothel managers. One report called the local police "rotten to the core," so it was no surprise that some enterprising hotel mangers also sought some graft from the taxpayers. The hotel bill for the Mounted Police's stay in Albuquerque became a political issue. Businessmen filed so many false claims with the fair committee that Fullerton was forced to intervene and declare which statements were true and which were bogus. The official tab for housing the rangers was $100.60. If the fair committee had paid all the fake claims, they might have needed to declare bankruptcy. Strange as it may seem today, none of the men who presented fake bills was prosecuted for attempted fraud.[34]

The next week the mounted lawmen mustered in Las Vegas for the northern fair held in the Meadows City. The Las Vegas fair committee had also agreed to pay the rangers' travel expenses after Governor Otero had made it clear that the Mounted Police budget contained no provision for this type of public relations event. The committee was better prepared to handle the Mounted Police's accommodations than Albuquerque had been.[35]

These two fair parades were the only times that the complete corps of Fullerton's Rangers were ever assembled at the same place at the same time; two policeman had missed the muster call and swearing-in ceremony. It would have been very enlightening to be a silent observer as these eleven territorial lawmen took the measure of each other. Fullerton's Rangers established the precedent of the territorial/state fair duty now preformed by the New Mexico State Police during the annual New Mexico Expo, the state fair held at Albuquerque each fall.

The two 1905 territorial fairs proved to be a pleasant diversion for the territorial police. Some of the men, like Sergeant Bob Lewis, even brought their families with them to the festivities.[36] Ever so quickly, however, the fun faded and duty called. While Fullerton and his men where in Las Vegas, the governor's office received urgent requests for Mounted Police assistance, so telegrams were sent asking that the Mounted Police return to patrol duty and aid local authorities in Guadalupe and Rio Arriba counties.[37] The other rangers returned home and renewed the business they had left unfinished.

Lieutenant Baca and Rangers McGrath and Putman took the passenger train south from Las Vegas to Socorro. While en route, they prevented a holdup of the Santa Fe train just south of Belen. A newspaper account said that the presence of the heavily armed gray-clad rangers "frightened the would-be robbers, who escaped in the darkness."[38] Baca and Putman detrained at Socorro while McGrath continued on to Deming where he changed trains to reach Lordsburg.

Baca took time out from his Mounted Police duties to take part in a joyous family event. Mary's 24-year-old schoolteacher sister Ruby Hamilton Berry married 44-year-old John Ellsworth Griffith on Wednesday evening, November first. They said their vows before friends and family at the Episcopal Church of the Epiphany at Socorro. This was Ruby's first marriage and John's second. Three years later, the couple had a son they named William Ellsworth Griffith.[39]

* * *

"There have been, and still are, too many writers who, although they have never seen an Indian in their lives, have published tragical stories of their treachery and cruelty," wrote Simon Pokagon, chief of the Pottawatomie nation in 1897. The chief continued,

> Mothers, for generations past, have frightened their children into obedience with that dreaded scarecrow, "Look out, or the Injuns will get you!"; creating in the infant mind a false prejudice against our race, which has given birth to that base slander, "There is no good Injun, but a dead one." It is therefore no wonder that we are hated by some worse than Satan hates the salvation of human souls.[40]

President Theodore Roosevelt was on record expressing a negative option of Native Americans, saying, "I don't go so far as to think that the only good Indians are the dead Indians, but I believe that nine out of ten are, and I shouldn't like to enquire too closely into the case of the tenth. The most vicious cowboy has more moral principle than the average Indian."

The Mounted Police Act mandated that the rangers must deal with "marauding Indians or bands of hostile Indians." Using colorful nineteenth-century language, the *Socorro Chieftain* told the story. "The noble redmen of New Mexico are showing a reckless if not a contemptuous disregard of the game laws of the territory and also the laws regulating their absence from their reservations."[41] In early November 1905, Captain Fullerton wrote the territorial game-and-fish warden concerning the Indian troubles. "Lieut. Baca and Meyers [sic] will leave Rahma [Ramah] the first of the week, and go Southwest from there into the Datil country and will investigate those Indian affairs, and will arrest any and all [Indians] that [they] find out hunting and confiscate their belongings."[42]

Page B. Otero, serving his third year as the territory's first game-and-fish warden, was excited about the proposed help from the Mounted Police. "I am heartily glad that some action will be taken at once to stop the depredations of these raiding devils. I have repeatedly notified the Indian Agents, but with, apparently, no results." Otero suggested a plan to Captain Fullerton: "The only remedy which I can now see, is to arrest, prosecute, and give them the extent of the law." In concluding, Otero said, "I earnestly hope that Cipriano and Meyers [sic] will accomplish something, and should be glad to hear of it when they do."[43]

A few days later, Warden Otero wrote to the superintendent of the Navajo Indian Agency at Fort Defiance, Arizona.

> I am receiving letters from the settlers there [western Socorro County] complaining of these Indian Depredations. In many instances when game was scarce they have killed cattle & sheep. I have notified the New Mexico Mounted Rangers [Police] and a party of them left for the area the first of this week.

Otero also said he was concerned that if the killing did not stop "there will be serious trouble." He concluded, "My instructions to the Rangers are to arrest, prosecute and confiscate all carcasses."[44]

Baca and Meyer were in San Juan County finishing some court business connected with their recent outlaw roundup. When they completed their business, they planned to pick up their horses and pack gear at Bluewater, in western Valencia County, and head south into western Socorro County. The two men left Farmington via the Denver & Rio Grande Railroad, north into Colorado, then south along the Rio Grande into Santa Fe. The rangers left San Juan County just before a smallpox outbreak ravaged through the D&RG crew based in that area. In the City of Holy Faith the two rangers switched to the main Santa Fe line and traveled to Albuquerque then west on the Atlantic and Pacific rails toward Bluewater. This long, roundabout trip saved the lawmen days in the saddle. The *Santa Fe New Mexican* reported that Baca and Meyer had left Albuquerque on Sunday evening, November 5, explaining that the territorial lawmen were headed into the western mountains. The newspaper reported, "They went on duty."

Page Otero was the older brother of Governor Miguel A. Otero. He served as New Mexico's first game-and-fish warden and later as a New Mexico territorial ranger and a deputy U.S. marshal, but once had been a boomtown vigilante. Born in to a wealthy family, he died broke, in debt, and shunned by his own relatives (NMMP/AC).

A few days later, Captain Fullerton wrote to a Socorro County rancher concerning the Indian hunters and the Mounted Police's investigation. "They [Baca and Meyer] went by way of Albuquerque and from there to Bluewater where they had left their horses. From there they went to the Datil [Mountains]. I instructed them to arrest everyone they could find and bring them [the wayward Indians] in. We will see what the law will do for them."[45]

Native Americans, wards of the federal government, were illegally hunting on national forest lands, yet no federal officers would help with the search for the culprits. In fact, Marshal Foraker had expressed the sentiment that it was "high time that the Territorial officials of Arizona and New Mexico devoted some of their energies [manpower and money] in this behalf [law enforcement]."[46] To one of his Socorro County ranch neighbors, Fullerton wrote, "The [federal] government does not seem to care to take hold of the matter and we want to do all we can to stop the Indians from killing this game. I should have sent more men had I had them." The captain then brought the Patterson area rancher up to date on the rangers' search. "I sent two men about 10 days ago, Lieutenant Baca and Meyers [sic]. No doubt they will arrest all that they find and bring them in; that was the instructions I gave them. I am looking for them anytime."[47]

There is a motto that says a person cannot change every problem they face, but that nothing changes until they address the problem. Page Otero faced his Indian problems when he wrote Captain Fullerton that he had two reasons why he did not personally go after the Indian violators. He said that he paid his deputies on commission and that they would only receive money if they made an arrest and won the prosecution. "Where I to go out [looking for lawbreakers] I would soon be without anyone to help me." Otero's second reason also dealt with money; "I carry [life] insurance and have been warned on three different occasions when I went after Indians, not to do so again or my policy would be cancelled."

Otero told everyone who would listen or read his letters that he would appoint any rancher or settler in the territory as a deputy game warden if they would go after the rebellious Indians.

> The only thing I can see to be done, since the Government sees fit to recognize these Indians as citizens, is to organize for their own protection and relief. I think if the settlers would kill off a few of them it might be the means of attracting a little attention from the Department [of Indian Affairs] at Washington & bring about the desired result. I heartily wish this would be done.[48]

The tone of Page Otero's words is disturbing to individuals in this era because killing people to attract "a little attention" has the ring of a barbaric nature. Even so, we should not place our society's value upon the people of 1905 New Mexico Territory. Both Page Otero and John Fullerton had close encounters with hostile Indians during the 1870s and 1880s. The western Indian wars had been over for less than 20 years, but they still held vivid memories for Spanish, Anglos, and Native Americans because the ghosts of our youth never leave us. It would seem that a hatred of Indians still ran deep in the soul of the 47-year-old Page Otero and to a lesser degree in his younger brother, the territorial governor.

Fortunately for the wandering Apache and Pueblo Indians and the Anglo-Spanish settlers in western New Mexico, Captain Fullerton put duty above whatever personal feelings he may have harbored toward Indians. Fullerton took no action toward helping Game Warden Otero make deputies of Socorro County ranchers so they could legally hunt Indians and kill them on sight. He did not want another Indian war just to get "the desired results" of the Indians observing the territorial game laws. The game laws were new, and the Indians' hunting habits were centuries old. It was not a matter of right or wrong, but new laws versus old ways, and Fullerton felt the incident could be settled without the loss of human life.

"While Lieutenant Cipriano Baca was returning [to headquarters] the other day," reported the *Silver City Enterprise* quoting Captain Fullerton, "together with Private Myers [*sic*], from a scouting trip, they came upon nine San Felipe Indians who had in their possession four female deer hides." Baca did not make any arrests, because the Indians "were in an ugly frame of mind and that he would have had to kill some of them to accomplish an arrest, so he ordered them home, and will arrest them on the reservation later." Discretion is the better part of valor, and Baca understood that principle of law enforcement.[49]

Did Baca have flashback memories of a similar incident he had with a drunken angry mob of Pueblo Indians? It is possible that Baca recalled his Taos encounter just a year before when he faced death by upset Indians. It is only reasonable to assume that he did not want a repeat of that explosive situation.

True to his promise, Lt. Baca and Julius Meyer conducted an expanded investigation, and they discovered that 150 Indians from San Felipe, Jemez and Isleta Pueblos had been illegally hunting deer in Socorro County, out of season and without a permit. The *El Paso Times* reported that the two rangers had ordered all the Indian hunters "back to their respective reservations and that nearly all of them have complied with the order."

Lieutenant Baca and Page Otero had corresponded about a similar incident in October. Then the Mounted Police took no action because the federal Indian officers would do nothing to assist the rangers. This time the territorial officers, acting as deputy game wardens, went to the pueblos and with the help of the local Indian policemen found the homes of the suspects and had them arrested. Some considered this action unusual, but a few months earlier Page Otero had commissioned all of the Mounted Police as deputy game wardens. A territorial ranger could not earn any arrest fees, but a deputy game warden worked on a fee structure. A large number of Native Americans received citations for killing game out of season and were bound over to the district courts because the alleged hunting incidents had occurred off the reservation lands. None of the Indian hunters who where arrested are mentioned in Mounted Police reports nor are they reported in official territorial police records.[50]

Page Otero had been trying for months to get the territory's Indian superintendent, or any federal help, to restrain Indians from off-season hunting on federal forest reserves. Finally, Otero turned to the Mounted Police, and the rangers were quick to respond. Headlines across the territory heralded their actions. In the wake of this favorable press attention, Baca's slow-to-move federal pals now needed to save face, so they staged a raid on the Jemez Pueblo.

"Three Indians were arrested by Fred Fornoff, as I understand, for violation of game laws," wrote Page Otero to Captain Fullerton. "I do not understand by which authority Mr. Fornoff acts, or whether it is part of his duty. Anyhow the offense was committed in Socorro Co. & the Indians should be tried there. Will you look into this?"[51] The territorial game-and-fish warden was a former deputy U.S. Marshal and understood federal law, thus his question concerning Fornoff's authority to arrest the Indians. Once again, Fullerton's men cleaned up behind Deputy U.S. Marshal Fred Fornoff.

The whole affair was a *locum tenens*—stopgap measure. Indian hunters did not understand the nature of their crime because the truth was that someone had forgotten to inform the tribal leaders about the new hunting laws. The illegal hunting incidents ceased once the tribal leaders received an explanation of the new regulations and conveyed this information to their brothers. The territorial game-and-fish department had official notices printed in English and Spanish and widely posted. The new governor fired Territorial Game and Fish Warden Page Otero in early 1906.

* * *

The Christmas season, both religious and secular, did not gain wide popularity in the United States until the middle and latter half of the 1880s and over the decades has elicited strong emotions in Americans. Quite often, these feelings tend toward a rage against soulless material consumption. "There are worlds of money wasted, at this time of year, in getting things that nobody wants, and nobody cares for after they are got." Those modern-sounding words where written in 1850 by author Harriet Beecher Stowe and still ring clear even across the ages.

Cipriano Baca always enjoyed being around children, and he really liked to spend *La Navidad* with his family. A popular Baca family Christmas activity was Cipriano's bedtime reading of Clement C. Moore's poetic tale "A Visit from St. Nicholas" adapted to *Pancho Clos*' dropping by the Baca house. Can you imagine Baca dressed as Pancho Clos giving out red-and-white striped candy canes to the neighborhood kids? The Hispanic version of Saint Nicholas dressed in a big sombrero, a poncho worn over his red shirt, a face full of whiskers, and sandals. The family attended mass, together with their relatives, *en la Nochebuena*, on Christmas Eve. For well over half a century, the extended Berry clan would remain a stalwart family in their support of the Episcopal Church of the Epiphany in Socorro.

Unlike native Mexican neighbors, the Baca family did not wait for *El Dia de Los Reyes* (January 6, Epiphany or Twelfth Night, the day the Wise Men arrived with gifts for the Bethlehem baby) for their children to receive gifts from *Papa Noel* (Santa Claus). In the Baca household many holiday gifts were handcrafted, but they were given with much love and joy.

* * *

To Cipriano Baca the holiday must have seemed all too short, but duty was a strong motivator within Cipriano's character. "Do your duty in all things," Robert E. Lee had said. "You cannot do more; you should never wish to do less." Once Baca had read the former Confederate general turned college president's words, he took them as his own motto.

During the last days of 1905, some people considered Albuquerque's weather "frightful." Snow was so deep on the plains that railroad engineers where constantly concerned about windblown drifts blocking the tracks. On one day, the temperature even dropped to 15 degrees below zero at Laguna Pueblo. Closer to Socorro, a postman had his horse freeze to death under him as he tried to deliver the mail between Magdalena and Burley.[52]

On December 30, 1905, Lieutenant Baca loaded his pack gear and his saddle and weapons aboard an express car and then left Socorro on that Saturday-morning train headed east into the central range country. He spent New Year's Eve in Las Vegas and the next morning loaded his tack on two rented horses and took up the trail of some stock thieves. For the next 18 days, Baca slowly made his way across San Miguel and Guadalupe counties. On this scout, Baca always seemed to be moving just one day ahead of bad weather. The area around Vaughn had 15 inches of snow on the ground with "prospects of more," and the Pastura country had over two and a half feet of snow base. Baca kept daily watch for Rangers Julius Meyer and Rafael Gomez whom he expected to join him in Guadalupe County and help make this winter patrol through east central New Mexico.

Charles Ilfeld, a wealthy Las Vegas retail and wholesale merchant and large Guadalupe County sheep rancher, had complained to his friend Governor Otero that he had suffered some recent raids on his herds. Otero, who, in partnership with J.W. Raynolds, the territorial secretary, owned the 30-mile-square Salado Livestock Company along 30 miles of the Salado River, understood the problem and requested a Mounted Police investigation. The *Washington Post* had once commented upon Miguel Otero's ranch, saying, "The governor is one of the most extensive sheep breeders in the southwest and his flocks in Guadalupe County aggregate 65,000 head."

Large sheep herds moving in large valleys guarded by lone herders made it easy for a quick-acting band of night raiders to slip among the woolies and drive away a few head on a moonless night. Six sheep one night, eight on another night, and so in a short time thieves could gather a substantial herd gleaned from many outfits. The sheep rustlers would quickly move the sheep out of the area and sell them in a market across the territory.[53]

Charles M. O'Donel, general manager of the Red River Valley Company that operated the three-quarters-of-a-million-acre Bell Ranch and Farm lying along the Canadian River in eastern San Miguel and Guadalupe counties, wrote to Captain Fullerton in November 1905, seeking help to stop fence cutters and cattle and horse stealing on the Bell property. One of the big problems for the Bell Ranch operation was the fact that it required a one-hundred-and-forty-mile fence to enclose the outer boundary of the property. Since large sections of this fence line crossed through heavily timbered terrain, it was easy for longropers to slip into an area behind the line riders, cut the fence, and drive out a small herd. They could just as easily bring in a wagon at night, kill and butcher some beef, and escape before daylight.[54]

On most occasions, ranchers welcome the spring and summer rains because on the average one cow will drank about 15 gallons of water a day during the warm months. The Bell Ranch, which was running about 25,000 head of cattle, needed about 375,000 gallons of water per day during this period. Deep water wells with wind-powered pumps and earth impounds were a major necessity for survival of the herd. No one dreamed that New Mexico's eastern rangelands could ever receive too much rain, but the unexpected happened.

The Canadian River basin experienced phenomenal rains during the last days of September 1904, and the U.S. Geological Survey reported that these rains caused the worst flood ever measured in New Mexico, over 36 feet above the riverbed. Records suggest that at least six people lost their lives and many small river settlements, as well as large sections of railroad track, were destroyed, while on the Bell Ranch hundreds of acres of farmlands and orchards, as well as buildings and livestock, were washed away.[55] Now, a year after the massive flood the economic loss was being compounded by livestock deprivations. Each cow had an economic value and must be accounted for as a profit or loss. In 1895, O'Donel's predecessor had set the tone: "I am opposed to cow stealing in any form and I cannot afford to be slack about it."[56] This 1905–1906 loss was just as unacceptable to the ranch company's current board of directors and investors.

Captain Fullerton was cognizant of O'Donel's leadership role in the New Mexico Cattle and Horse Growers' Association as well as the American Live Stock Association. He also understood Ilfeld's financial influence within the Republican Party's Central Committee. The dual requests from Ilfeld and O'Donel, and the encouragement of Governor Otero, for a ranger patrol in the east range country was reason enough for Fullerton to require Baca's presence in San Miguel and Guadalupe counties in the midst of a winter snowstorm.[57]

It was a slow and arduous journey for Baca and his horses. He spent most nights under the stars, but on rare occasion, a line cabin or vacated homestead made a welcome shelter. While Baca was cutting a trail through winter snow, Wall Street investors were blazing their own trail into the history books. On January 12, 1906, the Dow Jones Average closed above the 100 mark for the first time in the history of the New York Stock Exchange.

One day a Santa Fe newspaper reporter asked Captain Fullerton if the recent winter storms were impeding the operation of the police. "The severe weather in central New Mexico has interfered with the work of the police to some extent.... I don't like to talk too much about their movements just at present because it might prevent the capture of several of the outlaws." A short time later, Captain Fullerton was able to tell the media that he had received a report from Lieutenant Baca informing him that he had arrested the leaders of the "Robber's Roost" rustlers.[58]

Thirty days after Lieutenant Baca set out on his scout of the winter range country, he sat down at a typewriter and composed an outline of his activities. Baca described his trip thus:

> January 1st 1906 went to Gallinas Springs [in San Miguel County] about 40 miles east of [Las] Vegas; 2nd to Bell Ranch twelve miles south of Gallinas Springs; 3rd [went to second] Bell Ranch southwest of first Ranch (Bell Ranch) which is two miles south of Casaus [in Guadalupe County]. From 5th to 16th inst. I rode to different sections of this county [Guadalupe] getting evidence against horse and cattle thieves and locating horses stolen from difference [sic] counties, and whereabouts of criminals; 17th inst. I went to Pintada [still in Guadalupe County] thirty miles east of here [Casaus]; 18th inst. I arrested three horse thieves; 19th inst I rounded up horses and cattle.... On the 20th inst. I brought my three prisoners to Bell Ranch two miles from Casaus Post Office; on account of witnesses I returned with my prisoners to Ilfeld Sheep Ranch; 22nd inst., after arriving there Justice of the Peace would not act on account of not having Blanks [legal forms used to record the actions of a preliminary hearing] or any Law Books; I returned with my prisoners to Casaus 23rd inst; witnesses arrived 25th inst from Ilfeld Ranch; hearing held 26th; prisoners waived examination; committed by Justice of the Peace to Santa Rosa Jail on default of bond."[59]

Captain Fullerton arrived in Santa Fe on Friday afternoon February 23, 1906, for a scheduled meeting with Governor Hagerman. A reporter met him at the railroad depot and asked the captain about reports that outlaws had murdered Sergeant Lewis. Fullerton explained that Sergeant Lewis was not dead as had been rumored by the Santa Fe press, but he had received a telegram two days before from Lewis, who was in Old Mexico on assignment, and that he was very much alive and in good health. Fullerton then mentioned that Lieutenant Baca and his police squad had "just about cleared out the organization of cattle rustlers and horse thieves who have been operating in that neighborhood [Robber's Roost] for so long. I received a dispatch from him at noon today saying that he had just arrived in

Santa Rosa with a man who had stolen four horses. He recovered the animals and brought them into town."

The *Albuquerque Morning Journal*, in an expanded account of the longroper arrests, called Baca's captives a "desperate gang of cutthroat horse thieves" and said that they had "terrorized a wide section of country for a number of years." The ranger lieutenant, "after riding most of the time, night and day, for a week he effected [*sic*] the arrest near Mesa Arason." The newspaper said that some of the missing "animals were in the corral of the robbers who had just begun the butchering of the sheep" as Cipriano rode up to three men. Baca arrested Elisio Chavez, Gregorio Romero, and Liborio Lucero and took them up the Pecos River to Anton Chico and then to the Juan Pias place, both settlements in northwestern Guadalupe County, looking for a peace justice to hold a hearing, but "in each case the justice was 'out.'" Later, Captain Fullerton explained to a Santa Fe reporter Baca's dilemma. "This was necessary because local justices of the peace did not like to take the responsibility of trying the men at preliminary hearings for fear that they would be injured by other members of the gang. This outfit is thoroughly organized and has been carrying on this work for a number of years."[60]

Santa Rosa was the center of ranching country that dated back to the early 1820s. The town was now also headquarters to the area's developing railroad system. The influx of railroad men caused the creation of other businesses in the form of saloons, dance halls, gambling dens, and an assortment of general undesirables, including women of ill fame. Since Santa Rosa had no town police force, and the community was the county seat, the sheriff and his deputy had their hands full keeping the lid on troublemakers and little time to patrol the rangelands. This lack of rural law enforcement gave Guadalupe County the nickname "Robber's Roost."

A reporter asked Captain Fullerton how Lieutenant Baca had been able to capture the three leaders of the roost rustlers without firing a shot. "Since the force was mustered in last April, not a man has been killed, although several of them [rangers] have been under fire. Most of the outlaws, however, surrender as soon as the police find them, which speaks well for the men of service." What Captain Fullerton did not need to mention was that Cipriano Baca had become a living legend among the Hispanic population. They considered him a man of courage who did his sworn duty and sought justice for all people; one man with courage makes a majority.

A few weeks after a territorial ranger rode into Guadalupe County, newspaper headlines were proclaiming a successful raid. Baca's official statement said that he arrested four men; the forth man was Lucero's father who owned the corral that contained the stolen livestock. Chavez and Romero were bound over to the Guadalupe County Grand Jury where they were indicted for larceny and held for trial; the lucky father and son were released pending further investigation. Baca's rustler raid netted four horses, two cows, and a calf stolen from ranches in Socorro, Guadalupe, Bernalillo, Union and San Miguel Counties. The 148 recovered sheep belonged to Charles Ilfeld's sheep operation.[61]

The leader of the "Robber's Roost" rustlers, a 27-year-old widower named Elisio Chavez from the hamlet of Cohalleta, received two years in the territorial penitentiary at his trial in April 1906. The five-foot-tall day laborer had a knife cut on the inside of his right thigh. The second man brought to trial was five-foot-eight-inch-tall Gregorio Romero, a 27-year-old married day laborer. Convicted as charged, he got a one-year sentence at

Santa Fe. Both men received reduced time because of their work on road gangs building the Scenic Road north to Colorado.[62]

Sheriff Felipe Sanchez y Baca reluctantly accepted the suspected livestock thieves because the Guadalupe County courthouse was under repair, and the jail was not as secure as it would otherwise have been. The sheriff had sent most of the county's inmates to Quay County during the remodeling process, but in one of those twists of fate, three of the Guadalupe County prisoners escaped from custody during their stay in Tucumcari. These escapes, coupled with a suspected collusion with local cattle thieves, caused Captain Fullerton to request that Governor Herbert J. Hagerman investigate Quay County Sheriff Alex Street for malfeasance in office. Hagerman ordered Attorney General George Prichard to examine the public performance of both Street and the local district attorney Merritt C. Mechem. The issue of nonperformance was never resolved before Hagerman, Prichard, and Fullerton were all out of office. Street joined the Mounted Police force in 1910, and Mechem became a state governor and U.S. senator.[63]

The *Sun* was the Santa Rosa newspaper. It almost certainly published an account of Lieutenant Baca's extended journey across the frozen snow-covered rangeland of central New Mexico, his capture of the three suspects, and their final incarceration in the local jail. Unfortunately for the historical record, no known issues of the *Santa Rosa Sun* have survived from the era when Fullerton Rangers rode the range.

The region Cipriano Baca had traveled through had two and a half feet of snow on the ground in the low country and over three feet in the mountains according to a weather report published in the *El Paso Times*. "Stock and sheep are suffering greatly from lack of food," said an *El Paso Evening News* report and added that some ranchers were "at present cutting down pine trees for the starving animals to feed on." The territory's remote areas had another problem as wild animals were also on the hunt for food during these days of fierce weather. "The coyotes are still plentiful around Tres Piedras. They come right into town before dark and keep the dogs barking all night."[64]

History is often composed of strange phenomena. A century after the December 1905 blizzard hit north central New Mexico, the weather gods replayed the scenario and again blanketed the same area with a massive layer of snowfall. The weather stranded travelers for days as the twelve northeastern counties received over 30 inches of ground snow with 10- to 15-foot drifts. The National Guard used aircraft to drop feed to starving livestock and rescue missions. It took weeks to dig out of the storm, rescue stranded hikers, and resume normal business activities. The state's highway condition hotline came under attack for failure to update their information in a timely manner. This information lag needlessly stranded many motorists in troubled areas.[65]

In late January 1906, Rangers Julius Meyer and Rafael Gomez were finally able to reach Casaus and their delayed rendezvous with Lieutenant Baca. "On account of snow, bad weather and long distance they were delayed on [the] road from 26th December 1905 until January 22nd 1906." These two bone-weary rangers had traveled horseback through two feet of snow on muddy roads, and continued daily bad weather, for 28 days to reach Lieutenant Baca. Gomez, a former Santa Fe County officer, had replaced the rebel ranger Dick Huber on December 14, thus becoming the last man to be commissioned a Mounted Policeman under Captain John F. Fullerton.[66]

A.B. Harris, a large Guadalupe County ranch manager located near Sunnyside, complimented Captain Fullerton for the "good work of the Mounted Police under your command." He elaborated further by saying, "I have the pleasure to report that the recent operations of your men in the Salado Pastura district resulted in the capture of nearly all the known law breakers of the locality."[67]

Lieutenant Baca's Mounted Police strike force did not take a well-earned vacation. Now supplemented with Ranger John Brophy from Clayton, they roamed the plains of northeastern New Mexico where more cattle rustlers were at work. The *Tucumcari News* took note of the new trouble spot and told readers,

> The New Mexico Mounted Police should run these desperados out of the country as soon as it is possible to do so, and we understand Cipriano Baca is doing it as fast as he possibly can. He with two or three other [territorial] police have been making it warm for this class of criminals in Union County lately. The stockmen and farmer should render every assistance possible to the police and local officials until these depredations are history in New Mexico.

A week later, the Clayton *Enterprise* was able to cap this longroper roundup tale by reporting the success of the mission with seven men arrested, 150 stolen sheep found, and a number of horses and cattle recovered. "This breaks up one of the most thoroughly organized gangs of desperados in northeastern New Mexico."

The actions of Baca and his men in Union, Quay, San Miguel, and Guadalupe Counties were a public relations coup for the Mounted Police; a squad of Fullerton's Rangers had broken up another gang of long riders. The rangers' captain told the *Socorro Chieftain* that Lieutenant Baca's patrol "has the worst assignment of the whole force, but is doing effective work. Baca has orders not to quit till he has cleaned out the whole gang that has been terrorizing eastern New Mexico." Many would-be livestock thieves changed their ambitions and continued their honest endeavors instead of chancing an encounter with the ghostlike Territorial Mounted Police.[68]

Within weeks of taking the oath of office as territorial governor, Herbert J. Hagerman received a lengthy petition signed by some citizens of Anton Chico concerning the harassment of two fellow residents by a "Mounted Policeman" and condoned by Lieutenant Baca. The matter under investigation concerned night-rider fence cutters operating in the region. Hagerman sent letters to Captain Fullerton and C.M. O'Donel inquiring about the alleged incident.

The Bell Ranch manager was quick to reply to Governor Hagerman's request. "The gist of the whole matter is this. Those Anton Chico people are nearly all of them, up to their neck in this fence-cutting business." *Los Culpables*, the guilty ones, in this complaint were the citizens of the community in question. O'Donel went on to explain that two locals had provided him and Baca information implicating them and some of the men who signed the petition sent to the governor in the local depredations. His summation was concise,

> The allegation that Lieut. Cipriano Baca countenanced the employment of force or threats to obtain these statements is not worthy of a moment's belief. I have had abundant opportunity to form an opinion of that officer's efficiency. I have found him to be most intelligent and thoroughly well informed as to the nature and value of evidence- as well as cool and determined and tireless in the pursuit of criminals.

O'Donel ended his letter to the governor saying, "I thank you very much for the opportunity afforded me to put you in possession of the facts as I know them."

Meanwhile in Las Vegas, Lieutenant Baca took a few moments to compose a three-page report for Captain Fullerton detailing the rangers' fence-cutting investigation and Jose Sosteno Baca's role as a "fake" territorial policeman. The turncoat fence cutters Pilar Martinez and Monico Chaves faced arrest along with some of the men who signed the petition to Governor Hagerman. It was a long time before anyone cut Bell Ranch fences allowing their cattle to wonder off the home range, and no one ever again impersonated a Mounted Police officer. Following ten weeks of cold camps and wretched backcountry trails, lonely stakeouts and tough detective work, Lieutenant Baca dismissed his small squad of range riders. The *Socorro Chieftain* bragged that Cipriano's ranger team was "a good example of the service which the Mounted Police force as a whole is rendering the territory."[69]

John Brophy returned to Clayton, deciding he missed his wife and two sons too much during long ranger patrols. By the end of March he had found a new job as the town's night marshal. Rafael Gomez returned to Santa Fe, and in mid–March 1906, the *Santa Fe New Mexican* said, "Lieutenant Cipriano Baca of the mounted police has returned to his home in Socorro after two months of active service in suppressing law breakers and capturing criminals."

C.M. O'Donel requested that a ranger remain in the region because the fence-cutting raids had stopped "due in great measure to the presence in our camp of a member of the Police Force." Captain Fullerton ordered Julius Meyer to stay in Guadalupe County and make his headquarters at Casaus, near the Bell Ranch range. O'Donel wrote that Meyer was "a very efficient officer" and "his knowledge of Spanish and acquaintance with the native people render him well qualified for work of this kind [territorial policeman]." Meyer's wife, at this time, was of Hispanic heritage and uncertain of his assignment status; she left their home in the Anglo hamlet of Estancia and moved back with her parents in Albuquerque.[70]

* * *

With the advent of warmer weather, Captain John F. Fullerton issued orders that during the spring of 1906 his rangers would ride nonstop scouts until the long riders were all captured, killed, or driven from the territory. Sergeant Lewis was on assignment in Old Mexico, and the other rangers were covering their patrol areas. Captain Fullerton told the *Santa Fe New Mexican* that Lieutenant Baca's March scout had netted six rustler suspects, 40 head of stolen sheep, and the same number of lost or missing horses. The *Socorro Chieftain* added that some of "the thieves captured had been stealing cattle, butchering them and selling the beef in the [railroad] grading camps on the Belen cut-off [connecting the eastern railroads with the main Santa Fe line running down the Rio Grande]." The account continued, saying, "A lot of [cattle] hides were found hidden under the rocks near the house in which the thieves were arrested." One of the men taken in this raid was the man who disposed of the booty gathered by two Socorro County rustlers brought east to the railroad construction line. "Needless to say, the wild and picturesque career of this sweet trio has been interrupted for a time at least."[71]

In early February 1906, Col. Robert Hannigan, a young rancher residing in western Socorro County, had been kidnapped and held for ransom. The *Santa Fe New Mexican* editorialized that "extraordinary efforts should be made by officials of Grant and Socorro Counties and by the mounted police to apprehend Holliman, the desperado who was the chief actor, and his confederates" who staged the kidnap. The newspaper opined that the outlaws' capture, trial and conviction will mean much for the cause of justice in the Sunshine Territory. The New Mexican is of the opinion that Captain Fullerton of the Mounted Police will take effective steps to rid that section of New Mexico of these lawless characters, if he has not already done so.

The newspaper account concluded with a challenge, saying,

> If Captain Fullerton and his men should be successful in arresting the crowd of rustlers said to be located in the Mogollon country they would add a beautiful feather to those already in their hat for good work done.[72]

Cipriano Baca had developed into a clever undercover investigator, and in March 1906, his intended foe was the bandit Bob Holliman. The Mounted Police held a warrant for the kidnapper's arrest, and Baca knew that Holliman had been reported hiding in central Texas near his parents' property at Brady, a farm and ranch community on the stage route halfway between Abilene and Austin. Other reports had Holliman sighted along the Mexican boarder in Santa Cruz County, Arizona. The Texas Rangers, the Arizona Rangers, and local law enforcement officers had not been able to locate Holliman in their patrol area.

A Deming businessman provided New Mexico's territorial police with a confidential tip that Holliman's wife and teenage daughter were living in north central Arizona. Baca went to Arizona Territory to work his tracker's magic. Globe's *Arizona Silver Belt* reported that "Cypriano Baca, a ranger of New Mexico," had been in the area. "It is said that Holliman's wife is a resident here which led the New Mexico officer to believe that Holliman would very likely be found in this vicinity." The concept was sound, but the timing was amiss. The *El Paso Times* reported that Baca "has left Arizona without his man." It rained on Baca during the trip.

Cipriano Baca had missed Holliman by one day, but the case remained near the top of the Mounted Police's active case list. Sometime later, Lieutenant Baca and Sergeant Lewis arrested two men implicated in the kidnapping plot. Due to the failure of the Grand Jury to return an indictment against the two suspects, the court released the men. The Mounted Police closed their case. A California deputy sheriff finally located Mrs. Holliman and her daughter staying with her father at San Jose in Santa Clara County. Her husband was not located.[73]

* * *

The year 1906 held promise of being a milestone year for the citizens of New Mexico Territory. President Roosevelt and the Congress were considering legislation that would finally grant statehood to New Mexico, and the territory had a young, enthusiastic, and progressive governor. New Mexico's company of Mounted Police was looking forward to their first birthday and a continued growing level of community support.

The *Albuquerque Morning Journal* reflected this positive sentiment, saying,

> The force has recovered hundreds of head of stolen cattle and horses and sheep and it has apprehended a great many stock thieves and most important of all it has spread its moral influence among the lawless characters of the thinly settled districts, and has thus put an end to stock thieving, which up to the time of creation of the force [in March 1905], flourished almost without interruption.

The account also contained some editorializing by saying,

> That the Mounted Police force has been a very powerful influence for the preservation of order and the protection of property there can be no question. It is just now getting on an effi-

While doing detective work, Fred Fornoff was slow and methodical. One of his favorite comments was, "Give it time," but when action was called for, he led the charge. The former Rough Rider was a very effective ranger captain, but Fornoff has never received the credit he deserved as a peace officer (Fred Fornoff Papers, NMMP/AC).

cient basis; after several false starts, due to natural mistakes in organization of such a force. To abolish it now would undo much of the good work it has done.

The *Santa Fe New Mexican* also lent its voice to praising the Mounted Police, commenting,

> The record of the police since its organization is very good and so far has justified the passage of the act creating the force. Much has been done towards suppressing cattle rustling and stock depravations generally by its members and the expenses incurred in its maintenance so far have been made up several times over by the good work done.

Lt. Cipriano Baca had been the stabilizing force that kept the ranger concept alive during those early difficult days.[74]

Governor Herbert J. Hagerman fired three of his department heads that had loyally served under his predecessor, Miguel A Otero, three months after taking office as territorial chief executive. In late March 1906, Hagerman removed Otero's brother Page as the game-and-fish warden and asked Holm O. Bursum to give up his post as superintendent of the territorial prison. The governor was not impressed with Captain Fullerton's leadership, so he just let the captain's ranger commission expire and named a new chief for the Mounted Police. Fullerton's men were not sure what to do about the removal of their captain and were even less sure of their own fate.[75]

The new ranger chief, former deputy U.S. Marshal Fred Fornoff of Albuquerque, quickly called a summit with the rangers for Monday afternoon, April 2, 1906, at the new Mounted Police office at the territorial capitol in Santa Fe. Fornoff may have first congratulated the Mounted Police on their past year of hard work, reassured them of his support in that continued effort, and then promised them a new style of field leadership. There was a brief exchange of questions and answers, and the newly formed Company II of the New Mexico Mounted Police went into service.

C.M. O'Donel was quick to congratulate Fornoff upon his appointment and just as quick to praise Cipriano Baca. "I hope that the report I have seen in the newspapers to the effect that Lieutenant Baca will be retained in that rank is correct. I have had occasion to see something of that officer's work and have formed a very high opinion of his energy and ability."[76]

Fornoff may have used the opportunity to confer with Baca and Lewis concerning the operation of the police and their duty expectations. Fornoff said he needed someone to cover the office when he was in the field so he was going to request that Governor Hagerman reappoint Dick Huber to assume Octaviano Perea's vacated post. There is no record that Baca cautioned Fornoff about Huber, so Fornoff learned his own lesson of friendship-versus-leadership. Fornoff did not recommend reappointment when Huber's 1906 commission expired.

In other personnel matters, it is likely that Lieutenant Baca recommended Grant County deputy sheriff John Collier as a candidate to replace John Brophy as the seventh ranger. Baca may have also taken the opportunity to express support for Will Dudley's retention on the force. Will had been a strong supporter of Captain Fullerton, and Fornoff may have been concerned about the level of commitment he could command from this highly educated former schoolmaster. Next to Baca and Lewis, Dudley's arrest record and commitment to duty was one of the best of Fullerton's Rangers. After due reflection, Will Dudley's commission was renewed.

When Fred Fornoff became caption of the New Mexico Territorial Mounted Police, the rangers started wearing a hand-engraved silver star and carrying a small pocket commission as identification of their authority. Only one of these ranger badges has survived (NMMP/AC).

Baca told Fornoff that he had come to the Santa Fe meeting to assess the situation and would discuss the new arrangement with Mary and let him know in a few days whether he would continue to perform his duties as the Mounted Police lieutenant. Baca returned to Socorro, and following a family meeting, he executed his new oath of office on Saturday, April 7. A few weeks after the Santa Fe meeting, Fornoff fired Rhea Stewart of Aztec and named veteran Las Cruces officer Robert Burch as the eighth ranger. By early September, Fornoff felt he had his team in place.

Lieutenant Baca spent about a week in

early April 1906 inventorying the Mounted Police's equipment and arranging to sell the office furnishings because it was cheaper to acquire new items than to ship the secondhand furnishings from Socorro to Santa Fe. The lieutenant sent the Mounted Police's records, via Bob Putman's care, to Captain Fornoff. A small two-room suite on the first floor of the capitol, near the south entrance, served as the new headquarters. Fornoff furnished the territorial police's office with secondhand equipment from other government departments.[77]

An office in the territorial capital was part of the arrangements that Governor Hagerman and Fornoff had agreed to as a consideration of Fred's accepting the ranger command. The office relocation was in direct violation of Section 8 of the 1905 Mounted Police Act that directed that the ranger headquarters should be located in "the most unprotected and exposed settlement of the territory."[78] This requirement did not fit Santa Fe during the pre-statehood era, so the 1909 Mounted Police reorganization act designated Santa Fe as the headquarters city. The prestige of an office in the capitol was not the main reason that Fornoff wanted to be in Santa Fe. The new captain desired quicker access to the governor's office, other government department heads, and the legislative leadership when the territorial assembly was in session. This lack of ready communications had proved to be a political, social, and public relations disadvantage to Captain Fullerton, and Fred Fornoff did not plan to make the same mistake.

With the closing of the Mounted Police's Socorro office the headquarters action that had centered at the Chambon Building was no longer present. Baca, Lewis, and Putman now used Sheriff Leandro Baca's office as a defacto ranger station when they where in town. A desk job, however, was not Baca's idea of crime prevention, so the lieutenant, Lewis, and Putman were quick to return to the backcountry searching for new signs of the "outlaw trail."

* * *

The nation followed the news with shock. It came from the western ocean at seven thousand miles an hour and hit land under the 36-year-old lighthouse at Point Arena about 90 miles north of San Francisco. The fabled sin city by the Bay, home of splendor and degradation, was calm and peaceful at 5:13 that Wednesday morning, but a few seconds later, millionaires' mansions and working-class shanties alike where struck equally by a tremendous tremor from the depths of the earth. It was April 18, 1906, and the nightmare terror had begun. The nation's newspapers were still reporting the aftermath for weeks after the quakes had stopped and they had brought the conflagration under control. A century after the fact, the death total was still uncertain, but recent evidence suggests the loss reached nearly 3,000 people and the property loss is confused with estimates ranging toward a half a billion dollars in 1906 value and relief aid that amounted to about $10 million. Geologists continue to warn that nature will repeat the Great Earthquake tragedy along the San Andreas Fault by 2032 with more devastation than 1906, yet the city continues to grow with blatant disregard of the prophecy of a Sodom and Gomorrah II. City leaders have always downplayed the magnitude of the 1906 crisis because San Francisco is a tourist city, and none of the city fathers or the Chamber of Commerce leadership wanted to discourage any dollar-spending tourist from visiting the Bay Area.[79]

It is uncertain where Cipriano Baca was when he first heard about the destruction that rained down upon his boyhood home country. It was, however, days before Baca received news about the safety of his California family. In the midst of the continuing news about the San Francisco area devastation, a fresh tip from Arizona officers again sent Baca in search of the suspected kidnapper Bob Holliman, but the lead was cold. The *Socorro Chieftain* completed the tale: "Lieut. Cipriano Baca of the Mounted Police force returned home in this city Tuesday morning from a trip over into Arizona." All Baca got for his labor was a free train ride across the desert southwest.

A penciled note in the Mounted Police files suggest that while Baca was in Douglas he spoke with a bawdyhouse inmate named Rosa Reed. His report provides no details. A woman using that name died in Douglas in July 1925 and was buried in Calvary Cemetery. The woman's death certificate said she was the daughter of Belle Starr. The displaced Missouri farm girl Myra Belle Shirley had a daughter with the outlaw Cole Younger that she named Pearl. Later, Belle married an Oklahoma Indian outlaw named Jim Reed, and they had a son named Ed. Pearl often used the Reed name. Belle acquired her most famous name from her next Indian lover, the outlaw Sam Starr. Pearl first became a prostitute in Fort Smith, Arkansas, using the name Rosa Reed. Following a long career operating "sporting houses," she settled in Douglas. Baca's Rosa Reed and Belle Starr's daughter may have been the same person.

In early May, Baca made a trip through Lincoln County. The *El Farol* (The Lantern) of Capitan made note of that Monday, May 8, visit saying, "*Sr. Cipriano Baca, tentiente de la Policia Montada, paso ayer para Lincoln, procediente de Socorro.* (Mr. Cipriano Baca, Mounted Police lieutenant passed by yesterday on his way to Lincoln from Socorro.)" The Mounted Police lieutenant was a trial witness during the district court session held at the Lincoln County courthouse at Lincoln. He and Rangers L.F. Avant of Capitan and Will Dudley from Alamogordo in neighboring Otero County found some time to discuss a projected summer raid into the Sacramento Mountains.

The hard-riding Mounted Police where causing a stir across the southwest, and the highly respected *Denver Republican* took note. In mid–May, the newspaper carried a feature account about Cipriano Baca and his small squad of rangers under the headline "Riding the Territory of Bad Men" and congratulated New Mexico's lawmakers for creating the force. Later that May, the *Socorro Chieftain* expanding on the *Denver Republican*'s theme, said, "Lieut. Cipriano Baca, of the Mounted Police force, arrived home yesterday morning from an absence of five weeks on official duty in various parts of the territory." Baca arrested an accused horse thief on that scout, and the *Albuquerque Evening Citizen* told readers that when Baca was undercover on the hunt, he often looked like a "bad man" himself; thus he was able to fool the men he was hunting.[80]

* * *

In late May 1906, the Bacas were planning little Ruby's first birthday party, but on Thursday morning, three days before the magic June 3 date, the infant died suddenly. The *Socorro Chieftain* said, "The grieving parents have the heartfelt sympathy of a large circle of relatives and friends in their bereavement" and then described Ruby as having been an "exceedingly pretty and bright child." Ruby Hamilton Baca had received Christian baptism at a family service on Wednesday, March 14, at the Episcopal Church of the Epiphany, yet her funeral service was held at the Bacas' home and was led by the Rev. H.M. Perkins, the Presbyterian minister in Socorro. They interned the infant in the Berry Family Plot in the

Socorro Cemetery. The grave site is not marked. Even in this time of sorrow, the extended Berry family rejoiced in the knowledge that Mary Baca was again pregnant and was expecting in late November.

It is unclear what Baca's religious affiliation was at this time. His family's heritage was in the Roman Catholic Church where he had been baptized and raised in the faith, yet Cipriano often attended the Episcopal Church. He sometimes attended the Presbyterian Church, yet had been married in the Methodist-Episcopal Church. He was buried with a funeral mass from the Roman Catholic Church.[81]

The summer of 1906 was hot in Socorro County, but the weather did not stop local rustlers. Lieutenant Baca tried to relieve his sorrow over the loss of his daughter by going back out on "the road," but when he was preparing for the trip, he discovered he had lost his official railroad passes and could not afford to travel without the free transportation. According to the *Socorro Chieftain* a few "dodgers" placed around Socorro "brought the passes to light in less than twenty-four hours" and Baca made a day trip up the Santa Fe road to Magdalena to check on the livestock shipping site and "nose around," getting a feel for the local bad guys.

A short time later Baca returned to the Magdalena country. This time he was able to slip up on Louis Gallegos and Victoriano Garcia, arrest them for horse stealing, and escort them to the Socorro County jail to await the arrival of Quay County Sheriff Alex Street to take the two men back to Tucumcari for trial. Street told his hometown paper that Baca was "doing some very excellent work in Socorro and adjoining counties." A few weeks later, the *Clayton Enterprise* said that Cipriano's arrest of Ruperto Gonzales broke up a horse-stealing ring in the Datil Mountains in western Socorro County. Just as quickly, according to the *El Paso Times*, Miguel Garcia of Magdalena, another bandit leader, landed behind bars charged with sheep stealing. The *Tucumcari News* commended the Mounted Police lieutenant for these arrests and made special mention that Garcia was "a noted bad man in that section of New Mexico for the past two years."

The *Tucumcari News* reported that Miguel Garcia had once been a resident of Quay County, "but development here drove him west." The reporter added that Garcia was now under indictment in Torrance County for stealing 300 head of sheep from the McIntosh herds grazing the range around the village of Torrance, the county seat. Garcia had secretly stolen the herd while working for the owners "and got away with them so perfectly that he was not suspicioned for some time afterwards." The newspaper added final praise for Garcia's captor by saying, "Baca is said to be a fearless and capable officer, speaks both languages fluently and has a natural instinct to hunt criminals."

William Frazier owned the sheep. At the time of the theft's discovery, in September 1905, Mounted Policeman Dick Huber went looking for them and was able to recover 103 head from a range about 14 miles south of Albuquerque and returned them to their owner. The remainder of the stolen sheep was never located. It would seem that when Baca immersed himself in the hunt for rustlers he became almost maniacal. It is doubtful that Cipriano ever forgot the infant Ruby; he just rechanneled his grief into determination.[82]

* * *

Socorro had suffered about 15 small earthquakes, of 20 seconds or less, during six weeks in February and March 1904. A reporter for the *El Paso Herald* had written that Socorro had mass damage to the community and that these mini-earthquakes were punishment for past wickedness, and the town was receiving "a touch of the experience that was administered to Sodom and Gomorra." The *Socorro Chieftain* editor replied to this "fantastic nonsense" saying that the Texas reporter was suffering from "a too liberal indulgence in the fluid extracted of either Texas corn or Arizona cactus." All of this excitement took place while the Baca family was living in Albuquerque, so they had not personally experienced this natural phenomenon.

Beginning on July 2, 1906, and lasting into early 1907, the 1,500 inhabitants of Socorro suffered a series of earthquakes with magnitudes ranging between 4.5 and 6.0 on the Richter scale according to geologists at the New Mexico School of Mines who maintained seismic records for the National Weather Service. Prior to the first Socorro quake, the earth had shaken in Illinois, Utah, Pennsylvania, Ohio, and California with tremor activity reported in South Dakota, Wyoming, and Washington State. None of the Socorro rumbles where comparable, in size or devastation, to the April 1906 earthquake that had hit San Francisco, but the citizens were still in a panic. These central New Mexico events where unusual enough that in 1911 Harry Fielding Reid of the Seismological Society of America gathered official accounts and wrote a feature story about the Socorro earthquakes of 1906 and 1907 for the society's first publication.

The first shock rattled buildings in Socorro at about 3:15 A.M. on that Monday morning, and a second 4.5 shock hit about 15 minutes later. Eight more shocks moved the earth before noon and tremors continued into the evening. Contemporary accounts indicate that the people felt the sharp shocks within a 50-mile radius of the Socorro County courthouse.

"I remember that first night. Father was not home and Mama was very concerned. She was pregnant and due in a few months," recalled Cipriana Randolph. "Mother sent word for Father to come home." A second shock series hit Socorro before Baca could reach his home. These were about 1:30 A.M. and again at 4:10 on Saturday morning July 7, and a 3:00 A.M. shock hit Magdalena. "We children remembered how Father's family had survived the San Francisco disaster earlier that spring. Socorro had very little property damage and no one was seriously injured; no deaths."

Almost a week after the second shock series, on Thursday morning, July 12, just before dawn at 5:15, a 5.5-scale shock lasting about 15 to 20 seconds was felt north up the Rio Grande to Albuquerque, west to Fort Wingate near the Arizona border, and south to El Paso. People reported ground fissures and visible waves on the surface. The walls of adobe houses cracked and some brick chimneys fell down. Four days later, Socorro rocked with a 5.8 jolt people felt as far north as Raton Pass on the Colorado state line, west to Douglas, Arizona, and east across the mountains and plains toward Roswell. The epicenter was about 16 miles west of Socorro at a calderas, a volcano crater left after all the magma has blown out, called the Bursum Calderas. This shock was marked at a 7.0 intensity level, and the eastern press carried sensationalistic accounts of mass devastation.

Under a page-one headline, "Town Being Shaken Down," the *New York Times* said, "Shaken continually for two days by earthquake shocks, which were counted up to fifty-two, practically two-thirds of the town of Socorro is falling down. The Court House is in ruins and the people of the town are in terror." The news account, datelined from El Paso, reported that the Santa Fe Railway had sent boxcars to Socorro to evacuate the women and children. The next day, the *Times* follow-up story was on page two. "The people continue to live out of doors, very few spending the nights inside their homes. The inhabitants are largely of Indian blood and of the Catholic faith, and during the height of the earth shocks were seen in large groups on their knees in the streets, praying for life."

Socorro town leaders needed to do damage control, so they drafted a public relations statement for the Associated Press correspondent. To the editorial credit of the *New York Times,* they did print Mayor Holm Bursum's statement concerning the real state of affairs in Socorro. The mayor said that the courthouse was still standing but had lost some ceiling plaster and the toppling of two old chimneys. Some buildings, like the Winkler Hotel, sustained moderate damage, but the town was not devastated, as some sensational wire service accounts had claimed. T.J. Matthews, superintendent of the Socorro telephone company, claimed his system was working fine, and the only damaged homes were adobe houses that had seen more than a half century of life.

The *Cincinnati Post* told readers in the Ohio River Valley, "Provisions are getting scarce and real distress is found among the refugees. Not a house in town is safe to enter and chimneys and walls topple with each recurrent tremor." The *Albuquerque Morning Journal* reported, based upon tales told by refugees like District Attorney Elfego Baca and his family, that "fire, smoke, lava, cinders, flames and brimstone have converted the place into a miniature Hades." Mrs. J.J. Leeson claimed she had been in earthquakes in Los Angeles and San Francisco but had experienced nothing "so sickening [sic] as these prolonged rockings and jerkings of the earth at Socorro."

Elfego Baca, in hiding at his in-laws' in Albuquerque, claimed that when he ran from Socorro, the town was experiencing the hardest rain it had seen in 50 years and this added to the discomfort of those left behind to camp in the streets. A few days later, an *Albuquerque Morning Journal* reporter learned the falsehood of Baca's deluge tale and wrote a humorous apology, saying, "It will probably not dare to rain in Socorro for another fifty years." Soon after he returned to Socorro, public sentiment caused Elfego Baca to resign his county prosecutor's post under a dark cloud of mistrust and he returned to private law practice in the county seat.

In answer to the widespread reports that numerous volcanoes were smoking around Socorro, Mrs. Randolph recalled, "Uncle John [Griffith] wrote the Santa Fe newspaper telling them that Socorro had not had any volcanic action like they had reported in their paper. People that had left town had done so on already planned vacations." A *Silver City Enterprise* reporter came to Socorro to view the devastation and write a firsthand account. He returned home with a nonstory; there was little structural damage, no one was injured, and no one was dead.[83]

Cipriano Baca had returned to his family. "Father was our foundation. We were not afraid with him around. He said that he had been in two earthquakes when he was a kid, so we shouldn't be scared," recalled Cipriana Randolph. "I was just four at the time and I was real frightened until father said his mother had told him not to be scared because God would care for them just like it was promised in the Psalms. This was a comfort to a little girl, but I was still scared."

Cipriano was referring to the first few lines of chapter 46 in the Book of Psalms. Some current Bible translations use the word earthquake in verse 2, so the modern reader has a clearer understanding of the passage's message. If Cipriana's memory of her father's comment was correct, this was a strong testament of faith for a man who at this point in his life had lost his mother and father, two wives, three young children, and other close relatives.[84]

The Socorro's summer earthquakes struck a raw nerve as people of the nation and the world were still processing their reaction to the 7.8 magnitude earthquake that had leveled central San Francisco in the pre-dawn hours of April 18 and devastated the city with aftershocks and a massive fire that burned for weeks. Jack London wrote, "An enumeration of the dead will never be made." The novelist's prophecy has proved true. Historians now estimate the human lose at between 3,000 and 6,000 people, and the property loses were uncountable as they reached into the millions of dollars in turn-of-the-century dollar value. This was America's most devastating earthquake to date.[85]

On Thursday, November 15, 1906, a 250,000-square-mile area around Socorro heard rumbling sounds and then felt a 5.8 earthquake that shook plaster from walls of buildings hundreds of miles north in Santa Fe. This act of nature may have been the final straw for Mary Baca. Based upon family tales concerning Grandma Berry's prejudice toward most "Mexicans," she may have influenced her daughter's request not to be alone, pregnant with three small children, in an area that had become a "Little Chihuahua" and was across the railroad tracks and on the other side of town from her family's homes. On Monday, November 20, Cipriano and Mary Baca sold their house and lot on Second Street for $150.00. The property was located near the Methodist Episcopal Church and bounded on the north by Smelter Street and on the south by property owned by Santiago Trujillo. The east-side property line was 79 feet wide, but tapered off to 60 feet for the west sideline.[86]

Due to the nature of the quick house sale, it is possible that Cipriano was anticipating possibly relocating his family not to a new site within Socorro, but to a new community. Captain Fornoff was in the process of reassigning the territorial police to remote crime-infested areas. He might have discussed his plans for Baca when the two were together in Estancia. In support of this thesis, it should be noted that Cipriano Baca's replacement as lieutenant was John W. Collier who was quickly posted to Estancia. If the reassignment scenario is accurate, then it is likely that Baca intended for his family to stay temporarily at the Berry Boarding House while he made permanent arrangements for them.

Another 4.5 quake hit Socorro on Wednesday, December 19, 1906, and put a dark cloud of anxiety over the Bacas' Christmas holiday season and the pending birth of a new baby.

* * *

Lieutenant Baca would spend weeks at a time on patrol duty. He rode the remote trails in the western mountains, ventured into the valleys of out-of-the-way mining camps, and isolated logging villages. He was always searching for signs that would lead him to some wanted man. The *Alamogordo News* told the story about Baca visiting Mounted Police headquarters and spotting Amada Barilla on the streets of the capital city. Baca promptly arrested the man on a warrant for setting a series of fires at Willard in Torrance County and delivered him to the Santa Fe County jail until a deputy sheriff from Estancia could arrive to claim his prisoner.

The month of July 1906 was an active few weeks for Lieutenant Baca. After a few days of range riding, he arrested Inez Montes on a charge of stealing "young cattle," according to the *Capitan El Faro*. The cattle brand was unknown to Baca and others, so the owner was not quickly identified, but the Torrance County resident caught with the herd was taken to the justice of the peace at Estancia for his preliminary examination. The justice found Baca's evidence convincing enough to place Montes under a $1,000 bond to appear before the district court that fall. His job done, Cipriano once again headed for home and a short visit before another patrol.

In late July, Baca and his squad struck again. The *Santa Fe New Mexican* summed up the action with one sentence: "Capt. Fred Fornoff of the Territorial Mounted Police has received word that Lt. Cipriano Baca and some rangers have captured a number of horse thieves in a raid in the Sacramento Mountains of Otero County." The *Albuquerque Morning Journal* told its readers that Baca's two companions had been Rangers Bob Putman and Robert Burch and said that the trio had arrested four rustlers who had been "operating in the Sacramento mountains for several years." The report also noted that the rangers recovered a small herd of horses marked with a mixture of Otero County brands during the surprise raid on the rustler camp. One of the news bulletins concerning the arrests explained that the "capture was effected after some nervy work on the part of Lieutenant Baca and his men and will put an end to the worst of these stock thieves in the Sacramento county. The [four] ring leaders are now in jail [at Santa Fe]."

Lt. Baca and Ranger Burch stayed in the eastern mountains. Ranger Putman left the patrol to take the squad's prisoners to jail. Meanwhile in Santa Fe, Captain Fornoff had reorganized the Mounted Police force. He reassigned Bob Putman from his Socorro home base to patrol the western mining districts and the high mountain range country along the Arizona border. Fornoff wired Lt. Baca to inform him of the reassignment. He also contacted Putman at Alamogordo and informed him of his new duty station. Ranger Putman took the train from Alamogordo to Socorro, via El Paso, to pack up his household and escort his wife and son to their new home in Silver City.[87]

In his departmental report to the governor concerning operation of the Mounted Police, Captain Fornoff told his friend Governor Hagerman, "One of the principal duties of the Mounted Police is to protect cattle, sheep and horses. We have been successful in making a great reduction in this class of crime by a vigorous enforcement of the law and by running down horse [, sheep,] and cattle thieves." Fornoff bragged a little by writing that during "the four months I have held the office [of captain] 50 arrests have been made" by his ten-man territorial police force. Captain Fornoff neglected to say that his lieutenant had been a principal player in 12 of those reported arrests.[88]

A few days later in August, a tired Cipriano Baca headed home. On the way he located, and arrested, a man named Dwight Craig. The *Albuquerque Evening Citizen* said the young man, wanted on a robbery charge in Socorro County, quickly became Lieutenant Baca's reluctant traveling companion to visit Sheriff Leandro Baca's county-supported hotel.

The trees had just begun to turn colors in the high country when Cipriano Baca and Ranger Robert Burch, the veteran officer from Las Cruces, teamed up to serve some warrants. The Socorro County Grand Jury issued felony indictments for three men that VXT wranglers claimed they caught branding caves belonging to their boss, H.M. Porter of Denver. Two of the three men were charged with stealing, false branding, and killing cattle taken from the VXT Ranch in the Gila River Country, while the third cowboy had only been charged with cattle stealing. Baca arrested the cowboys as they were working for the N Bar Ranch and took them to Socorro. Judge Amos E. Green set a $500-per-charge bail for each man.

The *Socorro Chieftain* said, "Ezra M. Glaze furnished his bond for $1,500 and left at once for the western part of the county to raise the required [$500] bond for his brother [Oliver]. [H.S.] Hall also furnished bond [$500] and was released until court convenes." A $1,500 bond was a huge amount for a $40 to $60 per month cowboy to finance. There was much hard feeling in western Socorro County over the charge and the arrest. Many old cowmen did not see a crime in branding maverick calves found roaming on the open range.

Within days of returning from the N Bar Ranch, Ranger Burch headed back to Las Cruces, and Baca had joined Sergeant Lewis for a railroad trip to the stockyards at Magdalena. Lewis had gotten out of the cow business himself by selling his two milk cows. It was just too difficult for Lewis' wife to care for their small children and the cows during his prolonged absences. The two Mounted Police spent a few breezy September days in Magdalena so they could check on the status of the regional livestock roundup and the progress of the fall shipping season. Dr. E.A. Drake, editor of the *Socorro Chieftain*, was just as dutiful in recording Cipriano's all-too-brief visits home with his family as he was in reporting Baca's faithfulness to his law enforcement duties.[89]

* * *

The official reason for Lieutenant Baca's attendance at the Socorro County Republican Party Convention of 1906 was that Governor Hagerman had authorized a Mounted Policeman to provide security for the delegates. The *Socorro Chieftain* reported a rumor floating about the convention that the real reason Cipriano Baca was in attendance was to demonstrate his availability to be the party's candidate for sheriff. The convention delegates understood that Baca was not openly seeking the nomination, but it was common knowledge that he would accept a draft nomination from the delegates.

When Governor Hagerman removed Leandro Baca, the incumbent sheriff, from office in early October and named Misais Baca as interim sheriff until the November election selected a full-term officer, Hagerman had considered appointing Cipriano Baca to the post and also giving him his full support for the fall campaign. It is unknown if Baca even knew about this proposition, but James G. Fitch, a Socorro attorney and leader in the county Republican Party, had heard such a rumor and was concerned about Baca's ability to hold on to the sheriff's office in the general election. Fitch wrote the governor to apprise him of his concerns:

> He [Baca] has no means to make it with; and I doubt whether the [house] property he owns here [in Socorro] is worth $500.00, so that he is not qualified under law [Title VII — County Officers, Chapter II — Sheriff, Section 396 — Real Estate Qualifications, *Laws of 1884*] to hold the office.

Fitch may not have known that Baca also owned mining property in Socorro County; the taxable value of these mining holdings is unknown. The lawyer continued his appraisal:

> I have always had a warm feeling for him [Baca], and know his efficiency as a peace officer. He is however scarcely regarded as a permanent resident of Socorro County, and has no relations or connections, who would be of any assistance to him, in case he were a candidate for the office this fall.

It is true that the Baca family had not resided in Socorro County between 1899 and 1905, but the family visited the area often to see Mary's mother and sisters. Sallie Berry operated a boarding house in the county seat, one of Baca's brothers-in-law was a prominent Socorro attorney with ambitions of becoming district attorney and another brother-in-law was a former deputy U.S. Marshal who was now a mining engineer.

Fitch also told Governor Hagerman, "In addition he has recently antagonized the [local] cattle men, so that he would probably have them against him." If there truly were a disagreement between Baca and some Socorro County ranchers, it may have stemmed from some incident at the fall shipping roundup at Magdalena or maybe it was just hard feelings concerning Cipriano's recent arrest of some popular N Bar Ranch cowboys. "I do not believe he could run this fall with any hope of success," wrote Fitch and concluded by saying, "and personally for the sake of his family I would dislike to see him give up his present position [as Mounted Police lieutenant] for a term of three months as sheriff, or make a fruitless campaign."[90]

It is reasonable to assume that Baca never knew about the statements made in James Fitch's letter, but he did have ears among the powers of government and may have guessed the reason for Misais Baca's throwaway appointment as interim sheriff. In spite of this understanding, Baca may have still held hope that the convention delegates knew about his stellar law enforcement record and would yet seek him out and disregard their inner doubts about his electability.

Destiny had not selected Cipriano Baca, and the call to public service did not come. Baca viewed the convention's action as a lack of confidence in him and his law enforcement abilities. Cipriano had ridden in numerous posses and conducted countless solo scouts across the mountains and plains of Socorro County, but always working as someone else's deputy. He had been denied his chance to be the top lawman again. This rejection may have cut Baca's ego to the core, eaten at his inner being, and caused his thinking to cloud, especially after the victory of Aniceto C. Abeytia in the general election. Abeytia was a one-term wonder that held the office that Baca should have had.

* * *

A few days after his dreams were crushed at the Socorro County Republican Convention, Baca was "back on his horse" doing his sworn duty. "The Mounted Police are having trouble [trying] to suppress fence cutters in the Casaus section up the Dawson [railroad line]," reported the *Tucumcari News*. Casaus was still home to Ranger Meyer, and Baca had returned to the area to help him once again quell the livestock raids. Within a short time both men took the train to Tucumcari to testify before the district court, presided over by Judge Edward A. Mann, in the trial of two men they had arrested for horse stealing. A week later, the same newspaper said Baca was back in town "on official business." The mission was to deliver some more guests for Quay County sheriff Alex Street's Bastille.

Mary Baca had sent word to her husband that he needed to return to Socorro to attend a family obligation. His sister-in-law Pearl Thompson Berry was to wed Alexander Walter Edelen on October 16 in a Tuesday-evening service conducted by W.R. Dye in the Episcopal Church of the Epiphany. As a child, Miss. Berry received baptism in that same church. The couple would later have three children.

A short time later, Baca rode the Santa Fe passenger north from Socorro to the railroad stop at Wagon Mound on the old Santa Fe Trail. The village was nestled at the base of the 6,930-foot-tall namesake mesa. Baca rented a horse and rode the backcountry trails checking creek banks and watering holes looking for any sign of a human traveler. He was "on the lookout for a convict who escaped from a detachment working on the Scenic Highway some time ago." After a few days and nights searching, Baca was still unable to locate the road gang escapee or any potential longropers working in the area. It had been an uncomfortable scout riding through the open and windswept grasslands, plains and foothills of Mora County during that fall's cool days and cold nights.

A few days after the election in early November 1906, Baca was at the American Lumber Company's Kettner logging camp in the Zuni Mountains, located 35 miles west of Grants in present-day Cibola County, investigating the attempted murder of Jose Padillo. Cipriano Baca uncovered no real leads before he closed the hunt and returned to Socorro.

The growing crime rate in the area around Grants and Gallup caused Captain Fornoff to station one of his men in Kettner about six months after Baca's visit. George Fred Murray, a tall and lanky former Rough Rider, possessed only minimal "book learning," but he became one of the Mounted Police's premier rangers in a force of stalwart officers. The late William A. Keleher, pioneer Albuquerque attorney and historian, knew Fred Murray and told the author the ranger was so dedicated to law enforcement that he would storm the gates of hell with a bucket of water to retrieve a wanted man.

A few weeks after Baca returned from Kettner, he and Lewis used their railroad passes to save Socorro County taxpayers a few dollars as they each escorted a new inmate to Las Vegas so they could take up residence at the Territorial Asylum. Sergeant Lewis was escorting a "native woman" until he took custody of an Oklahoma Territory fugitive, captured at the railroad junction of Rincon, wanted for "obtaining money under false pretences." Lewis stopped in Santa Fe to house his male prisoner in the territorial lockup to await extradition to Lawton before taking his female prisoner on to Las Vegas. When Baca had delivered his prisoner to the asylum, he caught the next southbound train to Lamy Junction, 14 miles southeast of Santa Fe, where he transferred to the Santa Fe Central system and made a trip south to confer with Captain Fornoff who was attending the Torrance County District Court being held at Estancia, the new county seat.

The next morning Cipriano started the eight-hour trip north over the Santa Fe Central Railroad to Santa Fe. He spent the next few days in the capital temporarily in charge of the Mounted Police office while court duties occupied Captain Fornoff. During one of the days that Baca was in Santa Fe, Bob Putman came up from Silver City, and the two men discussed the "doings" in Grant County. Neither man knew when they parted that cold day at Santa Fe that it would be 12 years before they would both again be wearing a Mounted Police badge.[91]

* * *

When Baca left the City of Holy Faith, he returned to Socorro and spent a few days with his family who were still reeling from the death in late May of baby Ruby, just three days short of her first birthday. Thirteen days after Socorro's November 15 earthquake, Mary Baca gave birth at their temporary home at her mother's boarding house. Mary delivered twin daughters, Mary Ann and Maisie, on Wednesday, November 28, 1906, and the *Socorro Chieftain* reported the event.

> The stork visited the home of Lieutenant and Mrs. Cipriano Baca in this city Wednesday morning and left a fine pair of girl baby twins as one would care to look upon. The mother and

daughters are doing extremely well and the father is greatly pleased with the remarkable additions to his family circle.

Once more, the cry of a baby and children's laughter echoed in the Berry-Baca household.[92]

* * *

Socorro's 1906 Christmas holiday earthquake put a dark cloud of anxiety over the season. Compounding the glum was the fact that snow blanketed New Mexico Territory from a devastating snowstorm. In the Carlsbad area, reports said a number of sheepherders and a mail carrier froze to death. "Wood and coal famine at Carlsbad, N.M., and thermometers at zero compels people to burn bacon to keep from freezing," said the *Ozona Kicker*, published in the West Texas cattle country. For a second winter of extreme weather, Cipriano was in the thick of the elements and Mary Baca was not happy to have her husband traveling in that kind of weather. Circumstances suggest that she told him that she wanted him to get a job with less danger and less extended away-from-home travel. The Bacas had a growing family that needed a healthy father near at hand.

Cipriano Baca ended 1906 by arresting a man wanted for murder at Portales, near the Texas border in Roosevelt County. Late in the year, Captain Fornoff had implemented a new method for the territorial police to report their arrests to headquarters. The arrest form was a thick paper file card about 8 × 4 inches in size with basic information printed on one side. Beginning in the early summer of 1907, the information from the arrest card was entered into a large bound record ledger for easy reference. Fornoff also used the ledger totals as a quick method to track the territorial police's arrest record for his biannual accounting to the governor and the Territorial Legislative Assembly.

Lieutenant Baca filed a Mounted Police Arrest Card for Encarnacion Calderon. Baca noted that the brown-eyed, five-foot-ten-inch husky Mexican "had in his possession [a] bunch of skilliton [*sic*] keys, several belonging to [the] Santa Fe [Railroad] Co. Car Keys." Planned or unplanned, Baca's journey with the New Mexico Territorial Mounted Police was coming to the end of the trail; the Calderon arrest would prove to be his last action as a territorial ranger.[93]

* * *

The Spanish phrase *haciendo des veredas* describes a person who is staggering drunk; "following two trails at once." This folk saying would play a part in the Baca saga and help to cloud the legacy of his territorial law enforcement career.

The Saturday, January 5, 1907, issue of the *Albuquerque Evening Citizen* contained a bold-faced lie proclaiming that an intoxicated Mounted Police lieutenant had smashed "a harmless and inoffensive telephone instrument in San Antonio Thursday night." The newspaper also said that the territorial officer had angrily destroyed a telephone housed in one of the village's saloons. "Baca wantonly, deliberately and with intent to maim, massacre and murder, grasped up a shovel and assaulted the talking box in a most vigorous manner, resulting in its practical demolition." The Sunday and Monday issues of the *Albuquerque Morning Journal* refuted their rival's tale of mayhem saying the *Evening Citizen's* account of Baca battling a telephone was a first-class fabricated fable.

An enterprising reporter for the *Albuquerque Morning Journal* had used the long-distance telephone line connecting Socorro with the Duke City to contact Baca concerning the *Albuquerque Evening Citizen*'s "harrowing account" of the events at San Antonio. The reporter asked Baca if he had seen the story about the telephone assault, and Baca said he had not. The unnamed reporter read Baca the *Albuquerque Evening Citizen*'s account and then asked for his comments. The Sunday edition of the *Albuquerque Morning Journal* published Baca's account of the incident.

> I'm sorry they [the *Albuquerque Evening Citizen*] think I'm cruel enough to smash an innocent and defenseless telephone, but if they think so I guess it is all off. Anyway, the telephone is smashed, although I did not do it, and it was not done with a shovel. The facts are few and brief. Myself, with several other friends, were in the saloon mentioned in San Antonio. So was the telephone. It was unfortunate for the telephone, but we could not prevent its presence. At any rate, we had a drink or so and presently several of the boys engaged in a friendly scuffle, in which somebody got shoved against the wall and the unfortunate telephone. The telephone got knocked from its fastenings and smashed. That is all there was to it. I do not think, however, that I should have been convicted of assaulting the telephone without a hearing.[94]

W.S. Burke, editor of the *Albuquerque Morning Journal*, sent a reporter to San Antonio on the Sunday train for a firsthand, on-site investigation of the telephone affair and then published the journalist's findings on Monday morning. "The effort to injure Baca is a plain case of dirty work. Baca came here [San Antonio] to accomplish certain public work. From current reports he has accomplished it or a considerable part of it and this may account for the effort to discredit him." W.S. Strickler, editor of the *Albuquerque Evening Citizen*, refused to retract their account even after witnesses to the actual event swore that the story was a lie.[95] Strickler was an old-guard Republican opposed to Governor Hagerman and his "progressive" movement, and this dislike included the rangers, the governor's "private police."

"Father was what you would call a social drinker," remembered Cipriana Randolph. "I know he enjoyed strong liquor, but I never saw him drunk or heard anyone say that they had." Baca enjoyed a glass of Old Crow fine Kentucky Bourbon. "I was just a child in 1907 so I don't know anything about that bar incident in San Antonio [New Mexico], but that doesn't sound like Father. He was not a drunk. He was always a gentleman."[96]

The "drunken" Baca incident was a "plant" by powerful political forces working behind the scenes to discredit the accomplishments of the Mounted Police in the public's mind, so that negative community opinion would force the upcoming session of the Territorial Legislative Assembly to repeal the Mounted Police Act. A majority of the territory's sheriffs, some shady businessmen, and a wide assortment of anti–Hagerman administration Democrats and Republicans were actively opposed to the rangers and had organized a campaign to rid themselves of their nemesis and its commander-in-chief. The Baca fable was just a small part of the grand scheme. The attempted coup failed, the Mounted Police survived the legislative attack and W.F. Brogan replaced W.S. Stickler as editor of the *Albuquerque Evening Citizen* in March 1907.

* * *

Many people have assumed that Cipriano Baca's departure from the territorial police was a result of the telephone incident because the announcement of his resignation by the Mounted Police office came after publication of the *Albuquerque Evening Citizen*'s fable. Baca never publicly countered this misperception, so the tale passed into history as fact. The truth is that the date on Cipriano Baca's letter to Captain Fred Fornoff resigning his position with the Mounted Police is two days prior to publication of the *Albuquerque Evening Citizen*'s tale.

It is not easy to ascertain when Baca began thinking about leaving the territorial police because he was active until the day he turned in his ranger badge. The lieutenant was under mounting stress and having difficulty dealing with his personal life: the sorrow and sickness, his mounting family debt, and his growing frustration over his inability to advance his professional status. In the first verses of the fifth chapter of his *Letter to Church at Rome*, the first century Christian evangelist Paul wrote that mankind should rejoice in suffering because that is what produces human perseverance, and perseverance develops character and character leads to hope. The perspective of time might lead one to believe that at this point in his life Cipriano Baca was not clinging to hope, but may have been operating in a fantasy world.

There was no tête-à-tête; Baca just sent Captain Fornoff a terse three-line resignation letter. "I hereby tender you my resignation as Lieut[enant] of Mounted Police. [The] Same to take effect at your pleasure. Thanking you for your many favors. I remain, yours truly, Cipriano Baca." Baca had addressed the letter in a formal "Dear Sir" manner unlike his usual "Friend Fred" or "Capt. Fornoff" style. In his distress of composing the resignation, he misdated the letter as "Jan. 3/06."[97] There is no record remaining to show that Captain Fornoff tried to dissuade Cipriano from resigning.

The *Albuquerque Morning Journal* of Tuesday, January 8, 1907, contained a dispatch from Santa Fe announcing that Baca was leaving the territorial rangers, "which comes as a complete surprise to the many friends of one of the most efficient men under Mr. Fornoff." The dispatch added a final comment: "Mr. Baca's headquarters have been in Socorro and he has done yeoman service during his incumbency in rounding up rustlers and other criminals and preserving order in his district." Other newspapers echoed the sentiments of the dispatch.

Baca never made public his reason for resigning his Mounted Police commission, so at this late date it is hard to determine a single reason that may have caused him to leave the territorial police. Maybe the deep sadness in the Baca household played a role in his decision. Baca had spent nearly two years in the saddle riding the backcountry searching for the scum of New Mexico Territory, and maybe he had just grown weary of the chase. In our modern work world, we might say that Baca had just burned out and suffered from job stress. The answer may also be as simple as the fact that Cipriano Baca needed more money to support his family.

Seven days into January 1907, Miss Clara Olson, the governor's private secretary, made the following notation in the Executive Record Book: "The Governor this day accepted the resignation of Cipriano Baca as Lieutenant of the Company of New Mexico Mounted Police." The New Mexico Territorial Mounted Police never again had a Spanish-surnamed senior officer.[98]

17

Private Detective and Company Police Officer

"There is nothing so easy but that it becomes difficult when you do it reluctantly"—
Publius Terentius Afer, 159 B.C.E.

It is difficult to pinpoint Cipriano Baca's movements during the first few weeks of 1907, but he was in Albuquerque and El Paso working his contacts looking for the right business opportunity. The former Mounted Police lieutenant was in Santa Fe for the opening session of the 37th Legislative Assembly on Monday, January 21, 1907.[1]

Baca was present in the House chamber and heard Governor Hagerman tell the lawmakers, "The organization of a force of Territorial Mounted Police by the last legislature had proven to be a wise measure and one which has resulted in great good to the people of the Territory." The chief executive recommended that all the privates receive a pay raise and that three more rangers and an office clerk be added to the department. Not all the legislators who heard Hagerman's remarks agreed with his assessment of the value received from the Territorial Mounted Police.

Governor Hagerman had based his requests upon a report given him by Captain Fornoff dated January 2, 1907. The captain had been optimistic when writing, "The work of the men speaks for itself and I have no doubt that a calm survey of their operations for the past twenty-one months will result in liberal treatment by the Honorable Legislature of this Territory." Fornoff had stepped on political toes with one statement: "I believe it could be easily shown that the money expended for the New Mexico Mounted Police has been productive of greater results than if the same had been expended by county officials." The battle for the survival of the territorial police was joined.

"Move to Wipe Out Ranger Force," was the bold *Albuquerque Morning Journal* headline about the intrigue in Santa Fe; "the movement to abolish the force is a strong one, well organized and aggressive, and it will not delay action long." The pro-administration newspaper defended the Mounted Police, saying,

> The force has recovered hundreds of head of stolen cattle and horses and sheep and it has apprehended a great many stock thieves and most important of all it has spread its moral influence, among the lawless characters of the thinly settled districts, and has thus put an end to stock thieving, which up to the time of the creation of the force, flourished almost without interruption.

Now the challenge sounded. "[T]he stock interests should make their wishes heard and at once, for the movement to abolish the force is a strong one, well organized and aggressive, and it will not delay action long."

The leadership of the Republican Party majority knew that Democrats, and some dissident Republicans, would make an exerted effort to abolish the Mounted Police. The unpopular governor's massive collection of political enemies, bipartisan fiscal conservatives, and most of the territory's sheriffs planned to use the new federal law prohibiting railroad companies from granting free transportation on their trains to territorial officials as a focus to shut down the highly mobile police. This increased operational expense was a keystone of the abolitionist movement.

"It is to the men who own sheep and cattle and horses and who run them in open country from the protection of the ordinary peace officers that he [sic] [the] mounted men have been of greatest service." The Albuquerque newspaper report ended with a supportive editorial comment, "To abolish it [the territorial police] now would undo much of the good work it has done."

Cipriano's legislative friends may have convinced him that the Mounted Police were a sinking craft and that he should leave the ship before it went under and the rangers "drowned" politically. The sergeant-at-arms for the 1907 House of Representatives was Baca's friend Leandro Baca, the former sheriff of Socorro County. All finance legislation originated in the House.

Within days of the governor's legislative presentation, lawmakers in both chambers introduced numerous bills to abolish the territorial police. The House passed one of their bills to repeal the Mounted Police law and sent it to the Council where it languished in committee while the Council debated their own goals for the territorial police. In the end, none of the anti–Mounted Police groups had the political strength to deliver a bill to the governor's desk, so the status quo remained and the territorial police received funding in the 1907–1908 biannual budget.

It is unknown if Cipriano visited with Fornoff during his brief sojourn in the capitol complex. There were rumors that Baca and Fornoff had a personal disagreement and that Baca felt hurt by the encounter to the point that he believed he could no longer work for the captain. Henry David Thoreau wrote that it takes two people to speak the truth; one person speaking and the other listening. The two men may have had some sort of a misunderstanding; if so it did not take the two officers long to get over their difficulty and renew their friendship over a meal. Piquancy to these two men was a thick, well-cooked beefsteak and enchiladas, a full glass of aged Bourbon, a fine Cuban cigar and a Hershey's chocolate bar for good measure.[2]

Cipriano Baca lived his life believing the biblical command recorded in Deuteronomy 16:20: "You must pursue justice, only justice." The former Mounted Police officer had spent months tracking what he felt were some new leads concerning the political assassination of Col. J. Francisco Chaves in 1904. It is possible that Baca and Fornoff disagreed on this investigation. The incident was a political hot potato, and Fred Fornoff was a political animal.

Baca claimed that he tried to contact Fornoff by telephone concerning his new Chaves case information, but the captain was unavailable to take his call. It is significant to note that Baca chose not to write to Captain Fornoff, but instead to Governor Hagerman. Baca told the governor that he had "entirely reliable" information concerning the Chaves assassins and the full nature of the conspiracy. Baca said the men could be "captured in short notice" if the right man was set on their trail, implying he was the right man. Public records contain no information concerning what, if anything, Governor Hagerman did with the leads Baca uncovered during his Chaves murder investigation. However, in February 1907, Mounted Policemen Dick Huber and Julius Meyer did arrest a suspect in the Chaves murder, but the district attorney never brought the case to trial and no one ever collected the $2,500 reward money.

Baca had earned $1,500 a year as second-in-command of the Mounted Police and could not accept reward money, but a private detective could earn all the reward money he could collect. Could this be the real reason Baca left the Mounted Police? Did Baca seek the reward money for the capture of Col. Chaves' killer?

A powerful political cabal was finally able to force Governor Hagerman out of office, and J. Wallace Raynolds, the interim governor, was not willing to pursue the Chaves killing matter. When George Curry was inaugurated governor a few months later, he showed no interest in stirring up political trouble over something that transpired years before his watch. Today the Chaves assassination is still an unsolved mystery from the annals of frontier New Mexico Territory.[3]

* * *

The double dose of happiness that surrounded the birth of the Baca twins did not last. Mary Ann was barely two months when, "after several days of painful illness," she died about five o'clock on Saturday afternoon, February 1, and Baca-Berry relatives and friends gathered to mourn the loss of a fourth Baca child. "There was a large attendance of sorrowing relatives and friends at the funeral service at the family residence Sunday afternoon and the remains of the little one were laid to rest in [the] Socorro cemetery," was the *Socorro Chieftain*'s account.

The infant Mary Ann Baca has her eternal rest in an unmarked grave in the Berry Plot in the Socorro Cemetery next to her sister Ruby. Mary Berry Baca was so distraught that her infant daughter, the namesake for her great-grandmother Mary Ann Lord Gilberson, was unbaptized when she died that the surviving twin Maisie had a hasty presentation before the Lord the next Sunday. The congregation of Socorro's Episcopal Church of the Epiphany was the believing body of witnesses to this profession of parental faith on February 10, 1907.[4]

The Baca family seemed to be under a dark cloud of mourning and a deep concern for their future. Cipriano's financial worries had compounded with the sickness and death of his baby daughter, but the family mood changed quickly when the head of the household received a new job offer. The 47-year-old ex-territorial ranger willingly accepted a temporary position as a special agent, commonly called a railroad policeman, with the El Paso and Southwestern Railroad Company, one of the subsidiary properties of a massive multifaceted company called the Phelps-Dodge Corporation.

Today the Phelps-Dodge Corporation is one of the world's largest copper and molybdenum mining operations with subsidiary divisions making and marketing gas by-products, wire, and cable. Almost 15,000 people worldwide work for PD, as Wall Street traders know the corporation. Yankee businessmen Anson Greene Phelps and William E. Dodge founded

Mary Baca took this family group picture in the backyard of the Bacas' Socorro, New Mexico, home in the early months of 1907 before Cipriano started his new job in El Paso. The boys are Gilverson and Florentino who is holding his father's large hat. Cipriana stands next to her father who is holding Maisie (Mary Baca Photograph Album/Cipriana Randolph).

the multi-billion-dollar conglomerate in 1834 as an import-export business. The two men started by shipping U.S.-grown cotton to England in exchange for tin, iron, copper and other metals essential for the expansion of the new American nation's Industrial Revolution. The Phelps-Dodge Corporation became part of Freeport-McMoRan Cooper & Gold, Inc on March 19, 2007.

Over the decades, Phelps-Dodge began to develop local copper-mining interests to use in making their special wire and cable. This led the company to invest in railroad development for transportation, timber and coal for fuel, and finally diversifying into molybdenum mining. New Mexico was a natural source for timber, coal, coke, copper, and molybdenum. By 1900, Phelps-Dodge had established massive corporate operations in Arizona and New Mexico Territories. The original section of El Paso and Southwestern Railroad track ran between Bisbee, Arizona, and El Paso. The EP&SW's parent company, the Phelps-Dodge Company, had added two more railroads to their holdings by 1905, the El Paso Northeastern Railroad with tracks running from El Paso north to Santa Rosa, and the Dawson Railway, a track system running from the mining camp east to Tucumcari. In May 1907, Phelps-Dodge leased the Rock Island Railroad track from Santa Rosa to Tucumcari; thus, the company was able to control the rail shipping system between their major mining operations in northeastern New Mexico and southeastern Arizona. In 1924, the

Southern Pacific Railroad system purchased all of Phelps-Dodge's 1,200-mile rail system and rolling stock.

The growth of railroads was a worldwide phenomenon that generated fanciful dreams. William Larrabee, in his 1893 book *The Railroad Question*, suggested that a rail system constructed across the Bering Strait could connect North America with Russia and via a Trans-Siberian system "finally reach London via St. Petersburg, Berlin and Paris." In a final, more grounded statement, Larrabee wrote, "It is very questionable whether such a line is at present feasible either from a technical or financial point of view, but the time will probably come when the railroad track will connect New York and London." Trans-Atlantic flight seems to have killed Larrabee's prediction of a trans-oceanic rail system, but he did correctly predicted the impact the new Interstate Commerce Commission would have upon uniform freight rates and operation procedures.[5]

* * *

In late October 1901, Cipriano Baca, then sheriff of Luna County, had a cup of coffee with Bill Darbyshire, the short-cropped, red-haired head of the El Paso and Southwestern Railroad construction crew, at Deming's Harvey House and discussed the EP&SW's impasse with the Southern Pacific Railroad. Baca had a fondness for the new road because it was providing easier access to the area south and west of Deming toward Hermanas and on to the Hachita mining district in the Bootheel. Baca understood how that area's remoteness hampered economic development.

The infant EP&SW had one big problem. The Southern Pacific tracks formed an east-west throughway on the south side of Deming's union depot, while the Santa Fe road's tracks terminated in the yards on the north side of the large two-story depot and rail yard. The EP&SW needed to cross the Southern Pacific tracks in order to connect with the Santa Fe line so they could retrieve supplies from the north via the AT&SF. It was an honored custom that established railroads extended line-crossing courtesy to their competitors, but in this instance, the Southern Pacific did not want to let the EP&SW have transfer service with their competitor. The established old dog wanted to receive a five-dollar-per-car switching fee, an exorbitant amount for that day, from the upstart pup. The EP&SW refused the demand, so the Southern Pacific posted guards along its tracks in the Deming rail yard to prevent any overt action by the EP&SW to construct a clandestine crossing.

Baca reminded Darbyshire how the Atchison, Topeka and Santa Fe Railway construction crew had used "misdirection" to capture possession of Raton Pass in February, 1878, and thus earned the right to enter New Mexico ahead of their rival the Denver and Rio Grande Western Railroad. Late at night on Tuesday, November 5, 1901, Bill Darbyshire launched his own "misdirection" raid.

The EP&SW supervisor dispatched a few of his men to a point several miles west of Deming. These decoys fired their pistols in the air, and the men guarding the Southern Pacific tracks in Deming hurried west to investigate, meanwhile Darbyshire rushed a work crew to his proposed crossing site. By the time the Southern Pacific men returned to their posts, the deed was a *fait accompli* and the imprisoned Santa Fe cargo was safely rolling south over EP&SW tracks. Completed in 1902, the EP&SW rail line between Bisbee and El Paso used a 1 percent grade to cross over the 4,739-foot Continental Divide.

Sheriff Baca investigated the "riotous incident" on the Southern Pacific tracks and even looked into the covert construction operation in the Deming railroad yards, but he could find that no laws had been broken. Never publicly identified with the Great Deming Depot Raid, the tale of Baca's "misdirection" suggestion circulated freely among the EP&SW leadership. When the time came, the railroad's new ownership rewarded Baca's past assistance.

The main EP&SW operations office in El Paso became Special Agent Baca's new headquarters. As a railroad special officer, Cipriano worked under the general supervision of veteran railroad detective Quinn Sadler. Headquartered at Tucumcari, the chief detective for the Phelps-Dodge railroad system worked mostly within the eastern New Mexico sector centered upon the El Paso and Northeastern Railroad. Chief Special Agent Sadler received a commission as a nonsalaried Special New Mexico Mounted Police ranger in 1909.

Baca's efforts were concentrated on the El Paso rail yards and the West Texas sector of the holding company's operation. On many days, after some routine patrol of the El Paso yards, visitors could find Baca sitting around the big headquarters potbelly stove reading the newspaper, writing reports or maybe in a neighborhood saloon awaiting a call to a crime scene.

An EP&SW special agent's daily duties involved protecting the rolling stock, shipment consignments, and physical property of the company. Sadler's detectives also investigated any crime committed against the El Paso and Southwestern Railroad. It is difficult to paint a comprehensive portrait of Special Agent Baca's activities during his assignment in El Paso, because the railroad company purged their old police case files in the 1970s to make room in storage for current case files. However, the *El Paso Times* reported some of Baca's cases in "railroad happenings" notices. Special Agent Baca's small leather-bound notebook indicates that he sought the perpetrators who stole merchandise from a locked boxcar, searched for young thieves who stole coal from a rail yard storage area, conducted an investigation for missing equipment from an engine warehouse, and trapped some vagrants who were tampering with junction switches.[6]

* * *

Mary Baca's only brother was a mining engineer in the Mexican state of Sonora. In late February 1908, Mary Carman Cortesy-Berry planned on joining her husband south of the border. The *Socorro Chieftain* reported on the occasion, saying, "Mrs. Berry expected to visit friends in Las Cruces and El Paso on her way."[7] It is unclear if she saw Cipriano as she passed through El Paso. On the day the Socorro newspaper told its readers of Mary Berry's plan to visit her Las Cruces friends, the community was jolted from its winter slumber by a front-page murder that would ensnare Cipriano Baca in its web. The couple spent the next 40 years in Mexico. James died in 1947 and rests in the Berry Plot at Socorro. Mary Cortesy-Berry lived to become a centenarian.

* * *

It was Leap Year Day, 1908, and in mid-morning on that Saturday, the 57-year-old former lawman Pat Garrett kept his appointed time to meet his fate. The place was a mesquite-covered desert crossroads called Alameda Arroyo on the desolate Mail Road a few miles east of Las Cruces. A chunk of lead slammed into the back of the Alabama native's head pushing some of his graying brown hair into his skull. The aging former lawman was knocked forward, hit the ground, and rolled over on his back as a second piece of hot lead bored into the front of his body.

Later that day, a local range hand named Jessie Wayne Brazel walked calmly into the Dona Ana County sheriff's office in the courthouse at Las Cruces and laid a Colt .45 on the desk in front of Deputy Sheriff Felipe Lopez. He said he had recently killed Pat Garrett. The deputy thought it was a joke until Brazel's companion, Carl Adamson, solemnly confirmed the story by saying that Wayne Brazel had killed the former lawman–bounty hunter in self-defense.

Territorial Governor George Curry, Attorney General James M. Hervey, and Captain Fornoff made the 280-mile train trip from Santa Fe to Las Cruces for Garrett's funeral on Sunday March 1. Curry and Hervey had known Garrett since the early days in Lincoln County. The governor served as one of the pallbearers. On Monday, Garrett's family buried him, with no religious service, in the Odd Fellow's Cemetery at Las Cruces. Meanwhile, Fornoff and Hervey took Adamson to the site of the crime for a show-and-tell-at-the-scene investigation. Over the decades since the trio's visit to the Garrett death site, numerous published accounts of what the three men found have caused historians concern since each account has had a different tale to tell.

On Tuesday, March 3, Wayne Brazel received a preliminary hearing before Justice of the Peace Manuel Lopez, and he entered a not-guilty plea because he had shot in self-defense. The justice bound Brazel over to the action of the next session of the Dona Ana County grand jury. On Monday, April 13, the grand jury considered the findings of the inquest conducted by a coroner's jury and voted a true bill against Brazel charging him with murder. The district court judge issued a warrant for Brazel's arrest. At his bail hearing, the judge ordered a $100,000 bond to set Brazel free until his appearance at the October term of the District Court. One of Dona Ana County's most respected citizens, William W. Cox, and six of his rancher friends posted the needed cash bond. Southern New Mexico received a clear message concerning Cox's support of Brazel's actions.

A few weeks later, Fred Fornoff left Santa Fe for a visit with Baca in El Paso. Fornoff had a special request for his former lieutenant. He needed him to work the informants of the railroad agents and his own underworld network in the Las Cruces–El Paso region to find out what they knew or had heard about who was behind the Garrett murder. It was a difficult request. Baca very

The Louisiana-born Patrick Floyd Garrett served as sheriff of both Lincoln County and Dona Ana County. He had been a Special Texas Ranger, a deputy U.S. marshal, and a buffalo hunter before he became a customs collector, a rancher, a bad-debt drunk, and a lousy gambler (NMMP/AC).

likely had to call in personal favors to elicit the dangerous information Captain Fornoff wanted.

The ancient Greek philosopher Plato caught Cipriano's judgment on Garrett when he wrote, "You can learn more about a person during an hour of play than you can in a year of conversation." Baca had known Garrett and, like Captain Fornoff, did not care much for him as a person. The two men had played poker, and Baca family tradition relates that on one occasion Cipriano had won a cut-down 44–40 caliber Winchester 73 rifle from the old bounty hunter. Cipriano gave this weapon to his son Florentino for his protection while he lived in Old Mexico; later the young man used the rifle as collateral for a loan while he was attending college and never reclaimed the weapon.

Baca and Fornoff met again in late spring 1908. In a quiet corner of an El Paso hotel dining room, the two men enjoyed their favorite meal of beefsteak and enchiladas. During their meal, Baca outlined for Fornoff the tale of a cabal that had gone wrong. Powerful and shadowy entrepreneurs had been operating a Chinese smuggling operation from the El Paso area north across New Mexico to the coal mines and farms of southern Colorado. The ring had been using Garrett's semi-deserted and isolated canyon ranch as a hiding place to hold the illegal aliens until arrangements could be made to smuggle them aboard northbound trains. The small group of conspirators, related through blood, marriage, and/or money, had first tried to buy the canyon ranch, but Garrett would not sell because, for some unknown reason, he believed that his land had some value as mining property. The old manhunter had been involved in unprofitable Mexican mining ventures with partners like George Curry and Albert Bacon Fall. Fall would serve as a defense attorney for Brazel.

Governor George Curry directed Mounted Police Captain Fred Fornoff to make an independent investigation into the murder of Pat Garrett, the sheriff who had killed Billy the Kid in 1881. Fornoff considered the young outlaw to have been "a viper and a danger to society." He often said, "A respectable history of New Mexico ought not have a picture of that little murderer." Fornoff held only slightly more respect for Garrett (Fred Fornoff Papers, NMMP/AC).

Next, the cabal of smugglers took advantage of Pat's less-than-stellar abilities at the card table and caused him to mortgage his ranch property to settle his gambling debts, but Garrett weaseled on his loans forcing his creditors to take him to court to extract payment. Once again, the conspirators lost because the jury sided with Garrett. Now the plot became more underhanded; the men decided to get Garrett entangled in a leased land agreement made with their surrogates. Garrett was still arguing over the terms of this lease, enacted in his name by his son, on the day he died.

Much intrigue surrounded Pat Garrett during his life, and his remaining personal papers, housed in the New Mexico State University Library, are just as perplexing. Garrett was a vile and mean-tempered greedy badman, a petty gambler of questionable skill, a disreputable public servant and grafter, a deadbeat godless drunk, and a cold-blooded killer. There were many reasons why Pat Garrett's demise was welcome news to many people in the southwest, and Dona Ana County in particular; maybe even his own family was included in these numbers. Public opinion strongly supported the contention that Pat Garrett's family was better off, or no worse off, after his death than while Pat was alive. Strangely, the Garrett family seemed to hold no ill will toward Pat's confessed killer or his public supporters. Mrs. Garrett, and her children, honored the controversial land-lease agreement and went on with their lives. You cannot put spilled milk back into a pitcher.

Cipriano Baca had learned, contrary to the present-day legend or the myths of his day, that the Pat Garrett killing had resulted not from any conspiracy to murder, but had been a crime of opportunity. One of Pat's old foes had become impatient with Garrett's continual roadblocks to his financial success, the nonpayment of his debts, and the threats Pat had made against his life and freedom for over a decade. This pent-up hate had caused William Henry "Bill" McNew to seize upon the unplanned occasion to rid himself and his friends of this nagging nemesis and shot the old manhunter from the ridge above where Garrett had stopped his buggy to urinate. Wayne Brazel had simply added the *coup de grace*.

Captain Fornoff combined Baca's information with what he had learned visiting the murder site and from other informants into a draft report that Page Otero, the Mounted Police office clerk, polished and typed. Fornoff gave his formal report to Governor Curry who passed it to Attorney General Hervey for use during the Brazel trial. Curry would later claim that he never read Fornoff's final document. Hervey wrote, before his death in 1953, saying, "Fornoff made the trip to El Paso and came back and said he had made a real discovery but he did not know whether he would ever be able to prove it." Cipriano Baca never sought public credit for his part in discovering the background to Pat Garrett's murder, and Captain Fornoff never offered the information.

The *El Paso Herald* somehow learned about the Fornoff Report, and a reporter asked Attorney General Hervey if he could review its contents. In the pre–Open Records Act era, New Mexico's chief law enforcer refused the journalist's request, claiming that the coming trail was the proper place to present the evidence so as not to taint a jury pool. At the fall 1908 court session, the judge postponed Brazel's murder trial until the spring of 1909. Meanwhile, Brazel continued to work as a range hand for W.W. Cox.

The Third District Court of New Mexico was presided over by Territorial Judge Frank W. Parker. He was the same judge who had presided over the trial in the summer of 1899 that had freed the men that Garrett, then Dona Ana County sheriff, had arrested for the killing of Col. A.J. Fountain and his young son in the White Sands. Parker was also a friend of Brazel's chief attorney, Albert Bacon Fall, and more than once had publicly expressed his own dislike of Pat Garrett.

Judge Parker convened Case No. 4112, the *Territory of New Mexico vs. Wayne Brazel*, at 9:00 A.M. on Monday, April 19, 1909. W.C. Field, a Baca friend, was the doctor who had examined Garrett's wounds at the murder scene and later performed the autopsy on the body and testified concerning the nature of the wounds. District attorney Mark B. Thompson presented the rest of his case with such appalling indifference and incompetence that he could have stayed at home and done a better job. The prosecution presented no evidence showing that Garrett was unarmed, urinating, and wearing a heavy glove on his shooting hand at the time he died. The prosecution used none of the information contained in Fornoff's report, and neither Captain Fornoff nor Carl Adamson testified about their visit to the crime scene. The Dona Ana County district attorney was a political ally of Albert Bacon Fall.

The defense presentation was equally short as they called only three character witnesses. In an odd twist of fate, one of Brazel's supporters was Territorial Mounted Policeman John A. Beal of Deming. The two men had known each other since their youthful days as cowboys in Brown County, Texas. The jury began their deliberations at 5:45 in the late afternoon, and within 25 minutes Jessie Wayne Brazel was a free man and on his way to supper. In fact, many people in southern New Mexico and west Texas where happy with Wayne Brazel's acquittal. They were equally pleased the region no longer was home to an unpleasant deadbeat like Pat Garrett, and even fewer had a desire to see the murderer caught or tried or convicted.

W.W. Cox had sat with Brazel, as a public show of his support, during the cowboy's preliminary hearing and again at his murder trial. Following the acquittal verdict and Brazel's release, Cox hosted a massive barbecue celebration at his vast San Augustine Ranch to honor Pat Garrett's confessed killer.

William Henry "Bill" McNew, the rancher Cipriano Baca fingered as Garrett's killer, also attended the feast. So did Jim Gilliland and A.P. "Print" Rhodes, two other suspect killers. "Deacon Jim" Miller, Adamson's cousin-in-law was a "rumored killer" plant to misdirect the public from focusing on the real Garrett conspirators and their game. A mob in Ada, Oklahoma, lynched Miller, while the Brazel trial was in session, for an unrelated crime.

Fate dealt many twists to the lives of the people involved in the final days of Pat Garrett's life. Oliver Lee, a Fountain murder suspect, served as a member of the 1919 State House of Representatives and served as president of the New Mexico State Cattle Growers' Association. He died a wealthy and respected rancher in December 1941, and today his ranch is a New Mexico state park named in his honor.

Jim Gililland, another Fountain murder suspect, was a friend of Governor George Curry. In 1910, Curry appointed Jim a special Territorial Mounted Policeman. In later years, Jim never talked about the Garrett or Fountain murders. He died in August 1946. Curry was also a long-time friend of Pat Garrett. He had campaigned for Pat to be sheriff of Lincoln County and a few days before Garrett's death Curry loaned Pat $50.

Pat Garrett had known the Brazel family during his Lincoln County days. Pat liked and trusted Jessie Wayne Brazel and his father. The Garrett ranch was a short distance from the Gold Camp School where Olive Boyd was a teacher in this one-room building. In 1910, she became Mrs. Wayne Brazel. Brazel homesteaded west of Lordsburg and settled on a small ranch until his wife died in 1911. Three years later, Brazel disappeared and walked into oblivion. Not even his lawman brother, and later his son, could locate him.

Territorial Attorney General James Hervey's father had been a friend of Pat Garrett. Hervey was a boyhood friend of western author Emerson Hough. Hough had gathered information for his book *The Story of the Outlaw* from Pat Garrett. The old manhunter earned about $200 for his help with Emerson's book. Pat Garrett's son, Jarvis, always believed that Adamson had been the triggerman in his father's murder. Hough advised the young man not to seek revenge for his father's death or his father's murderers would kill him also.

The web became more twisted. Herbert B. Holt, one of Wayne Brazel's defense attorneys, had been Pat Garrett's personal lawyer and was a political ally of A. B. Fall. Someone assassinated underworld strongman Emanuel "Mannie" Clements on December 29, 1908, in the crowded wine room of Tom Power's Coney Island Saloon in El Paso. Power was Garrett's close friend. No one admitted seeing who fired the fatal shot and El Paso newspapers hinted that the murder was payback for the recent killing of two Chinese immigration agents.

William Web Cox sued Brazel for recovery of the $574.80 he had fronted the cowboy for the goat herd on the Bear Canyon Ranch, and Cox got the goats and the lease on Garrett's land. Cox developed his livestock empire and was a powerful political boss before his death in December 1923. Ironically, Cox and Garrett rest in the same cemetery.

Albert Bacon Fall became a member of President Warren Harding's cabinet. He was disgraced in a national political scandal, and federal prison was his reward. Fall died, in poverty, a broken man in 1944. During A.B. Fall's federal conspiracy trial, resulting from Fall's misdealings while serving as secretary of the interior, George Curry testified as a character witness for his former attorney general. Because of his testimony in support of Fall, Curry lost his federal job, so the New Mexico Legislature created a job for him as state historian. Governor Curry died a poor man in Albuquerque's VA Hospital in November 1947.

Three men did serve federal prison time for their part in the cabal to ruin Pat Garrett and legally steal his secluded Bear Canyon property for use as a way station for a Chinese labor smuggling operation. One of these men was Santa Fe Railroad conductor Hiland D. Maynard, who had arranged the subversive transport to the Colorado mining fields, was convicted of bribery and sentenced to 18 months as a federal prisoner. Another conspirator was a 62-year-old federal Chinese inspection officer. The third man was Carl Adamson, Brazel and Garrett's traveling companion on the death ride. He earned 18 months for conspiracy. Paroled in July 1912, Adamson moved to Chaves County, married, and raised sheep for A.D. Garrett. The sheep venture failed following the bust in the sheep market after World War I and Adamson died in 1919. His grandson, Joe Skeen, grew up to become a congressional representative from the southeastern district of New Mexico.

After Baca told Fornoff what he had learned about the Chinese smuggling, political deals and the financial arrangements between multiple players along the El Paso–Las Cruces–Alamogordo corridor, he had no more involvement with the Garrett murder investigation. One of the political strategists aligned in the power play against Pat Garrett was William Ashton Hawkins, a brilliant attorney for Charles B. Eddy's El Paso and Northeastern Railroad. In 1905, Phelps-Dodge had become the parent company for the EP&NE Railroad system and all of its holdings.[8]

The Mounted Police continued to fight a losing battle against politically protected organized crime in New Mexico Territory. Following the growth of local self-government granted by statehood, disbandment of the state rangers in 1921, and the rise of a "live and let live" attitude toward the rise of society's darker lifestyle following the end of World War I, a new and more sinister crime machine was born in New Mexico. The El Paso–Las Cruces corridor again emerged as a haven for mob controlled unbridled illegal gambling dens, under age and after hours drinking, all-hours sex trade, illegal drugs, alien human trafficking for field hands and domestic laborers, and bribery of public officials. The brutal murder of a tiny 18-year-old Las Cruces girl named Ovida "Cricket" Coogler, who knew too much about the political racketeering in New Mexico, in March 1949 served as the catalyst that ended a century of one-party political corruption centered in Santa Fe and infecting all levels of business, government, and law enforcement. The 1949–1950 housecleaning reached from the governor's office, to state executive departments, to members of the state legislature, to the state police chief and some state police officers, to district and county judges, and to local officials. The mob bosses left the state and moved to Nevada, but a half century later, organized crime has returned to the Land of Enchantment.[9]

* * *

Baca knew that the El Paso and Northeastern Railroad's headquarters in El Paso would be his base of operation, but since he was uncertain about the nature or duration of his new job, he left his family in Socorro. In the Oasis on the Rio Grande, Mary had her family to lend moral support and sometimes financial assistance. Robert E. Lee once wrote his wife that among the calamites of war, the hardest to bear was the separation from family and friends. It is very possible that Cipriano Baca felt this pain even though he made a few short trips home and was able to spend some quality family time in Socorro during the Christmas and New Year holidays.

The couple made plans to relocate to the Pass City early in 1908, but the death of Mary's grandmother and namesake, Mary Ann Lord Gilberson, in early January changed those plans. The Berry family plot in the Socorro cemetery became Grandmother Gilberson's final resting place. It was also about this time that Mary discovered she was pregnant again. Cipriano and Mary agreed that she and the children would continue to live in Socorro to be near her grieving mother, and Mary's sisters were near in case she needed help during her pregnancy.

During the second week of September 1908, Mary Baca presented her husband with a third son. The *Socorro Chieftain* told readers that Cipriano had come to town to "bestow the parental blessing on a bouncing boy baby" that was baptized James, but the family quickly nicknamed him Jimmy. The boy's name honored both Mary's father and her brother. The revised plan had been to relocate the Baca family to El Paso following the new baby's birth, but in mid–September, the *Socorro Chieftain* told its readers that the Baca family was not moving to El Paso. Instead they would be going to Dawson, "where Mr. Baca has accepted a very desirable position." The "desirable position" was the post of town marshal for the coal-mining town.[10]

Mountainview, founded in 1895 along the northern bank of the Vermejo River in the coal-rich Sangre de Cristo Mountains of northern Colfax County, was renamed Dawson in 1900 in honor of the two brothers who owned the town-site property. The Dawson brothers bought 23,000 acres of the Vermejo River Valley in 1869, and after the discovery of coal on the property, they constructed a small mining and coking operation. A rail line from Tucumcari to the coal-mining town opened the enterprise to worldwide markets.

The Phelps-Dodge Corporation bought the Dawson brothers' coal deposit mineral claims, operating mine sites, coke ovens, and the plated town site in 1905. The conglomerate mining company started expanded operations in Stag Canon to provide the coal supply needed to run nearly 600 coke ovens that burned night and day near Dawson. These ovens made coke from hard coal and helped to extract coal gas. Coke transports easily, burns very hot, and produces very little smoke, so Phelps-Dodge had a ready market for their product with the steel mills in Colorado and Pennsylvania. They sold their coal gas as a heating and lighting fuel in regional markets.

Dewey Tidwell, a druggist at Dawson in the late 1930s, recalled the town decades later. "Dawson was a complete community, with the big company store [PD Mercantile], bank, churches, hotel, theater, golf course, barber shop, saloon [called the Snake], and just about every necessity."

An additional benefit that helped to enticed Cipriano Baca to accept the offer to be Dawson's marshal was Phelps-Dodge's health care plan. The company charged employees a small monthly fee that entitled the employee's family to full medical care at the company hospital. This family plan covered all care except for major injury or illness not resulting from work-related activity.

Dewey Tidwell recalled the social conditions in Dawson, saying,

> Phelps-Dodge did not tolerate racial discrimination. Names such as Gringo, Wop, Dago, Spic, Kraut, Limey, and Mick were bantered back and forth without any hostility, from those the nickname referred to, but say Okie, Arkie, or Texan and there was usually some trouble.

In Dawson, single miners and coke oven operators lived in ethnic boarding houses. Each house had a boarding boss of the nationality located in the house who was the house overseer. Family men were leased a small house, regardless of their nationality, along Family Row. Railroad workers lived in a separate suburb near the rail yard, a short distance from the miners' quarters and the coke makers compound.

The *Compiled Laws of New Mexico—1897* contains a section prohibiting mining and mercantile companies from paying their employees in company scrip. However, the scrip law did not prohibit these same conglomerates from providing company scrip or tokens as their sole means of change for purchases made at company-operated stores or saloons. Almost all of Dawson's 4,000 citizens traded at local businesses like the large company-owned mercantile store because the miners could easily cash their paychecks and make payments on outstanding credit accounts. "PD Mercantile, as it was commonly called, with its grocery, meat, dry goods, ladies' ready-to-wear, men's wearing apparel, shoe department, bakery, hardware department, and undertaking department, along with the drug department, flabbergasted me," Dewey Tidwell remembered. Few miners had personal transportation or the extra money to travel to nearby towns for their household supplies. Another evil labor practice was not changed until 1917 when a law was enacted requiring all employers to cease random pay periods and remunerate their employees at a standard time each month or each week.

The mine owners expected Town Marshal/Deputy Sheriff Cipriano Baca and his policemen to maintain order at the payroll office, serve as debt collectors for the company store, control drunks at the company saloon, keep any unhappy miners at their jobs, and generally maintain peace and order in the town. Dawson had no town jail, so Baca had to transport all his prisoners to the county lockup at Raton. The coal camp policemen usually led a lonely, ostracized life because they were often viewed as coldhearted thugs by the workers while the company managers saw them as an evil that they needed but that must be keep under tight control.

Cipriana Randolph cheerfully recalled the months her family lived in Dawson:

> I don't know exactly what Father's job was when we lived in Dawson. But, it was connected with that large company [Phelps-Dodge] that made coke. I was quite young when we lived there and we did not live there very long. The town was located in a nice green mountain valley

and the smokestacks were always working, day and night. I remember that we lived in one of the company houses. They were built in long rows for the company employees.

Today the coal mining camp Cipriana had trouble recalling is just a fading memory recalled by aged newspaper files, family scrapbooks and photograph albums, and marked only by a few foundation slabs, decaying coke ovens and a cemetery. The Dawson Cemetery is on the National Register of Historic Places because its rows of gray iron crosses mark the last resting place of 383 men who died in two of the nation's worst coal mine explosions.

Within a few months after Cipriano's arrival in Dawson, one of three things transpired: he completed his policing assignment in the camp, he became disenchanted with his job at Dawson, or his services were more useful back in El Paso. In any case, Baca turned in his marshal's badge and in early 1909 returned to his original job as a special agent for the EP&SW Railroad. Shortly after Cipriano Baca left Dawson, the new police chief, former Mounted Policeman Frank Vance, had to deal with an epidemic of homicides. The town witnessed six murders in less than a month.

In September 1910, former Mounted Police Sergeant Will Dudley replaced Vance. Will was good friends with EP&SW chief of detectives Quinn Sadler, who also lived in Alamogordo, so Dudley was an easy choice to head Dawson's six-man force of deputy marshals. Under Dudley's leadership, the police quickly restored order in the coal town. Two years after Frank Vance left Dawson, his family asked his Cimarron friend Mounted Policeman Fred Lambert to look into the circumstances surrounding Vance's assassination. Lambert gathered information that proved that the local mining camp police chief and his cronies had murdered Vance, but state and local Colorado authorities would not act on the evidence. Colorado's political machine was controlled by massive coal-mining trust companies that tolerated no "outside" troublemakers.[11]

Following his short sojourn in northeastern New Mexico, Baca brought his family to El Paso. Mrs. Randolph recalled that as a girl her family "lived upstairs over the office of the Stag Canyon Fuel Company" when they lived in El Paso. The fuel company was the retail outlet for the Phelps-Dodge Company's coal mined at Dawson. An El Paso city directory confirms Mrs. Randolph's recollection that the Bacas' apartment was at the southeast corner of North Virginia and St. Louis Streets, just northeast of El Paso's Chinatown area.

St. Louis Street, present-day Mills, paralleled the Southern Pacific tracks one block south. The railroad tracks ran down the center of Main Street with the depot between North Stanton and North Virginia Streets. The Baca living quarters were a few blocks up Virginia from a Chinese's temple, called a "joss house" in honor of one of the Orientals' pantheon of gods, and on a windy day the scent of incense could be detected. East of the Bacas' home, near the San Jacinto Plaza, the Chinese community operated numerous laundry shops and opium dens. The pleasure palaces might operate nightly until dawn due to ineffective patrols of the El Paso Police Department. The El Paso *Evening Tribune* even mentioned the problem: "Opium joints on South Oregon are a disgrace to our city." The opium dens remained active well into the 1920s.

Cipriano was not as concerned with the opium dens as he was with the alligators in San Jacinto Plaza. These descendants of prehistoric sea reptiles had made themselves at home sunning in the pond of the old plaza since 1883. Small neighborhood dogs were sometimes reported missing, and Baca was always concerned about his children's safety when they went to *Plaza de Los Lagartos* with the other neighborhood kids. The plaza was the center of the downtown business district and the town's gathering place. Horse-drawn carriages, or hacks, surrounded the place like a cabstand at a modern airport. Transient preachers shared their Gospel message from the protocol in a shady grove of trees, and children and adults played in the manicured grass. Night vandals mistreated the alligators, so in the mid-1960s the city government removed them from more harm, but today a fiberglass sculpture of a basking alligator greets all plaza visitors.

Records are unclear on this point, but it seems that Cipriano Baca joined the Railroad Association of Special Agents and Police of the United States and Canada. Founded to offer training, via an annual national convention, the association was supportive of railroad police departments. Baca was planning to attend the 1910 convention in San Francisco, but fate had a different plan.

* * *

In August 1909, the Berry-Baca family was making plans for Effie Hunter Berry's wedding and a celebration for little Jimmy Baca's first birthday. The family was also making plans to welcome yet another child to the family; Mary was four months pregnant. The *El Paso Morning Times* was not able to record these happy events before it reported another sad event in Cipriano Baca's life. "The infant son of C. Baca, special agent of the Southern, died at the home of his parents on Virginia Street. The remains were shipped to Socorro, N. M. Saturday night [August 7]." The Bacas buried their fifth child in the Socorro Cemetery, and Jimmy's grave, like that of the other Baca children, is now known only to God.

The life cycle continued. On Monday, November 22, 1909, the Baca family gathered in Socorro to witness the union of Mary's last unmarried sister to Clyde Eldon Stauder. Effie was 24 years old and, like her older sisters, worked as a schoolteacher. Stauder was a friend of the tall, handsome and popular bachelor John "Slim" Rusk, the veteran Mounted Policeman stationed at Chama, and was a relative of William G. Sargent, the territorial auditor, who would help the political conservatives to dismantle the Mounted Police in late 1913. The couple met while attending the School of Mines, and now they would establish their home on a sheep ranch, near Chama, along the Colorado border. Cipriana Randolph had fun at the wedding because she liked her Aunt Effie and her new husband. The young girl had no way of knowing how important they would both become in her life.

Mrs. Cipriana Randolph never forgot Friday, January 28, 1910.

> It happened to be my eighth birthday. I was very much upset to come home from school that afternoon expecting to have a party and finding a baby sister. Rachel [Encarnacion Baca] had just been born [and named to honor our fraternal grandmother]. Father told me I'd still have my party because Mama had managed to bake a cake that morning and Father had a couple of neighbor children in and we had a small party in the kitchen.

The official documentation of Rachel's birthday is another example of how family records and tradition can differ from government personal data files. One of the recorders in the El Paso County clerk's office maintaining the local birth index cards for the Texas Bureau of Vital Statistics mistakenly recorded that Rachel Encarnacion Baca's birthday was January 21, 1910.[12]

Family photographs taken when the Bacas lived in El Paso show that Cipriano had started wearing wire-rim eyeglasses during this period. He would wear some form of glasses the rest of his life. The eyewear did not seem to hinder Baca's fearless approach to law enforcement.

18

The Mogollon Years

"Former lieutenant of Mounted Police accepts task of straightening out tangle in mountain mining camp."—*Socorro Chieftain*, 3 September 1910

Mogollon had been a mining camp for over a quarter of a century. The community was made up of miners from numerous ethic origins, businessmen and shopkeepers who provided their needed services, a Catholic and a Presbyterian church for spiritual needs, families with enough children to fill a large two-story schoolhouse, and a motion picture house. The west end of town housed "Little Italy," a red-light district that was home to 18 white girls, while the east end of the canyon, near the Roman Catholic Church, contained a sporting house for Hispanics.

In 1910, Mogollon also had six saloons and two liquor stores. A camp resident commented about this type of business saying, "Two saloons are ample for a town the size of Mogollon." The camp's troubles revolved around money. The miners were not spending enough of their hard-earned money to support the camp's liquor business or the local gamblers, so they began to compete with each other. "The success of the mining industry is everything to the people of Mogollon. The liquor business is immaterial. Capital for developing our mines and turning them into steady producers is what we want most and what we must stick to when we get it," wrote a Mogollon citizen.[1]

In the late summer of 1910, Territorial Mounted Policeman John Beal and Mogollon Constable and Special Mounted Policeman Bob Putman, were investigating a series of stage robberies near Mogollon because the local deputy sheriff was less than effective in his enforcement of the law. He was, in fact, the cover man for the businessmen who wished to have a "wide open" town and was supported by the local peace justice in his effort to "not make waves." The Mounted Police quickly caught the stage robbers and then began systematically closing down Mogollon's numerous illegal saloon operations, gambling dens, and the unlicensed red-light district. Upon recommendation of the Mounted Police, a directive from Sheriff George E. Sanchez and the Socorro County Commissioners' Court fired both Charley Clark, Mogollon's saloonkeeper-deputy sheriff, and Christian Sorensen, a town merchant and justice of the peace.

Some local saloonmen and gamblers did not like that action, so they joined with the former deputy sheriff and former peace justice in a plot to discredit or kill the territorial officers. They sprung their trap in the former deputy's saloon. However, the conspirators had not counted upon the quick action and deadly automatic pistol of Mounted Policeman John Beal.

This view of the Mogollon mining camp from Mt. Eberle looks east down Silver Creek Canyon. In the spring of 2008 the author stood on this same spot to view the remains of the ghost town with Jim Stauder, a Baca relative, as a companion (Jim Stauder Photograph Collection).

Herman A. Hoover noted the confrontation in his August 27 diary entry: "Stage driver brought word up that Chas. Clark was seriously if not fatally shot last night at Mogollon by one of the Mounted Police ... heard Clark was taken to Silver City Hospital." The next day Hoover wrote, "learn[ed] that Chas. Clark died in Silver City today."[2]

The two territorial police soon found themselves confronting a mob of angry saloonmen and gamblers calling themselves a justice-of-the-peace posse acting by appointment of the dethroned Christian Sorensen. Years later, one of the men who was in that street gathering that had confronted the two rangers remembered the event. He recalled that the "posse" ordered the territorial rangers to give up their weapons and submit to arrest and that Beal had said no. The future ranger sergeant defiantly added, "If you guys want a fight, just turn your dogs loose." The mob leaders assessed the moment and slowly disbanded under threat of further lethal action by Beal and Putman.

The camp's shady element was now on the verge of vigilante action against the territorial officers. If Henry C. Brooks, the 33-year-old Texas-born local cattle inspector and Special Mounted Police from nearby Alma, had not arrived in Mogollon to support his fellow officers, Beal and Putman may have been forced into a bloody shootout with these disgruntled supporters of unrestrained free enterprise. Meanwhile, Captain Fornoff dispatched Sergeant John Collier to Mogollon to maintain order until Sheriff Sanchez could acquire a new deputy for the Mogollon area. Later, Fornoff traveled to Mogollon to assess the camp's disposition for himself and to hear firsthand about the troubles that plagued the community. The visit reaffirmed the captain's belief that his territorial rangers had done their duty.

Shortly after the street confrontation, Beal and Putman surrendered to Sheriff Sanchez and left Mogollon for a preliminary hearing before a judge in Socorro. A Socorro County grand jury indicted the two rangers for murder. The officers posted bail and were released from jail to await their trial date. In the spring of 1911, Mogollon saloon men employed a team of "big city lawyers" to help the county prosecutors present the case against Beal and Putman. The two rangers stood trial in the District Court at Socorro, and the jury acquitted both of them of all charges. The gunsmoke-inspired law-and-order legend of the New Mexico Territorial Mounted Police reached a new zenith.

In late August 1910, Cipriano Baca's world changed again. Mogollon was a tinderbox as the camp remained divided over the death of Charley Clark. Sheriff Sanchez needed a deputy who could settle the tempers and restore order, and the justice court needed a capable constable to replace Bob Putman, so Captain Fornoff recommended Cipriano. Sheriff Sanchez wired Baca, cosigned by Fornoff, offering him the Mogollon assignment and asking him to come to Socorro to discuss the offer. Cipriano later wrote his former commander, "I am very thankful to you for [your] kindness and I assure you [that] you will have no cause for regret from me [for your personal recommendation]."

Sheriff Sanchez and Baca were able to reach an agreeable financial arrangement, and Cipriano became excited about the new adventure. However, during these troubled days Baca's sense of fairness and duty once more surfaced. Cipriano, in a second letter to Fornoff, explained that his boss, Chief of Detectives Quinn Sadler, was not currently in El Paso, so Baca felt he needed to wait until he returned to tell Sadler in person about his plan to accept the offer to police Mogollon. Cipriano was no stranger to Mogollon, as he knew many of the business leaders in the community.

Baca fondly recalled Mogollon and its majestic vista. The mountain range runs about

100 miles north and south along the western boundary of the territory. The Mogollon Mountains proper rise about 5,000 feet above the surrounding valleys, 10,000 feet above sea level, and have a width of over 20 miles. Large volcanic lava flows created this formation, and the mountains are cut east to west by streams that form deep canyons. It is in these rugged canyons that prospectors located ore-bearing rock during the 1870s Apache Wars, and soon the mining camps were born.

A letter writer to the *Silver City Independent* held high hopes for the future of Mogollon. "We think that we have an officer in Cipriano Baca who is capable of sustaining the majesty of the law." The mystery writer believed this restored peaceful climate would create a favorable environment or investment capital and that the mining camp would continue to grow into a prosperous city.

Most of the population greeted Baca's second appointment as a Mogollon peace officer with much public praise. "There are good reasons for believing that Mr. Baca will make an efficient and satisfactory official [in a town] where conditions have been unfortunate for sometime," said the *Socorro Chieftain*. The *Albuquerque Morning Journal* noted that Socorro County Sheriff Pete Sanchez "believes his new deputy is the one man for the place at this time, when conditions to say the least, are a trifle complicated."

The deputy sheriff/constable-elect first went to Socorro to confer with Sheriff Sanchez and Captain Fornoff. Baca took his oath of office and then headed back to El Paso to settle family affairs. The next morning Cipriano was on the train to Deming and finally ended up in Silver City, the jumping-off point for the mining camps. Baca arrived in Mogollon about midnight Sunday, September 4, after having left Silver City at 6:00 A.M. aboard Charles W. Marriott's motor stage line. Marriot carried the mail and express, as well as passengers. This was a long, tiresome, overland trip even with a lunch and rest break, especially if the driver had to perform car maintenance or tire repair.[3]

An unknown philosopher once wrote that man should not fear tomorrow, because G-d was already there. It is certain that Mary Baca prayed for the safety of her husband during those fearful "days of tomorrow."

The Mogollon that greeted Baca on Monday had changed little since the late 1890s. It was still a single-main-street mining camp bustling with miners, mill workers, burro drivers, wood contractors and their choppers, mining engineers, and tradesmen like butchers, a shoemaker, a watchmaker, some cooks and restaurant helpers, and a doctor. There were also saloon operators, gamblers, and "ladies of the evening."

One of the first improvements that Baca noticed was that Mogollon connected to the rest of the territory and the nation via a long-distance telephone line to Silver City. Prior to the arrival of the telephone connection, the fastest means of communication outside the canyon was to send a telegraph request out of the camp with the mail stage to Silver City. The stage line driver delivered the wire request to the telegraph office and, if one was lucky, the message reached its destination within two days of leaving Mogollon. Since March 1909, a person seeking to send a telegram used the 15-member party line community telephone located in the McIntosh Mercantile, in the heart of the business district, to call the telegraph office in Silver City. The membership fee for the telephone cooperative was $10 per month. The Nova Scotia native made his profit by charging patrons $1 per call to connect their call to a long-distance operator. Ernest D. McIntosh was a 30-year-old bachelor who lived with his mother.

On his second day in Mogollon, the new deputy sheriff picked up a pencil and wrote Fornoff a status report. Baca found "every thing quiet," but he noted that "the camp people feel very bitter towards Beal & Bob, but just have to have patients [sic] and let them alone. I am sure after the trial all will think different." He sensed that most businessmen "feel pretty well towards me, but the town people wanted a man of the camp" as the new deputy sheriff/constable. "He is away [but] when he returns I will see him [and tell him the county commissioners refused to appoint him] and then [I will] get the businessmen to endorse me for constable so there will be no [bad] feeling and they can pay me something." Cipriano Baca understood small-town politics Mogollon style.

In another part of his letter, Baca touched upon finances. "Fred, I don't [sic] know of only $50.00 that I am getting [a month from Sheriff Sanchez] at present. I just cann't [sic] crowd these merchants a fig yet or any one else. I just got to handle this matter like a baby for a month at least and it costs like Hell to live here." Baca believed that if he could add the constable service fees to his bank account he could pay his bills. "I feel perfectly satisfied that all will come around OK, but it will take time and patients [sic] with these people." Baca closed his letter to Fornoff with a pledge to lend his aid to any assistance that Fornoff or the Mounted Police might need in the future.

Cipriano Baca celebrated his 51st birthday on September 26 with his new Mogollon friends. He was beginning to have a better reception among the ethnic groups, and he even attended mass at St. Francis Catholic Church to hear the French padre preach. Baca and the Frenchman both enjoyed fishing mountain streams. After he had reassured Mogollon's community leaders that he could maintain the law and preserve the peace, Cipriano settled into the routine of a constable serving a wide-open mining camp and a deputy sheriff assigned to patrol a remote mountainous region. Baca made his "headquarters" at the Bloated Goat Saloon and lodged at the nearby boarding house.

Later when a new road was being constructed from Mogollon to Silver City, Baca accepted the added duty of county road supervisor for the precincts at Mogollon and over the mountain at Cooney and Alma. He wanted to earn extra funds. Renting a house in the remote mining camp was expensive, and Baca wanted to own his own property.

H.A. Hoover's diary contains the following entry for February 11, 1911: "Heard today that Jim Vickery was shot yesterday [Friday], probably fatally." Vickery operated a slaughterhouse located about five miles out of Mogollon on the road toward Glenwood and supplied the meat sold in the local butcher shops. A traveler found Vickery badly injured along the roadside and took him to the doctor. Baca tried to question Vickery about who had shot him, but the man said he would tend to the matter when he recovered. Baca had nothing to base his investigation upon, since there was no evidence of a fight or robbery. Over the next few days, Vickery began to make a slow recovery from his chest wound. On February 17, Herman Hoover wrote in his diary, "Heard that Jim Vickery died at 9:30 last night [Thursday]." A blood clot had accomplished what the mystery assailant could not. The murder of Jim Vickery remains unsolved.

Baca continued to serve the people of the Mogollon country. The job settled into a routine of breaking up barroom fights, settling domestic disturbances, delivering legal process, and breaking up the "spitball" battles at the weekend movies. Hoover recorded one more killing in his diary for 1911. On October 8, the mine bookkeeper wrote in his journal, "A Negro killed a Mexican in Mogollon last night." The camp took little notice of the Saturday-night event, and Baca left no record of any investigation. After all, what was important about one Mexican's death or a Black man charged with his demise? There were half a dozen men ready to take their jobs come Monday morning. That was life in a remote multicultural, nonunion mining camp in the early 1910s.[4]

* * *

Numerous letters traveled between Mogollon and Socorro, and even though he was not living with his family, Cipriano did not forget his duty as head of the household.

> Father was always nice. Once I [Cipriana] was riding a horse and lost my balance. I fell and broke my arm. Father was out of town, so he wrote me a letter. Father thought it was funny, but he did warn me to be more careful when we rode next time. We missed him when he was away.[5]

A newspaper account of this incident had called it a serious accident. The two other kids riding with Cipriana also fell off the horse, but they where not injured.

Knowing that he might become snowed in for the winter, the 51-year-old deputy sheriff took advantage of the weather and made a trip home to El Paso to see his family in early December, 1910. The *Deming Graphic* took note of his presence in town during the layover between train connections: "Mr. Baca will be remembered as the first sheriff of Luna County." The days passed quickly, but the children enjoyed the early family Christmas. Baca reluctantly returned to Mogollon.

The *Socorro Chieftain* reported the results of Mary and Cipriano's relocation decision, saying the family "will not join him in Mogollon until several months."[6] Baca wanted to make sure Mogollon would not be a replay of the Dawson situation, so he decided to leave his family in El Paso until he could better assess his unstable economic future. School was another reason to keep the family in Texas. Gil, Cipriana, and Florentino attended a neighborhood school, and he needed to arrange suitable housing for his growing brood. Cipriano Baca had two family pictures with him; one was his children, and the other was Mary holding their baby. In spring 1911, Baca found housing for his family and moved them to the mining camp.

"I remember Mogollon as a very tough town and a hard place to raise a family. Father tried to make it a safe place for us, but he had a tough job," recalled Cipriana Randolph. "People liked Father; they didn't fear him. They were happy to be around him."[7]

In one issue of the Mogollon *Mines*, the editor pointed out how the denizens of the mining camp were proud of their school.

> The Little Red School House on the hill is a source of pride to all residents of Mogollon. The house is provided with modern school furniture, and only the best and most accomplished educators are employed by the Board of Trustees. The enrollment of pupils is 135, with daily average attendance of 100.[8]

Upon reflection, it would seem that the Baca children enjoyed their educational experience at the mining camp's hilltop school.

Cipriana Randolph fondly recalled life in Mogollon:

> So far as I remember Father was apparently happy with his work in Mogollon. Father always seemed to be very faithful and involved in any job he undertook. My mother possessed the ability to adjust to any surroundings and had the natural ability to cook and sew. We were always well fed and clothed. I feel that we were certainly not comfortable financially, but the Baca children were the best-dressed children at school or church.[9]

Left: Taken on the porch of their El Paso home on 12 March 1911, this photograph of the Baca children was a gift for their father at Mogollon. Gilberson is holding the always dour Maisie, Florentino is holding baby Rachel, and Cipriana is smiling for her dad (Mary Baca Photograph Album/Cipriana Randolph). *Right:* Taken on the porch of their El Paso home on 12 March 1911, this photograph of Mary Baca and the baby Rachel was a gift for her husband at Mogollon. Cipriano received this picture along with the picture of the children (Mary Baca Photograph Album/Cipriana Randolph).

Seven decades after she left Mogollon as a motherless-teenager, Cipriana Randolph, now an elderly widow and retired accountant, wished to see Mogollon again. Cipriana had developed cataracts, and even after an operation, she had trouble seeing well enough to drive her car. She also endured hip surgery and learned to walk slowly with a cane, and she suffered from arthritis in a couple of fingers of both hands but learned how to peck out a letter on her typewriter. Cipriana did not complain about how she got tired easily as she aged, but she did remark once to the author about not being able to sew as her mother had taught her; "[It] bothers me since I always made my clothes and the price of ready-made things is terrible."[10] Twice Mrs. Randolph planned a return to Mogollon.

The Hispanic community of Mogollon represented about 60 percent of the population, and the whole town joined in for a large parade and celebration on *Cinco de Mayo*. A couple of months later they all did it again on July 4. The wind drafts in the canyons around Mogollon made kite flying a fun sport for young and old. Mary Baca saved all the wrapping paper and ribbons from the family's Christmas packages and birthday presents so that Cipriano and the children could make high-flying monsters on sunny summer days. Cipriana Randolph also remembered that her father played baseball with the kids on the school grounds at Mogollon.

New Mexico held an election in early November 1911 to select the men who would compose the leadership of the new state government that expected to take office in early January 1912. The general feeling was that President William Howard Taft would sign the statehood proclamations as soon as the election results where accepted in Washington. Baca's friend Holm O. Bursum was the Republican standard-bearer to become the new state's first governor. His opponent was a Lincoln County rancher named William C. McDonald.

Voters rejected Holm Bursum while some of the other statewide Republicans won their office. Bursum once again turned his attention toward his mining interests in the Mogollon District. "Mr. Bursum takes his defeat like a philosopher," said the *Silver City Enterprise,* "showing none of that 'depressed' feeling that is usually attributed to defeated candidates."[11] Bursum was in Mogollon a week after the general election, and it is pretty certain that Baca and Bursum found time to have a friendly conversation, maybe talking about mining, road building and lost elections, over a big cup of black coffee, strengthened with a touch of aged Bourbon, and a cigar.

When Baca first brought his family to Mogollon in the spring of 1911, he rented a house, but by the end of the year, he and Mary had found they could afford to buy the house. On January 8, 1912, they concluded the house purchase from Clarence E. Tipton and his wife Sarah for $600. The lot, No 76 on the village plat map filed by George R. Brown, was the last home plot on the east end of the town site laid out on the north side of Silver Creek. The house was located near the entrance to Jack Canyon below the schoolhouse on the hill, St. Francis Catholic Church, and east of the Presbyterian Church across the creek street from the working-class homes and the boarding-house area. The recorded land deed said that the lot had a "frontage toward the south of 200 ft and a depth of 200 ft and which (was) surveyed in the name of Jake Kendall."[12]

Cipriana Randolph remembered the house. "We had a large cellar blasted out of a huge boulder in back of our house. Father had shelves built in it and you never saw so much canned fruit and vegetables." Cipriano's friend Peter Clark loved to hunt deer. "In the fall when deer season opened he was always the first one out and he always got a deer. He brought the carcass to Mama and you never saw so much jerked venison." Mary Baca also used the deer to make "some sort of what she called cheese and she made tripe of the belly. We kids did not care for the venison but Judge Clark was there often for venison dinners."[13]

On Thursday, December 28, 1911, Baca concluded the purchase of a half interest in a lode-mining claim registered to Ysidoro Jurado in the Cooney Mining District of Socorro County. The deed records do not divulge the amount of the transaction or the property's value, so it is impossible to estimate the degree of Baca's financial investment. The 47-year-old Jurado, a former Texan, was a wood contractor for local mining companies but did prospecting in his spare time from woodcutting. Jurado had a Mexican wife and a grown son and daughter living at home. Aleijo helped his father with the woodcutting business and did some digging at the mine.

The Jurado Mine was located in Hyde Canon, about a half mile from the Mogollon post office, near the Fanny Mine #2. The county clerk recorded the legal papers for the Jurado-Baca partnership at the Socorro County courthouse on New Year's Day, 1912.[14] It seemed like Baca's dream of regained prosperity was on the right course, but fate seemed to have other plans.

* * *

In a November 1910 election, New Mexicans had adopted an ultra-conservative state constitution and sent it to Congress for approval. In anticipation of congressional acceptance of the document, former governor Miguel A. Otero had a 47-starred U.S. flag made and presented it to his friend Governor William J. Mills. Word reached Santa Fe on August 21, 1911, announcing federal approval of the new constitution, with some suggested modifications, and authorization for the election of state officials in November 1911. Mills let his 12-year-old daughter Madeline raise Otero's flag over the capitol. Congress approved the results of the November 1911 election, and President William H. Taft officially declared New Mexico Territory's 62-year struggle to join the federal union ended on Saturday, January 6, 1912. The Sunshine Territory was now the Sunshine State, and Arizona Territory would become the 48th state a month later on St. Valentine's Day.

The day after President Taft proclaimed New Mexico statehood, John "Slim" Rusk died in an Alamosa, Colorado, hospital. He had contracted pneumonia while trying to serve extradition papers on a Colorado lawman wanted for a series of burglaries committed in Chama. Effie and Clyde Stauder, along with most of Chama, attended Rusk's funeral. He was the only State Mounted Policeman to die while on active duty. Ten days later, former Territorial Mounted Policeman Frank Vance died from "lead poisoning" in a Colorado mining camp while conducting an undercover investigation of local police corruption. It is unclear if Cipriano Baca had known Rusk or Vance, and he left no record of his reaction to their deaths.

On Monday, February 19, two heavily armed Mexicans entered the Mogollon Mercantile and killed the store manager and a clerk but spared the life of the bookkeeper. The bandits then fled with the money used to cash mine payroll checks. Men in the bar across the street had heard the two shots but first thought the sounds were the wind slamming the shutters. Witnesses saw the two bandits as they left the store, and the bookkeeper recognized one of the killer-robbers as a youthful miner he had seen in the camp and notified Deputy Sheriff Baca.

Baca used Ernest McIntosh's telephone to notify Sheriff Emil James, in Socorro, and officers in the surrounding area of the murder-robbery as a posse organized to trail the fugitives. Posses searched for the bandits' trail through the heart of the rugged Mogollon Mountain range. Sheriff James and a deputy had taken the train from Socorro to Silver City and rented horses to travel to Mogollon; en route they stumbled upon the outlaws' trail. A Silver City newspaper headlined the chase, "Bandits Run to Earth, One Killed, One Surrenders." Deputy Sheriff Scott Heaply killed 23-year-old Gregorio Torrango, while others wounded 18-year-old Francisco Granado and captured him along with the stolen money. Granado was tried for murder at Socorro, convicted, and sentenced to hang on April 25, 1913.[15]

* * *

"Women were urged by the health books and the doctors [at the turn of the 20th century] to indulge in deep preoccupation with themselves as 'the Sex'; they were to devote themselves to developing their reproductive powers, their maternal instincts, their 'femininity.' Yet they were told that they had no 'natural' sexual feelings whatsoever," wrote the authors of a sociological treatise on the history of women's health and hygiene. "They [women] were believed to be completely governed by their ovaries and uteruses, but to be repelled by the sex act itself. In fact, sexual feelings were seen as unwomanly, pathological, and possibly detrimental to the supreme function of reproduction." Doctors of that era seem to have accepted that men were sexual beings, so some medical men condoned prostitution on the grounds that the natural lust of males had an outlet other then their delicate wives or female companions. The educational tract continued,

> For the "well-bred" woman to whom sex really was repugnant, and yet a "duty," or for any woman who wanted to avoid pregnancy, "feeling sick" was a way out — and there were few others. Contraceptive methods were virtually unavailable; abortion was risky and illegal. It would never have entered a respectable doctor's head to advise a lady on contraception. Or to offer to perform an abortion. In fact, doctors devoted considerable energy to "proving" that contraception and abortion were inherently unhealthy, and capable of causing such disease as cancer. But a doctor could help a woman by supporting abstinence.

The two women authors' feminist expose concluded this subchapter on sex by asking the big question, "So who knows how many of this period's drooping consumptives and listless invalids were actually well [physically healthy] women, feigning illness to escape intercourse and pregnancy?"[16] Mary Berry Baca was not one of these women.

The Bible that Mary Berry grew up reading was the Authorized or King James Version first published in 1611. The Episcopal Church taught that the entry rite for eternal salvation for a woman was by the pain of childbirth. This teaching was based upon I Timothy 2:15 that said, "She shall be saved in childbearing. If they [women] continue in faith and charity and holiness with sobriety." Another treatment of the sacred word that gained popularity among Protestantism after its 1902 publication was *The New Testament in Modern Speech*. This translation expanded upon the original Greek text, saying, "Yet a woman will be brought safely through childbirth if she *and her husband* continue to live in faith and love and growing holiness, with habitual self-restraint." The phrase "and her husband" seems to bind a woman's life and her salvation to that of her husband's conduct and faith. This translation of Paul's teaching to his friend Timothy must have hung like a millstone around the neck of men who accepted this interpretation and lost a wife during or resulting from childbirth. Cipriano Baca may have been one of these men.

New Mexico's statehood in January 1912 brought many changes to the Land of Enchantment and the Baca family. Cipriano bought a house two days after the national flag gained a 47th star, and another son joined the clan in March. Cipriano named the boy in honor of his father Teofilo and his friend Judge Clark. It had been a very difficult delivery for Mary Baca, and nine days after the birth she was still bedridden, and even the infant was not gaining his strength. Arkansas-born Dr. Edward Manson Parham who came to Mogollon for his health attended the birth and recovery, but there was little that the Tulane graduate could do for mother or son. It is unclear if Dr. Parham had Mary admitted to the Mogollon Hospital, but at this time Cipriano sent word to Widow Berry that her daughter was still not recovering following the protracted delivery. In fact, Mary was growing weaker by the hour and only a miracle could save her life.

Cipriano's dream bubble burst on Tuesday morning, March 12, 1912, when 38-year-old Mary Ann Berry Baca gave up her fight for life. The *Socorro Chieftain* said, "She was a good wife and mother and a woman of unusually strong and admirable character." The *Silver City Enterprise* reported that Mary Baca had been "prominent socially in Socorro" for many years.

Mary's mother and her sister Ruby Griffith made the sad trip to Mogollon. They left Socorro via the railroad headed south toward Deming where they connected with the spur line up to Silver City. Early the next morning mother and sister began an eight-hour motor coach trip up to the 6,930-foot-high mining camp. When the two women reached Mogollon, they found Cipriano in a near state of depression. Mary had been the emotional, spiritual, and physical center of the Baca family and of her husband's world. Mother and sister now joined husband and children in grief.

Cipriana, then ten years old, later recalled her mother's death.

> Judge Clark was a good friend of Father's and he used to do a lot for us. Mama used to do a lot of his English-Spanish transcribing for him. He was so pleased that she could help him. He was the county judge [Mogollon's justice of the peace] and the town carpenter. He made the casket Mama was buried in. Grandma [Berry] remarked that it was made of such heavy wood.

T.J. Clark, who was in his early 70s, was a stonemason and builder by trade, so he also made Mary's grave marker. In June, Clark became very ill and his family took him to the Silver City Hospital. The Baca family was very concerned about Clark, but he soon recovered. It is uncertain if Cipriano could have endured the loss of his friend on top of losing his wife and son.

"Lord, make me an instrument of Thy peace," the 13th-century monk St. Francis of Assisi had written, but these words of the humble, gentle churchman where freely applied to Mary Baca.

> Where there is hatred, let me sow love; where there is injury, pardon; where there is doubt, faith; where there is despair, hope; where there is sadness, joy; where there is darkness, light. O Divine Master, grant that I may not so much seek to be consoled, as to console; not so much to be understood, as to understand; not so much to be loved, as to love.

This 700-year-old prayer was the legacy of Mary Ann Berry Baca to her family and friends

Mary Baca's memorial service at St. Francis Catholic Church in Mogollon drew her many friends. Burial was in the Mogollon cemetery, located a few hundred yards up the east fork of Jack Canyon past the Spanish red-light district, on a ridge between Mineral Creek and Silver Creek canyons looking down on Graveyard Gulch. Grandmother Berry and Ruby Griffith were making plans to return to Socorro when baby Teofilo Clark Baca lost his three-week fight for life. Judge Clark made the little casket for his namesake. Following a graveside service, Teofilo's little casket was buried next to his mother's grave.

Cipriana Randolph once recalled that shortly after her mother and brother's funerals the schoolchildren at Mogollon became upset over the news that the H.M.S. *Titanic* had collided with an iceberg. Most of the passengers, many small children, and crewmembers aboard the luxury liner drowned as the ship's band played "Nearer My God to Thee." The schoolchildren cried over the loss of so many lives, and the Baca children were again sad at their own loss.

We have no way of knowing what memories resurfaced within him during his state of grief, as Cipriano Baca dealt with other people's emotional state concerning the loss of life aboard the H.M.S. *Titanic*. The death of an old Mogollon pioneer miner he had known for a quarter of a century did touch is heart. The wife of the old Rebel solider-turned-miner was dead, and he had no living relatives, so few people joined Cipriano at the grave site. Deputy Sheriff Baca mourned another personal loss and again cursed the Angel of Death.[17]

19

State of New Mexico vs. Cipriano Baca: Murder

"Details of the affair are lacking."—*Albuquerque Morning Journal*, 27 May 1912

The Angel of Death had first claimed Marie and Eva I from Cipriano Baca; next, he took Mary to join their children Eva II, Sallie, Ruby, Mary Ann, James, and now a seventh infant, Teofilo. Cipriano's inconsolable grief and sense of loneliness soon became an internal rage; he was a strong man dealing with grief, self-doubt, financial worry, a growing lack of spiritual faith, and an omnipresent loneliness. The iron-willed Baca was on the verge of a breakdown.

Over night, Baca had become the sole parent for five children aged two to 14. Gil and Cipriana were able to help their father get a grip on reality and understand that they needed him. The household duties where divided up; a neighbor woman agreed to watch the infant Rachel while the older kids attended school. Days passed into weeks, and by spring, the Baca family life slowly returned to a semi-normal existence. Cipriano was doing his best to be both father and mother to his brood. Thousands of years earlier a sage of Israel wrote defining Baca's condition that has been preserved in the wisdom book of Proverbs: "Better is a dinner of vegetables where love is than a fatted ox and hatred within the home."

Baca received another punch in the nose when his friend Geronimo E. Sanchez unexpectedly left the sheriff's office and the county commissioner's appointed Emil James the acting sheriff. James quickly voided all supplemental financial arrangements with Sanchez's former deputies. Baca continued to serve as Mogollon's constable and as the county road supervisor for the area, so he still earned the fees accompanying these responsibilities, but not the stipend from the sheriff's office.

Not that it affected Cipriano Baca since he had already lost his deputy commission following his grand jury indictment, but Emil James won the Socorro County sheriff's race in November 1912. In January 1913, James replaced Sanchez's holdover deputies with his own appointees.

In the wake of these emotional days, it seems Baca may not have been functioning at his best. Events would indicate that Cipriano's good judgment and sixth sense clouded over when conducting his public duty.

* * *

In the Sherlock Holmes adventure *A Scandal in Bohemia* the consulting detective comments on the complexity of the case. He complains, "I have no data. It is a capital mistake to theorize before one has data. Insensibly one begins to twist facts to suit theories, instead of theories to suit facts." In his classic 1891 mystery, Sir Arthur Conan Doyle captured the dilemma that faces a historian examining the events surrounding Cipriano Baca's trial for murder.

Mogollon diarist H.A. Hoover made the following entry in his daily logbook for Thursday, May 30, 1912: "Red Simmons was buried today — died yesterday — was shot Saturday [25th] by Baca." The man left behind a grieving widow, three children, and a town divided over the nature of his painful death. The author found the grave of 56-year-old E.G. Simmons in the old Mogollon Cemetery. He is in the northwest section, just a short distance from the grave sites of Mary Baca and her son Teofilo, and an upright headstone containing his name, the year of his birth and death, an emblem signifying membership in a Masonic lodge and a poetic verse, marks his grave. The verse says, "No pains, no griefs, no anxious fear; Can reach our loved one sleeping here." A weathered three-foot-high wrought-iron fence encloses the grave guarded by a live oak.

In 1910, the Democratic-leaning *Silver City Independent* edited by former *Deming Headlight* editor W.B. Walton had commented upon Baca's law enforcement abilities. "He is a gentlemanly officer who in his long official career has never yet found it necessary to kill a man." The general populace never seems to have considered Cipriano a killer or a gunman for hire. In fact, the public, including Baca's political opponents, seems always to have viewed him as a highly qualified professional peace officer. He was not the typical fictional dime-novel-style two-gun marshal.

On Monday, May 27, 1912, the *Albuquerque Morning Journal* carried a story on page four headlined, "'Shock' Simmons Shot to Death at Mogollon." The Special Dispatch datelined from Socorro said,

> A telegram received this afternoon [Sunday, May 26] by Sheriff Emil James from his deputy at Mogollon announced the fatal shooting there today of "Shock" Simmons an old time cowman by Cipriano Baca, acting constable. Details of the affray are lacking, the message simply urging Sheriff James to come to Mogollon at once. It is not known whether Baca was arrested after the shooting or what provoked the tragedy.

The *Albuquerque Morning Journal* story went on to provide some background about Simmons, saying he "had lived in western Socorro county for many years. He was popular and always considered a law-abiding citizen. His friends are at a loss to understand how he could have become involved in any difficulty that would have caused the killing." The part of this story that remains a mystery is how did a "law abiding citizen" and a "gentlemanly officer" meet and the Death Angel have cause to take a life?

Ezra G. Simmons is the only man by that surname listed as living in Socorro County during the 1910 federal census, and this man was living in the Cooney settlement about a mile and a half north of Mogollon. In 1911, a flood destroyed much of the Cooney village, and soon after that natural calamity, the area experienced another setback with the decline in productivity at the area mines. Many people left the community to look for work. Some of these former Cooney residents moved to the bustling community of Mogollon. The Simmons family may have been one of these families.

On Tuesday, May 28, the *Silver City Independent* reported that Simmons had been "shot through the hip by Cipriano Baca, acting constable, Sunday morning. The bullet shattered the bone of the leg in a terrible manner, and while Simmons has a chance for life, he will be a cripple." This account provided comments concerning the circumstances of the arrest attempt gone wrong. "The two men had words over Mrs. Simmons, and Baca attempted to arrest Simmons. Simmons refused to go, and Baca got his Winchester while Simmons it is claimed armed himself with a six shooter."

The *Silver City Enterprise* published a graphic report on the nature of Simmons' wound. "The bullet, a soft-nosed missile, went through the upper center of the left thigh crushing the bone, cutting the artery and making a great hole where it passed out." Baca's one bullet created a massive injury causing Simmons to die a slow, painful death.

A week later, the *Silver City Independent* added further details to their coverage of the Simmons-Baca dispute. The newspaper reported that "Acting-Constable Baca" had been under the influence of liquor and entered into a conversation, on the street, with Mrs. Maud Simmons and that her husband objected to the exchange. The news report claimed that Baca had became angered at Simmons and drew a pistol on him, but the Last Chance Mine's engineer said he was unarmed and Baca's friends encouraged him to leave. However, around eight o'clock that Sunday morning, Constable Baca and two other unnamed posse men located Simmons sitting on his front porch bathed "in bright moonlight" and defiant of Baca's attempt to arrest him. The *Independent*'s account quoted Simmons as saying that he would not surrender to Baca, but he would give himself up to Deputy Sheriff Jim Harris. At this juncture, something went wrong with the arrest attempt, and Baca fired his fatal shot. The newspaper account went on to say the wounded man's wife blocked one of Baca's deputies from also shooting Simmons. Baca and his two deputies searched, or "ransacked," the Simmons' house for illegal weapons, but only found a .22 caliber pistol, with no ammunition, that belonged to Simmons's son Clay.

The Bill of Rights of the newly adopted New Mexico State Constitution contains two sections that are pertinent to the Baca-Simmons encounter. Section 10 is a safeguard against unjust search or arrest by police, and prevents a peace officer from invading a person's home and searching it without having a proper search warrant authorized by a court. Under the provisions of Section 6, a person may have firearms in his home for self-protection, but may not carry them concealed upon his person without the consent of the court.

Baca's chief defense was that he was acting in a lawful manner as a duly constituted peace officer. The prosecution never challenged that claim based upon the New Mexico's Bill of Rights or the legal status of Baca's constable commission issued by the Socorro County commissioners.

A few days later on May 31, the *Silver City Enterprise* reported on the Simmons shooting, but some of the basic elements differed from the *Albuquerque Morning Journal* account. "B.E. [sic] Simmons, better known as 'Red' Simmons, an engineer in the employ of the Ernestine Mining Co. at Mogollon, died in that camp Wednesday from effects of a gunshot wound inflicted by Constable Cipriano Baca Saturday evening. Simmons was aged about 40 years and leaves a wife and three children. He was well known and highly respected in the community."

Rumors concerning the Simmons-Baca shooting quickly spread around the region, and the *Silver City Enterprise* reported two of these. "One version is that Simmons was armed when shot and attempted to resist arrest, another alleges that Baca was intoxicated and had threatened Simmons owing to an old grudge and finally upon pretext of arresting him shot him. That Simmons was unarmed at the time of the shooting."[1]

One small detail in the Baca-Simmons relationship did not originally involve Cipriano. In the aftermath of the August 1910 incident that escalated from the killing of saloon keeper Charlie Clark, Red Simmons had been one of 16 people; many were saloon operators, appointed as an illegal "posse" organized by order of an illegal justice of the peace to arrest Territorial Mounted Policemen John Beal and Bob Putman. Did Baca's past association with the Mounted Police have some bearing upon Simmons's actions toward Baca or vis-à-vis Baca toward Simmons? This obscure piece of information could hold the key to why Baca's life took so many twists and turns following this Mogollon tragedy.

The *Silver City Enterprise*, the *Silver City Independent*, and the *Albuquerque Morning Journal* accounts discussed above raise some disturbing questions. If the dead man was so popular in Mogollon, why is there so much confusion about who he was or where and how he earned a living? Here are a few questions that need answers,

1. What was Simmons's real first name?
2. What was Simmons's nickname, and what did the moniker mean?
3. Was he a cowman? If Simmons was a "cattleman," Baca may have been investigating him as part of a group selling stolen beef to the local wholesale butcher shop for retail sales at area meat markets.
4. Was he a mine engineer? Baca was working with the Mounted Police to gather evidence concerning inside help in "piping off" recent ore shipments from area mines.
5. Was Simmons both a cattleman and a mine engineer or neither?
6. Was the arrest attempt an "old grudge" or a legal police action?
7. Who were Baca's two deputies or posse men, and why did he need a two-man posse to arrest one man?
8. When was Simmons wounded; on Saturday evening or Sunday morning?
9. Where was the lethal wound in Simmons's body?
10. What was Mrs. Simmons role in the whole incident?
11. What was Clay Simmons's role in his father death?
12. Was Baca really intoxicated at the time of the arrest attempt, or was that charge just another wild tale?

The *Silver City Enterprise* reported that the Ernestine Mine had registered the enterprise's best 20-day production period during the month of May 1912. The newspaper said that the mine had produced "21,724 Troy ounces of gold and bullion and 22,550 pounds of high-grade concentrates." The report also noted that the mine was up for sale. At this stage in his life, Baca was seeking mining investments for himself and his partner Ysidoro Jurado. Could this investment quest have played a part in the Simmons-Baca confrontation? Was it an investment offer scorned or gone bad? Racial tensions, class status, or some other real or imagined slight may have helped to trigger an argument that got out of control.

Mogollon's Dr. B.C. Kern first treated Simmons, but he soon sent to Silver City for the assistance of Dr. Angle. The region's medical dean arrived on Sunday, but soon after his initial examination of Simmons's wound, he realized the case was hopeless. Late Sunday, the physician returned to his home in Silver City.

Socorro County Sheriff Emil James arrived in Mogollon a few days after the shooting and formally arrested Baca, who waved a preliminary hearing in Mogollon, and accompanied Sheriff James to Socorro on Thursday morning. Based upon the findings of the coroner's inquest concerning the nature of Simmons's death presented at his bail hearing, held in the county seat, Cipriano was bound over to face a grand jury inquiry in September. Existing county jail records do not indicate that Baca was in jail prior to his bail hearing and his formal release on bond. Ysidoro Jurado's 24-year-old daughter Maria moved into the Baca house to watch over the Baca children while Cipriano was in Socorro. There is no clear picture of what Cipriano did after his bail hearing, but he most likely headed back to Mogollon to jump-start his financial future. He still had a family to support. Mogollon had a momentary surge of excitement in June with the discovery of a new gold vein. The *Silver City Enterprise* bragged, "Big Strike at Mogollon" and said the find was on the Iron Bear mine property. Baca and Jurado must have had renewed hope for their own mining claim.[2]

* * *

In late August 1912, Captain Fred Fornoff arrived in Silver City to attend the fall session of Judge Colin Neblett's District Court, and it is very likely that Fornoff and Baca met during this visit. As mentioned previously, Baca was helping his former chief with local gossip concerning current skims for "piping off" ore shipments from the Mogollon mines. Baca's suspension from his official duties, the grand jury investigation, his need for legal assistance, and his finances would have also been major issues of discussion.

Somehow, Baca was able to retain Edward A. Mann of the Mann and Venable Law Firm as his defense attorney. Mann was a former associate justice of the New Mexico Territorial Supreme Court. He and his partner John Venable had successfully defended Mounted Policemen John Beal and Bob Putman in their 1911 murder trail for killing Charlie Clark in Mogollon a year earlier. It is very likely that Captain Fornoff secured Judge Mann's legal counsel for Baca.

The first snow of the 1912 season fell during the first week of December and Baca was a sideline observer to one of the area's daring stage holdups. Two local men planned to rob the stage between Silver City and Mogollon, and small-spread rancher Jim Harris, Baca's replacement as deputy sheriff, was one of them. The would-be bandits tried to recruit the mail carrier from Silver City to be part of the heist, but instead he told the Mogollon postmaster about the plot. George Williams, the postmaster, notified the Silver City bank about the planned robbery, and a bank official requested help from Grant County Sheriff Herb McGrath. The sheriff notified Captain Fred Fornoff about the tip, and the Mounted Police chief came to Silver City where the two officers developed their plan to capture the would-be robbers in the act.

A week later, the *Silver City Enterprise* headlined their story "Alleged Bandits Walk into Trap Laid by Officers." The holdup had taken place as the bandits had planned, but not part of their plan was their own arrest. The stage robbers where arrested with bank bags, filled with cut up paper, in their possession. The *Santa Fe New Mexican* told readers that Fornoff was "detained in Grant County and may not be back [in Santa Fe] to eat Christmas dinner at home." A few days later, the *Silver City Enterprise* noted that Captain Fornoff was "in the city this week on official business," and in a different story headed "White and Harris Confess to Hold-Up," the newspaper said the would-be bandits broke under Fornoff's relentless questioning, and the captain was able to spend Christmas with his family.

Convicted of mail robbery, both bandits received sentences of ten years in federal prison. Socorro County Sheriff Emil James had egg on his face when the man he had appointed to replace Baca went to prison. A bad deputy had served Mogollon before Cipriano's appointment, another bad deputy replaced Baca, and the lawlessness had returned to the mining camp.

* * *

Cipriano Baca held high regard for Dr. W.C. Field. The two men became acquainted when Baca was a Grant County deputy sheriff in the 1890s. They became acquainted again in 1908 while Baca was investigating the circumstances surrounding the killing of Pat Garrett. It is uncertain if Baca was in Mogollon in mid–June 1912, during the time that Dr. Field and his family came to the mining camp to visit with Mrs. Field's mother. The doctor was also exploring an offer from the Mogollon Mining Company to reestablish his medical practice; he had worked for the company from 1886 until he left seven years later. In 1912, Dr. Field had a lucrative medical practice, a spacious estate northwest of the Dona Ana County courthouse used for "entertaining on a large scale during the social season," and 900 acres of irrigated farmland in the Las Cruces area; 50 acres comprised a very productive pear orchard. Two daughters blessed his household. In late summer 1912, Dr. Field accepted a $6,000-per-year salary to return to the Mogollon Mining Company as their resident doctor. The service contract allowed Field to conduct a private practice that could net him $3,000 in addition to his annual income.

Within a few months of accepting the mining company's offer, Dr. Field and his family settled in Mogollon. It would seem reasonable to assume that Baca and the doctor found an occasion to cross trails and perhaps enjoy a drink. Dr. Field was not just a "country doctor" but held the reputation as a first-class surgeon. What might have happened if he had treated E.G. Simmons's gunshot wound? Would the man have survived? Would Cipriano Baca's life have taken a different course?[3]

Baca always claimed publicly, as well as in court, that he had acted within the bounds of his legal authority and professed his rightness in using lethal force to attempt the arrest of E.G. Simmons. There is no record of his ever saying or writing anything different in private. Centuries before Cipriano was born the ancient Greek statesman-orator Demosthenes wrote, "Nothing is easier than self-deceit. For what each man wishes, that he also believes to be true." It is unlikely that history will ever know the whole truth concerning the Simmons-Baca confrontation, but we will attempt to reach some understanding of what transpired that fateful day in Mogollon as we explorer the complexities of the murder trial.

* * *

In the American justice system, the mission of a grand jury is to determine if the law enforcement officers have provided the government prosecution with enough evidence against an accused to bring a case to trial. If the grand jury believes enough evidence is not available to question the innocence of an accused person, the grand jury must issue a No Bill or no indictment. If the grand jury believes enough evidence is available to question the innocence of an accused person, the grand jury issues a True Bill or criminal indictment against the accused person demanding they stand trial as charged. At the trial, the judge charges a trial jury to determine the truth based upon the evidence presented to them.

In late September 1912, the Socorro County Grand Jury convened at the county seat to review the district attorney's presentations against suspected criminals. John Griffith, the Socorro County district attorney, chose not to take any part in the case against his brother-in-law, so his assistant J.A. Lowe represented the state's case to the grand jury session on the 24th. The panel heard testimony from Mrs. Maud L. Simmons, Clay Simmons, H.W. Johnson, Arthur Gore, Dr. B.C. Kern, Fred A. Lowe, P.M. McClellan, S.M. Hughes, and George Williams. All proceedings of a grand jury are secret and the records of the hearing are sealed. The system design is to protect grand jury witnesses, and the public will never know what caused the grand jury to issue a murder indictment against Cipriano Baca. The district attorney's office destroyed these records long ago.

Judge Edward A. Mann of Albuquerque, Baca's attorney, filed a motion to quash or annul the murder indictment. After hearing oral arguments, the court overruled or turned down the motion. Mann then filed a demurrer, a legal challenge suggesting the grand jury complaint was not sufficient to warrant any court action, but the court overruled this action also. Baca then had his formal arraignment before District Court Judge Merritt C. Mechem, an old friend. Cipriano entered a not guilty plea, was granted bond, and ordered to appear before the district court at the March 1913 session. The court placed appearance bonds on the prosecution's eight witnesses for the same court appearance. Later that day, Judge Mechem ordered that the state reimburse the witnesses for their travel expenses to Socorro and from Socorro to their homes.[4]

Following his grand jury murder indictment, the Socorro County Commissioners' Court relieved Baca of his constable's commission and his appointment as a county road supervisor. Cipriano's financial situation was in a desperate situation. He was barely coping by the winter of 1912, and the children's first Christmas without their mother was fast approaching. He no longer had his constable and road supervisor fees for income, so Baca accepted odd jobs and supplemented these finances by working day shifts at the Jurado Mine. On September 7, 1912, Baca had mortgaged his new house and lot for $500 to his friend, lumber mill owner Henry "Uncle Harry" Herman, a 68-year-old widower who was a native of Germany. The interest-free loan was due in six months. On January 3, 1913, Herman gave Baca an additional $100 and took possession of the house and lot.

Even as an elderly lady, Cipriana Randolph remembered Henry Hermann and other Mogollon citizens.

> I really don't know much about him [Hermann] except that he was an elderly man who lived up the canyon from us and every morning about 10 o'clock he would go by our house on horseback on his way down to get his mail. He apparently was well to do but I never got to go up and see where he lived. I remember the Coates & Moore store. Mrs. Coates worked in the post office. They had a son Eldridge about my age. We were all in school together. I would love to go back just to look [around] and run [up the canyon]. The last time I was there most of the houses were boarded up.

Cipriana also recalled the Bill Evans family,

> They lived a ways up [the canyon] from us on the other side of the creek. They built a lively new home but never lived in it. The story was told there about how Mrs. Evans used to get mad at him and roll him up in a sheet and beat [him].

Cipriana's best Mogollon friend was Hattie Shellhorn. "We were about the same age. Mrs. [Emma] Shellhorn later married the saloonkeeper — Mr. [Sylvester] Gamblin." Mrs. [John] Shellhorn was a widower from Ohio, and Gamblin was a bachelor from Texas, 18 years her senior. He had a playhouse built for Hattie, and the girls spent many hours playing dolls in the house, but the happy times were short lived.

Baca sold his half interest in the Jurado Mine to William Bates and Nicholas Ayon on February 26, 1913. The transfer document recorded in the Socorro County courthouse lists the sale price as "$1.00," but logic would suggest that this was not the correct sale price. Baca was a brave, proud, desperate man trying to cope and desperately trying to keep his family together.

It came too late for Cipriano Baca, but in the spring of 1913, Mogollon experienced a new burst of gold fever. The town repopulated almost overnight with a new breed of hard men each seeking a quick fortune. These months were a high point for the mining camp as miners extracted approximately $1.5 million in gold and silver from the area's mountains. That production record accounted for about 40 percent of New Mexico's precious metals produced during the second year of statehood. The conservative *Mogollon Mines* recorded its own assessment in a March issue. "It has been said that Mogollon is booming. It is not so but we have a steady and sure growth, based on legitimate business methods."[5]

Baca's central focus was his family's welfare. It is sometimes difficult to reconstruct events within the Baca household in late 1912 and early 1913. Cipriano left no written account of his personal life and even his children had trouble pinpointing exact dates of family events, so when the author gave Cipriana Randolph a copy of her mother's death notice, she replied, "I was surprised to see the date of my mother's death. I really did not know it." Mrs. Randolph explained her lack of knowledge saying that the Baca-Berry clan seldom discussed the events surrounding the breakup of her family. Grandma Berry saw Baca's murder trial as a dark shadow over the Berry family saga and locked the memory away. Cipriano was a blight upon the Berry family's honor and social status, a family embarrassment of the first order.

"Father had to make a difficult decision because he felt he could no longer care for us children and face the demands of his job." It was not his job so much as the stress of his lack of finances and his impending murder trial that gave Cipriano sleepless nights. What if a jury convicted him of murder and he went to prison or received a death sentence? Who would care for the Baca children? Cipriano sent letters to Mary's mother and her brother and sisters asking for their help with the children. Replies came and a plan developed.

Seventy years after Cipriana Randolph and her siblings left Mogollon for good she recalled that winter trip to Socorro,

> When Father took us to Socorro about a year after Mama died, we left Mogollon in a covered wagon with two-span of horses. We girls always stayed in the wagon. At night the boys and Father and Mr. Jurado took turns sleeping and keeping the fire going. The coffee pot was always on the fire. We first went to Silver City. Three days and two nights; the snow was still so deep and packed. It was a lonesome trip.
>
> When we left, Father would not let us take any of our toys and we gave them to Hattie [Shellhorn]. We [the girls] could each take a doll and I forgot mine and wrote and had Hattie go up to the Jurado house and get it and send it. But it got broken in the mail. It was the last doll Mama had dressed for me; was a bride doll. It was spreading sawdust around so [I] guess Grandma [Berry] got rid of it. I have often wondered that she did not keep the clothes for me. I never knew what happened to the doll or clothes.

214 Cipriano Baca, Frontier Lawman of New Mexico

We discuss Cipriana Baca's relationship with her Grandmother Berry elsewhere.[6]

It is very possible that the Baca children knew nothing, or very little, about their father having killed a man at Mogollon and his legal troubles. Fifteen-year-old Gilberson, now calling himself George, was the only sibling old enough to understand the family distress surrounding his father's trial, but he was not a witness to these events because he was out of the country living with his Uncle James Berry on a mining claim in Old Mexico during the trial and the aftermath.

Preteen Cipriana was tending livestock on a sheep ranch near Chama, in remote Rio Arriba County near the Colorado border, far removed from the events transpiring hundreds of miles away in Socorro County. She was staying with her beloved Aunt Effie and Uncle Clyde Stauder. Cipriana never discussed her father's murder trial with the author since she had no firsthand knowledge of her father's brush with a prison term or the hangman's rope.

Aunt Ruby and Uncle John Griffith and their son took in school age Florentino. It is conceivable that the nine-year-old boy may have overheard talk about his father's troubles from schoolchildren in Socorro or maybe from his cousin whose father was the district attorney. This may help explain some of Florentino's later difficult relationship with his father.

Also living in Socorro was six-year-old Maisie, cared for by Grandmother Berry, and her baby sister Rachel who joined the family of Aunt Pearl and Uncle Alex Edelen. All the adults understood that this child-care arrangement was only temporary pending the outcome of Cipriano's legal and financial troubles.

On Tuesday afternoon March 4, 1913, Thomas Woodrow Wilson took his first oath of office as president of the United States and then told the nation, "Our life contains every great thing, and contains it in rich abundance." It is doubtful that Cipriano Baca

The district court chamber in the Socorro County courthouse was the scene of the 1911 murder trial of Mounted Police John Beal and Bob Putman for killing a saloon owner in Mogollon. Two years later, Cipriano Baca faced a jury also accused of murdering a man at Mogollon (Jim Stauder Photograph Collection).

held this viewpoint as he and his wife's family nervously awaited the start of his trial for murder.[7]

The spring 1913 court term of the state's Seventh Judicial District convened in mid-March in the district court chambers in the courthouse at Socorro. The sheriff's office summoned a pool of qualified citizens for possible jury duty and deputies were busy delivering legal papers requiring attendance at the court session. The *Silver City Enterprise* commented on the pending Baca murder trial, saying, "This case promises to be hard fought."[8]

The criminal docket and court journal of the Seventh Judicial District held in session at Socorro during the spring of 1913 contain the legal records of Baca's trial, Cause No. 3669. These brief official records seem to create more questions than they answer. One interesting entry in the court docket concerns a woman named Mildred Marquette. She earned $29.20 for being the court stenographer. What function did she play during Baca's murder trial? Was there a transcript made of the trial testimony? No trial transcript is contained in the court records. If a trail manuscript still exists, it could be in some long-forgotten file. A copy of the trial transcript could be an important assist in answering this case's many unanswered questions.

Sadly, copies of the *Socorro Chieftain* for the era surrounding the weeks before and after the Simmons shooting in May 1912 and the murder trial in March 1913 no longer exist in the newspaper's history files or in the Socorro County courthouse newspaper collection. Conspiracy buffs might find it of interest to learn that no known copies of the *Socorro Chieftain* covering the entire year 1913 have been located anywhere.

Colin Neblett was a native of the Commonwealth of Virginia and a lifelong Democrat. He had married Mazie Moore of Los Angeles, and they had a daughter. Neblett had attended Bethel Military Academy and received his law degree from Washington and Lee University in 1897. He had practiced law in Silver City, served in the territorial assembly, and as Grant County school superintendent before his appointment as a district court judge in 1907. In early November 1911, Neblett had an appendectomy done by Dr. Westlake at Silver City's Ladies Hospital. Two months later Sheriff Herb McGrath had the same operation by the same doctor at the same facility. In the summer of 1912, the judge was a delegate to the 21st Democratic National Convention that nominated Thomas Woodrow Wilson, a native Virginian, for president. In 1917, Neblett became the second man appointed as judge of the federal district court of the State of New Mexico. Judge William H. Pope had died in office, and President Wilson named Neblett as his successor. Neblett would serve as judge until 1948. He died in 1950 and his family buried him in Albuquerque. Today a large state wilderness area, containing the beautiful Cimarron River Canyon and Palisades in Colfax County, honors the judge's memory.[9]

Neblett was serving as the judge of New Mexico' Sixth Judicial District, sitting at Silver City in the spring of 1913, when he agreed to replace Merritt C. Mechem as Baca's trial judge. Judge Mechem had recused or disqualified himself from hearing this case because of his friendship with Baca and the fact that he had been the presiding judge for the trial of Mounted Policemen Beal and Putman two years earlier. Mechem was a seasoned jurist and longtime friend of veteran Quay County sheriff and Mounted Policeman Alex Street, so he understood that men involved in a face-to-face shooting incident did not shoot to kill the other; they shoot to stay alive. The *Silver City Enterprise* reported that Mechem came to "finish the present term of court here." Nesbitt opened court in Socorro on Monday morning, March 24, 1913.[10]

District Attorney John Griffith also recused himself from being part of the prosecution of his brother-in-law. Griffith had led the territorial team that had prosecuted Beal and Putman two years earlier. The district attorney also had another reason for not involving himself in the Baca case: the stress of a murder case. In the spring of 1913, the 50-year-old Griffith was showing signs of liver disease that would take his life later that fall. Griffith's two assistant district attorneys, J.A. Lowe and Milton J. Helmick, prosecuted the state's case against Cipriano Baca.

Baca and his chief attorney received a copy of the potential jury panel during an open court session on Thursday morning, March 27. Over the weekend, Baca and his legal team reviewed the panel list and made final preparations for voir dire questions and their trial strategy. On Monday, the thirteenth day of the court session, Judge Neblett began the voir dire process, the questioning of prospective jurors by the attorneys of both sides as they tried to expose possible improper biases prior to the selection of the actual jury to hear the case. The lawyers had not finished selecting an 11-man jury before the "hour of adjournment" had arrived, and Judge Neblett postponed the jury selection process until Tuesday. The men impaneled on the first day were Vicente Jaramillo, Rafael Sanchez, Bernabel Ortega, Jose M. Montoya, Manuel Alderete, Manuel Rivera, David Montoya, David Pineda, Frank Zengerly, Jose Estrada and Herminio Gallegos. They represented a cross section of Socorro County voters; Manuel Alderete was selected chairman of the jury.

At nine o'clock on Tuesday morning, Sheriff Emil James presented the court with a ten-man Special Petit Jury Venire No. 6. One of these men would fill the 12th position on Baca's trial jury. All the men were sworn and then presented questions "touching their qualifications to serve as Petit Jurors" before Judge Neblett dismissed three men from consideration. The names of the remaining seven men went into a box, and Juan Baca was randomly selected to be the twelfth juror. The completed jury panel was "sworn to well and truly try the issues joined in this cause pending" and "true deliverance make between the prisoner at the Bar and the State of New Mexico, and a true verdict render according to the law and evidence submitted."[11]

"As it is," said the *Mogollon Mines*, "the miner who is summoned as a juror is oftimes [sic] unable to bear the expense incident to a journey of this kind [a 580-mile trip from Mogollon to Socorro to attend court], and the business man cannot afford to lose the time."[12] The prosecution witnesses, mostly from Mogollon, had been in the county seat for over two weeks waiting to tell their story to the judge and jury, and some witnesses where upset about the inconvenience of the trip and the delay of the court in getting to the Baca case. This session of the district court had already heard two other murder cases before calling Cause 3669. Many courthouse spectators wondered if the two not-guilty verdicts where an omen for the outcome of Cipriano Baca's case.

Following a lunch break, Judge Neblett asked the prosecution team to lay out the state's case against Baca. The second day's session adjourned before the state rested its case, so the judge ordered, "The jury is allowed to retire until the incoming of Court to-morrow morning at nine o'clock." The jury was sequestered and guarded all night by two court bailiffs.

Lowe and Helmick completed the state's case in the morning of the third court day.

The official records do not mention it, but extant regional newspaper accounts of the trial hint that Baca took the stand and told his version of the incident. The state's attorneys were unable to break Cipriano's story or the account told by his witnesses. The court journal reflects Wednesday afternoon's action, saying,

> The jury now having heard all the evidence submitted; having heard all arguments of counsel, and having been fully instructed by the Court; and the trial of this cause being concluded, retire to consider their verdict in charge of Solomon Pino and Walter Davenport, two duly sworn bailiffs of this Court.

The jury gathered in the jury room to discuss the case and reach a verdict.

The *Silver City Independent* headlined their report on the deliberation "Cipriano Baca Acquitted." The newspaper said, "It was claimed that there was no reason for arresting Simmons nor any good reason for shooting him. The jury held other wise." The *Albuquerque Morning Journal* reported, "After being out but fifteen minutes the jury in the case of the State vs. Cipriano Baca ... returned a verdict of not guilty on the first ballot." This newspaper then explained a possible reason for the verdict: "Baca who was an officer at the time of the shooting maintained that he shot Simmons in discharge of his duty, a defense the prosecution was unable to break down."

After jury foreman Manuel Alderete read the verdict, Judge Neblett immediately issued a final decree. The typed text remains clear on the aging journal pages of the court logbook,

> W-h-e-r-e-u-p-o-n, it is ordered by the Court that the said verdict be filed in open court; that the jury be discharged from further consideration of this cause; and that the defendant, Cipriano Baca, go hence without day as to the charge contained in the indictment herein, and that the sureties upon his appearance bond herein be, and they hereby are discharged.

Judge Neblett ordered the court to pay the eight witnesses a total of $597.20 for their expenses during their 14 days in Socorro and a 580-mile trip from Mogollon. Dr. B.C. Kern earned $189 for his "expert test'my," and Clay Simmons was paid $55.50, while H.W. Johnson, Arthur Gore, F.A. Lowe, Pete McClellan and George Williams earned $57 each. Mrs. Maud Simmons was paid $67.70 for her 794-mile trip from her new home in Arizona. Members of the jury received token payment for their three days of public service. The *Silver City Enterprise* reported that Johnson, McClellan, Gore, and the young Simmons returned home on Thursday morning. It is unclear when Mrs. Simmons, Williams, Lowe, or Dr. Kern left Socorro to continue the rest of their lives.[13]

"If there is one to be buried and one to be tried, I'm going to be the one tried," Elfego Baca says in one of his fanciful autobiographies. He called this bloody motto his philosophy for dealing with adversity.[14] Cipriano Baca had followed his old nemesis' axiom, and he was the one that stood before the bar of justice. However, unlike Elfego, Cipriano Baca did not glory in his victory. Cipriano had won his freedom and his life, but he had lost his soul. "If someone is burdened with blood of another," wrote a sage in what is now known as Proverbs 28:17, "let that killer be a fugitive until death; let no one offer assistance."

The ordeal seems to have cast a gray cloud over the rest of Baca's life. He was financially ruined and never regained more then a paycheck-to-paycheck lifestyle. It is unclear how Baca paid his legal bill or if he ever did.

Cipriano Baca left no known written record or verbal reaction to the "not guilty" verdict, and even move strangely, there are no known Baca or Berry family remembrances of the occasions surrounding the trial. It is very possible that none of the Berry family attended the trial. This void is deafening to a biographer, yet the silence itself speaks with a thunderous roar and says volumes about the present-day relationships among Cipriano Baca's many descendents.

20

A Broken Family

"[My husband] never would talk about his father, due to a grudge he held against him for putting him in an orphanage in Albuquerque."—Mrs. Florentino (Louise) Baca, 12 August 1982

"It was difficult for Father to break up the family," recalled Cipriana Randolph. "Nothing was ever the same again. I only saw Father a few times after the family separated. I went to live with Aunt Effie and Uncle Clyde Stauder on a Chama sheep ranch. We [the Baca children] didn't see each other much after that cold winter trip [to Socorro]." Cipriana seems to have always had kind words to say about her siblings, but in later years, the siblings did not always reciprocate this same compassion.[1]

John Amos, one of Cipriano's grandchildren, explained that his mother always spoke of her older sister "with extreme vitriol" but did display "a semblance of affection" for Gilberson, Florentino and Rachel, "though she seldom spoke of any of them." Maisie was six when she moved into the Widow Berry's home and was treated as a daughter. Even John Amos referred to Sallie Berry as his grandmother because he never knew his real grandmother, Mary Berry Baca. Maisie Hill Baca became a "Berry," and like Rachel and her older brothers, retained little affection for their father or for the Baca family heritage.

Grandma Sallie Berry even referred to Cipriana as her "dirty little Mexican" grandchild because the girl loved her father and retained her sense of being a Baca; she also had the feminine version of her father's name. The Berry matriarch believed that Cipriano Baca had "stolen" her daughter, forced her to live in an alien culture, and finally killed her by his lust for sex causing her daughter to bear more children then she was physically capable of sustaining. Grandma Berry died in Socorro in January 1936, and was buried in the Socorro Cemetery's Berry family plot alongside her long-mourned husband and her mother Mary Ann Lord Gilberson who had died in Socorro in January 1908. Four of Grandma Berry's grandchildren lay interned in the Berry family plot, three infant Baca children and the baby Alexander Edelin Amos.[2]

* * *

We have mile markers pointing the way, but there is no full account of the road Baca now traveled. Much of the trail is now dimly lit or dark and covered with dust. Some mileposts are bright on the horizon and serve as beacons to help keep us on the path, while others are just stumbled upon in the dark, broken and discarded. Events are somewhat

Cipriano Baca and his horse are standing in front of the Presbyterian Church in Mogollon following Baca's return to the town after his 1913 murder trial acquittal at Socorro (Mary Baca Photograph Album/Cipriana Randolph).

foggy over the next few months following Baca's trial, but the circumstantial evidence indicates that Baca returned to Mogollon, leaving most of his children in the care of the Berry family, to regain his social and financial footing.

Robert "Stuttering Bob" Lewis, the former Mounted Police sergeant, joined the influx of carpenters that had descended upon Mogollon during the 1913 boom strike. Baca also wanted in on the boom. Baca and Florentino, unable to stay in Socorro with the Griffiths due to the district attorney's deteriorating health, shared a boarding-house room with Lewis. It is unclear how Baca earned a living during these summer months, but it is possible that he returned to butchering to help feed the influx of transients while 10-year-old Florentino helped in the shop. "I think Father tried to make enough money to have us back together again," recalled Cipriana. "But something went wrong and Father lost all his money."

A person's focus is his reality, and that focus can change from moment to moment. A person can also experience multiple realities. Some realities are delusional, and these can grow into a paranoia that can lead to a state of madness. Most of our dreams or fantasies never go beyond the realm of reason, and soon our "real-word" surroundings cause our make-believe reality to give way to the truth. This truth becomes a person's true reality. This fact happened to Cipriano Baca.

The Mogollon boom of 1913 was short-lived. The records are unclear as to how long Baca followed his dream of becoming a wealthy mining man, but one day his vision cleared and he faced reality. Baca needed a new jump start to his life and a more stable source of income than butchering in a busted boomtown. Cipriano renewed his connections with Phelps-Dodge and the Santa Fe Railway and became a transient policeman, guard, or enforcer for the company's joint operations in northern New Mexico and southern Colorado. Family memories recall that Florentino attended school while father and son where at Cripple Creek, Colorado, a mile marker on the ghost trail.[3]

Sometime around 1915, Cipriano and Florentino returned to New Mexico. They settled in the coal mining camp of Blossburg, near Raton, where Baca became the local "lawman" serving as resident livestock inspector and part-time coal mine guard. He was also a special deputy under Colfax County Sheriff Abe Hixenbaugh. The sheriff's wife Nora had spent part of her childhood in Tombstone, Arizona Territory, living next door to Wyatt Earp and his wife. Nora's father, Andy Neff, and Earp were mining partners, and she enjoyed her youthful visits with the lawman-gambler.

Natives discovered coal in Dillon Canyon in 1820, but it was not until 1881 that mining camp enterprises begin furnishing high-grade coal to the Santa Fe Railway for its locomotives. The Maxwell Land Grant Company leased Dillon Canyon to a local stock company called the Rocky Mountain Coal and Railroad Company, and the lessees hired Col. Edward Savage to run the new development. He established a principal settlement he named Blossburg in honor of his hometown in coal rich Pennsylvania. Col. Savage billed the rapidly expanding community as "the Pittsburg of the West." In the early 1880s, Blossburg boasted a weekly newspaper called the *Pioneer*, and by the turn of the century, the town had a community band, a baseball team, two active churches, a Knights of Pythias lodge, a dozen business houses, and a new school building.[4]

By the time Baca arrived in the last half of the 1910s, Blossburg was home to only about a hundred people, and the mercantile store was the liveliest establishment in the village next to G.B. Janolini's saloon. The stockyards were a seasonal business that expanded the village's economy and kept two livestock brokers in business. The shipping yards also kept Baca occupied conducting cattle and sheep brand and disease inspections. A few horse herds also passed through Baca's inspection station. Year by year the area became less and less a mining camp or livestock shipping point and more and more farm country. Today no one lives in what was once Blossburg, and only a few stone-and-mortar walls are visible in the old town site. A large grove of trees and one two-story building stand as the lone sentinels to a colorful past and a milestone on Baca's ghost trail.

A moment of speculation suggests that Cipriano Baca might have crossed paths with his successor as lieutenant of the Mounted Police during his years in Colfax County. John

Wesley Collier was a special officer for the St. Louis, Rocky Mountain and Pacific Railroad Company and their mining interests in Colfax County. Collier, his wife Lizzie, and young daughter Coral lived in Raton and later on a ranch near Ute Park. The Cimarron River community was the western terminus of the railroad and the southern entrance to the Baldy Mountain mining country. The tall, lanky, transplanted Texan was a tough force when dealing with mine labor union bosses and radical railroad workers for six years before he resigned and moved to Kansas in the early 1920s.[5]

There are Baca family tales, ghost trail mile markers, concerning the teenaged Florentino working in the coal mines surrounding Raton. Where did the future mining engineer work; Sugarite, Yankee, Gardiner, Brilliant, Swastika or maybe Blossburg? The old mine payroll records are no longer available, and due to Florentino's reticence to discuss that part of his youth with his family, it is hard to determine the truth of the youthful coal miner tale.

The Spanish first visited the area surrounding the present-day settlement of Madrid, in the Oritz Mountains of Santa Fe County, in the 1600s, and they named the countryside for Don Francisco de Madrid. The area hills held deposits of lead, and this mineral started the mining interest in the region before the discovery of coal in the 1830s. By the late 1860s, a mining center had developed and the coal production increased annually until it reached a peak in the early 1920s. The Madrid coalfield is unique because it contains anthracite, hard coal, and bituminous or soft coal. In 1889, the Santa Fe Railway built a branch line to Madrid, located a few miles northeast of Albuquerque on the high road to Santa Fe, so that the soft coal became economical to ship. The hard coal sold commercially for home and business use.

In 1896, the railroad company leased the Madrid property to the Colorado Fuel and Iron Company that operated the mines until 1906 when they gave up the venture because of recovery difficulties. Former federal deputy marshal turned Albuquerque banker and businessman, George A. Kaseman, owner of the Hahn Coal Company in the Duke City and distributor of Madrid mined smithing coal, decided to mine the coal himself. He bought up the mineral lease and had Oscar Huber, his sales manager, oversee the Madrid-mine productions of the new Albuquerque and Cerrillos Coal Company. Electric lighting was provided by a company-generating plants, streets where paved, and a hospital was constructed. Constructing a reservoir high up in the mountain range and using gravity to distribute the liquid to points below met the water supply need.

In the 1920s and 1930s, Madrid became famous for not only high-quality coal production, but also its massive lighted Christmas display. Following George Kaseman's death in 1938, Oscar Huber bought the Madrid town site and all rights to the area's mineral deposits. He continued the company until 1954 when the coal mines were shutdown due to low coal demand. Today the once-bustling mining camp has recreated itself as a center for the arts and has become a tourist destination.[6]

It had taken Baca almost three years to reestablish himself after he left Mogollon in 1913, but he finally settled down in Santa Fe County. Kaseman, Cipriano's old friend from the federal marshal's office, had Oscar Huber hire Baca as a mine guard and then secured Baca's appointment as the deputy sheriff at the Madrid mining camp. Florentino lived with his father during this period, went to work in the coal mines by day, and studied by night.

21

The Wartime Rangers

"During 1918 the [mounted] police performed very valuable service to the state and nation." — Walter M. Danburg, General Secretary, State Council of Defense, State of New Mexico

When the Sunshine Territory faded into history on Saturday, January 6, 1912, so did the New Mexico Territorial Mounted Police. At that moment of death, the Sunshine State was born, and with it, the new state's first police force vested with statewide authority. The New Mexico State Mounted Police now earned their own reputation for fearlessness in enforcing the law.

By the time the second session of the First State Legislature met in the spring of 1913, the Mounted Police had arrested members of the State Senate, the legislature's upper chamber, on charges of accepting a bribe. These Republican lawmakers had taking money to cast their vote for a certain candidate during the selection of the new state's U.S. senators. Up until the 17th Amendment to the Constitution of the United States, ratified in 1913, mandated a popular vote by a state's citizens as the method to select U.S. senators, the different state legislatures or general assemblies had selected that state's federal senators.

Within days of convening the second session of the First State Legislature, a senator introduced a bill to abolish the Mounted Police in the State Senate, and a lengthy pro-and-con debate followed. Governor McDonald made it clear that he would veto any measure to abolish the state police. The legislative kingpins were not sure that they could muster the votes needed to override a gubernatorial veto, so they did a sure thing. The members of the House Committee on Finance "forgot" to provide funding for the Mounted Police Department. They knew the governor supported the Mounted Police, but they also knew that he would not veto the mandatory biannual legislation to fund the state government; no money, no police.

Captain Fornoff sued the state auditor, Will Sargent, citing section 12 of the Mounted Police Act of 1905 that specified the territorial police be paid from a special property tax collected annually and placed in a special Mounted Police Fund to be used to fund the rangers. This trust fund was a dedicated account within the territorial/state general accounts, and by the start of the state's first fiscal year, the special Mounted Police tax was generating $18,000 a year. Captain Fornoff wanted to spend that money to support his small company of state police.

The state district court at Santa Fe upheld the Mounted Police's point of view in "State of New Mexico ex rel. Fred Fornoff vs. William G. Sargent, 18 NM 272," but the attorney general appealed this decision to the New Mexico Supreme Court. The high court, in a quick review, reversed the lower court judgment claiming that the 38th Legislative Assembly in 1909 had amended the Mounted Police Act of 1905 and eliminated the special tax and the special account by the new legislation. The Supreme Court ruling also said that since the money collected under authority of the Mounted Police Act of 1905 was now being absorbed into the state's general revenue fund, it would take an approved legislative appropriation to remove these funds from the state treasury. Thus, the Mounted Police Department ran out of authorized funding on December 1, 1913.

The high court justices, in their haste to render a timely opinion, seem to have missed a pivotal point in this case. Francis Wilson, the plaintiff's attorney, didn't ask the court why, if the receipts from the special Mounted Police tax were placed in the state's general fund as of 1909 as the state auditor claimed, both the state treasurer and the state auditor found it necessary to continue to maintain separate account ledgers for the Mounted Police Fund.

The answer is simple. The territorial treasurer, and later the state officer, continued to collect the Mounted Police tax after the 1909 legislation repealed the separate tax to maintain the territorial police operation. The tax collection continued after the deactivation of the state police in December 1913. State lawmakers refused to allocate the Mounted Police Fund money for the Mounted Police during the 1915 and 1917 legislative sessions, yet the treasurer and auditor account ledgers testify to the use, over the years, of these funds to support selected state police functions. What authority had authorized the use of these dedicated funds?

Another interesting point to consider is that the state auditor and the state treasurer maintained the Mounted Police special fund ledgers until the 1923 fiscal year; two years after lawmaker repealed the Mounted Police law in 1921. It was at this time that state lawmakers quietly took the $84.32 remaining in the Mounted Police Fund and absorbed it into the state's general operating account.[1]

The New Mexico Mounted Police was a paper force during the years 1914–1917. The Mounted Police law remained on the statute books, but with no funding, the paid officers had their commissions revoked. Governors William C. McDonald and Washington E. Lindsey continued to issue "special without pay" state police commissions to select peace officers, like railroad police and range detectives who worked in more than one county under a provision of the Mounted Police Reorganization Act of 1909.

When Governors McDonald and Lindsey faced a law enforcement crisis that needed a public face, they called on Fred Fornoff, but if the assignment called for stealth action, they turned to a lone ranger named Fred Lambert. The governors paid Lambert and Fornoff from their office contingency fund and/or the Mounted Police Fund covered travel expenses.

Fred Lambert held a special trust from both chief executives, working under a special Mounted Police commission, and at the direction of the governor. He became a "Phantom Force," and he seemed to be everywhere there was trouble. Lambert called Cimarron home, but in 1914, he transferred to Santa Fe. He served as a deputy special officer of the U.S. Indian Service for the suppression of the liquor traffic on the state's Indian reservations and as a deputy U.S. Marshal, but federal officers granted the governor use of Lambert's service when the state needed him. Later, Charles Catron, of the Catron law firm of Santa Fe, employed Lambert to manage one of his large land grant holdings and continued to make Fred's ability as an investigator available to the governor.

Following the border incursions of 1916 by Mexican raiders, hundreds of men residing in the southern tier of New Mexico's counties received short-term nonsalaried Mounted Police appointments as special militia/police designed to function during an emergency in support of their county sheriff and later their county War Defense Committee. These special Border Trouble Rangers never saw state service.[2]

* * *

August 1914 became a pivotal year in world history as much of Europe marched into a continental conflict that would become the Great War. The Central Powers were composed of the vast empires of Germany, Austria-Hungary, Turkey, and Bulgaria. They opposed the allied forces of Great Britain, France, Russia, Italy, Japan, Portugal, China, Greece, and certain Latin American countries. As this global conflict dragged into 1916, both sides made overtures to have the United States join their cause, but President Wilson continued to enforce neutrality in spite of the Imperial German Navy's continued attacks upon American merchant shipping in the North Atlantic.

Historians still debate the reasons, but in early March 1916, Mexican revolutionary leader Jose Doroteo Arango Arambula, commonly called Poncho Villa, sent an invasion force to attack the U.S. Army base and the citizens of Columbus, in Luna County, along the New Mexico–Mexico border. Eighteen Americans died in the rebel raid, and President Wilson responded by sending General John J. Pershing into Mexico at the head of a 6,000-man Punitive Expedition to hunt down Villa and his rebels.[3] Meanwhile, Mounted Policeman Fred Lambert arrived in Columbus and with some of the region's special Mounted Police reestablished civil order in the area.

A few minutes past two o'clock on Sunday morning, July 30, 1916, a massive explosion, now estimated as a 5.5 magnitude quake, destroyed the tiny Black Tom Island, located about a mile from the Ellis Island home of the Statue of Liberty in the New York harbor. The Lahigh Valley Railroad owned the island, and the government used the area as a munitions storage site and dock area for shipments to the Allied forces in Europe. The island, covered with freight cars and pier-side barges, connected to the mainland near Jersey City by a railway causeway. In an act of sabotage, German agents had slipped past the island's lax security and placed a time bomb that resulted in a blast felt 100 miles away in Philadelphia, while jolting people out of bed in the massive New York harbor area. Seven people died in the attack. The sky glowed orange for hours as the ground fires grew and more boxcars exploded. When firefighters finally extinguished the massive waterfront fire, 13 dockside warehouses were charred ruins; six piers had disappeared into the bay while hundreds of railroad freight cars had become ashes and twisted steel.

Later, authorities discovered that the saboteurs almost drowned in the waves their work had caused. They hid out among members of the German spy network in Hudson County, New York, before they made their way to Mexico. Few people at the time believed that the explosion was a terrorist act ordered by the Imperial German government, and it took the American intelligence network years to understand the vastness of Germany's 1914–1917 sabotage effort in the United States. A postwar Mixed Claims Commission composed of German, American, and nonaligned representatives took years to determine that Germany was liable for reparations. In 1939, Hitler's Nazi government refused to honor Germany's Great War debt, and the Black Tom case remained unsettled until after the German state was defeated in a second world war. In 1979, Germany made its final payment toward the $95 million reparation owed the United States.[4]

Nearly a year after the U.S. Army marched into Mexico, President Wilson ordered Pershing and his command home without having captured Villa. That same month, February 1917, Arthur Zimmermann, the foreign secretary of the Imperial German Government, sent a coded message to Heinrick von Eckhardt, the Imperial German ambassador in Mexico City, which was intercepted by British intelligence and passed on to the U.S. government. The intercept, referred to as the Zimmermann Telegram, suggested that Mexican president Venustiano Carranza's government should join with Imperial Germany and her Central Powers allies to defeat the aims of the Allied Powers. The telegram suggested that Mexico should send her army into the American southwest and recapture Texas, Arizona, New Mexico, and California and claim them as a war prize at the conclusion of the European conflict and the defeat of the United States; it was Mexico's manifest destiny of *Tierra y Libertad*, land and liberty, to reclaim her lands stolen by the North American Yankees.[5]

The Mexican national anthem is almost unknown outside the confines of that republic, but one line is worth noting in connection with the 1917 threat against the United States. "Mexicans, at the cry of war, prepare the steel and steed, and may earth shake at its core to the resounding roar of the cannon." The leadership in Mexico City was favorable to the Central Powers, but wisely chose not to accept the Imperial German offer to join in a war against the United States.

The relations between Mexico and her northern neighbor remained lukewarm until the Mexican government stopped all friendly pretence and openly supported Adolph Hitler's Nazi Germany in the 1930s. The Mexican government often gave preferential treatment to German commercial ships and the Nazi navy during their visits to Mexico's sunny harbors, as in the Great War when the Mexican government provided a safe haven for Imperial German spies.

Some historians and sociologists are beginning to question why Mexico's government has never joined with the world community to fight in any engagement against terrorist or totalitarian regimes threatening peace and stability in the world. Why have so many worldwide crime families found a home in Mexico? Is this national cowardliness, greed, national passivism, or a dislike of democratic values and capitalistic principals?

During the last century, the Mexican people have suffered a succession of corrupt and ineffective state and national governments. These officials have been unable, and/or unwilling, to overcome a continuous runaway inflation economy, rampant poverty, an out-of-control birthrate, a corrupt police and court system, increasingly lucrative and brutal underworld of criminal cartels, and oppressive religious traditions that chain people to the past. To escape this morass in their homeland, many Mexican nationals have fled northward, flooding the U.S. labor market and straining their northern neighbor's social services system. It is not a burning desire for political freedom, but a lust for money that fuels this invasion. This illegal migration has effectively reclaimed Mexico's lost southwestern lands and is now penetrating into the small villages and metropolitan areas of America's heartland. The result is not Hispanic assimilation into American's heritage, but a cultural segregation designed to reshape America's culture, language, and national values.

When the State Department released the intercepted Imperial German diplomatic cable to the press in March 1917, it caused heightened concern in Santa Fe, but it also galvanized national public opinion against the cause of the European Central Powers. The prospect of a second Mexican-American War was a serious political and military concern in America and a real possibility during this period of tense international relationships. War Defense Committees in New Mexico's southern tier of counties put their community Mounted Police units on alert and hoped that the crisis would just blow away in the desert wind. This proved a false hope. In April, Congress confirmed that the United States was now at war with the Central Powers led by Imperial Germany. America joined with the Allied Powers, pledging "to make the world safe for Democracy."[6]

On Tuesday, May 1, 1917, Governor W.E. Lindsey addressed a special session of the Third State Legislature meeting in Santa Fe. The governor told the lawmakers he had four "prime requisites for the successful prosecution of the war" effort within the state that he wished for them to address. Lindsey wished to find the means to recruit the state's full quota of men for the armed forces, increase the state's output of "foodstuffs," officially "constitute the War Council" he had established by executive order, and finally the chief executive said the "accomplishment of these and other necessary activities in this time of stress will require the appropriation of money."

Governor Lindsey was very concerned about the worldwide food shortage. He believed New Mexico farmers could assist to alleviate the problem.

> All of us have to live from day to day, and few, if any of us, have escaped till now, having our attention most strikingly called to the unprecedented high cost of living. The staple articles of food commonly regarded as necessary, demand an unprecedented price. What then may we expect considering the fact that there is not now in the world enough food to sustain the human race for a longer period than six months? The shortest sighted [person] should readily see that our future existence depends upon the coming harvest.

Lindsey asked that the legislature provide funding to send county farm agents into every part of the state to assist "our farmers on the land." He also asked for funds to loan to farmers so they could buy seed and suggested that all unemployed boys "from fourteen to nineteen years of age, should be listed [sic] at once and mobilized for work in planting, cultivating and harvesting crops."[7]

Early in 1918, the United States was gearing up to send more troops to the Great War in Europe, and Congress enacted legislation to conserve the nation's resources for the war effort. Many perceived Daylight Savings Time as a way to reduce energy consumption by shifting an hour of daylight to late in the afternoon to expand the daylight working hours. The Standard Time Act was the first federal legislation to establish designated time zones across the nation to regulate intercontinental commerce; the major railroads had used a standard time system since 1883 to coordinate train movements. Until the Standard Time Act, most of the nation's business activities operated by local time or the sun's natural time. Some historians credit Benjamin Franklin with first proposing the daylight savings concept in 1784, but it took over 130 years and a world war before the idea gained its chance. Many people did not have clocks or pocket watches and an animal's natural clock did not accommodate an artificial clock. One can almost hear Cipriano Baca making a clip like, "You can't teach a rooster to crow an hour before sunrise." Daylight Savings Time never became very popular, and lawmakers repealed the law after the war ended.

The idea of a national "wartime" daylight savings plan was reinstated during the Second World War only to be repealed after that conflict ended. Local customs again ruled summertime commerce, but this mix mash became standardized with the 1966 Uniform Time Act and all of its subsequent amendments. One wag suggested that, if the Congress could change the time of day, then why could not the government raise the freezing point so that people would feel warmer in winter.

President Wilson's national wartime mobilization plan called for a quick presence of American troops on French soil, so he federalized all the state National Guard units to help supply this first contingent to see combat in Europe. Federal troops and New Mexico's guardsmen were among the soldiers sent to eastern bases for shipment to Europe. This action left the State of New Mexico's common border with the Republic of Mexico's northern states of Chihuahua and Sonora unprotected from an enemy invasion from the south. In light of the strong feelings about the border conditions in New Mexico, this development posed a real threat to the security of the southwest and provided a potential natural entry into the American heartland.

Governor Lindsey supported border security and encouraged the New Mexico State War Council to provide joint funding, along with the state's Cattle Sanitary Board, to reactivate a full-time company of the Mounted Police to patrol the border and serve as livestock inspectors and range riders to protect the vital food supply and other natural resources. These new state rangers and their special unpaid auxiliary were to be guardians of civil order and the "eyes and ears" against a sneak attack through Mexico.

The *Silver City Enterprise* offered editorial support to the governor's plan, saying,

> In reviving and reorganizing the New Mexico Mounted Police, Governor Lindsey [a Republican], the New Mexico Council of Defense [a Republican-controlled administrative body], the New Mexico Cattle and Horse Growers' Association and the New Mexico Cattle Sanitary Board, have sought only the protection of the property and the safety of life and limb of the people of the state. The organization begins on a non-partisan basis, and it will be maintained on that high plane. Every member of the organization is directed by regulations to refrain from taking any active part in political campaigns.

Governor Washington E. Lindsay selected Herbert James McGrath, longtime Democratic sheriff of Grant County and a former Mounted Police under Captain John Fullerton, to lead the new company. Vic Culberson, a member of the Council of Defense, recommended his friend Cipriano Baca as one of the 16 full-time state rangers, and Baca welcomed the opportunity to once again round up border outlaws, unpatriotic "war slackers" and livestock thieves. As a state police officer, Cipriano earned a $150-per-month salary.[8]

When state officials were considering reestablishing the Mounted Police as a full-time agency again, Fred Fornoff contacted Fred Lambert about accepting a salaried appointment under Captain McGrath. Lambert really wanted to return to New Mexico and ride with the new state police, but he had promised his wife that he would help her ailing brother operate his livestock brokerage house in Missouri. A few years later, after her brother's death, the Lamberts did return to New Mexico, and before Fred's death in 1971, the state honored him as the last living member of the territorial police and the dean of New Mexico's peace officers

Shortly before his death, Fred Lambert recalled his memory of the new ranger captain.

> I had some dealings with Herb McGrath when he was sheriff of Grant County. I was on an undercover mission [for the Mounted Police] and got arrested by the Silver City marshal, and I

got McGrath to get me out of jail. I completed the case and returned home only to be called back south to work with McGrath again. He was a well-mannered gentleman. A widower if I remember right; well liked by the people in Grant County. He had a ranch just outside of town, but McGrath lived in a big brick house in town. As I recall McGrath's daughter died while he was Mountie captain and he blamed himself for her getting sick. He tried to resign the Mountie Service, but the governor wouldn't let him go. His men seemed to have liked him enough to give him a gold badge. That's respect![9]

McGrath took his oath as Mounted Police captain on Tuesday, April 16, 1918, and the official muster for the new full-time state police was set for Wednesday, May 1. It was, however, two weeks later before the payroll contained the last ranger's name. The official Mounted Police records are not clear concerning Cipriano Baca's assigned duty station, but since most of McGrath's force served in the southern half of the state, it seems likely that Baca also lived in the area.[10]

McGrath's Mounted Police were to do the same type of work as the men who had served with Fullerton and Fornoff, but the new rangers had a few additional special assignments. During the war emergency the Mounted Police were to assist federal officers and the local and state Council of Defense representatives to detect and prevent the spreading of Central Powers propaganda or other violations of the Selective Service Act, the Espionage Act, the Food and Fuel Control Act, the Sabotage Act, and the Sedition Act. The Mounted Police were also required to enforce state and federal laws against gambling, prostitution and the sale of alcoholic spirits near military instillations, in addition to ticketing speeders and drivers who did not have license tags on their automobiles. The old horseback-mounted, livestock-thief-chasing ranger legend of the Fullerton-Fornoff Mountie Service had entered a new era of law enforcement for New Mexico.

McGrath had been a member of Fullerton's Rangers in 1905 and served a number of terms as sheriff of Grant County. He had a large ranch near Silver City and a home in the town. He was the only Democrat to serve a head of the rangers. He killed two men in gunfights (NMMP/AC).

* * *

Due to the uncertain demands of being a Mounted Police constantly on assignment, Cipriano felt he was unable to continue the day-to-day care of Florentino, so the teenager stayed on in Madrid and continued to work in the mines. Following the war's conclusion, the nation suffered a depressed economy and many mines closed. Florentino lost his job and had to live at an orphanage in Old Town Albuquerque where he stayed for about nine months before going to live with his Grandmother Berry in Socorro. Florentino worked a variety of jobs, including teaching, running a stock room, working at the power plant, and doing assay work. During this period, he enrolled in the School of Mines prep school. When he was 20 years old in 1923, Florentino Baca became the youngest person to earn a bachelor of science in mining engineering, with honors, from the School of Mines. During these years, young Baca became friends with a Socorro schoolteacher named Louise Nazarene, the daughter of a doctor from Dallas Center, Iowa. Miss Nazarene followed Florentino Baca to Bolivia and married him while he was working as a mining engineer in La Paz.[11]

* * *

Newspapers across the United States carried reports of how the American Expeditionary Force was advancing on the Western Front in France and Belgium during October 1918, and there were reports that the European conflict would be over soon. Germany was fighting a last-ditch holding action as men continued to die in the bloody trenches of no-man's land. While the world's attention was focused upon the battlefield, another more deadly killer carried by the winds started its global march. It was the Spanish influenza, and the *London Times* opined that not since the Black Death had such a plague swept the world; an estimated 20 to 40 million people died.

In fact, more Americans, at home and abroad, died from this flu pandemic, an estimated 600,000 to 750,000 people, than lost their lives to bombs and bullets in all of America's previous wars, including the Great War, up to that point in the nation's history. The 1918–1919 flu moved like a tidal wave from the East Coast to the Pacific, and within weeks, the nation became paralyzed with death and sickness. New Mexico experienced about 50,000 Spanish Flu cases, in a population of approximately 360,000 citizens, and suffered about a 10 percent mortality rate.

Albuquerque, the state's largest population center at nearly 15,000 people, is known as the "Heart of the Well Country" due to its central location in New Mexico's healthy climate. The motto notwithstanding, thousands of people became sick, and before it had run its course, "The Bug" had killed over 160 people in the Duke City. The *Albuquerque Morning Journal* played the public servant and provided its readers some guidelines on "How to Dodge the 'Flu.'" The newspaper said a person should " keep feet and clothing dry; avoid crowds; protect your nose and mouth in the presence of sneezers; gargle your throat three times a day with a mild antiseptic if only salt and water; don't neglect a cold; keep as much as possible in the sunshine; don't get 'scared.'"

The war effort had called many of the nation's doctors and nurses to uniform, so the domestic health care shortage quickly became a crisis. The Albuquerque city government prohibited public gatherings; churches, entertainment establishments, restaurants, schools, and factories closed their doors. People who had never prayed in their lives now found a need to speak to G-d. Heads of households could not work due to business closings or their own sickness, and many families quickly found that they had no money to sustain them. The few charities that existed in New Mexico had their resources strained to the breaking point and were left with little ability to continue providing meaningful assistance.

Mogollon can serve as an example of how the epidemic affected the isolated communities of the state. Many in the mining camp were bedridden, and whole families became stricken. The two resident doctors could not handle the load, so the army sent a doctor and nurse up from Fort Bayard to assist. One of the military medical corps ordered local residents to kill some deer so the hospital staff could make soup for the families unable to care for themselves. No one seemed concerned that it was illegal to hunt deer during this season of the year.

People were dying so quickly in Mogollon that the grave diggers could not blast out holes fast enough to keep up with the demand. Resident diarist H. A. Hoover recalled that the bodies were stored in a dance hall to await burial. "It is said that cats found their way into that building and gnawed on the faces of the dead — a gruesome thing." Fifty-two people died in Mogollon due to the quick moving pandemic, and one of these deaths was 18-year-old Hattie Shellhorn, Cipriana Randolph's childhood friend, who died on October 11, 1918, and was buried in the town cemetery. The "flu bug" disappeared as quickly as it had arrived, but it was not until 1943 that scientists developed the first vaccine to combat the disease.

Dr. Charles V. Chapin wrote in the January 1916 issue of the *American Medical Association Bulletin*, "It is unfortunate that a state with a population which now numbers nearly a half million should do nothing whatever for public health." New Mexico "is the only state of which this can be said." Governor Lindsey issued a proclamation prohibiting all public gatherings in the state, but this measure was voluntary because New Mexico had no statewide mechanism to establish health directives to enforce the governor's order. With no health mandate, the State Mounted Police had no authority to enforce any state quarantine or any other health safety issues like safe drinking water and milk supplies or the proper disposal of human waste. The price of this legislative void was costly in human lives, and at the November general election, New Mexico's voters demanded that their state government eliminate this flaw. The pride of many New Mexicans was hurt when doctors rejected them for military service during the Great War due to their poor physical condition. Tuberculosis infected many men.

A new governor took office in January 1919 and proposed the creation of a state health department in his legislative message to the Fourth State Legislature. The lawmakers heard the message and passed House Bill 118, as amended, creating a multi-level health department system, and Governor O.A. Larrazolo signed the bill into law honoring his youngest son who lost his life to the Spanish influenza. The legislation created a state health laboratory, a bureau of vital statistics, maternal and child care health services, dental and mental health programs, a public health nursing system, and proper sanitation services.[12]

* * *

The Great War reached a climax with an across-the-battlefields general armistice on November 11, 1918. Washington Lindsey's single term as governor ended on New Year's Eve and so did the authority of the Mounted Police. The protocol that established the state police specified that the rangers' commissions would expire on December 31, 1918, unless the governor disbanded the rangers sooner or extend the mandate for the police beyond the expiration date. Governor Lindsey felt he had completed his job as a wartime leader, so he left the fate of the Mounted Police to his successor. NMMP Company Three, like Fullerton's Rangers and Fornoff's Boys, held no formal ceremony to disband the unit and turn in their equipment. Like the smoke of a campfire, they disappeared with the wind.

In fact, some of McGrath's men were in the field when they learned that days earlier their commissions had expired. McGrath lobbied the State Council of Defense for months trying to get his men paid for the six days they had worked in January 1919, but the auditor refused payment. The state owed Baca $30 at the time he unceremoniously left the state service. Once again, he had paid himself to do a law enforcement assignment.

The *Magdalena News* praised the state rangers' service, saying,

> As a body, and as individuals, they (the Mounted Police) are selected because they are fearless and law-abiding, reputable men, and their duty is to enforce the laws as they are found on the statute books of the state, and this they do without fear or favoritism.

During their eight months of field operations, Captain McGrath's Mounted Police established a new standard of excellence for public service. These state officers made 452 major arrests and conducted 118 important investigations that were still open cases when the company was decommissioned. To understand the magnitude of this eight-month arrest record, one can compare it to the 72 arrests made during the year that John Fullerton led the first Mounted Police or that Fred Fornoff's 11-man ranger force took three years to account for 450 arrests. Since none of the Mounted Police arrest reports survive, it is hard to evaluate Baca's individual level of performance.[13]

Captain McGrath's 16 rangers were also responsible for almost $2,000 in fines and fees collected by local courts. The company's final report noted that the Mounted Police had recovered stray stock, returned to the owner, valued at nearly $9,000 and unclaimed stray stock valued at almost $3,000 that was delivered to the Cattle Sanitary Board for sale by that agency. McGrath's Mounted Police also proved they were more than stock detectives by actively enforcing laws like the state's new automobile code, the hotel license law, and the occupation tax law.

Herb McGrath devoted days of nonpaid time, over a five-month period, closing his unit's accounts with the State Council of Defense. He sent the state police records to the new headquarters at Las Vegas, closed the Silver City office, sold the office equipment, and arranged to sell his Ford Flivver. McGrath originally purchased the auto for $521.05 and was only able to sell the well-used vehicle for $150 ten months later. Captain Sena purchased himself a new Dodge touring car for $1,264.65 and bought new furniture for his Las Vegas office.[14]

The new captain chose not to recommend Cipriano Baca as one of his officers because he was not "flexible" enough to adjust to new law enforcement standards. Baca was a member of the Republican Party, but his current lack of political influence with the new party bosses who influenced Governor Larrazolo, his age, and his notable record of impartial law enforcement had become a liability.

Governor Octaviano A. Larrazolo reestablished the Mounted Police on Thursday, January 2, 1919, under authority granted him in the Public Defense Act of 1917. The national war crisis was over, but now the nation faced the "Red Scare" of the Bolshevik, or Socialist, and the anarchist movement. New Mexico was not exempt from the fear that gripped the industrial heartland and the mining sections of America.

Governor Larrazolo had witnessed the results achieved by McGrath's Rangers, and he quickly recognized the usefulness of such a police force and understood that the wartime need to project a public image of a bipartisan state government was no longer politically required. He appointed a new captain, Apolonio A. Sena of Las Vegas, who was a prominent

Hispanic member of the Republican Party. When the Fourth State Legislature convened later in January 1919, the governor asked the lawmakers to fully fund his police and expand the size of the department.

Governor Larrazolo made no pretense of the state government's concern about personal freedom and equal justice for all of New Mexico's citizens. The Great War was over, and Americans wanted to return to an era of normalcy. The government removed the austere measures of the war years. The young warriors returning from Europe wanted a different life than the one they had known before the war. They were the "Lost Generation," and they wanted quick wealth and personal pleasure. They welcomed the advent of the Roaring Twenties with open arms and a disregard for laws against "pleasurable sins" like gambling, the sale of alcoholic beverages in backroom "speakeasies," and other vices. The leadership in Santa Fe was also ready to return to the old system of ruling-party, iron-fisted power brokering and "feathering your own nest" party-line politics.[15]

One tragedy of the transition of the Mounted Police command and headquarters was that McGrath transferred 118 open investigations to the new ranger company. Captain A.A. Sena, who was determined to make his own mark on the Mounted Police Service, wanted none of McGrath's unfinished work or any of his men. He did not pursue most of these cases, and the result was that many potential felons got a pass from the reorganized state police. The state's media was strangely silent on the subject.

A party-line vote granted the governor his fully funded and expanded state police, so in mid-year, 1919, Sena's command increased to five sergeants and 16 policemen divided into five service districts. Captain Sena's police force soon became the "boss enforcers" for wealthy businessman and the politically connected. In the final months of 1919, the governor ordered the whole Mounted Police force to Gallup to maintain "civil order" during the coal mine strikes; they were taxpayer-paid strike busters. The golden age of the Mounted Police headed toward an abyss.

A.A. Sena's Mounted Police recorded 114 arrests for 1919 and 103 arrests in 1920. Sena resigned as Mounted Police captain in the fall of 1920 to run for statewide office; he lost. Merritt C. Mechem, the former district court judge, became governor in January 1921, and tapped former San Miguel County Sheriff Lorenzo Delgado, also a Republican, to be the fifth and final head of the Mounted Police.

In late 1920, a special legislative finance committee released a recommendation to abolish the State Mounted Police and establish a three-man state marshal team in their place. The committee, headed by former Territorial Governor Herbert J. Hagerman, believed this approach would still keep a state police function, but would save the state treasury $40,000 per year. Mechem agreed with his fellow Republicans and publicly endorsed the proposal with the understanding that Lorenzo Delgado would be the chief marshal.

A bill to abolish the State Mounted Police quickly passed both legislative chambers. Governor Mechem signed the emergency legislation on Tuesday, February 15, 1921, 16 years to the day after the Mounted Police had been born, and unceremoniously dismissed Delgado's small force. The anti-state police lawmakers and the sheriff's fraternity who used the guise of fiscal responsibility to win their war against a central police authority had duped Mechem. The coup de grace came when state lawmakers omitted the state marshal plan from their legislative agenda.

The tradition of fair and impartial law enforcement established by the Mounted Police now lives in the heritage of the men and women of the New Mexico State Police. In 1933, the state organized a ten-man motorcycle unit to be a courtesy patrol of the state's highways serving as goodwill ambassadors to weary travelers and as visible guardians of highway safety. Two years later, New Mexico Motor Patrol became the nucleus of an independent New Mexico State Police when the legislature created that law enforcement unit. Since 1986, the State Police have been one of seven divisions operating under the jurisdiction of New Mexico's Department of Public Safety.[16]

22

The Sunset Years

"People will forget what you say, People will forget what you did, But people will never forget how you made them feel." — Anonymous

At some time around the turn of the 20th century, an immigrant miner named Honeyky established a copper-mining operation in the Burro Mountains about one and a half miles northeast of Silver City. A short time later, a small settlement of miners took root and was called Tyrone in honor of Honeyky's native home in Ireland. Phelps-Dodge had bought up all the surrounding mining claims and created a new town site northeast of the original location by 1909. The conglomerate enacted a dream of Mrs. Dodge to build a well-planned luxurious company town by contracting with world-renowned architect Bertram Goodhue to design a Mediterranean Spanish-style community. The project had cost over $1 million by its completion and occupation in 1915. The new town contained a Torbernite Drive, Bornite Street, Chalcopyrite Avenue, Tenorite Court and naturally a Cooper Court was part of the business and residential sections. The community contained a school, and a hospital, along with its palatial residences for the company executives. Within a few years of the town's construction, about 7,000 people inhabited it.

In early January 1919, Cipriano Baca found he no longer had his state ranger post, but his past association with the Phelps-Dodge Company once again provided a helpful assist. Phelps-Dodge needed a qualified guardsman for their massive investment at Tyrone, so when Baca's services were again available, they enticed him to return as their law enforcement agent. The local management of the Tyrone mine supported the election of John E. Casey as sheriff of Grant County in November 1918. When he took office on January 1, the new sheriff became aware of Baca's availability. Casey knew of Baca's law enforcement reputation and his past connection with the Grant County sheriff's office, so he did not hesitate to appoint Cipriano as his deputy for Precinct 22, the area encompassing the Tyrone mining site.

The 60-year-old Baca rented a cabin in Fontana Canyon and had as his only neighbors a fellow deputy sheriff named John N. Parrott and John Reding, a cigar and tobacco salesman. The 38-year-old Reding and his wife Stetter and their two young children had come to Grant County from Michigan. Parrott and his wife Euca were native Texans as were three of their four children. Parrott had been a marshal at Deming before becoming one of the two sergeants of McGrath's Mounted Police in 1918. Baca and Parrott had been friends for years.

Baca's Tyrone assignment worked out admirably for the sheriff and for the mining company. Baca renewed old acquaintances and made new ones. As the months passed, Cipriano performed his new duties with the same enthusiastic fervor that he had always shown when wearing a peace officer's badge in Grant County.[1]

* * *

During the early 1920s, Cipriana Randolph visited her father at his Fontana Canyon home near Tyrone. During the visit, she made a sentimental return to Mogollon and found a few people still living in the semi-ghost town. To her surprise, some of these hardy old-timers still remembered her father and the Baca family, and she was able to locate her mother and brother's graves.

In the summer of 1984, Cipriana Randolph underwent surgery for a growth on her thyroid. On the day before she entered the hospital she wrote, "I hope I can get back to New Mexico during the coming year. I would like to go to Mogollon once more. I know it is practically a ghost town now but I have a desire to go." Mrs. Randolph's operation was successful. "I am fine health wise — just slower ... the scar is hardly visible. I call it my 'Masterpiece.' Now I take thyroid and feel fine."

Cipriana Randolph, and her sister-in-law Louise Baca, made a final visit to Mogollon over a half century after her 1920s nostalgic return to the site of so much family joy and sadness. Louise Baca told the author about the final journey,

> Ana [Cipriana] and I searched for her mother's grave on her last visit to Mogollon, but we couldn't find it or the one for her baby brother. The place was a ghost town when we visited it in the summer of 1985. Ana was able to locate the site of her girlhood home, but nothing remained of the structure. [A 1914 flood had destroyed much of the area around the Baca home; a 1915 forest fire and the ravages of time did the rest.] Even today, Mogollon is a remote place, so back then it must have really seemed isolated. The place had many good memories for Ana, but it was still the place that a ten year old girl lost her mother.

On her final visit to Mogollon, Cipriana found no one who remembered her father or her family's stay in the camp. At the time of Mary Baca's premature death, the *Socorro Chieftain* had expressed the hope, "May she rest in peace." Mrs. Randolph found the newspaper's request fulfilled.[2]

Today a community group has undertaken the monumental task of restoring the old burial ground. The decades have altered the look of the hilltop. Tall, thin pine trees reach toward the heavens and obstruct the view of the campsite below because no one today cuts them down for mineshaft supports or firewood. The old footpath is now a forest service road, but it is just as steep and rough to traverse as a century ago. It took strong men to transport a casket up Graveyard Gulch.

In the spring of 2008, the author and Jim Stauder, a descendent of Effie Berry, made a pilgrimage to Mogollon seeking the spirit of the Baca-Berry family. A search was made of this mystical mining camp seeking the sites that were important in Cipriano Baca's life. Some sites were easy to locate, and we approximated the location of a few others, while many have eroded and vanished. Harsh weather and time have taken their toll on the Mogollon cemetery so that today at least 140 graves are unmarked; among these are Mary Ann Berry-Baca and her baby son Teofilo. A systematic search of the cemetery revealed no new information, but the trip up to the hilltop did provide the researchers a sense of a long-gone era.

* * *

Cipriana Baca Randolph (in glasses) made her last visit to New Mexico in June 1984. During her stay, she made a nostalgic journey to Socorro and Mogollon to visit the area of her childhood. The stately Mrs. Randolph and her friend from school days in Albuquerque say goodbye at Albuquerque's SunPort as Cipriana prepared for her flight back to the West Coast (NMMP/AC).

Tyrone was a prosperous operation until the copper market crash of 1921 ended Phelps-Dodge's ability to sell their copper, and the corporation closed the Tyrone mine as unprofitable. Miners moved away as did most other residents of the dream town, including Cipriano Baca and Manuelita Paiz and her children.

Dust gathered on the Tyrone site until 1969 when copper prices made it profitable for the owners to begin a strip mine operation that eventually destroyed the old Tyrone town site. A third location, still called Tyrone, now exists a few miles north of the early 1900s town site.

A typhoid fever outbreak, caused by infected milk production, hit Grant County in early 1920. The desire to live in an area with better health and sanitation caused Baca to look favorability upon relocating to Albuquerque. Cipriano left Grant County for the last time and sought a new future as a shipping inspector for the New Mexico Cattle Sanitary Board, with his headquarters located in the Duke City. During these early years in Albuquerque, Baca occasionally had a visit from his children that still lived in the state.

As a state brand and disease examiner, Baca was empowered to enforce sanitary board quarantines and branding regulations, and to approve the legal transporting of cattle to auction houses or meat market. Baca had learned early that a close "look see" at a herd might uncover altered brands or latent disease, and this experience proved advantageous to cattlemen in central New Mexico.

In July 1923, the *Gallup Independent and Carbon City News* front-paged a story titled

"2 Prisoners Confess Part in Butchering Stolen Cattle." The McKinley County newspaper told readers how Cattle Inspector Baca and the sheriff arrested two suspects and convinced one of the men to show them where they had hidden the hides from the stolen and butchered cattle. The press account reads as if it was just a routine day's occurrence for Baca to break up a gang of rustlers. Baca had made the difficult task of manhunting look so easy for so many years that the public had come to expect positive results when the old lawman took up the trail. Baca had become a living legend.

During Baca's era, a longroper might end up on the wrong end of a looped rope around his neck, but if a rustler is caught today he is more likely to receive a slap on the wrist by a judge, or if he is a repeat offender, he may earn some prison time and a large fine. Time has not changed everything. The sticky-roper is still able to exploit absentee owners, busy auction barns, and the ageless way cattlemen do business with a handshake and little paperwork. The large cattle trailer and good highways changed the method that a thief uses to transport his stolen herd, but understanding livestock is still a prerequisite for a successful cattle theft. A rustler still has to know how to handle, move, and load cattle. He must also understand how to dispose of the product; it is still not a job for a novice or a "city-boy" Saturday-night cowboy.

The 1923 death of Warren G. Harding, an Ohio native son, took place very suddenly while he and the First Lady were on a cross-country tour to explain his administration's programs and to gauge the feelings of the nation. He called the trip a Voyage of Understanding. Baca most likely had some discussions with his friends concerning the mysterious circumstances of the chief executive's death and maybe what would the new "Yankee" president, Calvin Coolidge, do to help working people gain a portion of the nation's thriving economy.

The livestock inspector's job gave the 65-year-old Baca enough financial security so that in 1924 he bought a small house situated upon a lot and a half located at 1510 North First Street, just west of the Santa Fe Railroad right of way. Today the site is a vacant lot in the warehouse district a few blocks south of the east-west interstate highway that bisects Albuquerque. Baca took out an $800 mortgage, with 8 percent interest, payable in 40 monthly installments of $20 each from the Realty Sales Company. Sometime later, Baca built a small "shanty" on the back of his property and rented the place. The appraised value of Baca's house and property was $1,200 in 1930, but the investment value dropped during the Depression era to only $700 in 1940.[3]

By 1925, the Duke City had become a gathering point for former Mounted Police. Baca was a cattle inspector, and J.R. Galusha was the Albuquerque city marshal. A. A. Sena, former captain and wishful politician, was the editor of the Spanish newspaper *La Graceta*. John H. McHughes was a truck farmer working the west slopes of the Sandia Mountains, and the legendary Fornoff was a private detective working out of his home on West Roma Street. It makes fun speculation to consider the possible social interplay between these intrepid, aging former rangers.

These men all lived in a small trading community centered within the blocks between Old Town on the Rio Grande and a few blocks east of the railroad tracks toward the University of New Mexico on the heights. Did these old territorial warriors see each other socially? Did they have occasion to interact professionally? On the other hand, did they each just travel their own path? We may never have a full answer to these questions, but we

Cipriano Baca saw his children only a few times after the family disintegrated in 1913. One of those occasions was in the late 1920s. Left to right are Florentino, Maisie, Gilberson and their father (Jim Stauder Photograph Collection).

do know that Fornoff, McHughes, and Galusha played poker together. Baca and Fornoff also visited each other as old friends.

Four years of livestock inspections on the open range or at the stockyards was enough for the 69-years-old who was beginning to show the aftereffects of his youthful active outdoor life. Bernalillo County Sheriff Felipe Hubbell came to Baca's rescue and gave him the opportunity to become an office deputy and court bailiff. Cipriano was happy to accept the new challenge.

John Amos once remarked that his grandfather "always seemed to have a presence in my life." He also expressed his concept concerning his grandfather's philosophy of law enforcement and Baca's own ancestral heritage.

> I do know that if my grandfather Baca were alive today his sentiments with regard to the flood of illegal immigrants we are experiencing would be with those of most Americans. While his heritage may be Spanish, he would never claim to be a hyphenated American. Through and through he was 100 percent American. I have no doubt that he would be highly offended if anyone ever referred to him as "Hispanic."
>
> While he may have apprehended first time illegals he would nonetheless return them back across the Rio Grande [or the line in the sand between New Mexico and the Mexican State of Chihuahua] out of simple benevolence, but if he caught them a second time he would incarcerate them and have them deported.

Cipriano Baca was a competent sheriff's deputy in Albuquerque. It was a nice job while it lasted, but political change again cost Baca his law enforcement post.[4]

In January 1930, a butcher's meat cleaver replaced Baca's deputy sheriff star. In 1906, two federal laws, the Pure Food and Drug Act and the Meat Inspection Act, changed the sanitation rules for operating a chophouse, but the basic premise remained the same—killing and dressing out animals for meat. It was a bloody, revolting and smelly job and had its own element of danger, as the meat cutter would wield a meat clever or a butcher knife in the course of preparing the meat for sale.

Being a meat chopper was not a long-term vocation for a man with aging muscles and a spine misaligned because of long days in a saddle and nights sleeping on the hard ground. A couple of years later, Baca lost his meat-selling business, not because of his physical ailments but because of the nation's severe economic depression.

A few price examples can give a clear picture of the nation's economic downturn. The price of a pound of hamburger in 1920 was 11 cents; the same price Baca was getting in 1930. The average family income had dropped from $2,160 to $1,600 in one year. Postage was up from two cents to three cents, rent went from $15 per month to $22, and the cost of a movie was up a dime to 25 cents. Eggs cost six cents more for a dozen, and a pound of bacon increased from 16 to 30 cents while coffee was at 37 cents, up from 12 cents a pound. The price of an average home had dropped almost 50 percent in value and gasoline was down a few pennies a gallon, but few families could afford an automobile or a house. When his meat-cutter job failed, Cipriano accepted a night watchman's badge, a ring of keys and a flashlight just to keep food on his table.[5]

Captain Fornoff stayed in Santa Fe after the Mounted Police office closed in December 1913. Officially, he worked for the state tax office, but he also did special Mounted Police projects for Governor McDonald. In 1915, Fornoff moved to Torrance County and formed a salt-mining partnership with a couple of Estancia businessmen. A few years later, a decade after New Mexico statehood, the old ranger chief settled his wife Lullie, sons Fred, Jr., and Howell, and a stepdaughter, Dorothy Bowman, in Albuquerque.

Fred Fornoff, Jr., died at age 95 in April 2007. On a bright Saturday afternoon in late March 1991, the author and his wife had the privilege of an extended visit with Fred, Jr., a decorated World War II hero, and his lovely wife Lois in their Albuquerque home. During our wide-ranging discussion, Fred, Jr. fondly recalled Cipriano Baca.

> He had the manners of a real gentleman and mother liked him. She didn't have much use for many Mexicans, but she liked Mr. Baca. I can't say that I knew Baca very well. Remember, I was a teenager then and didn't have much to do with adults. He came to supper once [in the 1920s] when we lived over on West Roma. Momma told Howell [Fred Jr.'s younger brother] and me to behave during dinner and then go outside and play and leave Mr. Baca and dad alone. Dad was in bad health and did some kind of detective work then and maybe he and Baca were talking business. I don't know what they talked about, but the two of them sat out back smoking cigars, playing poker and drinking some of dad's bootleg whiskey.

Whiskey was illegal during Prohibition, but alcohol was easy to locate in Albuquerque.

> Lois and I had married the first time in September 1934 and we lived with Mother there on West Roma. Money was tight then so we were able to help support each other. Sometime after dad was sent up to Sheridan, Wyoming [to the Veteran's Hospital in 1926] Baca came into the store looking for a new pair of shoes. He said I looked just like my father. I didn't remember him until he told me he was Cipriano Baca and he had worked with my dad. He was much older and had a full beard. Still stood straight and had nice manners. I remember the quiet tone of his voice; you never forget that about someone. His old shoes were well worn and he paid for the new shoes with small change. I don't know why I remember that now, because nobody had much money during the Depression years. I never saw Mr. Baca after that, but [I] remember when he died. It was about a year or so after my dad [had died in 1935] and Mother read about it in the paper. She said that another one of dad's rangers had died. She said that there surely must have been a big poker game in heaven that night.[6]

What an honor roll: Captain Fornoff, Will Dudley, Dick Huber, Herb McGrath, Page Otero, Slim Rusk, Frank Vance, Julius Meyer, Captain Fullerton and now Baca. What a poker game.

* * *

In the *Book of Proverbs* it is written, "Gray hair is the crown of glory" gained by a righteous life. Florentino and Cipriana were the only Baca children that kept in regular contact with their father. Mrs. Randolph lived in California, and Florentino resided in Hot Springs, present-day Truth or Consequences, south of Albuquerque in 1936.

Baca's namesake daughter maintained a special relationship with her father.

> I saw Father a few times when I came to Albuquerque to attend the high school and later when I came back to attend business school. Aunt Effie and Uncle Clyde Stauder came with me [from the sheep ranch near Chama] during the winter months when I was in high school. She [Aunt Effie] was a good friend of Elmer and Irene Fullerton, they were Captain John F. Fullerton's son and daughter-in-law, and Uncle Clyde was the brother-in-law of Ed Sargent [territorial/state auditor from El Rito]. When I moved to Las Vegas [to work and to attend Highland University] and later after I married [Walter Randolph] I would see Father from time to time. He would [take the train and] come visit me there [in Las Vegas]. It was sad when we had to move to California.[7]

This photograph commemorates the visit of the author and his wife with Lois and Fred Fornoff, Jr., in their Albuquerque home in March 1991. Fred is holding the Winchester .44–40 rifle used by his father when he was captain of the New Mexico Mounted Police. Fornoff recalled meeting Cipriano Baca when he was a young man (NMMP/AC).

The numerous tales of his kindness toward people in trouble and his special love for children in general does not reflect itself in Cipriano Baca's latter day rocky relationship with most of his own children. Neighborhood kids seem to have always had a special friend in "Mr. Baca." One woman recalled her youth and of knowing Cipriano as an elderly gentleman.

It was the Great Depression time. He was not well to do, but nobody was living too good in them days. Yet, he always seemed to have a small bag of candy for us kids. He loved to sit and watch us play baseball in the vacant lot down the street, always giving words of encouragement even when one of us did something wrong. The boys were better behaved when Mr. Baca was at the game and they even let us girls play. He had a kind voice, but we kids all knew he was someone to show respect to and we did.

I have a petrified mammoth tooth Mr. Baca gave me one day. My name is Jennifer, but Mr. Baca would always call me Miss Jenny. I liked that because it made me feel grownup. One day my [older] brother Chris was trying to show me how to ride his bicycle and I fell off and skinned my knee. But the worst part was I ripped a hole in my stockings [long cotton socks worn by girls] and they was my Sunday pair and I knew Momma would be real upset with me 'cause she told me not to dress up and play in my Sunday best. Them stockings was Lord's Day dress and not for play. I knew I would have to go to confession about this and [I] didn't want to 'cause the priest had real bad breath.

Mr. Baca gave me this here mammoth tooth and told me that he found it back 30 or 40 years before [around the turn of the 20th century] near Deming and it had brought him good luck. I would carry that tooth in my school pencil box and cried one day when I thought I had lost it. I even had it as "something old" on my wedding day. It's sad, but I remember Mr. Baca better than I remember my own father. He [Baca] seemed to care more about us kids. I don't know what happened to Mr. Baca, because Daddy got a job in one of the mines out near Gallup and we moved away and never saw him [Baca] again. I still have the mammoth tooth and my daughter will get it for her wedding [as something old].

The story of Cipriano Baca finding a mammoth tooth gained some additional support in November 2000, when a rock hunter discovered two mammoth tusks in a ravine about ten miles northeast of Deming. These ancient remains are on display at the New Mexico Museum of Natural History in Albuquerque.[8]

23

The Question of Eva Paiz

"Life is the first gift, love is the second, and understanding is the third."—Author Unknown

In this chapter, we discuss the discovery of one of the buried trail markers along the path to tracing the life of Cipriano Baca. In one of her reflective moods Cipriana Randolph told the author that she believed her father may have had a "companion" after her mother's death, but her Hispanic heritage would not sanction her talking about it even if she wanted to discuss the subject. On another occasion, Cipriana Randolph told the author she had once discovered that she had a sister named Eva who was not her mother's child. The author assumed that Cipriana meant that her father and his first or second wife had a girl they named Eva, but the author could never locate information to support that assumption. Genealogists Alexander V. King is the discoverer of the identity of the "real" Eva who is the subject of this chapter.

* * *

Tierra Amarilla translates into English as "yellow earth" and refers to the natural clay pigment found in the region used to color native-made pottery for generations before the Spanish arrived in the 1830s. Even today the mostly Hispanic settlement on the banks of the Rio de Tierra Amarilla is only a village, but in 1880 the territorial assembly designed the hilltop community, nicknamed TA, as the county seat of the almost 6,000-square-mile Rio Arriba County. The present-day two-story brick Grecian-style columned courthouse, constructed just before the First World War, is the largest building in the county. In June 1969, the courthouse was the site of a siege and bloody gun battle between police and Reies Lopez Tijerina and fellow members of the *Alianza Federal de Mercedes* militant land grant claimants. In an attempt to heal the mental anguish of the attack, workers repaired the bullet holes in the outer walls of the Rio Arriba County courthouse, but to older generations the anguish, the mistrust, and feelings of betrayal run deep and remain.

Rio Arriba means "upper river" in Spanish and designates the area as the northernmost section of the Rio Grande in New Mexico. The county was one of the original seven *partidos* established under Spanish rule and continued under Mexican authority. When the United States gained control following the war with Mexico, the county structure remained. Rio Arriba County is home to the vast Jicarilla Apache Reservation and the Pueblos of San Juan and Santa Clara. The Chama, the Brazos, and the upper Rio Grande are important to the county's agriculture and sheep-herding industries. Today these mountain waterways are also a source of recreation.[1]

Pedro Montoya was born in *Las Partidos de Rio Arriba de Condicion de Nuevo México de Republica de México* in June 1830. He was in his late teens when his homeland became part of the United States because of the Treaty of Guadalupe Hidalgo ending the United States' war with Mexico. Pedro never learned to read or write English, but he was semi-literate in speech. He worked as a day laborer, earned enough to buy a house in Tierra Amarilla, and in 1873, at 43, he married. His bride was 38 years old and like her husband could speak, but not read or write, English. Dorotea gave birth to a son in June 1877, whom the couple named Jose; eight years later, she delivered a second child christened Manuelita.

Manuelita Montoya was born in Tierra Amarilla on Sunday, July 4, 1886, and she spent her childhood in the area. She attended the local school for about four months a year, when it was open, and learned her religious beliefs at the Santo Nino Catholic Church. A Mexican social tradition, *La Quinceanera*, recognizes a young woman's journey from childhood to maturity. The celebration highlights G-d, family, friends, music, food, and dance; Manuelita celebrated her *quinceanera* with the dawn of the new century, and a year later on January 2, 1902, she married Francisco Paiz, eighteen years her senior. This was a first marriage for each of them, and from that point forward, they lived a working-class life. Their dream started in "the land of the yellow earth."

The couple made their home at Velarde, a farming community along the Rio Grande in southern Rio Arriba County where Francisco worked as a section foreman for the narrow gage Denver and Rio Grande Western Railroad. Francisco's parents lived next door. Lucario and Maria were 70 and 52 respectively and had parented six children, but only their sons Francisco and Vicente lived. Vicente, his wife Franciscita, and their two young sons Sostenez and Elenterio also lived in Velarde. Vicente was a section hand working for his brother on the Chili Line.

Francisco and Manuelita's first child died as an infant. A second child was born in 1905 and named Magin. He got a baby sister, Luisita, two years later, and in 1908, Jose joined the family. Another son, Marcelino, was born during the winter of 1909–1910, and a year later Abdon added another son to the growing Paiz clan. In 1914, Lucadio became the baby of the family.

At some point prior to 1916, Francisco and Manuelita left the family compound at Velarde and moved their five rambunctious sons and one daughter south to Bland in Sandoval County. There was no railroad that served the community, so it is unknown what Francisco did to support his brood. It is possible that he worked at one of the many timber-cutting or milling operations, or more likely, he took up mining. The demand for gold and silver during the years prior to America's entrance in the European conflict was on a steady increase. The need for skilled "gang boss" leaders who could handle the ethnic mine laborers was in high demand, and Francisco had that kind of experience.

The Bland community was crammed into a 60-foot-wide canyon in the Jemez Mountains west of Upper Horn Mesa. In 1900, over 3,000 people lived in this gold and silver mining camp. The settlement boasted more than a dozen saloons, a couple of brothels, an opera house, a boarding house, four sawmills, a stamp mill, a mercantile store, a telephone company, a water company, two banks, a few blacksmith shops, a stage line, a stock exchange, and a Methodist-Episcopal Church. Former Deming newspaperman J. Marvin Hunter operated a weekly newspaper called the *Herald*. Twenty years after the camp's founding in 1896, the ore supply that had reached a million dollars a year started to decline, and today the ghost town remains are on private property.

The Paizes' son Alfonso had been born on April 28, 1916. He grew up, became loveable "Uncle Alfonso," and died in 1998 at age 82. Sometime after Alfonso's birth, the growing Paiz family left Bland. This time the family moved with six sons and the one daughter.

The Paiz family settled in Madrid. It was here that Francisco and Manuelita became acquainted with Cipriano and Florentino Baca. Maybe they met at a social function; the business and social life in Madrid was much like that of any other New Mexico mining camp of the late 1910s. Maybe the two men encountered each other at the mine, or maybe Baca took his laundry to Manuelita. We may never know the answer to how Cipriano and Manuelita came to know each other, but they would be part of each other's lives for the next two decades.

Shortly after the United States entered the Great War in Europe, the labor movement began a campaign to enlist New Mexico's large population of immigrant miners into the coal miners union. At Madrid, the union made a "strenuous effort" in August 1917 to sell its cause and used the notoriety of Arizona's "Bisbee Deportation" to convince local miners to join a "sympathy" strike in support of miner mistreatment at Gallup. Police arrested many New Mexico miners, of European descent, under provisions of the national Espionage and Sedition Laws. It is unknown if Francisco Paiz was a union miner or if he took part in any strike effort.

Francisco Paiz died at Madrid in 1918, most likely one of the unlucky that perished in the great Spanish flu epidemic. The 34-year-old Manuelita was alone to provide for her seven children aged two to thirteen years. Both sets of grandparents were dead, and Manuelita's only other relatives where her older brother Jose and Francisco's younger brother, her brother-in-law, Vicente. These two men were not in a financial position to provide her with much assistance, as they had to struggle just to make a living to support their own large families.[2]

* * *

On Wednesday, November 19, 1919, a girl was born to the widow Manuelita Montoya Paiz while she was living in Old Tyrone in Grant County. The infant Eva accompanied her mother and her older siblings to the Duke City in the early 1920s. She grew up and married Arthur T. Sanchez in Albuquerque in 1938. Eva and her first husband had two daughters and a son before they divorced in 1949. A few years later, Eva married Wallace Flores and had another son in 1953. Eva Paiz Sanchez Flores died at Albany, Alameda County, California, on August 18, 1998. Seven years earlier, her mother Manuelita Montoya Paiz had died in Albany on August 16, 1981.

Eva Paiz Sanchez Flores's niece Adele Camacho, daughter of her youngest brother Alfonso, attended a Vaca/Pena family reunion in California in 2005 and claimed that her late aunt had been a daughter of Cipriano Baca. Adele Camacho's claim was not new information within the Paiz family, but its public revelation was unexpected and out of character within the Hispanic culture.

* * *

23. The Question of Eva Paiz

Cipriano Baca, a year before his death, with his Amos and Randolph grandchildren in the front yard of his Albuquerque home. Joan Amos stands in front of her oldest sister Ruth, while John Amos stands behind the toddler Margaret Ann Randolph (Cipriana Randolph).

The national census taken in early 1920 was the first resident count enumerated since New Mexico statehood; the previous seven federal censuses were under a territorial government. The 14th U.S. Census takers enrolled Precinct 22, the area around Tyrone in late January. Living in a rented house identified, as 168-A Bachimba Canyon in the miner's section of the Old Town community was 32-year-old Manuelita Paiz, a widow, and her eight children. Paiz supported her family as a laundress working out of her home. Manuelita lived with her 15-year-old son Magin, her 13-year-old daughter Luisa, her 12-year-old son José called Joe, her 11-year-old son Marcelino, her nine-year-old son Abdon, her six-year-old son Lucadio known as Leo, Alfonso who was almost five, and the bright-eyed month-old Eva.

Manuelita Paiz and her children had accompanied Cipriano Baca to Grant County when he took up his duties as a Mounted Police officer during the summer of 1918, and they went with him to Albuquerque in the early 1920s when he relocated to that community for his new job. When Baca bought a house in November 1924, he built a "shanty" on the back half of his lot and rented it to Mrs. Paiz. The Paiz family was still living at that address when Cipriano died in 1935 and continued to live there for a few years after Baca's death.

Early in this century, the former Eva Paiz's only living sibling was her brother Leo, then in his 90s, who vividly recalled when Baca would come to visit the family in Old Tyrone and that he was always riding a big white horse.[3]

Cipriana and her husband Walter Randolph and their daughter, Margaret Ann, returned to New Mexico from Los Angeles in September 1935. They made a sentimental stop in Socorro to see Cipriana's 80-year-old Grandmother Berry who was in ill health; she died in January 1936. The Randolphs continued on to Albuquerque for an afternoon visit with her father and her sister Maisie. Maisie and her three children lived near Bernalillo at the time.

Recorded in the 17 chapter of Proverbs is the statement that grandchildren "are the crown of the aged, and the glory of children is their parents." At least part of this ancient wisdom was true when applied to Baca's relationship with his children and his grandchildren.

The two Baca daughters saw their father at his North First Street home in Albuquerque, and Cipriana took pictures of the grandchildren with their grandfather. John Amos, who was six the time he last saw his Grandpa Cipriano, has tried to recall the events surrounding the photographs taken in front of the Baca house during that 1935 visit, but could not. When John Amos learned that his grandfather's grave was unmarked, he showed a grandson's love and placed a prestigious maker on the site in August 2004.

It is possible that at some point during this last visit with her father Cipriana met Manuelita Paiz and her half sister Eva. It is also possible that Cipriana had first met Mrs. Paiz and her baby during her visit to her father's home at Tyrone in the early 1920s. Cipriana may have encountered both mother and daughter during one of her visits to see her father when she attended high school in Albuquerque and later when she attended college at Las Vegas.

John Amos speculated on Cipriana's knowledge of Eva,

> I find it difficult to believe that Aunt Ann would not have known that her father had sired another child after her mother's death. Aunt Ann was closer to her father than any of his other children and it is highly unlikely that Cipriano would have kept her in the dark for seventeen years about another sister. That would be totally out of character for him.

We may never know the truth of these speculations because Cipriana Randolph never openly spoke on this subject.

If Cipriano Baca had introduced Eva as his daughter during the 1935 visit, or if Cipriana's sister even suspected the relationship, this could explain Maisie Amos's near hatred of her father the rest of her life. John Amos recalled, "I don't remember her [his mother] ever speaking of Cipriano — or my own father, for that matter — and it remained thus until the day she died. My mother lived in the past and knew how to hate."

It is almost certain that Florentino knew about, or strongly suspected, a relationship between his father and Mrs. Paiz. He was with his father in Madrid; later lived at Hot Springs, present-day Truth or Consequences, 150 miles south of Albuquerque on the Rio Grande, during the early 1930s, and occasionally would drive up to Albuquerque to check on his father's welfare. "I do find it a bit tragic that Florentino, Uncle Forty, never was able to reconcile himself fully with his father," reflected John Amos. "I don't think he [Florentino] ever really comprehended Cipriano's situation. Moreover, I think this carried over into his relationship with [his wife] Louise and his two daughters. How sad!"[4]

Carrie Louise Nazarine married Cipriano Baca's son Florentino in April 1945. She and Cipriana Randolph became friend and in later years enjoyed researching the Baca family history. Both women helped the author with this biography (NMMP/AC).

The Randolphs continued their 1935 motor coach trip east toward Missouri and a less strained atmosphere surrounding the visit to Walter's family. On their return trip to California, the Randolphs spent a few days in Chama with Cipriana's surrogate parents, Clyde and Effie Stauder.

* * *

In November 2006, genealogical researcher Alexander King, author of the as-yet-unpublished tome *Three "Baca"/"Vaca" Families: Their New Mexico Ancestry and California "Descendancy,"* put a period to the Eva Paiz saga as far as this biography of Cipriano Baca is concerned. King wrote the author, saying,

> I understand that Cipriano and Manuelita never publicly claimed that Eva was their daughter and no official records seem to support the claim. Well, the sad fact is that omission is never proof or disproof of anything! We cannot ignore or under value the differences in social culture

of the time—especially of New Mexican Hispanic culture, which was and is still somewhat different from Anglo-American culture. Cipriano was a prominent citizen, even in old age, and because Ms. Paiz was certainly Catholic and cognizant of his status and her religious imperatives, any relationship they may have had would have been kept under wraps. This is the essence of Hispano family secrets; putting on a silent public front to a very different private reality.

They would live in separate households. She would accept that his "real wife and family" were to be his heirs. And so all would appear as would be expected of a man of his status. That generation would seal their lips and leave little to no documentation—and would leave a very large obstacle for future researchers to surmount.

I do give weight to the mere existence of the oral history related by Ms. Paiz's family. Two generations later, there's little reason to keep the secret and outright fabrications usually die within the generation. So, the fact that this belief persists in the Paiz family after all this time makes me think "where there's smoke, there's likely fire." It is clear that Cipriano's paternity of Eva is and was a long-held belief among Manuelita Paiz's descendants.[5]

One more reason for Manuelita Paiz to conceal Eva's illegitimate birth within the family was to maintain the family's acceptance in the Roman Catholic Church. The church played a central role in the life of a Hispanic family during this era. The parish priest was the "father figure" who oversaw the community's social life, church educational system, and in many areas the economic opportunities for his parishioners. The Church of Rome also controlled the spiritual life and salvation of the flock.

A century has made a difference in how many Hispanics historically view the influence of the Roman Catholic Church in their daily lives. The Baca descendents are among this group. It would seem that over four generations Cipriano's lineage has adopted a more freewheeling lifestyle than their ancestors.

24

Crossing the Great Divide

"I am giving out so I will close. Good Bye."—Cipriano Baca's last letter to his daughter Cipriana, 22 August 1936

"Draw your chair up and hand me my violin, for the only problem we have still to solve is how to while away these bleak autumnal evenings," said Sherlock Holmes in what is called the "Adventure of the Noble Bachelor." Cipriano Baca may never have read one of Sherlock Holmes' adventures, but if he had, he certainly could have identified with the hero. The term *ennui perplexed* means a person in a state of weariness and discontent that comes from having no occupation or interest combined with a degree of mental bewilderment. This accurately described Cipriano Baca's last months on earth.

Baca had a "joining neighbor" to his North First Street home named Jasper T. Hobbs. The native of Massachusetts had been a machinist in the Santa Fe Railroad shop in the Duke City. At some point prior to 1936, Hobbs lost his Irish-born wife. Baca once wrote his daughter Cipriana that Hobb's sister-in-law would occasionally fix the two old men a home-cooked meal, do their laundry, and clean their houses. In the letters Cipriana retained from her father, he never once mentioned Manuelita Paiz, but this does not prove that she did not also perform domestic duties for Baca.[1]

Time came when Baca's weakening health would no longer allow him to work, and even reading and playing checkers became more difficult. The long days in the saddle, the hard ground and cold camps, and continued economic stress compounded by the onset of colon cancer finally claimed their toll. Cipriano had been a chain smoker most of his adult life. Due to the rapid cancer growth, the last months of Cipriano Baca's life were a living hell for the aged warrior.

Manuelita Paiz, in a sworn affidavit filed with the Bernalillo County Probate Court, told how she had found a dejected Cipriano Baca on the first Sunday in May 1936. In her statement, Mrs. Paiz claimed she found Cipriano sleeping on the lawn near the street, and she helped him because "he was about starved from hunger, ragged, and dirty." Mrs. Paiz said that from this point forward she became "a nurse, a chambermaid, and a cook for Baca."

> I put him to bed, gave him clean clothes, washed him and bathed him, thereafter, I kept him clean, in body and clothes. I had to wash his clothes, and his bedding, had to feed him special food, as he could not eat what a healthy person eats. He was continually bed ridden, and I had to care for him as if he was a baby for he could not get up, for his daily needs, when he would

get his bed soiled I had to clean his sheeting. He was so nervous that we had to tip toe in order to keep from making noise. I had to care for him day and night, as he demanded care at night as well as during the day. He needed the care [a] baby does and that kind of care was given by me to him.

Mrs. Paiz made a $270 claim against Baca's estate for these services. In her statement, Mrs. Paiz said that she paid some of Baca's drugstore bills and doctor fees. Paiz also claimed that her teenage daughter Eva helped her with some of these health care duties. It should be noted that Mrs. Paiz's signed affidavit, filed as part of her claim on Cipriano's estate, made no mention that Eva was Baca's "love-child" daughter, so the probate court ruled that Cipriano Baca's only living heirs were his children with Mary Ann Berry Baca.

Following protracted probate procedures, the court settled Baca's estate in 1940. When the back taxes where paid on his North First Street property, only $255.82 remained in the estate account to settle other claims; Mrs. Paiz received $83.75 for her personal care and $11.75 for cleaning and painting the walls of Cipriano's house before the new owner could rent the house.[2]

* * *

It is the destiny of all humanity to die thus releasing their soul to return to the Creator of Life. It seems that when humans realize that their time on Earth is limited they value it more and try to take full advantage of their allotment. Cipriano Baca was no exception. In his last days, Baca seems to have appreciated all the kindnesses shown him by friends and those who had recently befriended him. He understood that his life was waning, and he seemed to reflect an inner peace in letters to his daughter Cipriana. Baca may have reconciled himself to the fact that he would never again have a close relationship with any of his children, except Cipriana, his beloved namesake daughter whom friends and family called Ann.

During July and August 1936, Cipriano Baca spent over three weeks at Albuquerque's St. Joseph's Sanatorium and Hospital. "I am feeling good today that is why I am writing such a long letter," he wrote Cipriana. "[I] have lost 10 lbs [and] am very weak but feel some better ... received your letter [a] few days ago. It made me feel better, tell your Aunt Jovita that next time I feel as I am feeling today I will write her. I have not seen Florentino for 2 months."

Cipriana Baca Randolph and her family were living in Long Beach, California, near her father's sister. She had sent her dad the latest picture of her daughter Margaret Ann along with her letter. Baca had last seen his daughter and his 21-month-old granddaughter the year before. Baca wrote Cipriana concerning the new photograph. "Margaret will always be full of Life & Happy, that is a natural gift to Her." Following her mother's death, Margaret Ann chose to distance herself from her mother's Hispanic heritage and her Baca family relatives.

Three days after he returned home from the hospital, Cipriano again became very ill and his friend Hobbs talked to a sympathetic county commissioner concerning Baca's health. Doctor J.W. Hannett arranged to check on Baca's health. The doctor quickly determined that Baca needed immediate around-the-clock medical care, so he ordered Cipriano's readmittance to the hospital. In early September 1936, Baca packed a cardboard box with a few personal items and made his final move to a room in St. Joseph's Hospital.

During his adventuresome life, failure had discouraged Cipriano, and that failure had made him sad. However, he did not dwell upon the failure; it did not keep him captive. Baca would get up and try something different. He never failed for lack of trying. He never gave up hope.

In his last letter to Cipriana, the old lawman wrote, "I really don't know who is paying for this treatment." Baca may have felt this would be his last letter so he told his daughter, "There is nothing against my property, but back ½ of my 1936 taxes which became delinquent 1st of last May." Baca explained that his only income was "$3.00 per month rent on that back shanty" he had on his North First Street property. During the three and a half years between Baca's death and selling his house to settle his estate, the rent fluctuated between $6.00 and $10.00 per month.

Cipriano was not sure what the medical staff intended to do concerning his case. "I will let you know in case I [am to] be operated [on] or not." Baca was unable to keep that promise. He had addressed his daughter as "Dear Sister" and gave "Best wishes to Walter & your self & children & to Jovita & Jack." Cipriano ended the letter by saying, "Good Bye Father."[3]

On Thursday, September 17, 1936, Cipriano Baca underwent an operation on his lower colon, but the procedure proved to be too late, and Baca's condition grew worse daily. His once sandy blond hair was now gray, and the once bright sparkle of his blue eyes had dimmed. Cipriano never made it back to North First Street nor was he able to play checkers with his old friend Hobbs again. On Tuesday, September 22, at 2:45 A.M., Cipriano Baca died from the effects of colon cancer. He was 77 years, 11 months and 27 days old, and now he walks forever in the Elysian Fields of Paradise with other heroes and people who did the work of the Good Lord on this Earth.

In the *Albuquerque Journal*'s obituary, titled "Veteran Officer Dead," the newspaper told readers that Baca had been "a law enforcement officer in New Mexico for 52 years" as "a member of the territorial mounted police, a railroad secret officer, and served as law officer for live stock associations." Four sentences of newsprint had summed up a man's life. Cipriano Baca's earthly journey was complete, and the Creator of Life's promise made in II Kings 22:20 was fulfilled: "I will gather you to your ancestors and you shall be gathered to your grave in peace."[4]

Cipriano Baca had spent 48 days at St. Joseph's Sanatorium and Hospital and his estate was charged $144, three dollars per day, for his room and board. He was also billed $10 for the operating room, laboratory fees were $19, the X-ray fee was $100, drugs and other supplies amounted to $20.35, and Baca's surgical dressing cost $1.90. By the time Cipriano Baca died, he had amassed a $209.25 hospital bill, not much by today's standard, but it was a princely sum during the Great Depression era.

It is likely that Manuelita Paiz, his daughter Eva, other members of the Paiz family, and a few neighbors where Baca's only mourners. None of Mary and Cipriano's five living children, except possibly Florentino, attended their father's viewing in the Chapel in the Garden at the French Mortuary or the funeral mass held at the Immaculate Conception Catholic Church, on Copper Avenue NW near the corner of Sixth Street near Central Avenue.

Even with his father's death, Florentino could not, his wife said he would not, forgive the man he felt had broken up his childhood family and had abandoned him to an orphanage. Carrie Louise Nazarine Baca said that she never knew her father-in-law and that she and her daughters only learned about him after reading a magazine biography written by the author. Florentino would not talk about his father, and he provided only minimal family history to the person who made out Cipriano's death certificate.[5]

The French Funeral Home's final statement listed fees for embalming, casket, and other services totaling $138. The Baca estate was charged $5 to cover the fee for digging the grave site and then levied an additional $60 charge so that the gravesite would be tended "with care" over the years at the funeral home's new Sunset Memorial Cemetery. The administrator of Baca's small estate allocated no funds to mark the gravesite, and none of his children ever felt the desire or had the financial resources to place a headstone on his grave. John Amos, Baca's grandson, placed a stone on the site in 2004. Cipriano Baca's grave is located about a half mile northeast of the site of where he spent the last 12 years of his life.

* * *

Contained among the mystic writings of ancient Israel, the sages of old left us a shining insight. They caught the eternal meaning of a life led by men like Cipriano Baca. It is recorded within the Zohar (4:152 a) that the "fool sees only the outer garment of a person; the wise man sees his inner garment — his character." Cipriano Baca had lived a life of honor and character.

Cipriano Baca rode the ebb and flow of the middle-class working man from the era of President McKinley's "Full Dinner Pail" prosperity right into the dark days of President Roosevelt's Great Depression. His life had spanned a golden era from horseback travel, gas lighting, and wood-burning cookstoves to automobiles, electric ranges and incandescent

In 1936, Cipriano Baca died in Albuquerque and was buried in the city's seven-year-old beautifully landscaped Sunset Memorial Part. The grave site remained unmarked until the spring of 2004 when Baca's grandson John Amos placed a headstone on the site (NMMP/AC).

light, motion pictures with sound and color, and airplane travel. Clyde Tombaught had seen beyond the Kuiper Belt, a span of space that is billions of miles beyond the planet Neptune and is a breeding ground for new worlds, and discovered the "planet" Pluto just six years before Baca's death.

Meanwhile, the planet Earth was on the verge of a second worldwide conflict between the forces of freedom and the forces of conquest and directorship. The world was also set to start a journey into the awesome and mysterious Atomic Age and the realm of space travel.

The newspapers and radio dramas of the 1930s contained many stories about a new breed of crime fighter. These federal government officers were popularly called G-men, and, along with radio heroes like the Lone Ranger and Tonto and numerous "cowboy" and adventure movie heroes, these agents were the backbone of the decade's fascination with crime fighters and gangsters.

The contemporary population of New Mexicans has no collective memory of the state's old territorial police or their fight to bring law and order to the eastern desert, the western plains, and the high mountain country. The New Mexico Mounted Police's flight into historical oblivion had begun. Only a few Duke City residents could recall the deeds of the soft-spoken Spanish lawman who had once been a living legend. Cipriano Baca had simply outlived his era.[6]

Cipriana Randolph once told the author that Psalms 84:07 was G-d's mission for her family. "Passing through the Valley of Baca they make it a place of springs; yea, the early rain clotheth it with blessings." Maybe she was right.

25

Epilogue

"The gentleman does not needlessly and unnecessarily remind an offender of a wrong he may have committed against him. He cannot only forgive; he can forget, and he strives for that nobleness of self and mildness of character which imparts sufficient strength to let the past be put in the past."
— Robert E. Lee

Cipriana was Cipriano and Mary Baca's oldest daughter, and the author knew her as a lovely lady who cared deeply about her family and her dual heritage: "I am deep in genealogy on both the Baca and Berry sides. Is quite an endeavor but becomes more interesting all the time." After Cipriana read the author's first magazine account of her father's life, she said she was excited to learn so much about her family. "I was surprised to see the date of my mother's death. I really did not know it. In fact, I have worked out quite a lot of dates and information from that article. How sad we [her family] did not pursue a lot of this information years ago." Cipriana and Walter had one daughter and two grandchildren. Cipriana Baca Randolph died in Orange, California, on June 20, 1998, and rests in Whittier's Rose Hill Memorial Park. Walter Randolph had died on September 12, 1988.

Cipriana's surrogate parents, Effie and Clyde Stauder, sold their Chama interests and returned to Socorro in the late 1930s to purchase the historic Park House on the southeast corner of the historic plaza. They invested in a local bank and built a large home they called the Castile a few blocks south from their hotel. The house still stands, but new owners tore down the hotel to make room for a large supermarket. Effie and Clyde E. Stauder, Sr., rest together in the Berry family plot in the Socorro Cemetery along with their son Lt. Col. Clyde E. Stauder, Jr., and his wife.

Maisie Hill Baca, raised by her Grandmother Berry, attended the grade school at the School of Mines in Socorro where she met Charleston, West Virginia, born John Pierpont Amos. John's mining job took the young couple to Peru before they settled in Socorro. Maisie and her three oldest children visited Grandfather Cipriano a few times in Albuquerque during the 1930s, but after his death, she refused to acknowledge her Hispanic heritage or discuss her father.

Twenty-three-year-old Maisie lost her husband a few months after his 30th birthday, and he was laid to rest in the Socorro cemetery on September 17, 1931. Maisie took a job in Chicago, later married twice, finally settled in California, and died in the San Francisco Bay area on Christmas Eve, 1974. Her death certificate listed her name as Mary Amos McCabe.

Her Uncle James Berry and his wife raised Rachel Encarnacion Baca in Pachuca, Mexico. Jim worked as a mining engineer and later as the general superintendent of a large mining operation in the town. Rachel refused to acknowledge her Baca family legacy, always claiming Jim and Mary Berry as her parents and that their children were her brother and sister. She married Arthur Lonergan, and in the mid–1930s they lived in New York City and later moved to the Los Angles area where her husband was the art director for MGM studios. Rachel and Cipriana were the last of the Baca children still alive when the author began research on this biography.

Gilberson, or George, spent some time in an Old Town Albuquerque orphanage before his father was able to reclaim him. He would seldom talk about his childhood or his family. He served in the Navy during the First World War and after his discharge settled at Lake Buff Village in Shields Township, near the Great Lakes Naval Training Center, where he operated a very successful sales and service business. He died in April 1968, and, buried with military honors, rests in the National Cemetery at Santa Fe, New Mexico.

At 20 years of age in 1923, Florentino Baca became the youngest student to earn a bachelor's degree with honors in engineering from New Mexico School of Mines. Eleven years later, he earned a master's degree. He designed mining equipment and received several patents for his work, but he was never able to forget the sad memories of his youth. The widely traveled Florentino Baca died at Ottumwa, Iowa, in June 1972.

Members of the Manuelita Paiz family openly discuss their relationship to Cipriano Baca, and always express warm feelings toward him. Manuelita Montoya Paiz and her daughter Eva both died in Albany, California, and are buried in that community.[1]

* * *

This work has attempted to resurrect the life and legend of Cipriano Baca, and now history is the final judge of our deed.

> "[He was] a loyal friend and a chivalrous gentleman. Let that now and forever be enough for us."
> — Sherlock Holmes, "The Adventure of the Illustrious Client"

Chapter Notes

Chapter 1

1. Fray Angelico Chavez, *Origins of New Mexico Families: A Genealogy of the Spanish Colonial Period* (Santa Fe: Museum of New Mexico Press, 1992. Revised Edition) pp 141–145.
2. Nancy M. Brown, *Baca: Origenes Espanoles* (Belen, NM: Spanish History Museum, 1992).
3. A copy of Don Juan Manual Vaca's notebook is in the author's collection, CB/AC.
4. Patricia Black Esterly (compiled by), *Census of 1821: New Mexico Province, Santa Fe Parrish* (Albuquerque: New Mexico Genealogical Society Inc., 1994) p 91.
5. See C. Gregory Crampton and Steven K. Madsen, *In Search of the Spanish Trail: Santa Fe to Los Angeles, 1829–1848* (Salt Lake City: Peregrine Smith Books, 1994) for a readable account with understandable maps of this historic trading route.
6. See Wood Young, *Vaca-Pena Los Putos Rancho and the Pena Adobe* (Vallejo, CA: Wheeler Printing and Publishing Inc., 1965) for a history of the ranch and grant.
7. Seventh Census of the United States 1850, Family 02 (Manuel Vaca), Solano County, CA, Microfilm M432, Roll 36, NA.
8. Conversion formula developed by the Mathematics Department of the University of Oregon.
9. Young, *Vaca-Pena Los Putos Rancho and the Pena Adobe*. The author also made extensive use of the Baca-Pena family genealogical records collected by Los Angeles researcher Alexander King in 2007 for use in his projected publication concerning these early California settlers.
10. Seventh Census of the United States 1850, Family 02 (Manuel Vaca), Solano County, CA, Microfilm M432, Roll 36, NA.
11. William Cary Jones, *Report of the Subject of Land Titles in California made in pursuance of instructions from the Secretary of State and the Secretary of the Interior together with a translation of the Principal Laws on the Subject and some other papers relating thereto* (Washington: Gideon & Co., Printers, 1850).
12. Jonathan A. Ortega, "Vacaville, California Founded by New Mexico Baca Family," *Nuestras Raices: Journal of the Genealogical Society of Hispanic America*, Spring 1997, p 8.
13. Baca family land records, copies CB/AC.
14. Letters: Cipriana Randolph to author, 8 Sept 1982 and 10 Oct 1982, CB/AC.
15. Letter: Cipriana Randolph to author, 12 Dec 1984, CB/AC.
16. The author has numerous copies of Baca's personal letters and official documents that support this point of view, CB/AC.
17. A youthful Lincoln studied grammar and math at a private school conducted by Azel Dorsey for a short time in 1824. The school tablet is at the Abraham Lincoln Presidential Library and Museum located in Springfield, IL.
18. Mark Twain, *Roughing It* (NP, 1872).
19. *San Francisco Daily Alta California*, 9 Oct 1865; *Harper's Weekly*, 18 Nov 1865.
20. "The Earthquake in the Interior," *San Francisco Daily Morning Call*, 22 Oct 1868.
21. "Destruction of Property in Various Part of the City," *San Francisco Daily Morning Call*, 22 Oct 1868.
22. "Destruction of Property in Various Part of the City"; "Dispatching the News East"; and "The Earthquake in the Interior," *San Francisco Daily Morning Call*, 22 Oct 1868.
23. Mark Twain, "The Great Earthquake in San Francisco," *Early Tales & Sketches*, vol. 2, *1864–1865* (NP: 1865) p 304.
24. Letter: Cipriana Randolph to author, 23 June 1984, CB/AC.
25. Conversation Notes: Cipriana Randolph and author, 21 June 1984, Notes CB/AC.
26. Cipriana Randolph gave the author a copy of the telegram, CB/NMMP.
27. *Vallejo (CA) Chronicle*, 7 July 1877.
28. Letter: Cipriana Randolph to author, 13 Dec 1982, CB/AC.

Chapter 2

1. Letters: Cipriana Randolph to author, 23 June 1984 and 30 Oct 1985, CB/AC.
2. Tenth Census of the United States 1880, Family 68 (Don A. Sanford), Cienega Valley, Pima County, Arizona Territory, Microfilm T 09 Roll 36, NA.
3. *Tucson Citizen*, 2 Jan 1875 and 4 Dec 1880.
4. Frederick Bechdolt, "Stories of the Old West: Tombstone's Wild Oats," *Saturday Evening Post*, 8 Nov 1919, pp 41–42, 45–46.
5. Conversation: Cipriana Randolph and author, 21 June 1984, Notes CB/AC; Letter: Cipriana Randolph to author, 23 June 1984, CB/AC. Stuart N. Lake wrote a series of articles about Wyatt Earp for the *Saturday Evening Post* prior to the 1931 publication of his classic Earp biography. It is unknown if Baca ever read Lake's *Wyatt Earp, Frontier Marshal*. There were 226 episodes of "The Life and Legend of Wyatt Earp" starring Hugh O'Brian, with Lake serving as the historical consultant, that where broadcast on ABC-TV between Sept 1955 and June 1961. The series zenith happened during the 1957–1958 season when it was ABC-TV's highest-ranking program in the A.C. Nielsen ratings (32.6) with a sixth-place position. The network canceled the program before the series

dealt with Earp's bloody Vendetta Ride and the death of John Ringo.
6. Tenth Census of the United States 1880, Family 08 (J.D. Kinnear), in the country, Pima County, Arizona Territory, Microfilm T 09 Roll 36, NA.
7. Fifteenth Census of the United States 1930, Family 235 (Cipriano Baca), Pct 21, Bernalillo County, NM, Microfilm T626 Roll 1392, NA.
8. Letter: Cipriana Randolph to author, 10 Oct 1985, CB/AC.
9. *Salt Lake City Tribune*, 21 June 1881; *Arizona Weekly Star* (Tucson), 13 Feb 1881 and 23 June 1881; *Arizona Daily Citizen* (Tucson), 21 May 1882; C.M. Chase, *The Editor's Run in New Mexico and Colorado* (NP, 1882) p 127.
10. Letter: Everett B. Pomroy to Wayne McVeigh, 23 June 1881, Attorney General Records, Arizona Territory 1881, NA; William Henry Bishop, "Across Arizona," *Harper's Monthly Magazine*, March 1883.
11. *Arizona Weekly Star* (Tucson), 23 June 1881; Adolphus Henry Noon, "Arizona: Incidents of the Journey from Casa Grande to Tucson," *Chicago Tribune*, 5 Dec 1879.
12. *Arizona Daily Star* (Tucson), 7 May 1882; *Kansas City* (MO) *Journal*, 15 May 1883.
13. Letter: Cipriana Randolph to author, 23 June 1984, CB/AC; Chuck Hornung and Gary L. Roberts, "The Split: Did Doc & Wyatt Split Because of a Racial Slur?" *True West*, 2001, pp 58–61.

Chapter 3

1. See F. Stanley (Stanley Francis Louis Crocchiola), *The Deming, New Mexico Story* (Pantex, TX: Private, 1963) for a brief history of the community.
2. David F. Myrick, *New Mexico's Railroad: An Historical Survey* (Golden, CO: Colorado Railroad Museum, 1970) pp 20, 28, 58 and 59; C.M. Chase, p 128.
3. C.M. Chase, p 127; Interview: Mrs. Ed Pennington by Frances E. Tetty, 1 Aug 1938 at Deming, NM, WPA Writers' Project/New Mexico, Library of Congress.
4. *Silver City Southwest Sentinel*, 25 Feb 1884; *Silver City Enterprise*, 14 Dec 1882.
5. See R.K. DeArment's groundbreaking article, "Deadly Deputy," *True West*, Nov 1991, and Bob Alexander's biography *Dangerous Dan Tucker: New Mexico's Deadly Lawman* (Silver City, NM: High-Lonesome Books, 2001) for an in-depth look at this man.
6. "Doc Gilpin," *Silver City Enterprise*, 31 Oct 1884.
7. C.M. Chase, pp 140–141.
8. New Mexico Territorial Census 1885, Deming Precinct, Grant County, NMSRCA; C.M. Chase, pp 99, 124–125.
9. "Sheriff Baca," *Deming Herald*, 7 May 1901.
10. *Deming Tribune* and *Lake Valley Herald*, 25 Dec 1884.
11. J. Brad Baker, "Every Moving Thing," *American Philatelist*, March 2002, p 10.
12. *Deming Tribune* and *Lake Valley Herald*, 25 June 1885.
13. Grant County Corporation Record Book #1, unpaginated, County Clerk's Office, Grant County Administrative Center, Silver City.
14. Tim Vanderpool, "What Became of the Mimbres?" *American Archaeology*, Fall 2007, pp 39–43; See F. Stanley (Stanley Francis Louis Crocchiola), *The Lake Valley, New Mexico Story* (Pep, TX: Private, 1964) for a brief history of the community.
15. *Deming Headlight*, 12 Oct 1888.
16. "Curbstone Gossip," *Deming Headlight*, 28 Sep 1888.
17. *Deming Headlight*, 5 April 1889.
18. *Deming Headlight*, 1 Feb 1889 and 16 Aug 1889.
19. *Marriage Register for Grant County, NM 1872–1898*, No page number, County Clerk's Office, Grant County Administrative Center, Silver City.
20. "The Tardy Ivanhoe," *Seattle Press-Times*, 20 Oct 1894.
21. Ninth Census of the United States 1870, Family 106, Pct 1, 12 Ward (San Francisco), San Francisco County, CA, Microfilm M593 Roll 85, NA; Tenth Census of the United States 1880, Family 127, Winters, Yolo County, CA, Microfilm T09 Roll 86, NA; New Mexico Territorial Census 1885, Family 391, Deming, Grant County, NM, Microfilm RG TANM Roll 40, NMSRCA.
22. *Deming Headlight*, 24 June 1882.
23. "Professional Card" and "Deming Locals," *Deming Tribune* and *Lake Valley Herald*, 25 Dec 1884; "The K.P. Ball at Deming," *Silver City Enterprise*, 6 Jan 1893.
24. Territory of Arizona vs. Morgan Earp, et al., Justice of the Peace Hearing, Document #94, Township #1, Cochise County, Arizona Territory. The author owns two versions of the Pat Hayhurst typescript made in the 1930s as part of a WPA project to preserve the now lost original handwritten testimony given at both the Coroner's Inquest (Document #48) and the monthlong hearing before Justice of the Peace Wells Spicer (Document #94); Thomas Keefe's testimony is recorded on pages 85–89. In the second version of Keefe's testimony, a note written after his name says, "Keefe knew May Woodman, 'the Bodie Road Runner.'" The note's intended meaning is unclear unless it is meant to imply that Keefe associated with notorious women.
25. *Bodie* (CA) *Morning News*, 24 and 25 Oct 1879.
26. *Bodie* (CA) *Daily Free Press*, 26 Oct 1880.
27. Ron W. Fischer (Ed.), *The Tombstone Business Directory 81880–1884* (Tombstone, AZ: Ron W. Fisher Enterprises, 2002) pp 9, 20, 81; Coroner's Inquest #117, 23 Feb 1883, County Clerk's Office, Cochise County Courthouse, Bisbee, AZ.
28. The word "canon" is Spanish for the English word "canyon," and is used in the Southwest by old-timers even today. In this spirit, "canon" has been used throughout the text.
29. C.M. Chase, p 127; *Silver City Southwest Sentinel*, 25 Feb 1884; Pennington interview, 1 Aug 1938.
30. Harvey Howard Whitehill won the election by 17 votes. He had served as sheriff from 1875 to January 1883. He was not reelected in 1890.
31. J. Marvin Hunter, *The Story of Lottie Deno, Her Life and Times* (Bandera, Texas: 4 Hunters Press, ND) pp 142, 143.
32. C.L. Sonnichsen, *Billy King's Tombstone* (Caldwell, ID: Caxton Printers, 1942) pp 142–160.
33. *Silver City Independent*, 26 Sept 1913; "Horse-Bicycle Race," *St. Johns* (AZ) *Herald* as reprinted in the *Lordsburg Western Liberal*, 27 Sept 1888.
34. "Curbstone Gossip," *Deming Headlight*, 21 Sept 1888.

Chapter 4

1. This book is part of the author's Cipriano Baca collection.
2. "Curbstone Gossip," *Deming Headlight*, 15 Feb 1889.
3. *Silver City Enterprise*, 23 Jan and 16 Jan 1891.
4. "Bronco's Break," *Silver City Enterprise*, 13 March 1891.
5. *Silver City Enterprise*, 20 Feb 1891.

6. "Bronco's Break," *Silver City Enterprise*, 13 March 1891.
7. Interview: J. Evert Haley with Walt Birchfield, 2 Nov 1939, J.E. Haley Collection, Haley Memorial Library, Midland, TX.
8. "Bronco's Break," *Silver City Enterprise*, 13 March 1891.
9. "Salty John" Cox transcribed by Eve Ball, "Salty John Cox and Bronco Bill," *True West*, May–June 1977, pp 24–25 and 48–89.
10. *Arizona Republic* (Phoenix), 19 Dec 1898.
11. Mounted Police Biography Files, NMMP/AC; "Title XIV — Fees and Salaries," *Compiled Laws of New Mexico 1897* (Santa Fe: New Mexican Printing Company, 1897) pp 474–490.
12. "Deplorable Tragedy," *Silver City Enterprise*, 28 Aug 1891.
13. "May and December," *Silver City Enterprise*, 9 Oct 1891.
14. *Santa Fe Daily New Mexican*, 21 Aug 1891.
15. *Silver City Enterprise*, 28 Dec 1894.
16. "Another Killing," *Silver City Enterprise*, 15 July 1892.
17. "Foul Play Suggested," "Shooting at Pine Cienega" and "Mysterious Murder," *Silver City Enterprise*, 21 Oct 1892.
18. "The K.P. Ball at Deming," *Silver City Enterprise*, 6 Jan 1893 and "Silver Convention," *Silver City Enterprise*, 30 June 1893.
19. *Deming Headlight*, 10 June 1893.
20. *Deming Headlight*, 2 Sept 1893.
21. E. Benjamin Andrews, *History of the United States from the Earliest Discovery of America to the End of 1902*, vol. 5, *1888–1902* (New York: Scribner, 1903) pp 107–137; "Local Items," *Deming Headlight*, 23 Sept 1893.
22. "Political Profligacy," *Silver City Enterprise*, 19 Oct 1893.
23. "Taken to the Pen," *Deming Headlight*, 9 Dec 1893.
24. *Silver City Enterprise*, 5 Jan 1894.
25. Andrews, *History*, vol. 5, pp 138–140; "Desperadoes Defy Deputies," *Silver City Enterprise*, 27 April 1894.
26. Theodore Roosevelt, "Social Evolution," *American Ideals*, 1897.
27. *Silver City Enterprise*, 29 June 1894.
28. "County Jail Delivery," *Silver City Eagle*, 22 Aug 1894.
29. "An Attempt at Rape," *Silver City Eagle*, 29 Aug 1894; "Held on $2,000 Bail," *Silver City Eagle*, 5 Sept 1894; *Santa Fe New Mexican*, 7 Nov 1895; *New Mexico Territorial Penitentiary Record Book of Convicts 1884–1904*, Prisoner 879, NMSRCA.
30. "For Sheriff," *Silver City Enterprise*, 17 Aug 1894. This business-card style advertisement is similar to those placed in other Grant County newspapers.
31. "Candidates and What They Want," *Deming Headlight*, 29 Aug 1894; "Sold at Sheriff's Sale," *Silver City Eagle*, 5 Sept 1894.

Chapter 5

1. "Republican Convention," *Silver City Enterprise*, 21 Sept 1894; Editorial Comment, *Deming Headlight*, 28 Sept 1894.
2. "Democratic Convention," *Silver City Enterprise*, 21 Sept 1894, "Candidates and What They Want," *Deming Headlight*, 29 Aug 1894.
3. The *Seattle Telegram* interview was reprinted in "The Tardy Ivanhoe," *Seattle Press-Times*, 20 Oct 1894.
4. Andrews, *History*, vol. 5, pp 138–152; dollar conversion tables, Federal Reserve Bank.
5. "The Tardy Ivanhoe," *Seattle Press-Times*, 20 Oct 1894.
6. "Water Front," *Seattle Press-Times*, 15 Sept and 27 Sept 1894.
7. "About the Ivanhoe, Who the Passengers Were That Sailed on the Ship," *Seattle Press-Times*, 7 Dec 1894.
8. "Shipping News," 11 Oct 1894; "Ship Ivanhoe Overdue," 15 Oct 1894; "Storm Off the Cape," 17 Oct 1894; "Two Ships Arrive, They Bring No Tidings of the Derelict Ivanhoe," 18 Oct 1894, *Seattle Press-Times*.
9. "The Ship Ivanhoe," *Seattle Press-Times*, 17 Oct 1894; "The Tardy Ivanhoe," *Seattle Press-Times*, 19 Oct 1894.
10. The *Seattle Telegraph* interview was reprinted in the *Seattle Press-Times*, 20 Oct 1894; "The Ship Ivanhoe," *Seattle Press-Times*, 22 Oct 1894.
11. "About the Ivanhoe," *Seattle Press-Times*, 7 Dec 1894; *Silver City Enterprise*, 16 Dec 1894.
12. "Republican Candidates Coming," *Deming Headlight*, 2 Oct 1894.
13. "The Sentinel," *Silver City Enterprise*, 26 Oct 1894.
14. *Silver City Enterprise*, 2 Nov 1894.
15. "Political Profligacy," *Silver City Enterprise*, 19 Oct 1894.
16. "The Baca-Fox Matter," *Deming Headlight*, 19 Oct 1894.
17. *Silver City Enterprise*, 26 Oct 1894.
18. *Silver City Enterprise*, 26 Oct 1894 and 2 Nov 1894.
19. Final Vote Chart, *Silver City Enterprise*, 9 Nov 1894.

Chapter 6

1. *Silver City Enterprise*, 25 Jan 1895.
2. "County Division," *Mogollon Mines*, Nov 1909.
3. *Silver City Enterprise*, 27 July 1894.
4. H.A. Hoover, *Tales from the Bloated Goat: Early Days in Mogollon* (El Paso: Texas Western Press, 1958); Father Stanley, *The Mogollon [NM] Story* (Pep, TX: Private, 1968).
5. William T. Thornton, *Report of the Governor of New Mexico to the Secretary of the Interior 1895* (Washington, DC: Government Printing Office, 1895) pp 49–50.
6. Biographical notes from the Holm O. Bursum Papers, CSR/UNM.
7. "Of Home Interest," *Socorro Chieftain*, 19 July 1895.
8. Letter: Holm O. Bursum to Cipriano Baca, 2 Aug 1895, H.O. Bursum Papers, CSR/UNM.
9. *Socorro/Chloride Black Range*, 6 Dec 1895.
10. "Notice to the People of Mogollon," *Socorro Chieftain*, 12 Aug 1895.
11. "Of Home Interest," *Socorro Chieftain*, 25 Oct 1895.
12. "Of Home Interest," *Socorro Chieftain*, 1 Nov 1895.
13. "From Mogollon," *Socorro Chieftain*, 7 Aug 1896. This was the first time that this newspaper mentioned that Baca was a peace officer at Mogollon.
14. See the booklet *The Healer: The Story of Francis Schlatter* (Santa Fe, NM: Sunstone Press, 1989) by Norman Cleveland for a readable account of this man's life and ministry.
15. Francis Schlatter as told to Ada Morley, *The Life of the Harp in the Hand of the Harper* (Denver, CO: Smith-Brooks, 1897); Agnes Morley Cleveland, *No Life for a Lady* (Boston: Houghton Mifflin, 1941) pp 220–226.
16. *Silver City Eagle*, 9 April 1896; Miscellaneous papers, Cipriano Baca Collection, CB/AC.
17. *Socorro/Chloride Black Range*, 28 Aug 1896.
18. Baca's certificate of election, Holm O. Bursum Collection, CSR/UNM.

19. *Socorro Chieftain*, 23 Oct 1896.
20. *Silver City Enterprise*, 30 Oct 1896.
21. Ted Raynor (Ed.), *Old Timers Talk in Southwestern New Mexico* (El Paso: Texas Western Press, 1960), E.D. McIntosh, *Recollections of Mogollon* (Private, ND) pp 75–76.
22. *Socorro Chieftain*, 18 Dec 1896.

Chapter 7

1. Inaugural Address of Calvin Coolidge, March 4, 1925, The Avalon Project at Yale Law School, Yale University, New Haven, CT.
2. *Socorro Chieftain*, 22 Jan 1897.
3. *Socorro Chieftain*, 5 Feb, 12 Feb and 02 April 1897.
4. *Socorro Chieftain*, 23 April 1897.
5. *Socorro Chieftain*, 14 May and 23 April 1897.
6. *Socorro Chieftain*, 28 May and 25 June 1897.
7. *Socorro Chieftain*, 9 July 1897.
8. *Socorro Chieftain*, 23 July 1897.
9. Letter: Cipriana Randolph to author, 1 April 1985, Conversation Notes: Cipriana Randolph and author, 21 June 1984, CB/AC.
10. Warren A. Beck and Ynez D. Haase, *Historical Atlas of New Mexico* (Norman: University of Oklahoma Press, 1969) pp. 46–47.
11. Dr. Adam Smith, *An Inquiry into the Nature and Causes of the Wealth of Nations* (London: Methuen, 5th edition 1789, 1904 printing).
12. *Socorro Chieftain*, 22 Oct 1897.
13. Letter: Cipriana Randolph to author, 1 April 1985, CB/AC.
14. Kevin D. Randle, "Aurora, Texas and the Great Airship of 1897," *Fate*, March 2003, pp 34–36; Brad Bailey, "An E.T. Yarn That Won't Go Away: The Tale of the Aurora Spaceman," *Sunday Express-News* (San Antonio, TX), 14 April 1982.
15. Conversation Notes: Cipriana Randolph and the author, 18 May 1984, CB/AC; "Strange Phenomena," *Nebraska Nugget* (Holdrege), 14 June 1884, Nebraska State Historical Society, Lincoln; "Aviator Nixon Made Daring Flight Here," *Deming Graphic*, 28 Nov 1913.
16. *Socorro Chieftain*, 9 April and 23 April 1897; *Albuquerque Daily Citizen*, 30 April 1897; *Deming Headlight*, 9 April 1897; Wayne Clark, "Inventing History," *NOLA Quarterly*, Jan–March 2007, pp 30–38.
17. *Socorro Chieftain*, 23 April and 2 July 1897.
18. "An Outrageous Attack," *Socorro Chieftain*, 2 July 1897.
19. Jeff Burton has published three accounts of the different Black Jack Gangs. These works are a must for basic research on the subject of this outlaw band.
20. William French, *Some Recollections of a Western Ranchman, New Mexico 1883–1899* (London: Methuen, 1927), pp 205, 218–219.
21. Jeff Burton's *Black Jack Christian: Outlaw* (Santa Fe, NM: Press of the Territorian, 1967) is an excellent account of the hunt for the original Black Jack; *Silver City Independent*, 20 May 1897; *Silver City Enterprise*, 21 May 1897.
22. Conversation Notes: Cipriana Randolph and the author, 18 May 1984, CB/AC.
23. Letter: Miguel A. Otero to E.P. Lamborn, Leavenworth, KS, 5 Jan 1937, E.P. Lamborn Papers (156), Box 3, File 4, Kansas State Historical Society. Even the highly respected Robert K. DeArment relied upon French's misguided notion and wrote in *George Scarborough, The Life and Death of a Lawman on the Closing Frontier* (Norman: University of Oklahoma Press, 2000) p 176, that Baca had served as the killer marshal of Clifton, Arizona.
24. Most issues of the 1898 *Socorro Chieftain* are missing from microfilmed newspaper files, and only a few miscellaneous issues of the newspaper for this year survive.
25. *Silver City Enterprise*, 27 July 1894; *Socorro Chieftain*, 30 July 1897. Robert A. Smith's *A Social History of the Bicycle, Its Early Life and Times in America* (New York: American Heritage Press, 1972) is an excellent study of the bicycle's imprint upon America's social and moral fiber.
26. *Sears, Roebuck and Co. Catalogue*, no. 104, 1897 (Chicago, IL) pp 611–613, 710–716, 752–754; *Sears, Roebuck and Co. Catalogue*, no. 117, 1908 (Chicago, IL) p 168.
27. Letter: Cipriana Randolph to author, 1 April 1985, CB/AC.
28. Jim Shaw was the former High Five Gang member who had led Fred Higgins's posse to Black Jack Christian's hideout.
29. Telegrams: US Marshal Foraker to/from Sheriff Bursum, 18–20 Aug 1897, US Marshal Papers (USMP), CSR/UNM.
30. Letters: US Marshal Foraker to Cipriano Baca at Dry Creek, NM, 29 Aug 1897; US Marshal Foraker to Attorney General McKenna, 26 Oct 1897, USMP, CSR/UNM.
31. Letter: U.S. Marshal Foraker to Attorney General McKenna, 25 Oct 1897, USMP, CSR/UNM.
32. Letter: U.S. Marshal Foraker to Attorney General McKenna, 26 Oct 1897, USMP, CSR/UNM.
33. *Graham County Bulletin* (Solomonville, Arizona), 20 August 1897. In their highly researched biography of the outlaw George Musgrave, Karen and John Tanner misattributed this reprinted story to the *Deming Searchlight*. Really titled the *Headlight*, this New Mexico newspaper used the masthead in reference to the town's roots as a pioneer railroad community.
34. Letter: US Marshal Foraker to Attorney General McKenna, 2 Nov 1897, USMP, CSR/UNM.
35. *Graham County Bulletin* (Solomonville, Arizona), 29 Nov 1897; *San Francisco Chronicle*, 30 Nov 1897.
36. *Socorro Chieftain*, 3 Dec and 31 Dec 1897.
37. Walter Hovey, "Black Jack Ketchum Tried to Give Me a Break!," *True West*, April 1972, p 48.
38. *Socorro Chieftain*, 17 Dec 1897.
39. *Santa Fe New Mexican*, 26 April 1901.
40. *Socorro Chieftain*, 26 Nov 1897; *Socorro Chieftain*, 3, 10, 17, 24 and 31 Dec 1897.
41. *Albuquerque Morning Journal*, 8 Jan and 9 Jan 1898.

Chapter 8

1. Gilberson-Berry Family Records provided to the author by John Amos, Sandy, UT; the history of Saint Mark's Cathedral was provided by the church rector's office.
2. James and Sallie Berry Family Records, CB/AC; the history of Saint Mark's Cathedral was provided by the church rector's office.
3. *Las Vegas Optic*, 24 Aug 1884; James and Sallie Berry Family Records, CB/AC.
4. *Socorro Chieftain*, 18 Nov 1892; James and Sallie Berry Family Records, CB/AC. Park City or La Smelta was the name given to the area just southwest of Socorro and until 1894, this was the site of the Billing's Smelter. Today the area is part of a Socorro housing development. In the early 1990s, the federal Environmental Protection Agency's attempt to clean up the old slag dump caused a political firestorm. Rene Kimball, "Century-Old Emergency?," *Albuquerque Sunday Journal*, 8 July 1990, pp 1, 3.

5. "Extracts from Exchanges," *Las Vegas Daily Optic*, 26 Feb 1903.
6. James and Sallie Berry Family Records, CB/AC.
7. Fourteenth Census of the United States 1920, Family 70 (Sallie Berry), Pct. 24, Socorro County, New Mexico, Microfilm T 625 Roll 05, NA.
8. *Roll of Students 1898–1899*, New Mexico School of Mines Bulletin, Special Collections, New Mexico Tech Library, Socorro; *Socorro Chieftain*, 28 April 1900.
9. *Socorro Chieftain*, 9 June 1900.
10. *Socorro Chieftain*, 8 Sept and 13 Oct 1900.
11. *Socorro Chieftain*, 21 Dec 1900.
12. *Socorro Chieftain*, 27 April 1901.
13. Thirteenth Census of the United States 1910, Family 44 (John B. Griffith), Pct. 24, Socorro County, New Mexico Territory, Microfilm T 624 Roll 918, NA; *Parish Register*, 1885–1937, Episcopal Church of the Epiphany, Socorro, NM.
14. *Capitan Progress*, 12 July 1901.
15. *Parish Register*, 1885–1937; *Roll of Students*, 1898–1905.
16. *Socorro Chieftain*, 20 July 1900.
17. *Socorro Chieftain*, 8 Sept 1900, 16 Feb 1901, 30 Sept 1901 and 18 Oct 1902.
18. James Berry biography, *New Mexico School of Mines Bulletin 1905*, Special Collections, New Mexico Tech Library, Socorro. James Berry studied mine engineering when he attended the School of Mines. Nine decades later the scope of study at the old college has changed. In the fall of 1996 the New Mexico Institute of Mining and Technology's (New Mexico Tech) Energetic Materials Research and Testing Center began a new direction. The new field of study was born of tragedy. In April 1995, the federal building in Oklahoma City was blown up, killing many people. The Counter Terrorist Explosives Research Center is designed to examine ways to prevent future terrorist assaults, upon people and buildings, with blast-resistant technology. "New Mexico Tech Begins Counter-Terrorist Research," *Midland* (TX) *Reporter-Telegram*, 24 Nov 1996.
19. *Socorro Chieftain*, 2 June 1900 and 5 July 1902; *Parish Register*, 1885–1937; Berry Family Tales, Conversation Notes: James Stauder and author, summer 2007, CB/AC.
20. Pearl Berry was one of seven girls in the 1901 confirmation class at the Church of the Epiphany. *Socorro Chieftain*, 12 July 1902; *Roll of Students*, 1898–1905; *Parish Register*, 1885–1937.
21. Baca-Berry Family Records, copy in CB/AC; *Parish Register*, 1885–1937.
22. Letter: Cipriana Randolph to author, 12 Dec 1984, CB/AC.
23. "Of Home Interest," *Socorro Chieftain*, 22 May 1896.
24. Conversation notes: Cipriana Randolph and author, 15 Dec 1984, CB/AC.
25. Barry family traditions conveyed to the author by Jim Stauder, summer 2007, CB/AC.

Chapter 9

1. When the author first wrote about Cipriano Baca in his 1971 *The Thin Gray Line: The New Mexico Mounted Police*, he mistakenly claimed that Cipriano was a relative of Elfego Baca. This erroneous information had been provided by an old Socorro County resident who had known both men when he was a young man.

The eminent historian Dr. Larry D. Ball repeated the author's mistake in his 1992 book on Arizona/New Mexico sheriffs and in his 1992 biography of Elfego Baca. Ball wrote that Cipriano and Elfego were cousins and that Cipriano and Leandro were brothers, but according to Cipriana Baca Randolph's family records both of these statements are untrue.

Jeff Burton ("Bureaucracy, Blood Money and Black Jack's Gang," *The Brand Book*, English Westerners' Society, Winter 1983 and Summer 1984) also mistakenly reported that Cipriano was a brother to Socorro City Marshal A. B. Baca. The two men were not related, but Abdenago or A. B. Baca was the older brother of Elfego Baca.

Oscar Caudill said (as told to Eve Ball in "Hell on the Largo," *Frontier Times*, Dec/Jan 1972, p 41) "Elfego Baca, sheriff at Socorro, sent his brother Leandro, who was at that time [1920] his deputy, to Quemado." These two Baca men were not brothers.

2. Twelfth Census of the United States 1900, Family 16 (Leandro Baca), Frisco, Socorro County, New Mexico Territory, Microfilm T 623 Roll 1003, NA; *Socorro Chieftain*, 5 Aug 1892; Deed Books L, 26, 37, and 52, County Clerk's Office, Socorro County Courthouse, Socorro, NM; Leandro Baca Biography File, NMMP/AC.

3. Magdalena *Mountain Mail*, 1 Nov 1888.
4. *Socorro Chieftain*, 5 May 1893, 9 June 1893, 4 Nov 1892, 6 Jan 1893, 21 Sept 1893.
5. Holm Bursum Biography File, Leandro Baca Biography File, NMMP/AC.
6. Deed Book 52, County Clerk's Office, Socorro County Courthouse, Socorro, NM.
7. "Still They Come," *Deming Graphic*, 12 Jan 1906.
8. *El Paso News*, 30 June 1906; *Albuquerque Evening Citizen*, 22 Sept 1906; *Executive Record Book No. 6*, pp 366–369, NMSRCA.
9. Miguel A. Otero, *My Nine Years as Governor of the Territory of New Mexico 1897–1906* (Albuquerque: University of New Mexico Press, 1940) p 329.
10. "The Sheriff's Office," *Socorro Chieftain*, 22 Oct 1906; *House Journal*, 1907, NMSRCA.
11. Appointment Notice, oath of office, NMMP/NMSRCA; "Sergeant Lewis Promoted," *Socorro Chieftain*, 21 March 1908. Governor George Curry had served as the clerk of the Fifth District Court during 1895–1896. This duo federal/territorial court covered Lincoln, Chaves, Eddy and Socorro counties. It was during this time that Curry became acquainted with Leandro Baca. Mounted Policeman George Fred Murray had killed a man he found sleeping with his wife and was convicted of manslaughter and sentenced to the territorial penitentiary. He served ten months and 12 days of his three-year sentence. In 1911, he was appointed a Special Mounted Police and served until the corps was disbanded in December 1913.
12. Elfego Baca wrote Captain Fornoff, "Mr. [Leandro] Baca is a poor man; [but] a very honorable man." Letter: Baca to Fornoff, 21 Dec 1909, Letters Received, NMMP/NMSRCA. Leandro Baca had made eight arrests and recovered much stolen property during the 18 months that he served as a territorial ranger. Mounted Police Arrest Reports, NMMP/NMSRCA.
13. Letter; Leandro Baca to Gov. Miles, 19 Aug 1910, Letters Received, Governor William J. Miles Papers, NMSRCA.
14. Leandro Baca was elected as a commissioner to serve from the Second District. This district covered the mountain range lands around Quemado. H.O. Bursum was one of his two bondsmen. Baca took his oath as

a Special Mounted Police on 11 Oct 1919. Appointment Notice and Oath of Office, State Mounted Police Records 1919, NMSRCA.

15. Leandro Baca Biography File, NMMP/AC.

16. Elfego Baca, *Political Record of Elfego Baca and a Brief History of His Life*, private printing, 1924. Elfego seems to have always celebrated his birthday on 27 February, but the official records show that he was born on 10 February and was baptized five days later. *Socorro Book of Baptisms*, 1854–1865, Archives of the Catholic Archdiocese of Santa Fe, NM.

17. Kyle Crichton was an Albuquerque advertising company executive who interviewed Baca a few times in the fall of 1927. He took these interviews and then expanded Baca's 1924 political pamphlet into a 219-page book that was published by the parent company of the *Santa Fe New Mexican* in July 1928. Baca and Crichton jointly held the copyright. In 1997, a national "western book dealer" was asking $450 for a first edition of the Crichton book.

18. "Socorro County Troubles," *Silver City Enterprise*, 7 Nov 1884. The *Albuquerque Evening Democrat* was the only newspaper that published most of the testimony given during Elfego Baca's three-day murder trial.

19. *Socorro Chieftain*, 20 Sept 1895.

20. See Larry D. Ball's *Elfego Baca in Life and Legend* (El Paso: Texas Western Press, 1992) and Howard Bryan's *Incredible Elfego Baca: Good Man, Bad Man of the Old West* (Santa Fe: Clear Light Publishers, 1993) for unencumbered and readable accounts of Baca's life.

21. The social columns of the *Socorro Chieftain* during this period.

22. Letter: James G. Fitch to Governor H.J. Hagerman, 3 Oct 1906, Letters Received, Gov. H.J. Hagerman Papers, NMSRCA. Cipriano Baca had considered the idea of being sheriff of Socorro County even before Leandro Baca had been officially removed from office. *Albuquerque Evening Citizen*, 23 Aug 1906.

23. *Executive Record Book*, no 6, 17 March 1905, Gov. H. J. Hagerman Papers, NMSRCA. Elfego Baca felt he was pressured to resign as district attorney due to his actions in causing the arrest of a federal officer he had charged with illegally carrying a firearm while not on duty (*Albuquerque Evening Citizen*, 12 April 1906). The case against the federal peace officer was finally dismissed in court (*Socorro Chieftain*, 7 Dec 1907).

In January 1888, Elfego Baca's name first appeared in the record books of Socorro County. He bought two lots in the Park City development, southwest of Socorro, from Robert Simpson. Three years later he bought two more lots. Over the next two decades, Baca bought mining claims at Carthage and Mogollon; bought and sold large herds of cattle and horses and once he even bought a container of barbershop supplies. Deed Books, County Clerk's Office, Socorro County Courthouse, Socorro, NM.

24. Ball, *Elfego Baca*, p 87.

25. *Socorro Chieftain*, 18 June, 30 July 1921 and 5 Nov 1922.

26. Cipriano Baca burial records, Sunset Memorial Park, Albuquerque.

27. The author enjoyed the TV series and collected the comic books and other product tie-ins. Some of the TV episodes where edited into two 78-minute motion pictures called *The Nine Lives of Elfego Baca* (1958) and *Six Gun Law* (1962) that were shown in Europe. In December 2005, the Disney Studios issued a special limited edition DVD containing three of the Baca TV shows.

Chapter 10

1. The Baca-Berry marriage was recorded at the Socorro County courthouse on April 7, 1898; *Silver City Enterprise*, 11 Feb 1898 and 25 Feb 1898; *Silver City Independent*, 1 March 1898.

2. William A. Degregorio, *The Complete Book of U.S. Presidents*, 3rd edition (New York: Barricade Books, 1991) p 363.

3. Song/Sheet Music: Charles K. Harris, "Break the News to Mother" (New York: Chas. K. Harris Publishers, 1897), CB/AC.

4. The 2nd US Volunteer Cavalry, Torrey's Rocky Mountain Riders, was organized by Judge Jay L. Torrey of Wyoming. The 3rd US Volunteer Cavalry was commanded by Melvin Grigsby from men in the Dakota Territory and Montana and Nebraska. They were called Grigsby's Cowboys. These two regiments never received the same public status as the Rough Riders.

5. During the first half of 1899, Col. Theodore Roosevelt's account of the Spanish-American War was serially published in *Scribner's Magazine*. Later that same year the six articles were combined, along with several self-serving footnotes and four appendices, into a book called *The Rough Riders* (New York: Scribner, 1899). Appendix A contains an unofficial roster of the regiment.

6. Editorial, *New York Times*, 24 August 1898; Miguel A. Otero, *My Nine Years as Governor of the Territory of New Mexico 1897–1906* (Albuquerque: University of New Mexico Press, 1940) p 35.

7. Camille E. Cazedessus II, *The Rough Riders and New Mexico* (Baton Rouge, LA: Rendezvous Books, 1994) pp 4, 10. In celebration of the centennial of the Long Island encampment, the Montauk Historical Society published a compendium of the area newspaper accounts and the letters that Roosevelt wrote from the camp. The book, called *Bully!*, contains over 500 pages of primary material edited by Jeff Heatley.

8. See Frank Freidel's *The Splendid Little War* (Boston: Little, Brown, 1958) for a clear, readable presentation of the Spanish-American War.

9. Letter: Holm O. Bursum, Socorro, NM, to E.P. Lamborn, Leavenworth, KS, 12 April 1933, E.P. Lamborn Papers (156), Kansas State Historical Society, Topeka.

10. Letter: Holm O. Bursum to William S. French, 16 July 1897, Letter Book, Holm O. Bursum Collection, Center for Southwest Studies, UNM.

11. Gilberson Baca File, CB/AC; Baptismal Records, Church of the Epiphany Episcopal Church, Socorro.

12. *Socorro Chieftain*, 27 Jan and 3 Feb 1899.

13. Letter: Creighton Foraker to C. Baca, 6 April 1898, USMP.

14. *Socorro Chieftain*, 27 Jan and 3 Feb 1899.

15. Conversation Notes: Cipriana Randolph and author, 21 June 1984, CB/AC.

16. Letter: Foraker to Baca, 16 June 1899, USMP.

17. *Santa Fe New Mexican*, 7 Feb 1899.

18. Letter: Cipriano Baca to H.O. Bursum, 23 Feb 1899, Holm Bursum Papers, CSR/UNM.

Chapter 11

1. Otero, *My Nine Years as Governor*, pp 101–102.

2. *Report of the Standing Committee of the Council on Penitentiary Operations*, 23 Feb 1887, NMSRCA.

3. The *Santa Fe New Mexican*'s coverage of the prison riot was compiled in the *Holocaust at New Mexico*

State Penitentiary, Feb. 2–3, 1980 (Lubbock, TX: C.F. Boone Publisher, 1980) and the tale was expanded by Roger Morris in *The Devil's Butcher Shop: The New Mexico Prison Uprising* (Albuquerque: University of New Mexico Press, 1983).

Sixteen years after the great riot, the *Albuquerque Journal* did an investigative feature on the New Mexico state prison system and commented that, "New Mexico's six prisons can be dismal compounds wrapped in razor wire and despair." The newspaper study said that New Mexico ranked fourth in the nation with a per-inmate spending of $75 per day and a total annual prison budget of $138 million. Only 6 percent, $8.2 million, of that budget was spent on rehabilitation programs. In 1996 the New Mexico prison system had a 38 percent recidivism rate.

"Spending taxpayer money to teach and treat criminals isn't popular (in New Mexico). Half the New Mexicans surveyed in a *Journal* poll in September (1996) said they want no-frills prisons that emphasize punishment. They want criminals locked up. Warehoused. Out of sight." Carla Crowder, "The Prison Dilemma, Hard Time vs. Good Time," *Albuquerque Journal*, 29 Dec 1996. The saga of the New Mexico prison system continues.

4. Morris, *The Devil's Butcher Shop*, pp 31–53.
5. William T. Thornton, *Report of the Governor of New Mexico to the Secretary of the Interior, 1895* (Washington, DC: Government Printing Office), pp 42–43.
6. Otero, *My Nine Years as Governor*, p 109–110.
7. "Flowers and Criminals," *Detroit Free Press*, 18 March 1906.
8. "Bursum Is Appointed Senator to Replace Fall," *Albuquerque Morning Journal*, 12 March 1921; Kevin J. Fernlund, "Senator Holm O. Bursum and the Mexican Ring 1921–1924," *New Mexico Historical Review*, Oct 1991, pp 433–543.
9. *Albuquerque Daily Citizen*, 3 May 1899.
10. *Socorro Chieftain*, 11 Aug 1900.
11. *Socorro Chieftain*, 5 May and 9 June 1900.
12. *Socorro Chieftain*, 9 June and 8 Sept 1900. The newspaper had correctly reported that Effie Berry had gone to Santa Fe in June to spend the summer, but it then confused the Berry sisters by saying that it was 11-year-old Pearl Berry who had returned to Socorro in late August 1900.

13. Miguel A. Otero, *Report of the Governor of New Mexico to the Secretary of the Interior 1902* (Washington, DC: Government Printing Office, 1902) p 191. Letter: Mrs. Louise Nazareth Baca to author, 12 Aug 1982, CB/AC.

Chapter 12

1. *Silver City Enterprise*, 30 Oct 1896.
2. *Socorro Chieftain*, 5 Jan 1901.
3. *Socorro Chieftain*, 12 Jan 1901.
4. New Mexico Mounted Police Arrest Records; New Mexico Penitentiary Prisoner Records, 1900–1920, NMSRCA.
5. *Socorro Chieftain*, 26 Jan 1901 and 13 Oct 1900.
6. Otero, *My Nine Years as Governor*, p 82.
7. *Socorro Chieftain*, 16 Feb 1901.
8. *Executive Ticker*, 11 Feb 1901, p 179, M.A. Otero Papers (21P), Box 04, CSWR/UNM.
9. *Socorro Chieftain*, 16 Feb 1901; "Territorial Topics," *Las Vegas Daily Optic*, 12 Feb 1896; *New Mexico Health Resorts* (Topeka: Santa Fe Railroad Passenger Department, 1902).
10. Messages of Governor M.A. Otero, Legislative Assembly 1901, Territorial Archives of New Mexico, Microfilm Roll 150, NMSRCA.
11. Luna County Data, 22nd United States Census 2000, NA.

Chapter 13

1. *Lordsburg Western Liberal*, 5 April 1901.
2. *Santa Fe New Mexican*, 2 April 1901.
3. "Our County Officers," *Deming Herald*, 9 April 1901.
4. "The Officers Appointed," *Deming Headlight*, 6 April 1901.
5. *Socorro Chieftain*, 6 April 1901; *Silver City Enterprise*, reprinted in the *Socorro Chieftain*, 13 April 1901; *Deming Herald*, 7 May 1901.
6. *Deming Herald*, 30 April 1901.
7. *Deming Herald*, 27 May 1901; *Lordsburg Western Liberal*, 12 April 1901.
8. *Socorro Chieftain*, 18 May 1901.
9. *New Mexico Territorial Penitentiary Record Book of Convicts November 2, 1884–April 4, 1904*, Prisoner Numbers 1441–1445, NMSRCA.
10. Letter: Foraker to Baca, 30 April 1901, USMP, CSR/UNM.
11. J. Marvin Hunter, *Autobiography*, as quoted in F. Stanley, *The Bland [NM] Story* (Pep, TX: Private, 1964) p 07.

12. David Wallechinsky and Irving Wallace, *The People's Almanac* (Garden City, NY: Doubleday, 1975) p 273; *New York Times*, 4 March and 5 March 1897.
13. Margaret Leech, *In the Days of McKinley* (New York: Harper & Brothers, 1959) p 575.
14. "President's Day," *Deming Herald*, 7 May 1901; William Allen White, *Autobiography* (New York: Macmillan, 1946) p 251; *Washington Post*, 3 March 1897.
15. Otero, *My Nine Years as Governor*, pp 172–174.
16. Letter: Cipriana Randolph to author, 1 April 1985. The author has the McKinley funeral book, CB/AC.
17. William G. Clotworthy, *Homes and Libraries of the Presidents* (Blacksburg, VA: McDonald & Woodward Publishing, 2003) p 177.
18. *Socorro Chieftain*, 25 May 1901; *Deming Herald*, 7 May 1901.
19. *Deming Herald*, 20 Aug 1901; *Deming Headlight*, 14 Sept 1901. Baca bought this land, Lots 57 and 58 of Block 74 in the Boles Addition, on 26 April 1902 and sold them on 24 Aug 1903, but the deed of sale, for some unknown reason, was not recorded until 17 Feb 1909. Baca bought Lot 15 of Block A on 12 Aug 1901 and sold it on 2 Jan 1903, Deed Book 2, County Clerk's Office, Luna County Courthouse, Deming, NM.
20. *List of Purchasers, Old and New Mexico Improvement Company*, Deming, NM, Sale No. 6 Sheriff Cipriano Baca, Lots 16, 17, 18, 19 of Block A, p. 100, Deming-Mimbres Museum Archives, Deming, NM.
21. *Deming Herald*, 28 May 1901.
22. "Passing of the Bad Man," *Deming Herald*, 7 May 1901.
23. *Socorro Chieftain*, 22 June 1901.
24. "How We Do In Luna," *Deming Headlight*, 20 July 1901.
25. Letter: Creighton Foraker to Cipriano Baca, 20 June 1901, USMP.
26. Letters: Creighton Foraker to Cipriano Baca, 13 Aug and 9 Sept 1901, USMP.
27. *Deming Herald*, reprinted *Socorro Chieftain*, 22 June 1901; Letter: Cipriana Randolph to author, 1 April 1985, CB/AC.
28. "Bold Daylight Robbery," *Deming Herald*, 11 June 1901; "A Bold Holdup," *Deming Headlight*, 15 June 1901.
29. *Deming Herald*, 18 June 1901; *Socorro Chieftain*, 22 June 1901; *Deming Herald*, 25 June 1901.
30. *Deming Herald*, 25 June 1901;

Deming Headlight, 29 June 1901; *Socorro Chieftain*, 29 June 1901; *Deming Herald*, 2 July and 9 July 1901; Letter: Cipriana Randolph to author, 12 Dec 1984, CB/AC.

31. *Deming Herald*, 25 June 1901, 4 Feb 1902, 9 July 1901; *Deming Headlight*, 13 July 1901; *Deming Herald*, 16 July 1901; *Proceedings of Board of County Commissioners—Book 1*, 1 July 1901, County Clerk's Office, Luna County Courthouse, Deming, NM.

32. David F. Myrick, *New Mexico Railroads: An Historical Survey* (Golden, CO: Colorado Railroad Museum, 1970) pp 82–88; "Jack Finley Slain; Stabbed to Death," *Deming Headlight*, 3 Aug 1901; *Lordsburg Western Liberal*, 9 Aug 1901; *Deming Herald*, 13 Aug 1901; "A Startling Discovery," *Deming Herald*, 3 Sept 1901.

33. The real quotation was "Now look! That damn cowboy is President of the United States," and was credited to Senator Mark Hanna, a Republican from Ohio, as spoken in September 1901.

34. David Wallechinsky and Irving Wallace, *The People's Almanac* (Garden City, NY: Doubleday, 1975) p 273.

35. Letter: Cipriana Randolph to author, 1 April 1985, CB/AC. The book that Mrs. Randolph remembered was Col. G. W. Townsend's *Our Martyred President, Memorial Life of William McKinley*, published in 1901 by D.Z. Howell. It is part of the CB/AC.

36. See Eric Rauchway, *Murdering McKinley, The Making of Theodore Roosevelt's America* (New York: Hill and Wang, 2003) and A. Wesley Johns, *The Man Who Shot McKinley, A New View of the Assassination of the President* (New York: A.S. Barnes and Company, 1970) for case studies of the assassination and the era it ushered upon America and the world.

37. William Allen White, "One Year of Roosevelt," *Saturday Evening Post*, 4 Oct 1902, pp 3–4.

38. *Deming Headlight*, 28 September 1901, 19 October 1901; *Proceedings of Board of County Commissioners—Book 1*, 11 Oct 1901, County Clerk's Office, Luna County, Deming, NM.

39. Deming *Herald*, 8 Oct 1901; *Socorro Chieftain*, 5 Oct and 12 Oct 1901.

40. *Deming Herald*, 11 Oct 1901; Gov. Otero's speech, 16 Oct 1901, Otero-Stinson Papers, CSR/UNM.

41. *Deming Herald*, 22 Oct 1901.

42. *Deming Herald*, 12 Nov 1901; *Socorro Chieftain*, 16 Nov 1901; *Deming Herald*, 22 Nov 1902; *Socorro Chieftain*, 30 Nov 1901; *Deming Herald*, 24 Dec 1901.

43. *Proceedings of Board of County Commissioners—Book 1*, 6 Jan 1902, County Clerk's Office, Luna County, Deming, NM; *Lordsburg Western Liberal*, 6 Dec 1901. The Luna County Commissioners' Court, in 1996, authorized a plan for charging inmates a $10 booking fee and a $5 bonding fee to help defray the cost of operating the county jail. The jail administrator was quoted as saying, "Obviously the best way around these fees is not to go to jail." Presently $15,000 to $20,000 is budgeted from these fees. The year before, Luna County had joined Otero County in assessing inmates a portion of the bill for their medical costs. "Jail to Charge Booking, Bonding Fees," Lubbock (TX) *Avalanche-Journal*, 28 Dec 1996. Bernalillo County and Taos County each now charge inmates room and board fees. A prisoner may pay these fees in cash or by doing community service. "Taos Prisoners Now Must Pay for Meals," Lubbock (TX) *Avalanche-Journal*, 12 May 1997.

44. *Deming Herald*, 28 Jan 1902.

45. *Socorro Chieftain*, 11 Jan 1902.

46. *Deming Herald*, 21 Jan 1902.

47. *Socorro Chieftain*, 1 Feb 1902; Birthday conversation: Cipriana Randolph and author, 28 Jan 1985, Notes in CB/AC.

48. "Female in Male Attire," *Socorro Chieftain*, 18 Jan 1902.

49. "Deming National Bank to Open," *Santa Fe New Mexican*, 9 Sept 1903; Chuck Hornung, "Wyatt Earp's New Mexico Adventures," *Old West*, May 1999, pp 17–24. For a good biography of Lottie Deno, read Jan Devereaux's *Pistols, Petticoats, & Poker, The Real Lottie Deno: No Lies or Alibis* (Silver City, NM: High-Lonesome Books, 2009).

50. *Deming Herald*, 4 Feb and 18 Feb 1902; *Deming Headlight*, 8 Feb 1902; *Deming Herald*, 8 April 1902; *Socorro Chieftain*, 19 April 1902; *Proceedings—Book 1*, April–Sept 1902.

51. *Deming Herald*, 27 May and 10 June 1902; *Deming Headlight*, 21 June 1902; *Deming Herald*, 24 June 1902; *Socorro Chieftain*, 21 June, 12 July and 5 July 1902.

52. *Deming Herald*, 15 July, 23 Sept and 5 Aug 1902.

53. *Socorro Chieftain*, 16 Aug 1902; *Deming Herald*, reprint *Socorro Chieftain*, 30 Aug 1902.

54. Miguel A. Otero, *My Life on the Frontier I* (New York: Press of the Pioneers, 1935) pp 32–33; Conversation: Cipriana Randolph and author, 21 June 1984, notes CB/AC; Buffalo Bill's show advertisement, *Deming Headlight*, 27 Sept 1902; *Deming Graphic*, 23 Feb 1912; Clarence Gartman, "Last Days of Buffalo Bill," *Golden West*, Feb 1973, pp 35–37, 44–45; Harry E. Webb, "Buffalo Bill as I Knew Him," *The West*, Nov 1967, pp 34–37, 64.

55. *Deming Headlight*, 11 Oct 1902; *Socorro Chieftain*, 25 Oct 1902; *Deming Herald*, 11 Nov 1902.

56. "Speech to Luna County Citizens," 29 March 1901, Gov. M.A. Otero Papers (21 P), Box 4, Folder 11, CSWR/UNM. By 1916, M.A. Otero had changed his party loyalties. In a speech he gave at a Roswell meeting, Otero said he would vote for the worst Democrat over the best Republican candidate for any post. Otero even served as a delegate to the Democratic Party National Conventions in 1920 and 1924.

57. *Lordsburg Western Liberal*, 5 April 1901; *Socorro Chieftain*, 8 Nov 1902; *Proceeding—Book 1*, 10 Nov 1902, p 35.

58. *Deming Herald*, 18 Nov and 22 Dec 1902; *Deming Headlight*, 27 Dec 1902; *Deming Herald*, 30 Dec 1902; *Deming Herald*, reprint in *Socorro Chieftain*, 30 Aug 1902; Letter: Miguel A. Otero to E.P. Lamborn, Leavenworth, KS, 21 Dec 1936, E.P. Lamborn Papers (156), Box 03, File 04, Kansas State Historical Society, Topeka.

59. "Deming Item," *Albuquerque Daily Citizen*, 14 Jan 1903; *Deming Graphic*, 15 April 1903.

60. *Proceedings*, 5 Jan 1903. In April 1906 the Roswell city council was considering an adjustment of its water rates. The local paper printed a comparison chart of towns with "the same grade as to accessibility of water." Deming was included in this study. Deming received its water supply from "shallow deposits." *Roswell Register* newspaper clip, April 1906, CB/AC.

61. Otero, *My Nine Years as Governor*, p 83; *Socorro Chieftain*, 27 Dec 1902; *Deming Graphic*, 3 June, 22 July, 26 Aug and 16 Sept 1903; Den Galbraith, "The Lost Ledge of Governor Otero," *True West*, March–April 1964, pp 45, 50–51; "Deep Down Mine," *El Paso Herald*, 17 Feb 1904; Fayette Jones, *New Mexico Mines and Minerals* (Santa Fe: Private, 1905) p 134.

62. *Deming Graphic*, 3 June 1903; Conversation Notes: Louise Baca and author, 9 Nov 1996, CB/AC.

63. *Deming Graphic*, 13 Nov 1903;

Silver City Enterprise, 5 Feb 1904; *City Directory of Albuquerque* (NP: 1904); "New Mexico Nut Rustlers Cashing in on Pecans," *San Angelo* (TX) *Standard Times*, 23 Jan 1991, A11.

Chapter 14

1. *Report of [to] the Secretary of the Interior by the Governor of New Mexico*, 1904, Gov. M.A. Otero Papers, NMSRCA. U.S. Marshal C.M. Foraker, as a courtesy, provided Governor Otero with a copy of his department's annual report and financial statement. In 1904, the governor included Foraker's data in his own State of the Territory report to the secretary of the interior. Cipriano Baca is listed as a deputy US marshal in this report.
2. Letters: C. M. Foraker to/from Joseph McKenna, Letter Book, 9 Aug 1897–25 Aug 1898, USMP/CSR.
3. *United States Code*, Appropriation Act for Department of Justice, Fiscal Year 1897–1898, Section Nine — U.S. Marshals.
4. Larry D. Ball, *The United States Marshals Of New Mexico and Arizona Territory, 1846–1912* (Albuquerque: University of New Mexico Press, 1978) pp 194–195, 197.
5. "Locales," *Deming Graphic*, 24 Feb 1904; Sir Arthur Conan Doyle, "The Adventure of the Priory School," *Strand*, Feb 1904.
6. Fred Lambert told the author that he was a spectator at the 1915 Fats-Leans baseball game. He was in Santa Fe working for the US Indian Service at the time. Fred could not remember the game score or who won, but he did remember that the two teams really teased each other during the game. Conversation notes in CB/AC.
7. Ball, *United States Marshals*, p 275 endnote 48.
8. Kaseman's letter describing his adventure on *Cerro Los Moqujino* is in a private collection dealing with the Jewish influence on the development of early New Mexico; Samuel Oshmier, "Pilgrimage to New Mexico's Mystery Mountain," *Ancient American*, Feb 2006, pp 2–4; Joseph C. Winter, "Riddle of the Mysterious Rock," *Albuquerque Journal Magazine*, 24 June 1984, pp 8–11, 15; "Did King Solomon's Navy Discover America?," Arutz Sheva: Israel National News.com, 17 Dec 2007.
9. *Albuquerque Evening Citizen*, 22 May 1906; *Portales Herald*, 12 April 1904; *Deming Graphic*, 27 April 1904.
10. John A. Gjevre, *Chili Line: The Narrow Rail Trail to Santa Fe* (Espanola, NM: Rio Grande Sun Press, 1971), p 30. This volume contains a reprint of the 1902 and 1905 time schedules used for the Santa Fe Branch of the Denver and Rio Grande Railroad. These charts where used to reconstruct Baca's trip.
11. Letter: Baca to Marshal Foraker, 30 Sept 1904, USMP/CSR.
12. *Santa Fe New Mexican*, 8 Oct 1904.
13. Letter: Baca to Marshal Foraker, 30 Sept 1904, USMP/CSR.
14. Letter: Marshal Foraker to Cipriano Baca, 1 Jan 1905, Letters Sent, USMP/CSR; *Santa Fe New Mexican*, 1 March 1905; Otero, *Executive Ticker*, 1 March 1905; Letter: Foraker to Attorney General, 14 March 1905, Letters Sent, Baca to Foraker, 22 March 1905, Letters Received, USMP/CSR.

Chapter 15

1. "Mounted Police Began Their Work," *Albuquerque Morning Journal*, 2 April 1905.
2. "Are Sworn into Office," *Santa Fe New Mexican*, 1 April 1905; "Mounted Police Began Their Work," *Albuquerque Morning Journal*, 2 April 1905; Letter: Cipriana Randolph to author, 1 Dec 1982, CB/AC.
3. For a general history see the author's *The Thin Gray Line: The New Mexico Mounted Police* (Fort Worth, TX: Western Heritage Press, 1971).

Chapter 16

1. For a readable, yet detailed, history of the first company of Mounted Police, consult the author's book *Fullerton's Rangers* (Jefferson, NC: McFarland, 2005).
2. Conversation Notes: Cipriana Randolph and author, via telephone, 21 June 1984, NMMP/AC.
3. Copies of the 1905 Mounted Police Oath of Office forms and the Fullerton's Rangers' Muster Roll, NMMP/NMSRCA.
4. "Are Sworn into Office," *Santa Fe New Mexican*, 1 April 1905.
5. *Socorro Chieftain*, 15 April 1905; *Deming Headlight*, 20 Oct 1910.
6. Weather was always a problem for Fullerton's Rangers. Here is a good example. "On account of snow, bad weather and long distance they [Julius Meyer and Rafael Gomez] were delayed on [the] road from 26th December 1905 until January 22nd 1906." The two rangers fought bad weather for 28 days before they were able to join Lt. Baca for an outlaw roundup. Report: Lt. Baca to Capt. Fullerton, 26 Jan 1906, NMMP/NMSRCA.
7. In 1903, the safety razor company sold 51 of their new razor kits at $5.00 each. Within three years, they sold over 300,000 razor kits and 500,000 replacement blades.
8. Conversation Notes: Lambert and author, 18 June 1967, NMMP/AC.
9. Pine tar soap is still formulated and marketed by Grandpa's Soap Company of Erlanger, KY. They have produced this specialty type of soap since 1878.
10. Comparison cost data from the Department of Commerce, Bureau of the Census Data Sheet.
11. *Deming Graphic*, 7 April 1905.
12. *Socorro Chieftain*, 8 April 1905.
13. "The 'Bad Men' Will Be Forced to Vacate," *Santa Fe New Mexican*, 18 April 1905.
14. *Acts of the Legislative Assembly of the Territory of New Mexico, Thirty-Sixth Session 1905, New Mexico Coded Law 1905* (Santa Fe: New Mexican Printing Co., 1905) chapter 9, "Mounted Police," pp 31–34.
15. "Wants New Mexico Rangers," *Alamogordo News*, 4 Feb 1905.
16. Letter: Capt. Fullerton to Elkins, 2 June 1905, Letters Sent, NMMP/NMSRCA.
17. Randall Hackley (AP), "Mexican Bandits Spark Threat of Range War," *Lubbock* (TX) *Avalanche-Journal*, 30 Jan 1983. Two border ranchers were killed in 1980 by drug smugglers. Other Mexicans cut fences and steal cattle and equipment because of lax border law enforcement. Ranchers go armed, and one said, "This is the wild, wooly West. Anything can happen"; "Smaller Towns Deal with Gangs," *Lubbock* (TX) *Avalanche-Journal*, 18 Dec 1995. Youth gang violence is spreading into many rural and remote sections of southwestern New Mexico.
18. *Silver City Independent*, 25 April 1905.
19. "New Mexico Crop Bulletin," *The Outlook* (White Oaks), 8 June 1905; Letter: Capt. Fullerton to W.C. Barnes, 27 July 1905, Letters Sent, NMMP/NMSRCA.
20. Letter: Capt. Fullerton to Whitney Company, 10 July 1905, Letters Sent, NMMP/NMSRCA; Reconstructed NMMP Voucher Records, NMMP/AC.

21. Letter: Capt. Fullerton to Lt. Baca, 14 July 1905, Letters Sent, NMMP/NMSRCA.
22. Letter: Baca to his wife, ND, Cipriano Baca Papers, Baca Family Collection, copy CB/AC.
23. Letter: Lt. Baca to Capt. Fullerton, 8 July 1905, Letters Received, NMMP/NMSRCA.
24. Many of the chants, songs and tales of the Tewa (Pueblo) nations were collected and translated by Herbert J. Spinden and published, *Songs of the Tewa*, by the Exposition of Indian Tribal Arts Inc. in 1933. The Indian exhibit was shown in the gallery of the Corcoran College of Art and Design at Washington, DC.
25. *Socorro Chieftain*, 12 Aug 1905; *Albuquerque Evening Citizen*, 9 Aug 1905; *Silver City Independent*, 15 Aug 1905.
26. *Farmington San Juan Index*, 25 Aug 1905; "Mounted Policeman Perea Makes Arrest," *Durango* (CO) *Evening Herald*, 29 Aug 1905.
27. Letters: Capt. Fullerton to Lt. Baca and the three wives, June–Aug 1905, Letters Sent, NMMP/NMSRCA; *Socorro Chieftain*, 22 July 1905.
28. This incident is covered in detail in Hornung, *Fullerton's Rangers*, pp 181–195.
29. Telegram: Sheriff Boone C. Vaughn to Capt. Fornoff, 19 May 1906, Letters Received, NMMP/NMSRCA.
30. Herb McGrath Report, 26 July 1905, Letters Received, NMMP/NMSRCA; *Silver City Independent*, 15 Aug 1905; "Mounted Police Chase Apache Kid And His Squaw," *Albuquerque Morning Journal*, 18 Aug 1905; Marc Simmons, "Hunting Expedition Came Back with Bigger Game Than Expected," New Mexican Scrapbook, *El Paso Times*, 2 Feb 1986; McGrath's athletic career was covered in college newspaper *The Collagist*, RCHC/NMSU. It is now believed that the Kid was not an Apache, but a member of the Yavapai tribe.
31. Letter: Capt. Fullerton to Dudley, 12 Sept 1905, Letters Sent, NMMP/NMSRCA; "Mounted Police Here for Parade," *Albuquerque Morning Journal*, 20 Sept 1905; "Territorial Mounted Police Appear in Parade," *Albuquerque Evening Citizen*, 20 Sept 1905; Letters: W.H. Greer to Gov. Otero, 8 Sept 1905, Otero to Greer, 12 Sept 1905, Letters Sent and Received, Gov. M.A. Otero Papers, NMSRCA; "Mounted Police in Fair Parade," *Albuquerque Evening Citizen*, 20 Sept 1905.
32. On 25 Oct 1905 Fullerton issued Mounted Police Voucher #57 for $30 and the territory paid the bill with Warrant #11728 on 5 Nov 1905. Interestingly, Fullerton deducted a $3 hat fee from each of the paychecks he wrote his men. No record has been located as to the dispossession of this $30. Letter: Captain Fullerton to rangers with paycheck, 14 Nov 1905; Voucher Records, NMMP/NMSRCA.
33. *Santa Fe New Mexican*, 21 Sept 1905; "Mounted Police Here for Parade," *Albuquerque Morning Journal*, 20 Sept 1905.
34. Letter: Capt. Fullerton to Dr. B.H. Briggs, 10 Oct 1905, Letters Sent, NMMP/NMSRCA.
35. The Las Vegas Fair had made the first arrangements for the Mounted Police to ride in a fair parade. However, the northern fair followed the Albuquerque show, so the rangers first appeared in the Duke City. Letters: R.E. Twichell to Gov. Otero, 23 Aug 1905; Otero to Twichell, 30 Aug and 2 Sept 1905, Gov. M.A. Otero Papers, NMSRCA.
36. *Socorro Chieftain*, 23 Sept 1905.
37. Telegrams: Rio Arriba County Sheriff B.C. Hernandez to Gov. Otero, 26 Sept 1905; C.M. O'Donell to Gov. Otero, 27 Sept 1905; J.W. Raynolds, Acting-Governor, to Capt. Fullerton, 27 Sept 1905; Fullerton to Raynolds, 27 Sept 1905; C.M. O'Donell to Otero, 29 Sept 1905; Raynolds to Fullerton 29 Sept 1905 and Fullerton to Raynolds, 29 Sept 1905, Telegrams Sent, NMMP/NMSRCA.
38. "Report of an Attempted Holdup on Santa Fe," *Santa Fe New Mexican*, 4 Oct 1905.
39. Perish Register, The Church of the Epiphany, Socorro, NM.
40. Simon Pokagon, "The Future of the Red Man," *Forum*, August 1897.
41. *New Mexico Coded Laws 1905*, chapter 9, "Mounted Police"; "Red Men Are Lawless," *Socorro Chieftain*, 16 Dec 1905.
42. Letter: Fullerton to Page B. Otero, 3 Nov 1905, Letters Sent, NMMP/NMSRCA.
43. Letter: Page B. Otero to Capt. Fullerton, 8 Nov 1905, Letters Sent, Fish and Game Warden Papers, NMSRCA.
44. Letter: Page B. Otero to R. Perry, 11 Nov 1905, Letters Sent, Fish and Game Warden Papers, NMSRCA.
45. *Santa Fe New Mexican*, 7 Nov 1905; Letter: Fullerton to W.M. Berrowdale, 9 Nov 1905, Letters Sent, NMMP/NMSRCA.
46. Letter: U. S. Marshal Creighton Foraker to the U.S. attorney general, 26 Oct 1897, Letter Book 1897, USMP/UNM.
47. Letter: Capt. Fullerton to James Patterson, 15 Nov 1905, Letters Sent, NMMP/NMSRCA.
48. Letter: Page B. Otero to Capt. Fullerton, 18 Nov 1905, Letters Sent, Game Warden Papers, NMSRCA.
49. *Silver City Enterprise*, 1 Dec 1905; *El Paso Times*, 2 Dec 1905; "Red Men Are Lawless," *Socorro Chieftain*, 16 Dec 1905; "Trouble with Pueblos," *Portales Herald*, 22 Oct 1904.
50. Letters: Lt. Baca to Game Warden Page Otero, 17 Oct 1905, Otero to Baca, 30 Oct 1905, Letter Book, Game Warden Records, NMSRCA; "Deputy Game Warden," *Western Liberal* (Lordsburg), 12 May 1905; "Indians Troublesome," *Santa Fe New Mexican*, 16 Dec 1905; *Roswell Register*, 26 Jan 1906.
51. Letters: Page Otero to Capt. Fullerton, 27 Nov 1905, Page Otero to Sheriff Boone Vaughn, 3 Jan 1906; Letters Sent, Game Warden Papers, NMSRCA.
52. "New Mexico," *El Paso Times*, 4 Jan 1907.
53. Letters: Charles Ilfeld, Gov. Hagerman and Capt. Fullerton exchange, Jan 1906, Letters Received/Sent, Gov. H.J. Hagerman Papers, NMSRCA; *Washington Post*, 17 Oct 1905.
54. Letter: Capt. Fullerton to C.M. O'Donel, 3 Nov 1905, Letters Sent, NMMP/NMSRCA.
55. *Destructive Floods in the United States in 1904*, USGS Water-Supply and Irrigation Paper No. 147 (Washington, DC, 1905) pp 128–129.
56. Letter: Arthur Tisdall to Frank Bloom, 28 June 1895, Tisdall Letterbook 1894–1897, Red River Valley Collection, CSR/UNM.
57. See William J. Parish, *The Charles Ilfeld Company: The Rise and Decline of Mercantile Capitalism in New Mexico* (Cambridge, MA: Harvard University Press, 1961) and David Remley, *Bell Ranch: Cattle Ranching in the Southwest, 1824–1947* (Las Cruces, NM: Yucca Tree Press, 2000) for profiles of these two men.
58. Baca's Field Report, 26 Jan 1906, Letters Received, NMMP/NMSRCA; "Historic Dates for the Dow Jones Average," Associated Press, Oct 1989 release; "Mounted Police Doing Good Work," *Santa Fe New Mexican*, 6 Feb 1906.

Notes — Chapter 16

59. Baca's Field Report, 26 Jan 1906, Letters Received, NMMP/NMSRCA.
60. "Sergeant Lewis Very Much Alive," *Santa Fe New Mexican*, 23 Feb 1906; "Mounted Police," *Clayton Enterprise*, 23 Feb 1906; "Lieutenant Baca of Rangers Raids Robbers' Roost," *Albuquerque Morning Journal*, 28 Jan 1906; "Mounted Police Doing Good Work," *Santa Fe New Mexican*, 6 Feb 1906.
61. "Lieutenant Baca of Rangers Raids Robbers' Roost," *Albuquerque Morning Journal*, 28 Jan 1906.
62. New Mexico Territorial Penitentiary Record Book of Convicts, book 2, April 5, 1904–Febuary 13, 1915, Convict #1984 and Convict #1986, NMSRCA.
63. Chuck Hornung, *Fullerton's Rangers* (Jefferson, NC: McFarland, 2005) pp 186–188.
64. "New Mexico News," *El Paso Times*, 8 Jan 1906; "New Mexico," *El Paso Evening News*, 17 Jan 1906.
65. Leslie Linthicum, "Heavy Snowfall Holds Up Travelers and Turns N.M. Into a Winter World," *Albuquerque Journal*, 30 Dec 2006; Charles D. Brunt, "Motorists Critical of Outdated Hotline Info during Storm," *Albuquerque Journal*, 5 Jan 2007; "Winter Storm Claims Lives of at Least 16, State Officials Say," *Albuquerque Journal*, 6 Jan 2007; "National Guard Rescues Stranded Camper, Weeks After Search Was Called Off," *Albuquerque Journal*, 14 Jan 2007.
66. Letter: Lt. Baca to Capt. Fullerton, 26 Jan 1906, Letters Received, NMMP/NMSRCA; "No Trains for Two Weeks," *Roswell Register*, 19 Jan and 2 Feb 1906.
67. Letter: A.B. Harris to Capt. Fullerton, 7 Feb 1906, Letters Received, NMMP/NMSRCA.
68. *Tucumcari News*, 10 Feb 1906; *Clayton Enterprise*, 16 Feb 1906; *Santa Fe New Mexican*, 10 March 1906; "Mounted Police Good Work," *Socorro Chieftain*, 17 Feb 1906; "Lieutenant Cipriano Baca," *Socorro Chieftain*, 3 March 1906.
69. "Lieutenant Cipriano Baca," *Socorro Chieftain*, 3 March 1906.
70. Letters: Lt. Baca's Field Report, 26 Jan 1906; Private Brophy's resignation, 20 March 1906; Lt. Baca to Capt. Fullerton, 13 Feb 1906, C.M. O'Donel to Capt. Fornoff, 7 April 1906, Letters Received, NMMP/NMSRCA; Letter: C.M. O'Donel to Gov. Hagerman, 12 Feb 1906, Letters Received, Gov. H. J. Hagerman Papers, NMSRCA.
71. *Santa Fe New Mexican*, 10 March 1906; "Lieutenant Cipriano Baca," *Socorro Chieftain*, 3 March 1906.
72. "After the Desperados in the Mogollons," *Santa Fe New Mexican*, 24 Feb 1906.
73. "On a False Scent," *Arizona Silver Belt* (Globe City, AZ), 15 March 1906; *El Paso Times*, 3 April 1906; Letters: Sheriff Frank Ross, Jr., to Capt. Fornoff, 16 July 1906; Sheriff J.C. Wall to Capt. Fornoff, 17 July 1906; Deputy Sheriff N.S. Jackson, 27 July 1906, Letters Received, NMMP/ NMSRCA.
74. "Move to Wipe Out Ranger Force," *Albuquerque Morning Journal*, 5 Feb 1906; "After the Desperados in the Mogollons," *Santa Fe New Mexican*, 24 Feb 1906.
75. "Fornoff for Captain of Mounted Police," *Santa Fe New Mexican*, 21 March 1906; *Albuquerque Evening Citizen*, 2 April 1906.
76. "Reorganization Mounted Police Effective Today," *Santa Fe New Mexican*, 2 April 1906; Letter: C.M. O'Donel to Capt. Fornoff, 7 April 1906, Letters Received, NMMP/NMSRCA.
77. The Mounted Police office location and interior description were described to the author by the last living territorial ranger, Fred Lambert of Cimarron. Lambert Notes, NMMP/AC. Cipriano Baca's work in moving the Mounted Police records and the disposition of the Socorro office equipment is contained in Baca's reports and the 1906 office inventory, NMMP/NMSRCA.
78. *New Mexico Coded Laws*, 1905, chapter 9 — Mounted Police, Section 8, NMSRCA.
79. See Gordon Thomas and Max Morgan Witts, *The San Francisco Earthquake* (New York: Stein and Day Publishers, 1971) for a very detailed account of this crisis; "Archivist Delves into Records Doubling Toll of '06 Quake," *Lubbock Avalanche-Journal*, 13 Dec 1984.
80. *Socorro Chieftain*, 24 April 1906; *Capitan El Farol*, 8 May 1906; "Riding the Territory of Bad men," *Denver Republican*, 13 May 1906; *Socorro Chieftain*, 26 May 1906; *Albuquerque Evening Citizen*, 22 May 1906.
81. *Socorro Chieftain*, 2 June 1906.
82. *Socorro Chieftain*, 9 June 1906; *El Paso Times*, 20 June 1906; *Clayton Enterprise*, 1 June and 20 June 1906; "Brings Criminals Back," *Tucumcari News*, 23 June 1906.
83. *Socorro Chieftain*, 19 March 1904; "Town Being Shaken Down," *New York Times*, 19 July 1906; "Earthquakes in Texas," *New York Times*, 20 July 1906; *Albuquerque Morning Journal*, 20 July 1906; *Cincinnati Post*, 23 July 1906; *Albuquerque Morning Journal*, 18 July 1906; *Socorro Chieftain*, 18 July and 21 July 1906; Conversation Notes: Cipriana Randolph and author, 21 June 1984, CB/AC; *Albuquerque Evening Citizen*, 12 July 1906; "Letter to the Editor," *Santa Fe New Mexican*, 20 July 1906; *Silver City Enterprise*, 27 July 1906.
84. Conversation: Cipriana Randolph to author, 21 June 1984, Notes CB/AC.
85. Associated Press wire story, "Lifting Fog on San Francisco's Great Quake," *Odessa* (TX) *American*, 16 April 2006.
86. Deed Book 62, County Clerk's Office, Socorro County Courthouse, Socorro, NM; *Socorro Chieftain*, 24 Nov 1906.
87. *Alamogordo News*, 28 July 1906; "The Livestock Robbery," *Capitan El Farol*, 17 July 1906; *Santa Fe New Mexican*, 1 Aug 1906; *Albuquerque Morning Journal*, 31 July 1906; *Socorro Chieftain*, 4 Aug 1906.
88. Fornoff's operations report is part of Governor Hagerman's report to the secretary of the interior 1906 (Washington, DC: Government Printing Office, 1906).
89. *Albuquerque Evening Citizen*, 14 Aug 1906; "For Stealing Cattle," *Socorro Chieftain*, 8 Sept 1906; *Clayton Enterprise*, 14 Sept 1906; *Socorro Chieftain*, 18 Aug and 15 Sept 1906.
90. Letter: James G. Fitch to Hagerman, 3 Oct 1906, Letters Received, Gov. H. J. Hagerman Papers, NMSRCA.
91. *Tucumcari News*, 6 Oct 1906 and 13 Oct 1906; *Parrish Register*, The Episcopal Church of the Epiphany, Socorro, NM, pp 42, 104; *Albuquerque Evening Citizen*, 26 Oct 1906 and 6 Nov 1906; *Socorro Chieftain*, 24 Nov 1906.
92. *Socorro Chieftain*, 4 Dec 1906.
93. "Late News," *Ozona* (TX) *Kicker*, 4 Dec 1906; New Mexico Mounted Police Description Card, Arrest Cards, NMMP/NMSRCA.
94. The "they" is assumed to mean the editors of the *Albuquerque Evening Citizen*, but "they" could also have meant Governor Hagerman and Captain Fornoff. Baca's statement is unclear as to what he intended "it is all off" to mean to his reader.
95. "Baca Denies He Smashed the

Phone," *Albuquerque Morning Journal*, 6 Jan 1907; "San Antonio People Say Story Is Fake," *Albuquerque Morning Journal*, 7 Jan 1907.

96. Letter: Cipriana Randolph to author, 1 April 1985, CB/AC.

97. Letter: Baca to Fornoff, 3 Jan 1907, Resignations, Gov H.J. Hagerman Papers, NMSRCA. Baca's resignation letter is dated the same day as the alleged smashing of the barroom telephone. This was two days prior to the publication of the *Albuquerque Evening Citizen*'s story.

98. "Lieutenant Cipriano Baca Has Resigned," *Albuquerque Morning Journal*, 8 Jan 1907; *Executive Ticker*, 6 Jan 1907.

Chapter 17

1. *Albuquerque Morning Journal*, 21 Jan 1907.

2. *Message of Herbert J. Hagerman, Governor of New Mexico to the 37th Legislative Assembly*, January 21, 1907 (Santa Fe: New Mexican Printing, 1907), pp 36–37; Mounted Police Department Report, 2 Jan 1907, NMMP/NMSRCA; "Move to Wipe Out Ranger Forces," *Albuquerque Morning Journal*, 5 Feb 1907; Defeated and Vetoed Bills, 37th Legislative Assembly, NMSRCA; Interview: Persy Sickles and author, Socorro, NM, 18 July 1970, NMMP/AC. Sickles had been a youthful friend of Cipriano's daughter Maisie Baca Amos.

3. Letter: Baca to Gov. Hagerman, 12 Jan 1907, Letters Received, Gov. H. J. Hagerman Papers, NMSRCA; *Albuquerque Morning Journal*, 21 Jan and 10 Feb 1907.

4. *Socorro Chieftain*, 2 Feb 1907; Parish Register, the Church of the Epiphany, Socorro, NM.

5. Myrick, *New Mexico Railroads*, pp 58–94; William Larrabee, *The Railroad Question* (Chicago: Schulte Publishing, 1893) p 89.

6. Myrick, *New Mexico's Railroads*, pp 83–88; Interview Notes: D.R. Thomas, Special Agent of the Atchison, Topeka and Santa Fe Railway Company and historian of their frontier railroad detectives, and the author, Lubbock, TX, 18 June 1977. Baca kept a list of his railroad detective investigations pasted in the back of an El Paso and Southwestern Railroad time schedule book.

7. "Locals," *Socorro Chieftain*, 29 Feb 1908.

8. Territory of New Mexico vs. Wayne Brazel, Cause #4112 — Murder, Third District Court Records for April 19, 1909, District Clerk's Office, Dona Ana County Courthouse, Las Cruces; *New Mexico Territorial Penitentiary Record Book of Convicts, April 5, 1904–February 13, 1915*, NMS CRA; Nancy Farrar, *The Chinese in El Paso* (El Paso: Texas Western Press, 1972) pp 19–22; Chuck Hornung, "The Fornoff Report," paper presented to the Sixth Western Outlaw-Lawmen History Association Convention, Craig, CO, 20 July 1996; Chuck Hornung "Surprising New Information on Pat Garrett's Death: Details from the Fornoff Report," *The Journal, Western Outlaw-Lawman History Association*, Spring/Summer 1997; Chuck Hornung "The Fornoff Report: New Light on the Death of Pat Garrett," *True West*, March 1998.

9. Paula Moore, *Cricket in the Web* (Albuquerque: University of New Mexico Press, 2008).

10. *Socorro Chieftain*, 7 Dec 1907, 12 Sept 1908 and 19 Sept 1908.

11. See Toby Smith, *Coal Town, The Life and Times of Dawson, New Mexico* (Santa Fe: Ancient City Press, 1993) for a very readable account of life in the mines, the town and its people; Dewey Tidwell, "Dawson, A Personal Recollection," *New Mexico Magazine*, June 1981, pp 53–55; Letters: Cipriana Randolph to author, 12 Dec 1984 and 30 Oct 1985, CB/AC; Frank Vance and Will Dudley biography files; Frank Vance Murder Case File, NMMP/AC.

12. *Worley Directory-El Paso, Texas 1910*, p 123; Letter: Cipriana Randolph to author, 13 Dec 1982, CB/AC; *El Paso Evening Tribune*, 18 Oct 1893; "Child of C. Baca," *El Paso Times*, 9 Aug 1909; *Socorro Chieftain*, 14 Aug 1909; Letters: Cipriana Randolph to author, 13 Dec 1982 and 12 Jan 1983, CB/AC; *Socorro Chieftain*, 15 Feb 1908.

Chapter 18

1. "Has Been," Letter to Editor, *Silver City Independent*, 17 Sept 1910.

2. H.A. Hoover, *Tales from the Bloated Goat: Early Days in Mogollon* (El Paso: Texas Western Press, 1958), p 43.

3. "Cipriano Baca to Be Deputy at Mogollon," *Albuquerque Morning Journal*, 3 Sept 1910; Letter: Baca to Captain Fornoff, 31 Aug 1910, Letters Received, NMMP/NMSRCA; "Has Been," Letter to the Editor, *Silver City Independent*, 17 Sept 1910; "A New Deputy at Mogollon," *Socorro Chieftain*, 10 Sept 1910.

4. Letter: Baca to Fornoff, 6 Sept 1910, Letters Received, NMMP/NM-SRCA; *Minutes of the County Commissioners Socorro County*, 13 April 1912, County Clerk's Office, Socorro County Courthouse, Socorro; H.A. Hoover, *Tales from the Bloated Goat: Early Days in Mogollon* (El Paso: Texas Western Press, 1958) p 47.

5. Letter: Cipriana Randolph to author, 1 April 1984, CB/AC.

6. *Deming Graphic*, 2 Dec 1910; *Socorro Chieftain*, 3 Dec 1910.

7. Letter: Cipriana Randolph to author, 13 Dec 1982, CB/AC.

8. "Mogollon School," *Mogollon Mines*, Nov 1909, p 42.

9. Letter: Cipriana Randolph to author, 13 Dec 1982, CB/AC.

10. Letter: Cipriana Baca to Clyde E. Stauder, Jr., 2 Oct 1989, copy in CB/NMMP.

11. "Personal," *Silver City Enterprise*, 14 Nov 1911 and 15 Dec 1911.

12. Deed Book 77, p 39, County Clerk's Office, Socorro County courthouse, Socorro.

13. Letter: Cipriana Baca to Clyde E. Stauder, Jr., 2 Oct 1989, copy in CB/NMMP.

14. Mining Deed Book 76, p 159, County Clerk's Office, Socorro County Courthouse, Socorro.

15. *Santa Fe New Mexican*, 21 Aug 1911; "Key Historical Facts & Dates in New Mexico," *New Mexico Blue Book* (Albuquerque: Secretary of State's Office, 2006); Michael Jenkinson, "Bonanza in the Mogollons," *Frontier Times*, Aug–Sept 1971, p 60; "Bandits Run to Earth, One Killed, One Surrendered," 1 March 1912, "Convicted of First Degree Murder," 05 April 1912, "Will Hang May 3rd," 12 April 1912, "Personal," 13 Oct 1912, *Silver City Enterprise*; *Socorro Chieftain*, 13 April 1913.

16. Barbara Ehrenreich and Deirdre English, *Complaints and Disorders, The Sexual Politics of Sickness* (Old Westbury, NY: Feminist Press, 1973) pp 30–31, 38–39.

17. "Mrs. Cipriano Baca Dead," *Socorro Chieftain*, 16 March 1912; "Personal," *Silver City Enterprise*, 15 March 1912; Baca family records, CB/AC. Letters: Cipriana Randolph to Clyde E. Stauder, Jr., 2 Oct 1989, Cipriana Randolph to author, 10 Oct 1982, CB/AC; *Silver City Enterprise*, 21 June 1913; "Death of Mogollon Pioneer," *Silver City Enterprise*, 19 April 1912.

Chapter 19

1. H.A. Hoover, *Tales from the Bloated Goat: Early Days in Mogollon*

(El Paso: Texas Western Press, 1958) p 48; "Letter to the Editor," *Silver City Independent*, 17 Sept 1910; *Socorro Chieftain*, 23 Oct 1896; "'Shock' Simmons Shot to Death at Mogollon," *Albuquerque Morning Journal*, 27 May 1912; *Silver City Independent*, 28 May 1912; "Red Simmons Dies of Injuries," *Silver City Enterprise*, 31 May 1912; *Silver City Independent*, 4 June 1912; Mogollon Cemetery Archives.

2. *Silver City Enterprise*, 31 May 1912; "Big Strike at Mogollon," *Silver City Enterprise*, 21 June 1912.

3. "Personal," *Silver City Enterprise*, 6 Sept 1912; "Personal," *Silver City Enterprise*, 6 Dec 1912; "Personal," and "Alleged Bandits Walk into Trap Laid by Officers," *Silver City Enterprise*, 20 Dec 1912; *Santa Fe New Mexican*, 23 Dec 1912; "White and Harris Confess to Hold-Up," *Silver City Enterprise*, 27 Dec 1912; *Albuquerque Morning Journal*, 23 April 1913; "Las Cruces Local and Personal Notes," *The Rio Grande Republican* (Las Cruces), 23 June 1911; *Silver City Enterprise*, 14 June 1912; "Dr. Field and Family to Leave," Las Cruces *Republican*, reprinted in *Silver City Enterprise*, 23 Aug 1912.

4. Record Book L, Seventh Judicial District State of New Mexico, Cause 3669, pp 51–53, Clerk of the District Court, Socorro County Courthouse, Socorro; *Silver City Enterprise*, 27 Sept 1912.

5. Deed Book 73, pp 200–202, and Deed Book 77, pp 280–281, Mining Deed Book 79, p 7, County Clerk's Office, Socorro County Courthouse, Socorro; Letter: Cipriana Baca to Clyde E. Stauder, Jr., 2 Oct 1989, CB/AC; Letter to the Editor, Mogollon *Mines*, 13 March 1913.

6. Letters: Cipriana Randolph to author, 7 Sept 1982; Louise Baca to author, 12 Aug 1982; Cipriana Baca to Clyde E. Stauder, Jr., 2 Oct 1989, CB/AC.

7. William A. Degregorio, *The Complete Book of U.S. Presidents* (New York: Barricade Books, 1991) p 418.

8. "Cipriano Baca on Trial," *Silver City Enterprise*, 4 April 1913.

9. Colin Neblett biography file, CB/AC.

10. "Personal," *Silver City Enterprise*, 14 July 1912; "Purely Personal," *Silver City Independent*, 25 March and 8 April 1913.

11. Record Book L, Seventh Judicial District State of New Mexico, Cause 3669, pp 171, 181–182, 184, 187–188, Clerk of the District Court, Socorro County Courthouse, Socorro.

12. "County Division," *Mogollon Mines*, Nov 1909, p 19.

13. "Cipriano Baca Acquitted," *Silver City Independent*, 8 April 1913; "Baca Is Acquitted of Murder on First Ballot," *Albuquerque Morning Journal*, 3 April 1913; Record Book L, Seventh Judicial District State of New Mexico, Cause 3669, pp 187–188, Clerk of the District Court, Socorro County Courthouse, Socorro; "Baca Acquitted," *Silver City Enterprise*, 4 April 1913.

14. Kyle S. Crichton, *Law and Order, Ltd., The Life of Elfego Baca* (Santa Fe: New Mexico Publishing Corporation, 1928) p 3.

Chapter 20

1. Letter: Cipriana Randolph to author, 13 Dec 1982, CB/AC.

2. Letter: John Amos to author, 13 Oct 2006; expanded in a telephone conversation on 21 Oct 2006, CB/AC.

3. Letter: Cipriana Randolph to author, 1 April 1984, CB/AC; See Paige W. Christiansen, *The Story of Mining in New Mexico* (Socorro: New Mexico Bureau of Mines and Mineral Resources, 1974) for an account of this frontier industry.

4. F. Stanley, *The Blossburg [NM] Story* (Pantex, TX: Private, 1962), pp 3 and 20.

5. Conversation Notes: Coral Collier Horton and author, Tucson, AZ, 29 Jan 2006, NMMP/AC.

6. See Joe Huber, *The Story of Madrid, New Mexico* (Private Printing: ND) for a personal account of his family's involvement in the ownership of the town and the mining operation.

Chapter 21

1. "State of New Mexico ex rel. Fred Fornoff, Appellee vs. William G. Sargent, Auditor of the State of New Mexico, Appellant (18 N.M. 272) No 1623, 16 Oct 1913," *Journal Supreme Court of New Mexico*, January Term 1913, pp 271–281; Territorial/State Treasurer Records and Territorial/State Auditor Records, NMSRCA.

2. See Chuck Hornung, *The Thin Gray Line, The New Mexico Mounted Police* (Forth Worth, TX: Western Heritage Press, 1971) and *Fullerton's Rangers, A History of the New Mexico Territorial Mounted Police* (Jefferson, NC: McFarland, 2005) for a discussion of the Mounted Police Fund and the Phantom Force.

3. See Col. Frank Tompkins, *Chasing Villa, The Last Campaign of the U.S. Cavalry* (Harrisburg, PA: Military Service Publishing, 1934) for a comprehensive military account of the Punitive Expedition of 1916–1917.

4. See *Sabotage at Black Tom: Imperial Germany's Secret War in America, 1914–1917* (Chapel Hill, NC: Algonquin Books, 1989) by former *Washington Post* journalist Jules Witcover for a detailed account of this and other sabotage incidents.

5. Dean Smith, "The Zimmermann Telegram 1917," *American History Illustrated*, June 1978, pp 28–37.

6. Lansing B. Bloom (Ed.), *New Mexico in the Great War* (Santa Fe: El Palacio Press, 1927).

7. *Message of W.E. Lindsey, Governor of New Mexico, to the Third State Legislature in Special Assembled*, May 1, 1917 (Santa Fe: New Mexico Printing Co., 1917).

8. "Politics in Discard," *Silver City Enterprise*, 10 May 1918; Walter M. Danburg, "New Mexico in the Great War—The State Council of Defense," *New Mexico Historical Review*, vol. 1, no. 2, April 1926, p 118.

9. Conversation: Fred Lambert and the author, 29 June 1969, Cimarron, NM, NMMP/AC.

10. Oath of Office, NMMP Appointment File 1918, State War Council Records, NMSRCA.

11. Florentino Baca Biography File, CB/AC.

12. "Mogollon Is Hard Hit by Influenza," *Silver City Independent*, 22 Oct 1918. See Richard Melzer, "A Dark and Terrible Moment: The Spanish Flu of 1918 in New Mexico," *New Mexico Historical Review*, July 1982, pp 213–236, for an overview of this health crisis; "How to Dodge the 'Flu,'" *Albuquerque Morning Journal*, 1 Oct 1918; Bradford Luckingham, *Epidemic in the Southwest, 1918–1919* (El Paso: Texas Western Press, 1984) pp 18–28, for an overview of the flu in Albuquerque; H.A. Hoover, *Tales from the Bloated Goat: Early Days in Mogollon* (El Paso: Texas Western Press, 1958) p 34; *New Mexico Laws of 1919*, chapter 85, NMSRCA; Myrtle Greenfield, *A History of Public Health in New Mexico* (Albuquerque: University of New Mexico, 1962).

13. Mounted Police Captain's Department Reports 1906–1909 and 1918, NMMP/NMSRCA, *Magdalena News*, 13 May 1918.

14. Mounted Police File, Records of the State Council of Defense, Adjutant General Records 1918, NMSRCA.

15. Letter: Charles Springer to Captain A.A. Sena, 31 Jan 1919, Adjutant General Records 1919, NMSRCA; "Apollonio [sic] A. Sena New Police Captain," *Silver City Enterprise*, 10 Jan 1919; See Roberta Strauss Feuerlicht, *America's Reign of Terror: World War I, The Red Scare, and the Palmer Raids* (New York: Random House, 1971) for an overview of this dark chapter in America's social and political history.

16. Chuck Hornung, *The Thin Gray Line, The New Mexico Mounted Police* (Fort Worth, TX: Western Heritage Press, 1971) pp 67–71.

Chapter 22

1. Fourteenth Census of the United States 1920, Family 856 (John N. Parrott), Family 858 (John Reding), Pct. 22 (Tyrone), Grant County, Microfilm Roll 1076, NA.

2. Letters: Cipriana Randolph to author, 14 July 1984 and 12 December 1984, CB/AC; "Mrs. Cipriano Baca Dead," *Socorro Chieftain*, 16 March 1912; Conversation Notes: Louise Baca and author, 9 Nov 1996, CB/AC.

3. "2 Prisoners Confess Part in Butchering Stolen Cattle," *Gallup Independent* and *Carbon City News*, 17 July 1923; Deed Book 14, 13 Aug 1925, p 364, County Clerk's Office, Bernalillo County Courthouse, Albuquerque.

4. *Albuquerque City Directory*, 1922–1936, Southwest Collection, Albuquerque Public Library; Letter: John Amos to the author, 30 Oct 2006, CB/AC.

5. Conversion formula developed by the Mathematics Department of the University of Oregon; Comparison cost data from the Department of Commerce, Bureau of the Census Data Sheet.

6. Conversation Notes: Fred and Lois Fornoff, Jr., and the author and his wife, Fornoff Home, Albuquerque, NM, 23 March 1991, NMMP/AC.

7. Letter: Cipriana Randolph to the author, 13 Dec 1982, CB/AC.

8. Interview notes: Mrs. Jennifer Waite and author, 8 June 1968, Southwest Collection Room, Albuquerque Public Library, NMMP/AC; "Researchers: Tusks Most Complete, Best Preserved In New Mexico," *Midland* (TX) *Reporter-Telegram*, 28 February 2001.

Chapter 23

1. Robert Julyan, *The Place Names of New Mexico* (Albuquerque: University of New Mexico Press, 1996) pp 292, 352–353; T.M. Pearce (ed.), *New Mexico Place Names, A Geographical Dictionary* (Albuquerque: University of New Mexico Press, 1965) pp 133, 165.

2. Twelfth Census of the United States 1900, Family 337 (Pedro Montoya), Tierra Amarilla, Rio Arriba County, New Mexico Territory, Microfilm Roll 1001, NA; *Raton Range*, 10 July 1917; *Roswell Daily Record*, 11 July 1917; *Santa Fe New Mexican*, 12 July 1917; *Las Vegas Weekly Optic*, 14 July 1917; *Albuquerque Evening Herald*, 3 Aug 1918; Francisco Paiz-Manuelita Montoya Paiz genealogy information was provided by Adele Paiz Camacho via genealogical researcher Alexander King of Los Angeles to author, 25 Jan 2007; F. Stanley, *The Bland [NM] Story* (Pep, TX: Private, 1964), pp 5–8.

3. Fourteenth Census of the United States 1920, Family 195 (Manuelita Piez) and Family 857 (Cipriano Baca), Pct 22 (Tyrone), Grant County, New Mexico, Microfilm Roll 1076, NA; E-mail: Charles Jensen, a genealogist, to the author, 9 Aug 2006, CB/AC; Eloise Delinda Sanchez provided information on her mother Eva Paiz Sanchez to John Amos, 17 Oct 2005, CB/AC.

4. Letter: John Amos to author, 30 Nov 2006, CB/AC.

5. Letter: Alexander King to author, 16 Nov 2006, CB/AC.

Chapter 24

1. Fifteenth Census of the United States 1930, Family 287 (Jasper T. Hobbs), Bernalillo County, NM, Digital Print, NA.

2. Proof of Claim, Mrs. Manuelita Paiz, 1 Nov 1938, Estate of Cipriano Baca #4343, Probate Court, Bernalillo County Courthouse, Albuquerque, NM.

3. Letter: Cipriano Baca to Cipriana Randolph, 22 Aug 1936, copy in CB/AC; Exhibit A — Receipts, Estate of Cipriano Baca #4343, Probate Court, Bernalillo County Courthouse, Albuquerque, NM.

4. Cipriano Baca Death Certificate, 3071, Vital Records Unit, New Mexico Health and Social Services Department, Santa Fe; "Veteran Officer Dead," *Albuquerque Journal*, 23 Sept 1936.

5. Letter: Louise N. Baca to author, 12 August 1982; Telephone Conversation Notes: Louise N. Baca and author, 9 November 1996, CB/AC; "Cipriano Baca, New Mexico Lawman" was first published in the December 1981 issue of *Real West* and republished in the *Real West Yearbook*, 1982. It was the yearbook version that the Baca family first read.

6. King Vidor's classic motion picture *The Texas Rangers* staring Fred McMurray was playing in Albuquerque the day Cipriano Baca died.

Chapter 25

1. Baca-Berry-Paiz Family Information, Baca Data File, CB/AC.

Bibliography

I. Primary Published Sources: Books and Articles

Acts of the Legislative Assembly of the Territory of New Mexico, Thirty-Sixth Session 1905, New Mexico Coded Law 1905. Santa Fe: New Mexican, 1905.

Baca, Elfego. *Political Record of Elfego Baca and a Brief History of His Life*. Private, 1924.

Bishop, William Henry. "Across Arizona." *Harper's Monthly Magazine*, March 1883.

Bloom, Lansing B. *New Mexico in the Great War: Report of the Council of Defense*. Santa Fe: Historical Society of New Mexico, 1927.

Catron, Thomas B., and William T. Thornton (Eds.). *Railroad Laws of New Mexico*. Santa Fe: New Mexican Book, 1881.

Chase, C.M. *The Editor's Run: New Mexico and Colorado in 1881*. Reprint, Fort Davis, TX: Frontier Book, 1968.

City Directory of Albuquerque. NP, 1904.

Cleveland, Agnes Morley. *No Life for a Lady*. Boston: Houghton Mifflin, 1941.

Committee on Public Information. George Creel, chairman). *How the War Came to America*. Washington, DC: Government Printing Office, 1917.

Compiled Laws of New Mexico, 1884. Santa Fe: New Mexican, 1885.

Compiled Laws of New Mexico, 1897. Santa Fe: New Mexican, 1897.

Coroner's Inquest #117, 23 Feb 1883, County Clerk's Office, Cochise County Courthouse, Bisbee, AZ.

Destructive Floods in the United States in 1904, USGS Water-Supply and Irrigation Paper No. 147. Washington, DC: Government Printing Office, 1905.

Doyle, Sir Arthur Conan. "Sherlock Holmes: The Adventure of the Priory School," *Strand*, Feb 1904.

Fischer, Ron W. (Ed.). *The Tombstone Business Directory, 1880–1884*. Tombstone, AZ: Ron W. Fisher Enterprises, 2002.

French, William. *Some Recollections of a Western Ranchman, New Mexico, 1883–1899*. London: Methuen, 1927.

Frost, Max, and Paul A.F. Walter (Eds.). *The Land of Sunshine: A Handbook of the Resources Products, Industries and Climate of New Mexico*. Santa Fe: New Mexican, 1906.

Harris, Charles K. "Break the News to Mother" song and sheet music. New York: Chas. K. Harris, 1897.

Hagerman, H.J. *Report of the Governor of New Mexico to the Secretary of the Interior, 1906*. Washington, DC: Government Printing Office, 1906.

_____. *Message of Herbert J. Hagerman, Governor of New Mexico, to the 37th Legislative Assembly, January 21, 1907*. Santa Fe: New Mexican, 1907.

History of Contra Costa County. San Francisco: W.A. Slocum, 1882.

Hoover, H.A. *Tales from the Bloated Goat: Early Days in Mogollon*. El Paso, TX: Western Press, 1958.

Hovey, Walter. "Blackjack Ketchum Tried to Give Me a Break!," *True West*, April 1972.

Jaffa, Nathan (Compiler). *Acts of the Legislative Assembly of the Territory of New Mexico, 1909*. Santa Fe: New Mexican, 1909.

_____. *Report of the Secretary of the Territory, 1907–1908 and Legislative Manual, 1909*. Santa Fe: New Mexican, 1909.

Jones, Fayette. *New Mexico Mines and Minerals*. Santa Fe: Private, 1905.

Jones, William Cary. *Report of the Subject of Land Titles in California made in pursuance of the instructions from the Secretary of State and the Secretary of the Interior together with a translation of the Principal Laws on the Subject and some other papers relating thereto*. Washington, DC: Gideon, 1850.

Larrabee, William. *The Railroad Question*. Chicago: Schulte, 1893.

Lindsey, Washington E. *Message of the Governor to the Third State Legislature in Special Session Assembled, May 1, 1917*. Santa Fe: State Printing Office, 1917.

McIntosh, E.D. *Recollections of Mogollon*. Private, ND.

Martinez, Manuel (Compiler). *Laws of the State of New Mexico, 1919*. Albuquerque: Albright & Anderson, 1919.

_____. *The New Mexico Blue Book or State Official Register, 1919*. Albuquerque: Albright & Anderson, 1919.

Mills, William J. *Report of the Governor of New*

Mexico to the Secretary of the Interior, 1910. Washington, DC: Government Printing Office, 1910.

Neel, George M. (State Engineer). *Surface Water Supply of New Mexico, 1888–1925.* Santa Fe: State of New Mexico, 1926.

New Mexican Staff. *Holocaust at New Mexico State Penitentiary, Feb. 2–3, 1980.* Lubbock, TX: C.F. Boone, 1980.

New Mexico Coded Laws, 1905. Santa Fe: New Mexican, 1905.

Otero, Miguel A. *My Nine Years as Governor of the Territory of New Mexico, 1897–1906.* Albuquerque: University of New Mexico Press, 1940.

_____. *Report of the Governor of New Mexico to the Secretary of the Interior, 1902.* Washington, DC: Government Printing Office, 1902.

_____. *Report of the Governor of New Mexico to the Secretary of the Interior, 1904.* Washington, DC: Government Printing Office, 1904.

Pocket Map and Shipper's Guide of New Mexico. Chicago: Rand McNally, 1905.

Raynor, Ted (Ed.). *Old Timers Talk in Southwestern New Mexico.* El Paso: Texas Western Press, 1960.

Roosevelt, Theodore. *The Rough Riders.* New York: Scribner, 1898.

Schlatter, Francis, as told to Ada Morley. *The Life of Harp in the Hands of the Harper.* Denver, CO: Smith-Books, 1897.

Sears, Roebuck & Co. Catalogue, vol. 104, 1897; vol. 111, 1902; vol. 117, 1908. Chicago: Sears, Roebuck.

Smith, Dr. Adam. *An Inquiry into the Nature and Causes of the Wealth of Nations.* London: Methuen, 5th edition 1789, 1904 printing.

Tanner, Karen Holliday, and John D. Tanner, Jr. (Ed.). *New Mexico Territorial Penitentiary 1884–1912: Directory of Inmates.* Fallbrook, CA: Runnin' Iron, 2006.

Thornton, William T. *Report of the Governor to the Secretary of the Interior, 1895.* Washington, DC: Government Printing Office, 1895.

Tidwell, Dewey. "Dawson, A Personal Recollection." *New Mexico Magazine*, June 1981.

Twain, Mark (Samuel L. Clemens). *Early Tales & Sketches*, vol. 2, 1864–1865. NP: 1865.

_____. *Roughing It.* NP: 1872.

Wilson, Woodrow. *Address of the President of the United States Delivered at a Joint Session of the Two Houses of Congress, April 2, 1917.* New York: Edward J. Clode, Grossest & Dunlap, 1917.

II. Interviews Not Conducted by the Author

Walt Birchfield by J. Evert Haley, 2 Nov 1939, Haley Memorial Library, Midland, TX.

Mary Foraker by Larry D. Ball, 26 Aug 1976, Larry D. Ball Collection, State University, AR.

Mrs. Ed Pennington by Frances E. Tetty, 1 Aug 1938, WPA/NM, NA.

III. Author's New Mexico Mounted Police Collection and Archives (NMMP/AC)

Captain John F. Fullerton Papers and Photographs, Susan Fullerton Leverett Collection (copies).

Interview notes with Irene LaFont Fullerton and Susan Fullerton Leverett.

Captain Fred Fornoff Papers, Photographs, and Archives Collection.

Interview notes with Fred and Lois Fornoff, Jr.

Cipriano Baca Papers and Photographs, Cipriana Baca Randolph Collection (copies).

Interview notes with Cipriana Baca Randolph and Carrie Louise Nazarine Baca.

Berry-Baca-Stauder Family Photographs, Jim Stauder Collection (copies).

Interview notes with Jim Stauder.

Berry-Baca Family Genealogical Records, John Amos Collection (copies).

Interview notes with John Amos.

Manuelita Montoya-Paiz Family Genealogical Records, Alexander V. King Collection, (copies).

Fred Lambert Papers, Photographs and Archives Collection.

IV. Secondary Published Sources: Books

Ailman, H.B. (Helen Lundwall, Ed.). *Pioneering in Territorial Silver City, H.B. Ailman's Recollections of Silver City and the Southwest, 1871–1892.* Albuquerque: University of New Mexico Press, 1983.

Andrews, E. Benjamin. *History of the United States: From the Earliest Discovery of America to the End of 1902*, vol. 5, *1888–1902*; vol. 6, *1903–1912*. New York: Scribner, 1903.

Alexander, Bob. *Dangerous Dan Tucker: New Mexico's Deadly Lawman.* Silver City, NM: High-Lonesome Books, 2001.

_____. *Harvey Whitehill, Silver City Stalwart: An Old West Lawman on the New Mexico Frontier.* Silver City, NM: High-Lonesome Books, 2005.

Baldwin, Neil. *Henry Ford and the Jews: The Mass Production of Hate.* New York: Public Affairs, 2001.

Ball, Larry D. *Desert Lawmen: The High Sheriffs of New Mexico and Arizona, 1846–1912.* Albuquerque: University of New Mexico, 1992.

_____. *Elfego Baca in Life and Legend.* El Paso: Texas Western Press, 1992.

_____. *The United States Marshals of New Mexico and Arizona Territory, 1846–1912.* Albuquerque: University of New Mexico Press, 1978.

Beck, Warren A., and Ynez D. Haase. *Historical Atlas of New Mexico.* Norman: University of Oklahoma Press, 1969.

Brown, Nancy M. *Baca: Origenes Espanoles.* Belen, NM: Spanish History Museum, 1992.

Brown, Richard Maxwell. *No Duty to Retreat*. Norman: University of Oklahoma Press, 1991.

Bruner, Robert F., and Sean D. Carr. *The Panic of 1907: Lessons Learned from the Market's Perfect Storm*. Hoboken, NJ: Wiley, 2007.

Burton, Jeff. *Black Jack Christian: Outlaw*. Santa Fe: Press of the Territorian, 1967.

_____. *Bureaucracy, Blood Money and Black Jack's Gang*. London: English Westerners' Society Brand Book, Winter 1984 & Summer 1984.

_____. *Dynamite and Six-Shooter*. Santa Fe: Palomino Press, 1970.

Cazedessus, Camille E., II. *The Rough Riders and New Mexico*. Baton Rouge, LA: Rendezvous Books, 1994.

Chavez, Fray Angelico. *Origins of New Mexico Families: A Genealogy of the Spanish Colonial Period*. Santa Fe: Museum of New Mexico Press, 1992, Revised Edition.

Christiansen, Paige W. *The Story of Mining in New Mexico*. Socorro: New Mexico Institute of Mining and Technology, 1974.

Cleveland, Norman (Ed.). *The Healer: The Story of Francis Schlatter*. Santa Fe: Sunstone Press, 1989.

Clotworthy, William G. *Homes and Libraries of the Presidents*. Blacksburg, VA: McDonald and Woodward, 2003.

Crampton, C. Gregory, and Steven K. Madsen. *In Search of the Spanish Trail: Santa Fe to Los Angeles, 1829–1848*. Salt Lake City: Peregrine Smith Books, 1994.

Dary, David. *Frontier Medicine: From the Atlantic to the Pacific, 1492–1941*. New York: Knopf, 2009.

DeArment, Robert K. *George Scarborough: The Life and Death of a Lawman on the Closing Frontier*. Norman: University of Oklahoma Press, 2000.

Degregorio, William A. *The Complete Book of U.S. Presidents*, 3rd Edition. New York: Barricade Books, 1991.

Devereaux, Jan. *Pistols, Petticoats, & Poker: The Real Lottie Deno; No Lies or Alibis*. Silver City, NM: High-Lonesome Books, 2009.

Douglas, James, L.L.D. *Notes on the Development of Phelps, Dodge & Co's Copper and Railroad Interests, 1906*. Reprint, Bisbee, AZ: Frontera House Press, 1995.

Ehrenreich, Barbara, and Deirdre English. *Complaints and Disorders: The Sexual Politics of Sickness*. Old Westbury, NY: Feminist Press, 1973.

Esterly, Patricia Black (Compiler). *Census of 1821: New Mexico Province, Santa Fe Parrish*. Albuquerque: Mew Mexico Genealogical Society Inc., 1994.

Feuerlicht, Roberta Strauss. *America's Reign of Terror: World War I, the Red Scare, and the Palmer Raids*. New York: Random House, 1971.

Freidel, Frank. *The Splendid Little War*. Boston: Little, Brown, 1958.

Gjevre, John A. *Chili Line: The Narrow Rail Trail to Santa Fe*. Espanola, NM: Rio Grande Sun Press, 1971.

Greenfield, Myrtle. *A History of Public Health in New Mexico*. Albuquerque: University of New Mexico, 1962.

Holmes, Jack E. *Politics in New Mexico*. Albuquerque: University of New Mexico Press, 1967.

Hornung, Chuck. *Fullerton's Rangers: A History of the New Mexico Territorial Mounted Police*. Jefferson, NC: McFarland, 2005.

_____. *New Mexico's Rangers: The Mounted Police*. Charleston, SC: Arcadia, 2010.

_____. *The Thin Gray Line: The New Mexico Mounted Police*. Fort Worth, TX: Western Heritage Press, 1971.

Hunter, J. Marvin. *The Story of Lottie Deno: Her Life and Times*. Bandera, TX: 4 Hunters Press, ND.

Johns, A. Wesley. *The Man Who Shot McKinley: A New View of the Assassination of the President*. New York: Barnes, 1970.

Julyan, Robert. *The Place Names of New Mexico*. Albuquerque: University of New Mexico Press, 1996.

Langston, LaMoine. *A History of Masonry in New Mexico, 1877–1977*. Roswell, NM: Hall-Poorbaugh Press, 1978.

Larson, Robert W. *New Mexico's Quest for Statehood, 1846–1912*. Albuquerque: University of New Mexico Press, 1968.

Leech, Margaret. *In the Days of McKinley*. New York: Harper & Bros., 1959.

Linton, Calvin D. (Ed.). *The Bicentennial Almanac*. Nashville, TN: Thomas Nelson, 1975.

Luckingham, Bradford. *Epidemic in the Southwest, 1918–1919*. El Paso: Texas Western Press, 1984.

Metz, Leon Clair. *Pat Garrett: The Story of a Western Lawman*. Norman: University of Oklahoma Press, 1974.

Moore, Paula. *Cricket in the Web: The 1949 Unsolved Murder That Unraveled Politics in New Mexico*. Albuquerque: University of New Mexico Press, 2008.

Morris, Rodger. *The Devil's Butcher Shop: The New Mexico Prison Uprising*. Albuquerque: University of New Mexico Press, 1983.

Myrick, David F. *New Mexico Railroads: An Historical Survey*. Golden, CO: Colorado Railroad Museum, 1970.

Parish, William J. *The Charles Ilfeld Company: A Study of the Rise and Decline of Mercantile Capitalism in New Mexico*. Cambridge, MA: Harvard University Press, 1961.

Pearce, T.M. (Ed.). *New Mexico Place Names: A Geographical Dictionary*. Albuquerque: University of New Mexico Press, 1965.

Randle, Kevin D. "Aurora, Texas and the Great Airship of 1897." *Fate*, March 2003.

Rauchway, Eric. *Murdering McKinley: The Making of Theodore Roosevelt's America*. New York: Hill and Wang, 2003.

Remley, David. *Bell Ranch: Cattle Ranching in the Southwest, 1824–1947*, Revised Edition. Las Cruces, NM: Yucca Tree Press, 2000.

Schlesinger, Arthur M., Jr. (Gen. Ed.). *The Almanac of American History*, Revised and Updated Edition. New York: Barnes & Noble Books, 2004.

Sherman, James E., and Barbara H. Sherman. *Ghost Towns and Mining Camps of New Mexico*. Norman: University of Oklahoma Press, 1974.

Smith, Robert A. *A Social History of the Bicycle: Its Early Life and Times in America*. New York: American Heritage Press, 1972.

Sonnichsen, C.L. *Billy King's Tombstone*. Caldwell, ID: Caxton Printers Ltd., 1942.

Stanley, F. (Stanley Francis Louis Crocchiola). *The Bland [NM] Story*. Pep, TX: Private, 1962.

_____. *The Deming [NM] Story*. Pantex, TX: Private, 1963.

_____. *The Kelley [NM] Story*. Nazareth, TX: Private, 1973.

_____. *The Mogollon [NM] Story*. Pep, TX: Private, 1968.

Tanner, Karen Holliday, and John D. Tanner, Jr. *Directory of Inmates, New Mexico Territorial Penitentiary, 1884–1912*. Fallbrook, CA: Runnin' Iron, 2006.

_____. *Last of the Old-Time Outlaws: The George West Musgrave Story*. Norman: University of Oklahoma Press, 2002.

Tate, Bill (Compiler). *Treaty of Guadalupe Hidalgo of 1848 and the Gadsden Treaty of 1853*, Reprint from New Mexico Statutes 1963. Truchas, NM: Tate Gallery, 1967.

Thomas, Gordon, and Max Morgan Witts. *The San Francisco Earthquake*. New York: Stein and Day, 1971.

Torrez, Robert J. *Myth of the Hanging Tree: Stories of Crime and Punishment in Territorial New Mexico*. Albuquerque: University of New Mexico Press, 2008.

Townsend, Col. G. W. *Our Martyred President, Memorial Life of William McKinley*. New York: D.Z. Howell, 1901.

Wallechinsky, David, and Irving Wallace. *The People's Almanac*. New York: Doubleday, 1975.

Witcover, Jules. *Sabotage at Black Tom: Imperial Germany's Secret War in America, 1914–1917*. Chapel Hill, NC: Algonquin Books, 1989.

Young, Wood. *Vaca-Pena Los Putos Rancho and Pena Adobe*. Vallejo, CA: Wheeler Printing and Publishing, 1965.

V. Secondary Published Sources: Journal, Periodical and Newspaper Articles

Apostolides, Alex. "Mogollon, the Treasure Town." *New Mexico Magazine*, ND.

Armstrong, Ruth. "Mogollon, The Way It Was." *New Mexico Magazine*, ND.

Arutz Sheva, Israel National News. "Did King Solomon's Navy Discover America?," 17 Dec 2007.

Ashcroft, Bruce. "The July 1906 Earthquakes in Socorro." *New Mexico Historical Review*, Oct 1974.

Associated Press from Deming, NM. "Jail to Charge Booking, Bonding Fees." 28 December 1996.

_____. "Researchers: Tusks Most Complete, Best Preserved in New Mexico." 28 February 2001.

Associated Press from Santa Fe, NM. "Despite High Ranking, New Mexico Struggles to Rehabilitate Inmates." 30 December 1996.

_____. "New Mexico Tops Texas in Inmate Spending." 17 Jan 1997.

Associated Press from Santa Fe, NM. "NM Governor Acting to Move Prisoner Out of State Prisons." 21 February 1997.

Associated Press from Sunland Park, NM. "Dinosaur Tracks Found on Private Land near Mount Cristo Rey Base." 27 Jan 2003.

Associated Press from Washington, DC. "Study Finds Pig Roll in 1918 Flu Pandemic." 14 July 2009.

"The Automobiles of 1904," *Frank Leslie's Popular Monthly*, January 1904. Reprint, Scotia, NY: Americana Review, 1961.

Baker, J. Brad. "Every Moving Thing." *American Philatelist*, March 2002.

Bechdolt, Frederick. "Stories of the Old West, Tombstone's Wild Oats." *Saturday Evening Post*, Dec 1919.

Blaney, Betsy. "Man Gets 99 Years for Rustling." *Odessa (TX) American*, 26 Aug 2011.

Eidsmoe, Col. John. "The Ten Commandments and the Los Lunas Mystery Stone." Foundation for Moral Law website, posted 5 March 2010.

Fernlund, Kevin J. "Senator Holm O. Bursum and the Mexican Ring, 1921–1924," *New Mexico Historical Review*, October 1991.

Fincher, Jack. "America's Deadly Rendezvous with the 'Spanish Lady.'" *Smithsonian*, January 1989.

Galbraith, Den. "The Lost Ledge of Governor Otero." *True West*, March–April 1964.

Haddrill, Marilyn. "NM Trek Leads to Discovery of Mammoth Tusk." *Dallas Morning News*, 5 August 2001.

Hornung, Chuck. "Cipriano Baca, New Mexico Lawman." *Real West*, December 1981.

_____. "Cipriano Baca, New Mexico Peace Officer." *Journal of the Western Outlaw-Lawman History Association*, Spring 1997.

_____. "The Fornoff Report." Paper presented to the Sixth Western Outlaw-Lawmen History Association Convention, Craig, CO, 20 July 1996 (unpublished).

_____. "The Fornoff Report: New Light on the Death of Pat Garrett, *True West*, March 1998.

_____. "Surprising New Information on Pat Garrett's Death: Details from the Fornoff Report." *The Journal, Western Outlaw-Lawman History Association*, Spring/Summer 1997.

_____. "Wyatt Earp's New Mexico Adventures." *Old West*, May 1999.

———. "Cipriano Baca of the Mounted Police." *The Roadrunner*, Summer 2005.

———, and Gary Roberts. "The Split: Did Doc & Wyatt Split Because of a Racial Slur?" *True West*, December 2001.

Hunter, J. Marvin. "The Deming I Knew." *Frontier Times*, May 1944.

Jansen, Charles. "Cipriano Baca, Famous New Mexico Lawman, Grandson of New Mexico Born Founder of Vacaville, California." *New Mexico Genealogist*, December 2004.

Jenkinson, Michael. "Bonanza in the Mogollons." *Frontier Times*, Aug–Sept 1971.

Jones, Jeff. "Winter Storm Claims Lives of at Least 16, State Officials Say," *Albuquerque Journal*, 6 Jan 2007.

Kreiser, Christine M. "Influenza 1918, the Enemy Within," *American History*, December 2006.

Lyon, Fren. "Over Catron County Way." *New Mexico Magazine*, March–April 1972.

Navrot, Miguel. "Some Livestock Still Isolated by Snowdrifts." *Albuquerque Journal*, 4 Jan 1998.

Ortega, Jonathan A. "Vacaville, California Founded by New Mexico Baca Family." *Nuestras Raices: Journal of the Genealogical Society of Hispanic America*, Spring 1997.

Oshmier, Samuel. "Pilgrimage to New Mexico's Mystery Mountain." *Ancient America*, Feb 2006.

Paulson, Tom. "Research Suggests Real Killer in 1918 Flu: Immune System." *Houston Chronicle*, 15 October 2006.

Pokagon, Simon. "The Future of the Red Man." *Forum*, August 1897.

Reid, Harry Fielding. "Remarkable Earthquakes in Central New Mexico in 1906 and 1907," *Bulletin of the Seismological Society of America*, vol. 1, no. 1 (1911).

Smith, Dean. "The Zimmermann Telegram, 1917." *American History Illustrated*, June 1978.

Tanner, John D., Jr. "Violence in New Mexico Territory: A Penitentiary Analysis." *Western Outlaw-Lawmen History Association Journal*, Summer 2003.

Tidwell, Dewey. "Dawson: A Personal Recollection." *New Mexico Magazine*, June 1981.

Unruh, Bob. "Explained? New Mexico's Hebrew Ten Commandments." WorldNetDaily website, posted 18 March 2010.

Vanderpool, Tim. "What Became of the Mimbres?" *American Archaeology*, Fall 2007.

Winter, Joseph C. "Riddle of the Mysterious Rock." *Albuquerque Journal Magazine*, 12 June 1984.

VI. National Archives and Records Center, Washington, DC (NARC)

Seventh Census of the United States 1850, Solano County, CA.

Eighth Census of the United States 1860, Contra Costa County, CA.

Ninth Census of the United States 1870, Contra Costa County, CA, and San Francisco County, CA.

Tenth Census of the United States 1880, Pima County, AZ, and Yolo County, CA.

Twelfth Census of the United States 1900, Socorro County, NM, and Rio Arriba, NM.

Thirteenth Census of the United States 1910, El Paso County, TX, and Socorro County, NM.

Fourteenth Census of the United States 1920, Grant County, NM.

Fifteenth Census of the United States 1930, Bernalillo County, NM.

VII. New Mexico State Records Center and Archives, Santa Fe (NMSRCA)

Governor William T. Thornton Papers 1893–1897 (MF Rolls 103–128).

Governor Miguel A. Otero Papers 1897–1906 (MF Rolls 128–155).

Governor Herbert J. Hagerman Papers 1906–1907 (MF Rolls 156–163).

Governor George Curry Papers 1907–1910 (MF Rolls 164–180).

Governor William J. Mills Papers 1910–1912 (MF Rolls 181–189).

Governor Washington E. Lindsey Papers 1917–1918.

Governor Octaviano A. Larrazolo Papers 1919–1920.

House Journal 1905 and 1907 (MF Rolls 17 and 18).

Journal of the Council 1899 and 1905 (MF Rolls 13 and 17).

New Mexico Mounted Police Records 1905–1912 (MF Rolls 91–93).

New Mexico Mounted Police Records 1918–1921 (Department of Public Safety Records 1991–2004)

Report of the Standing Committee of the Council on Penitentiary Operations 1887.

New Mexico Territorial Census 1885 (MF Roll 40).

New Mexico Territorial Penitentiary Records 1884–1912.

New Mexico Fish and Game Warden Records 1905.

VIII. Texas State Library and Archives, Austin

Index Birth Records, El Paso County 1910, Bureau of Vital Statistics Records.

IX. Kansas State Historical Society, Topeka

E.P. Lamborn Papers, Special Collections.

X. Maritime Museum of British Columbia, Victoria

Records concerning the sinking of the steamship *Ivanhoe*.

XI. New Mexico State and County Records

Bernalillo County (Albuquerque): Deed Books; Probate Court File #4343.
Grant County (Silver City): Sheriff's Records, Marriage Register, Corporation Record Book 1.
Luna County (Deming): Proceedings of the Board of County Commissioner's Book 1, Deed.
Books, Bounty Records, Sheriff's Records, District Court Records.
Sierra County (Truth or Consequences) Deed Books.
Socorro County (Socorro): Marriage Records, Deed Books, District Court Records New Mexico Health and Social Services Department, Vital Records Unit, Santa Fe.
New Mexico Cattle Sanitary Board, Santa Fe.
New Mexico Supreme Court Law Library, Santa Fe.

XII. Center for Southwest Research, University of New Mexico (CSR/UNM)

Holm O. Bursum Collection and Papers.
Otero-Stinson Collection and Papers (506).
United States Marshal for New Mexico Territory Records.
William A. Keleher Papers MSS 742 BC.

XIII. The Haley Memorial Library and History Center, Midland, Texas

Brand Book of the Territory of New Mexico 1900.
New Mexico Old-Timers Interview Collection.

XIV. Private Record Collections

Burial Records, Knights of Pythias Lodge, Socorro, NM.
Perish Register, Church of the Epiphany, Socorro, NM.
Mogollon Cemetery Archives, Mogollon, NM.

XV. Deming-Mimbres Museum and Archives, Deming, New Mexico

Cipriano Baca newspaper clip file.
Old and New Mexico Improvement Company List of Purchasers Record Book.
Unknown mercantile company sales ledger, 1902–1904.

XVI. New Mexico Tech University Library, Socorro, New Mexico

Roll of Students, New Mexico School of Mines, 1900–1907.
New Mexico School of Mines Annual Bulletin.

XVII. Arizona County Records

Cochise County (Bisbee), Coroner's Inquest #117.

XVIII. New Mexico Newspaper Collections/Archives

Alamogordo Daily Journal
Alamogordo News
(Alamogordo) Otero County Advertiser
Albuquerque Daily Citizen
Albuquerque Evening Citizen
Albuquerque Evening Democrat
Albuquerque Morning Journal
Albuquerque Herald
Albuquerque Tribune
(Aztec) San Juan Index
Captain El Farol
Capitan News
Capitan Progress
(Carlsbad) The Pecos Valley Argus
Carrizozo Outlook/ Southwest Outlook
Clayton Citizen
Clayton Enterprise
Clayton News
Deming Graphic
Deming Headlight
Deming Herald
Deming Tribune and Lake Valley Herald
Estancia News
Farmington Enterprise
Gallup Independent and Carbon City News
(Hillsboro) Sierra County Advocate
Las Cruces Citizen
Las Cruces Independent Democrat
(Las Cruces) Rio Grande Republican
Las Cruces Sun-News
Las Vegas Daily Optic
Las Vegas Weekly Optic and Live Stock Grower
(Lordsburg) Western Liberal
Magdalena Mountain Mail
Magdalena News
Mogollon Mines
Nogal Republican
Portales Herald
Raton Range
Roswell Register
San Marcial Bee
Santa Fe New Mexican
Silver City Eagle
Silver City Enterprise
Silver City Independent
(Silver City) New Southwest and Grant County Herald
Silver City Southwest Sentinel
Socorro Chieftain
(Socorro) Industrial Advertiser
(Socorro/Chloride) Black Range
Tucumcari News and Tucumcari Times

(Tucumcari) *Quay County Democrat*
White Oaks Outlook

XIX. Additional Newspaper Collections

Aberdeen (SD) *Saturday Review*
Bodie (CA) *Daily Free Press*
Bodie (CA) *Morning News*
Chicago Tribune
Cincinnati (OH) *Post*
Detroit Free Press
Durango (CO) *Evening Herald*
El Paso Daily Herald
El Paso Evening Tribune
El Paso International Daily Times
(Globe City) *Arizona Silver Belt*
Kansas City (MO) *Journal*
Lubbock (TX) *Avalanche-Journal*
Midland (TX) *Reporter-Telegram*
Odessa (TX) *American*
Ozona (TX) *Kicker*
(Phoenix) *Arizona Republic*
Salt Lake City Tribune
San Angelo (TX) *Standard-Times*
San Francisco Daily Alta California
San Francisco Daily Morning Call
San Francisco Examiner
Seattle Press-Times
Seattle Telegram
(Solomonville, AZ) *Graham County Bulletin*
St. Johns (AZ) *Herald*
Tombstone (AZ) *Prospector*
(Tucson) *Arizona Daily Citizen*
(Tucson) *Arizona Weekly Star*
Vellejo (CA) *Chronicle*
Washington Post

Index

Numbers in ***bold italics*** indicate pages with illustrations

Abeyta, Abram 77, 93
Abeyta, Aniceto C. 83, 175
Abiquiu, NM 130
Adams, Rev. S.L. 87
Adamson, Carl 186, 189–190
Alama, NM 81, 197
Alameda Arroyo, Dona Ana County, NM 185
Alamogordo, NM 142, 168, 173
Albuquerque, NM (The Duke City) 8, 9, 10, 74, 84, 85, 86, 92, 116–117, 130, 133, 137, 144, 148, 151–153, 157, 169–170, 180, 229–230, 237–238, 240–241, 249–251, 255
Allardyce, Edward 48
Alvarado-Baca, Maria Lugarda Susana 22, 33
Alverson, Leonard 72
Amos, Alexander 219
Amos, Joan ***247***
Amos, John 2, 219, 240, ***247***, 248–249
Amos, John Pierpont 256
Amos, Ruth ***247***
Ancestors 3–5
Ancheta, J.A. 45, 93
Anderson, Charles 114
Anton Chico, NM 160, 162
Apache Kid (Zenogalache) 151
Apodaca, Francisco 142
Arizona 89, 118, 139, 142, 164, 170, 183
Arizona Rangers 91, 139, 142, 147, 164
Arthur, Chester A. 18
Ashenfelter, S.M. 31, 52
Atchison, Topeka and Santa Fe Railway/Railroad 17, 19, 20, 26, 55, 73, 74, 102, 135, 148, 163, 175, 177, 184, 190, 221, 238, 251
Atkin, Dave 72
Atlantic and Pacific Railroad 56, 154
Avant, L.F. "Fate" (NMMP) 141, 151
Aztec, NM 149

Baca, A.B. 66, 67
Baca, Cipriano *ix*, *x*; Arizona adventures 12–18; boyhood 3–11; Deming businessman 19–32; deputy U.S. marshal 63–74, 132–138; detective/city marshal 180–194; election lost and wife's death 45–53; family life 87–93; family troubles 219–222; Grant County officer 33–45; last days 251–255; Luna County sheriff 104–132; Mary Berry 75–80; Mogollon 54–62, 195–205; Mounted Police 139–179, 223–234; murder trial 206–218; mystery family 244–250; prison guard 94–99; rambler 235–243; Silver City 100–103
Baca, David 63
Baca, Dolores Juana (Lola) 7, 25
Baca, Elfego 73, 82, 83, 84, 84–86, 171, 217
Baca, Estevan 81
Baca, Eva (I) 15, 206
Baca, Eva (II) 99, 102, 113, 116, 117, 118, 120, 206
Baca, Florentino 7
Baca, Florentino Berry "Uncle Forsty" 14, 65, 76, 130, ***183***, 187, 200, ***201***, 214, 219–222, 229–230, ***239***, 241, 246, 249, 253–254, 257
Baca, Gilberson (George) "Gillie" Briones 91, 99, 102, 111–112, 117, 125, 129, ***183***, 200, ***201***, 206, 214, 219, ***239***, 257
Baca, James "Jimmy" 191, 194, 206
Baca, Jose Manuel 22, 23, 33
Baca, Jose Sosteno 163
Baca, Justiano 82
Baca, Lenandro 81–85, ***82***, 167, 173–174, 181
Baca, Maria de Jesus 7
[unknown]-Baca, Mary (Cipriano's wife #1) 14, 15
Baca, Mary Ann 176, 182, 206
Baca, Maximiano 7
Baca, Misais 83, 174–175
Baca, Patricio 22, 23, 34
Baca, Placido de Jesus 7
Baca, Prudenciana (I) 7
Baca, Prudenciana (II) 7
Baca, R.L. 129
Baca, Ruby Hamilton 144, 168–169, 176, 182, 206

Baca, Sallie 101, 102, 113, 117, 120, 206
Baca, Sally Gilberson 8
Baca, Teodoro 14, 22, 23
Baca, Teofilo Clark 204, 205–207, 236
Baca-Amos, Maisie Hill 2, 176, ***183***, 214, ***239***, 249, 256
Baca-Lonergan, Rachel Encarnacion 194, ***201***, 206, 214, 219, 257
Baca-Pena, Luisa (Louise) 7
Baca-Pena, Maria Fidelena Manuela (Illena) 7, 25
Baca-Randolph, Cipriana (Ann) *ix*, 9–18, ***14***, 64–66, 69, 79, 92, 112–113, 115, 120, 125, 129, 133, 141, 143, 169–171, 178, ***183***, 192–194, 200, ***201***, 202, 205–206, 212–214, 219–221, 236, ***237***, 241, 244, 248–249, 252–253, 255–256, 256
Baca-Walker, Maria Jovita 7, 10, 15, 92, 124, 253
Baca Ranch at Palomas 22
Bandelier, Adolph 134
Barilla, Amada 172
Beal, John A. (NMMP) 189, 195, 197, 209–210, 215
Behan, John 70
Belcher, George, and wife 67, 68
Belen, NM 84, 90
Bennett, P.J. 23, 105
Bergman, E.H. 96
Bernal y Vaca, Maria Dolores 4
Bernalillo, NM 248
Bernalillo County, NM 84, 85, 133, 160, 240, 251
Berry, James Fielding, Jr. 77, ***78***, 102, 185, 214, 257
Berry, James Fielding, Sr. 75, 76
Berry-Baca, Mary Ann "Mamie" (Cipriano's wife #3) 65, 70, 75–80, ***78***, 87, 99, 101–102, 111–112, 116, 117, 119, 125–126, 129–130, 138, 144, 150, 166, 169–172, 174–177, 194, 198, 200, ***201***, 202, 204–207, 215, 236, 252–253, 256
Berry-Edelen, Pearl Thompson ***78***, 79, 102, 123, 175, 214
Berry-Griffith, Ruby Hamilton 77,

281

Index

78, 98, 99, 102, 116–117, 144, 153, 204–205, 214
Berry-Hill, May Lincoln "Maisie" 76, **78**, 123
Berry-Stauder, Effie Hunter x, **78**, 79, 99, 102, 120, 194, 203, 214, 219, 241, 249, 256
Biavaschie, G. 63
Bicycle-horse race 30–32
Big Four Regiment (USVI) 89
Billy the Kid 84, 85, 127, 187
Birchfield, Walt 35
Blackington, Dr. Charles F. 81
Bland, NM 245
Blonger, Sam, and Lou 121
Bloomfield, NM 149
Blossburg, NM 221
Bodie, CA 26, 28
Bolton, gambler 30
Boxer Revolt in China 90
Brazel, Jessie Wayne 186–190
Bridges Jeffrey x
Briones, Don Felope Santiago 7
Briones y Vaca, Maria de la Encarnacion 6, 7, 9
Brocius, William "Curly Bill" 13, 21
Brogan, W.F. 178
Brooks, Henry C. (NMMP) 197
Brophy, John (NMMP) 142, 143, 152, 162–163, 166
Brown-Martinez, Nancy x
Burch, Robert (NMMP) 173–174
Burk, Michael 110
Burkdoll, A.R. 130
Burke, W.S. 178
Bursum, Mrs. H.O. (Lulu M. Moore) 58, 96
Bursum, Holm Olaf 56, 57, 58, 60, 61, 64, 66, 71, 82, 90, 91, 93–99, **97**, 123, 130, 165–166, 170–171, 202
Bursum Road 58, 60

Calderon, Encarnacion 177
Calles, Andres **101**, 102
Capitan, NM 141, 168
Carper, Frank 96
Carrizalillo Springs, NM 114
Casaus, NM 159, 163, 175
Casey, John E. 235
Catron, Thomas Benton 92
Catron County, NM 84
Chama, NM 79, 241, 249
Chapin, Dr. Charles V. 231
Chase, C.M. 16, 21, 22, 29
Chaves, Col. J. Francisco 181–182
Chaves, Monico 163
Chaves County, NM 190
Chavez, Elisio 160
Childers, J.N. 51
China/Chinese 92, 111, 122, 133, 187, 190, 193
Chloride, NM 151
Christian brothers 68, 69, 70, 100
Cimarron, NM 193, 224
Civil War 88
Clanton, Billy 27, 28
Clark, Ben 67, 70

Clark, Charley 195, 197, 209–210
Clark, Peter 202, 204–205
Clayton, Jeff W. 30
Clayton, NM 142, 162–163
Cleaveland, Agnes Morley 60
Clements, Emanuel "Mannie" 190
Clifton, AZ 68, 69
Cochise County, AZ, Cow-boys 1, 13, 16, 17, 18, 70
Cody, William F. "Buffalo Bill" 121, 124–126, 126
Colfax County, NM 191
Collier, Lt. John Wesley (NMMP) 38, 166, 172, 197, 221
Colorado 170, 193, 221
Colson, David 116
Columbus, NM 33, 36, 121, 225
Contreras, Leopoldo 56, 81
Coogler, Ovida "Cricket" 190
Coolidge, President Calvin 63, 238
Cortesy, Mary Carman 78, 185, 257
Courtright, Isaiah "Long-Haired Jim" 24
Cox, Okie 116
Cox, "Salty John" 35, 36
Cox, William W. 186, 189–190
Craig, Dwight 173
"Crazy Molly" 123
Crichton, Kyle S. 84
Cripple Creek, CO 221
Crockett, Davy 86
Cuba 87–90, 117, 125
Culberson, Vic 39
Cullin, Ed 72
Curry, Governor (NM) George 83, 89, 98, 182, 187–190
Curver, Will 72

Darbyshire, Bill 184
Datil, NM 91, 155, 169
Dawson, NM 175, 191–193, 200
Delgado, Captain Lorenzo (NMMP) 233
DeMier, John R. 96
Deming, NM 1, 17, 19, 20, 22, 25, 26, 27, 34, 40, 47, 51, 52, 55, 78, 102–104, 106–109, 114–115, 119, 120, 122, 129, 184, 198, 204, 243, 245
Deming earthquake 30
Deming Meat Market 23
Demosthenes 211
Denver & Rio Grande Railroad (The Chili Line) 135, 154, 184, 245
Diamond A Ranch (Victoro Land and Cattle Company) 35
Dona Ana County, NM 72, 82, 93, 103, 135, 186
Douglas, AZ 129, 168, 170
Drake, Dr. E.A. 174
Dudley, William E. "Will" (NMMP) 142, 143, 166, 168, 193, 241
Duff, U. Francis 79
Durango, CO 149
Earp, Morgan 13, 17, 27, 70

Earp, Virgil 27, 70
Earp, Wyatt 1, 13, 14, 17, 18, 23, 27, 29, 70, 121, 221
Eaton, Col. Ethan D. 63
Eaton, Nestor P. 63
Edelen, Alexander Walter 79, 175, 214
El Paso, TX 20, 84, 129, 170, 173, 183, 185, 193–194, 197–198, 200
El Paso and Northeastern Railroad 190–191
El Paso and Northwestern Railroad 183
El Paso and Southwestern Railroad 114, 182–185, 193
El Pueblo de la Ascencion de Jesus, Mexico 33, 34, 60
Elephant Corral and Livery Stable, Deming, NM 25, 26, 30
Elkins, George (NMMP) 142, 143, 147
Embudo, NM 135–136
Estancia, NM 142, 163, 172–173, 176, 240
Everett, WA 47

Fall, Albert Bacon 187–190
Fergusson, Harvey B. 52
Field, Dr. W.C. 188, 211
Finley, John 114
Fitch, James G. 77, 174–175
Fleishman 22
Florida Mountains 115
Fluri, Flora 43
Folger, Allan P. 48
Foraker, Charles 133
Foraker, U.S. Marshal Creighton M. 70, 71, 72, 91, 92, 106, 111, 121, 130, 132–133, 135, 138
Foraker, Mary 133
Forbes, William R. 130
Fornoff, Captain Fred (NMMP) 1, 74, 83, 88, 111, 116, 127, 130, 141, 143, 151, 156, 172–173, 176–180, 186–190, **187**, 197–199, 210–211, 223–224, 228–229, 231–232, 238, 240–241
Fornoff, Fred, Jr., and Lois 241, **242**
Fort Bayard, NM 41
Fort Defiance, AZ 154
Fort Griffin, TX 121
Fort Wingate, NM 148, 170
Foster, James E. 46
Foster, William H. "Billy" 127–128
Fountain, Col. Albert Jennings, and Henry 59, 188
Fowler, Charles 67
Frank, Lori x
Franklin, Benjamin 33, 44, 51, 119, 227
Frazier, William 169
French, William 68, 69
Fronteras, Mexico 71
Fullerton, Capt. John Ferguson (NMMP) x, 1, 63, 68, 117, 141–**144**, 146, 148–156, 159–165, 228–229, 231–232, 241
Fuss, Ron, and Pat x

Index

Gallegos, Louis 169
Gallegos, S. 121, 123
Gallup, NM 148, 238, 246
Galusha, Jandon R. (NMMP) 238, 240
Garcia, Miguel 169
Garcia, Victoriano 169
Garfield, President James A. 15
Garrett, Patrick Floyd 1, 85, 127, 185–190, *186*, 211
Gilberson, Charles Malchus 75
Gilberson, Mary Ann Lord 75, 182, 191, 219
Gilberson-Berry, Sallie Bonham 75, *78*, 102, 126, 144, 172, 174–175, 204–205, 213–214, 219, 229, 248, 256
Gilliland, Jim 189
Glaze, Ezra M., and Oliver 174
Globe, AZ 114
Gomez, Miguel 43
Gomez, Nestor 43
Gomez, Rafael (NMMP) 158, 161, 163
Gonzales, Ruperto 169
Good, John 36
Goodell, Arthur S. 100, 102, 103
Gosper, Governor (AZ) John J. 17
Granado, Francisco 203
Grant, Frederic J. 48, 50
Grant, President Ulysses S. 108–109, 129
Grant County, NM 20, *37*–39, 42, 44, 57, 100–103, 105, 106, 142, 147, 152, 163, 166, 210, 228, 235–237
Grants, NM 176
"Great Nut Rustling Caper" 131
Green, Judge Amos E. 173
Green, J.H. 120
Green, Dr. R.R. 136–137
Greer, William H. 110, 113, 117, 120, 126, 140, 147, 151
Griffin, Captain Edward D. 47, 48, 49
Griffin, William E. (NMMP) 89
Griffith, John Ellsworth 77, 144, 153, 171, 175, 211, 214, 216
Griffith, William Ellsworth 76
Guadalupe County, NM 153, 158–163
Guam 90

Hachita, NM 114, 142, 184
Hagerman, Governor (NM) Herbert J. 82, 85, 97, 98, 150, 159, 161–162, 163, 165, 167, 173–175, 178, 180–181, 233
Hall, U.S. Marshal Edward L. 68, 76, 100
Hall, H.S. 174
Hall, Williard "Will" Berry
Hannett, Doctor J.W. 252
Hannigan, Robert 163
Harding, President Warren G. 190, 238
Harris, A.B. 161
Harris, Jim 208, 210

Hasty, George A. 87
Hawkins, Ashton 190
Hayes, President Rutherford B. 108–109
Heaply, Scott 203
Hearst, George, and Phoebe 121
Hearst, William Randolph 120
Herman, Henry "Uncle Harry" 61, 212
Hermanas, NM 114, 123, 184
Hervey, Attorney General (NM) James M. 186, 189
Higgins, Dan 67
Higgins, Fred (NMMP) 68
Hill, Dorothy Ardis
Hill, Willard Homer 175
Hixenbaugh, Abe, and Nora 221
Hobbs, Jasper T. 251–252–253
Hodgon, J.H. 119
Hoffman (Hovey), Walter 72
Holgate, Henry 35
Holliday, Dr. John Henry 27, 121
Holliman, Bob 164, 168
Holmes, Sherlock 120, 133, 136, 207, 251, 257
Holt, Herbert B. 190
Hoover, Herman A. 197, 199, 207
Hoover, Ike 115
Hot Springs (Truth or Consequences), NM 249
Hough, Emerson 189
Hubbell, Felipe 240
Huber, Charles Richard "Windy Dick" (NMMP) 142–143, 152, 161, 166, 169, 182, 241
Huber, Oscar 222
Hughes, Jim 111, 113–114, 116, 118–119
Hund, John 125
Hunter, J. Marvin 106, 245
Hutchinson, W.R. 128

Ilfeld, Charles 158–160
Indian Territory 89, 118, 137
Indian troubles 29, 153–157
Isleta Pueblo, NM 134, 156
Ivanhoe (ship) 48–50

James, Emil 203, 206–207, 211, 216
Jemez Pubelo, NM 156
Jensen, Charles x
Johnson, J.R. 52, 116, 118
Johnson, William "Kid" 90–91
Jones, James 127
Jones, W.W. 58
Jurado, Ysidoro 202, 210

Kaseman, George A. 133–134, 222
Keefe, Edward 26
Keefe, Katherine (Kate) 26, 28, 29, 33, 47, 50
Keefe, Sherry 26, 47, 50
Keefe, Dr. Thomas 26, 27, 28, 29, 33, 47, 50
Keefe-Baca, Mary Linda (Marie) (Cipriano's wife #2) 26, 29, 30, 32, 33, 34, 39, 44, 45–50, 54, 101, 206
Keene, Billy 151

Keleher, William A. 176
Kelly, NM 73, 76, 87
Kephart, T.S. 72
Kern, Dr. B.C. 209, 217
Ketchum, Thomas "Black-Jack" 67–68, 72
Kilburn, William Harvey 38
King, Alexander x, 244, 249
Kinnear, John D. (Arizona Mail and Stage Line) 14
Kittner, NM 176
Knight, Richard S. "Dick" 42, 46
Knights of Pythias 27, 40, 112, 221

Laguna Pubelo, NM 157
Laird, Andrew B. 27, 34, 39–44, 51
Lake Valley, NM 24
Lambert, Fred (NMMP) x, 102, 145–146, 193, 224, 228
Lamy Junction, NM 176
Larrabee, William 184
Larrazolo, Governor Octaviano A. 231–232
Las Cruces, NM 72, 92, 116, 135, 166, 173–174, 176, 185–186, 190
Las Vegas (The Meadows City), NM 57, 77, 117, 151–153, 157, 162, 232, 241
Lee, Minnie 34–35
Lee, Oliver 189
Lee, General Robert E. 64, 157, 191, 256
Leeson, Mrs. J.J. 171
Lewis, Alfred Henry 120
Lewis, Sgt. Robert W. "Stuttering Bob" (NMMP) 83, 141–143, 146, 153, 159, 164, 167, 174, 176, 220
Lillie, Gordon "Pawnee Bill" 126
Lincoln, President Abraham 75
Lincoln, NM 168
Lincoln County, NM 168, 189, 202
Lindauer, Albert 25
Lindsey, Governor Washington E. 224, 227–228
Lockhart, Col. James A., and George 25, 34, 35, 38–39
Loggia, Robert 86
London, Jack 172
Lone Ranger and Tonto 255
Lonergan, Arthur 257
Loomis, A.J. 43
Loomis, H.W. "Will" 68
Lopez, Felipe 186
Lopez, Manuel 186
Lopez-Baca, Mariana 22
Lordsburg, NM 38, 41, 51–52, 142, 144
Lowe, J.A. 212, 216
Lucero, Liborio 160
Luna, Maximiliano 90
Luna, Salomon 102, 104
Luna County, NM 1, 20, 23, 88, 102–106, 109–111, 119, 121–123, 127, 129–131, 184, 200

MacDonald, Allan 52
MacVeigh, Attorney General Wayne 16

Madrid, NM 222, 229, 246, 249
Magdalena, NM 61, 76, 81, 157, 169, 174–175
Magnum brothers 149–*151*
Mahoney, J.A. 113–114
Mann, Supreme Court Justice (NM) Edward A. 175, 210, 212
Margeson, Reverend 26
Marriott, Charles W. 198
Marshal, Henry 72
Martinez, Contra Costa County, CA 3, 4, 8
Martinez, Pilar 163
Masterson, William B. "Bat" 121
Maynard, Hiland D. 190
McCabe, John 144
McDermott, P.H. 46
McDonald, Governor William C. 202, 223–224, 240
McFle, Judge John R. 135, 137
McGalloway, Frank 100
McGilinchy, Frank 40, 109
McGinnis, William (Elzy Lay) 98
McGrath, Capt. Herbert (NMMP) 13, 142–143, 151, 153, 210, 215, 228–*229*, 231–232, 235, 241
McGrath, P.J. 26
McHughes, John H. (NMMP) 238, 240
McIntosh, Ernest D. 62, 169, 198, 203
McIntyre, Isaac "Jim" 24
McKeyes, B.Y. 105, 127
McKinley, First Lady Ida Saxton 108–109, 115
McKinley, President William 62, 69, 87–89, 107–109, 113, 115–116, 125, 126, 254
McKinley County, NM 148–149, 238
McLaury, Tom, and Frank 27–28
McMahan, Thomas 113
McNew, William Henry "Bill" 188–189
Mechem, Governor (NM) Merritt C. 84, 161, 212, 215, 233
Merrill, W.R. 105
Mesilla, NM 145
Mexican Rurales 147
Meyer, Julius (NMMP) 142–143, 148–151, 154–156, 158, 161, 163, 175, 182, 241
Miller, James "Decan Jim" 189
Mills, Governor (NM) William J. 84, 203
Milton, Jeff 72
Mimbres River Cattle Company 23, 24, 30, 38
Mine labor riots/strikes 42, 48, 246
Mining "Homestead" Act 129–130
Mogollon, NM 54, *55*, 56–58, 60, 68, 80, 97, 133, 151, 164, 195–200, *196*, 206–207, 210, 220, 230, 236
Monroe, R.W. 69
Montes, Inez 172–173
Montoya-Paiz, Manuellita *ix*, *x*, 237, 244–252, 257

Moore, Clement C. 157
Moore, M.P. 40
Mora, NM 130, 176
Morales, Benito 41
Morley, Mrs. William Raymond (Ada McPherson) 59
Morris, Ed 120
Mullin, Mrs. Dr. Irene 47–48
Murray, George Fred (NMMP) 83, 88, 176
Musgrave, George 68, 72

Nazarine-Baca, Carrie Louise 99, 130, 236, *249*, 253
Neblett, Judge Colin 210, 215–217
Nevada mining camps 28
New Mexico Cattle and Horse Growers' Association 139, 159, 189, 228
New Mexico Cattle Sanitary Board 228, 237
New Mexico Mounted Police *x*, 13, 71, 83, 84, 91, 93, 102, 108, 117, 138–182; arrest card 177, 185–189, 195, 197, 199, 209–210, 215; Company III 231–233, 238, 240, 248, 253–255; guidon 152; phantom force 221–224; uniform and badge *140*, 141, *166*, 176, 179; war time 225–231
New Mexico National Guard 143, 228
New Mexico Penitentiary 1, 94–99, 120
New Mexico Territorial Fair (Albuquerque) 151–153
Newcomb, W.H. 46
Northern New Mexico Territorial Fair (Las Vegas) 151–153

Oakes, H.L. 43
Oakley, Annie (Phoebe Ann Mosy, Mrs. Frank Butler) 124–125
O'Donel, Charles M. (Bell Ranch) 158–159, 162–163, 166
Oglesby, T.L. 122
Oklahoma 89, 118, 176
Olsen, Clara 98, 102, 179
Otero, Don Miguel A., Sr. 17
Otero, Governor (NM) Miguel A., Jr. 17, 27, 69, 77, 83, *88*, 89, 93, 94, 97, 99, 101–106, 109, 113, 117, 126, 128, 129–130, 138, 140–141, 143, 151–153, 158–159, 165, 203
Otero, Page Blackwood (NMMP) 154–156, 188, 241
Otero County, NM 142, 168, 173

Paiz, Francisco 244–246
Paiz-Sanchez, Eva *ix*, 244, 246, 249, 250, 257
Panic of 1893 40, 42
Parham, Dr. Edward Manson 204
Parker, Judge Frank W. 112, 119, 122, 188
Parrott, John N. (NMMP) 235
Pennington, Ed, and wife 19, 20, 24, 29, 105, 128

Perea, Octaviano (NMMP) 142–143, 148–149, 166
Perkins, Rev. H.M. 168
Perrault, George O. 46
Phelps-Dodge Corporation 182–185, 191–193, 220, 235
Philippine Islands 90
Phoenician Inscription Rock 134
Phoenix, AZ 36, 118
Pima County, AZ 12
Pinos Altos, NM 42
Pipkin, Daniel "Red" 68
Pokagon, Pottawatomie Tribal Chief Simon 153
Pomroy, Evertt B. 16
Portales, NM 137, 177
Porter, H.M. 173
Porterfield, Judge 51
Potter, Dell M. 51–52
Prichard, Attorney General (NM) George 161
Puerto Rico 90
Putman, Robert "Bob" (NMMP) 147, 167, 173, 176, 195, 197, 209–210, 215

Quey County, NM 161–162, 169, 215
Quick, Harry 120

Raithel 23
Ramah, NM 149, 154
Ramsey, Alexander 108
Ranchos de Taos, NM 137
Randolph, Margaret Ann *247*, 248–249, 252–253
Randolph, Walter 12, 241, 248–249, 253, 256
Raton (The Gate City), NM 126, 170, 184, 192, 221–222
Ray, Charles "Poney Diehl" 13
Raynolds, Acting Governor (NM) J.W. 83, 143, 158, 182
Reding, John 235
Reed, Rosa (Pearl Starr) 168
Reserve (Frisco Plaza), NM 84–85
Rhodes, A.P. "Paint" 189
Richardson, Granville A. 139–140
Rinco, NM 176
Ringo, John Peters 17–18
Rio Arriba County, NM 79, 153, 244–245
Rio Grande 26, 81, 134, 163, 245, 249
Rio Puerco 134
Robinson, Clarence A. 82
Rock Island Railroad 183
Rodeo, NM 114
Rodey, Hon. Bernard S. 123
Roman, Arturo *x*
Romero, Gregorio 160
Romero, Santiago, Jr. *x*
Roosevelt, President Theodore 42, 83, 88–89, 116–117, 127, 151, 153, 165
Roosevelt County, NM 177
Rosch, Julius 114
Rose, Will 42

Roswell, NM 139
Rough Riders (1st U.S. Volunteer Cavalry) 89–90, 98, 117, 176
Royal Canadian Northwest Mounted Police 143
Rusk, John B. "Slim" (NMMP) 101, 194; death of 203, 241
Rynning, Capt. Thomas Harbro (Arizona Rangers) 142

Sadler, Quinn 185, 193, 197
St. John, Walter 120–121
St. Joseph's Sanatorium and Hospital 252–253
St. Louis, Rocky Mountain and Pacific Railroad 222
Salsbury, Nat 125
San Antonio, NM 177–178
San Felipe Pubelo, NM 156
San Francisco, CA 4, 47–48
San Francisco eathquake 8–9, 167
San Juan County, NM 83, 148–150, 154
San Marcial, NM 77
San Miguel County, NM 158–160, 162, 233
Sanchez, Eloise ix
Sanchez, Geronimo E. "George" 195, 197–198, 206
Sanchez, Manuel 123
Sanchez y Baca, Felipe 161
Sandoval County, NM 245
Sanford, Alonzo 12, 13
Santa Fe (The Ancient City), NM 92, 94, 102, 119, 137, 144, 163, 166–167, 172, 176, 180, 223–224, 240
Santa Fe Central Railroad 176
Santa Fe County, NM 94, 99, 129
Santa Rosa, NM 160–161, 183
Sargent, William G. 194, 223–224, 241
Scarborough, George 35, 72
Schlatter, Francis "The Healer" 59, 60
School of Mines, Socorro, NM 78, 79
Sears, Roebuck & Company 69
Seattle, WA 47
Secret Service (U.S. Treasury Department) 88, 108, 130
Sena, Captain Apolonio A. (NMMP) 232–233, 238
Separ, NM 36, 41
Serna, Dolores 120
Shakespeare, George L. 113
Shannon, Baylor 46, 51, 52, 53, 56, 100
Shaw, James W. 67, 70, 71
Shellhorn, Hattie 213, 231
CSS *Shenandoah* 49
Sheridan, J.E. 52
Sherman, General William T. 108
Sierra County, NM 147
Silver City, NM 17, 19, 21, 34, 38, 40–41, 47, 52, 54–57, 68, 72–73, 78, 100–103, 105, 116, 142, 173, 176, 197–198, 204, 209–210
Silver Creek, Socorro County, NM 55, 196, 202
Simmons, Ezra G. 207–217
Simmons, William 96
Skeen, Joe 190
Smith 123
Smith, George 67–68
Smith, William 63–64
Socorro, NM 55, 72, 73, 81, 85, 87, 101–102, 105, 119, 138, 142, 150–153, 156, 163, 167, 169, 173, 175–176, 180–181, 191, 197, 204, 256
Socorro County, NM 1, 54, 57, 73, 81–86, 90–91, 97–99, 117, 127, 129, 150, 157, 168–175, 202, 206
Socorro earthquakes 169–172, 176
Sorensen, Christian 195, 197
Southern Pacific Railroad 14, 18–20, 26, 184, 193
Southwest Cattle Raisers' Association 15–16
Spanish-American War 87–90, 125, 139
Spanish influenza 230–231, 246
Starr, Belle (Myra Belle Shirley) 168
Starr, Sam 168
Stauder, Clyde E., Jr. 256
Stauder, Clyde Eldon 79, 194, 203, 214, 219, 241, 249, 256
Stauder, James x, 236
Stein's Pass train robbery 87
Stevens, George H. 17
Stevenson, George 96
Stewart, Rhea (NMMP) 149, 166
Stovall, Dr. R.F. 25–26
Street, James Alexander "Alex" (NMMP) 161, 169, 175, 215
Strickler, W.S. 178
"Subscription" deputy 37, 197, 199

Taft, President William H. 201, 203
Taos, NM 135–137
Taos County, NM 135–137
Taos Pubelo, NM 135–137
Tax assessor system in New Mexico 63–65
Taylor, W.H. 46
Taylor, William M. 108, 142
Territorial Fair 152–153
Texas 139
Texas Rangers 139, 142, 164
Thompson, Mark B. 188
Thoreau, Henry David 181
Thronton, Governor (NM) William T. 52, 56, 85, 96
Thrope, Mrs. James 87
Thurmond, Charlotte (Mrs. Frank) "Lottie Deno" 120–121
Thurmond, Frank 120–121
Tidwell, Dewey 192
Tierra Amarilla, NM 244–245
Tombaught, Clyde, and the Kuiper Belt 255
Tombstone, AZ 27, 28–29
Torrance County, NM 142, 169, 172–173, 176, 240
Torrango, Gregorio 203
Towle, J.E. 63–64
Trelford, Arthur 97
Trisel, Clara J. 26
Trujillo, Faustin 137
Trujillo, Santiago 172
Tucker, Dan 21, 29
Tucumcari, NM 161, 169, 183, 185
Twain, Mark (Samuel Langhorne Clemens) 8, 46
Tyrone, NM 235–237, 248

UFO/airship 65–66
Union County, NM 142, 148, 160, 162
Ute Park, NM 222

Vaca, Don Jose Teofilo 4, 5, 6, 7, 9, 10
Vaca, Don Juan Manuel 4
Vacaville, CA 6, 26–27
Valencia County, NM 90, 154
Valencia y Briones, Maria Manuela 7
Vance, Frank (NMMP) 193, 203, 241
Vaughn, Boone (NMMP) 84, 149–151, 158
Veeder, M.M. 77
Velarde, NM 245
Vickery, Jim 199
Vigil, Severo M. 61

Wagon Mound, NM 175
Walters, William "Bronco Bill" 35–36, 38, 72, 90–91, 97–98
Walton, W.B. 46
Warderman, W.H. 72
Washington, DC 96, 118, 202
Weety, J.W. 52
Wells Fargo Express Company 17–18, 72
White, Scott 71
Whitehill, Harvey Howard 17, 21, 30–31, 38–39
Wiley, John M. 133
Williams, George 210
Wilson, Francis 224
Wilson, President Thomas Woodrow 214–215, 226
Wister, Owen 148
Woody, Glen 135–136
World War I (The Great War) 88, 91, 190, 225–233, 246, 257

Young, Cole 68
Young, Ed 51, 52
Younger, Cole 168

Zamora, Barbara x
Zuni, Holly x

www.ingramcontent.com/pod-product-compliance
Ingram Content Group UK Ltd.
Pitfield, Milton Keynes, MK11 3LW, UK
UKHW050540150426
5217IPUK00026B/2015